Library of
Davidson College

WALLACE STEVENS' SUPREME FICTION

WALLACE STEVENS' SUPREME FICTION

A New Romanticism

Joseph Carroll

LOUISIANA STATE UNIVERSITY PRESS
Baton Rouge and London

Copyright © 1987 by Louisiana State University Press
All rights reserved
Manufactured in the United States of America
Designer
Patricia Douglas Crowder
Typeface
Linotron 202 Granjon
Typesetter
G & S Typesetters, Inc.
Printer
Thomson-Shore, Inc.
Binder
John H. Dekker & Sons, Inc.

10 9 8 7 6 5 4 3 2 1

LIBRARY OF CONGRESS CATALOGING-IN-PUBLICATION DATA

Carroll, Joseph.
Wallace Stevens' supreme fiction.

Bibliography: p.
Includes index.
1. Stevens, Wallace, 1879–1955—Criticism and interpretation. 2. Philosophy in literature. 3. Romanticism—United States. I. Title.
PS3537.T4753Z6227   1987   811'.52   87-4070
ISBN 0-8071-1367-0

Alfred A. Knopf, Inc., has granted permission to quote from the following copyrighted editions of the works of Wallace Stevens: *The Necessary Angel: Essays on Reality and the Imagination* (1951); *The Collected Poems of Wallace Stevens* (1954); *Opus Posthumous*, ed. Samuel French Morse (1957); *Letters of Wallace Stevens,* ed. Holly Stevens (1966). Some portions of this study originally appeared, in slightly different form, as "The Ancient and the Modern Sage," *Victorian Poetry,* XXII (1984), and "A Poet and a Gentleman," *Denver Quarterly,* XXIX (1985).

For Paula and Gwendolyn

Contents

Acknowledgments / ix
Abbreviations and Prefatory Notes / xi

Introduction / 1

CHAPTER ONE
The Imagination as Metaphysics / 13

CHAPTER TWO
Evanescent Symmetries / 29

CHAPTER THREE
That Slight Transcendence / 63

CHAPTER FOUR
The Pure Idea / 106

CHAPTER FIVE
A Landscape of the Mind / 153

CHAPTER SIX
The Essential Poem / 212

CHAPTER SEVEN
A Final Construction / 303

APPENDIX
In the Fold / 339
Works Cited / 345
Index / 349

Acknowledgments

I would like to express my gratitude to Leonard Michaels, who encouraged my first efforts to write about Stevens and was extraordinarily generous in judging the results. The students in my Stevens seminars at the University of Denver have all contributed to my understanding of the poetry. More specific debts to Rachel Matheis and Jim Clark are recorded in the text. My largest debt is to Ian Duncan, who read the manuscript closely, gave many helpful criticisms of it, and provided several fruitful suggestions about Stevens' possible sources.

In writing this book, I have benefited from research leaves granted by the University of Denver and the University of Missouri, Saint Louis.

Abbreviations and Prefatory Notes

Quotations from Emerson are drawn from *The Complete Works of Ralph Waldo Emerson* (12 vols.; Boston, 1904) and will be cited parenthetically as *RWE*. For parenthetical citation of Stevens' work, the following abbreviations will be used:

CP   *The Collected Poems of Wallace Stevens* (New York, 1954)
OP   *Opus Posthumous,* ed. Samuel French Morse (New York, 1957)
NA   *The Necessary Angel: Essays on Reality and the Imagination* (New York, 1951)
LWS   *Letters of Wallace Stevens,* ed. Holly Stevens (New York, 1966)

Quotations of the poetry of Wordsworth, Coleridge, Shelley, Keats, Tennyson, Arnold, and Whitman are taken from the editions designated in Works Cited.

All of Stevens' poems discussed in this study have been assigned a date in parentheses, usually when the title of each poem is first mentioned. When the date of composition can be ascertained, that is the date given. Otherwise, the date given is that of first publication, which for Stevens usually means publication in a magazine not long after the date of composition. A few poems can be dated only by their appearance in a volume of Stevens' poetry. Dates have been drawn from the following sources: *Letters of Wallace Stevens*; *Opus Posthumous*; Holly Stevens' selection of the poems *The Palm at the End of the*

Mind (New York, 1971); and J. M. Edelstein's *Wallace Stevens: A Descriptive Bibliography* (Pittsburgh, 1973).

Stevens wrote many poems in segments of several stanzas each. For those poems in which these segments consist either of an equal number of stanzas of the same type or of varying line and stanza pattern, I refer to the segments as cantos. For those poems in which these segments consist of an unequal number of stanzas of the same type (these are usually tercets), I refer to the segments as strophes.

WALLACE STEVENS'
SUPREME FICTION

Introduction

In a letter of 1938, Wallace Stevens wrote that he did not yet wish to publish a collected edition of his works because "I do not feel that I have yet said what I have to say. The few things I have already done have merely been preliminary" (*LWS*, 333). In the seventeen years between this letter and his death in 1955, Stevens said what he had to say. He defined an aim for his poetry that would enable him to use the accumulated force of his preliminary exercises and that would satisfy all but the most fantastic ambitions of his creative drive. Stevens' aim was the creation of a supreme fiction, that is, "a poem equivalent to the idea of God" (*LWS*, 369–70). In an autobiographical note of 1954, he succinctly identifies the idea that dominates his later poetry and that gives a teleological shape to his career. "The author's work suggests the possibility of a supreme fiction, recognized as a fiction, in which men could propose to themselves a fulfillment" (*LWS*, 820). In this note Stevens does not say what the supreme fiction is, but he does say what it is not. "There are many poems relating to the interactions between reality and the imagination, which are to be regarded as marginal to this central theme." What I propose in this study is to take Stevens at his word: to explain what he understood by the idea of a supreme fiction and to interpret his poetry and prose by adopting this idea as my guiding principle. I shall argue that the course of his poetic development can best be understood as a struggle to overcome the metaphysical limitations of a simple dualism and to achieve a poetic absolute.

In many passages of his letters, the Adagia, and his essays, Stevens explicitly avows the religious and transcendental character of his supreme fiction. Despite these avowals, his critics have been reluctant to acknowledge his visionary purpose and have chosen for the most part to explicate his poetry within the boundaries imposed by the dichotomy between reality and the imagination. For example, in one of the earliest book-length studies, Frank Doggett holds that "the concepts that are submerged in Stevens' poetry are usually some variation of the idea of the subject-object relationship." Doggett argues that "there is no dialectic to support" these concepts and that "throughout Stevens' poetry, the only continuous strand of thought is a fundamental naturalism that is immediately apparent in the poems of *Harmonium*." J. Hillis Miller employs the same categories but, by emptying them of content, transforms naturalism into nihilism. "After the death of the gods and the discovery of nothingness Stevens is left in a world made of two elements: subject and object, mind and matter, imagination and reality. Imagination is the inner nothingness, while reality is the barren external world with which imagination carries on its endless intercourse.... At the beginning Stevens is already as far as he ever goes." Although it "is not dialectical," this scheme is susceptible to simple inversion. "The nothing is not nothing. It is. It is being." Joseph Riddel, adopting a perspective somewhere in between Doggett's naturalism and Miller's phenomenological abstractionism, uses the same basic formula. He maintains that in Stevens' poetry "the images exist to relate the self to its world, not to any greater self or any transcendent world."[1]

In recent years, the standard dualistic paradigm has frequently been adapted to the doctrines and rhetorical forms of poststructuralism. (Miller and Riddel have both reformulated their interpretations in deconstructive terms.) Helen Regueiro's views may be taken to represent an intermediate phase in this process of adaptation. She argues that "the central concern" of all modern poetry is "the quest for wholeness" and that this quest always, necessarily fails. Poetry only "illuminates the dialectic" between imagination and reality that "it seeks constantly and unsuccessfully to resolve.... Whether withdrawing into the enclosed space of the intentional creation or dissolving into the natural world, the poet stands blind and speechless in front of a reality he cannot reach or re-create." By defining the motive force of

---

1. Frank Doggett, *Stevens' Poetry of Thought* (Baltimore, 1966), ix; J. Hillis Miller, "Wallace Stevens' Poetry of Being," *English Literary History*, XXXI (1964), rpr. in Roy Harvey Pearce and J. Hillis Miller (eds.), *The Act of the Mind: Essays on the Poetry of Wallace Stevens* (Baltimore, 1965), 145, 146, 157; Joseph N. Riddel, *The Clairvoyant Eye: The Poetry and Poetics of Wallace Stevens* (Baton Rouge, 1965), 32.

Stevens' dialectic as an illusory telos, Regueiro reduces his poetic enterprise to an elaborate exercise in futility. The dynamic principle of this enterprise is only a blind impulse that is condemned to perpetuating its hopeless longing for closure. The inevitable step beyond this sort of interpretation is to attribute to Stevens himself a consciously deconstructive motive. Paul Bové, among others, takes this step. He argues that Stevens "actively employs the *telos*-oriented quest metaphor against itself not merely to show that there is no center but to test in fiction various poetic and personal myths and metaphors in a world with no firm point of reference."[2]

Stevens' own view of his poetic enterprise answers neither to the reading based on a static dualism nor to the reading that converts this dualism into an ironic exercise in linguistic irresolution. In a letter of 1948, he declares, "I do seek a centre and expect to go on seeking it. I don't say that I shall not find it or that I do not expect to find it. It is the great necessity even without specific identification" (*LWS,* 584). The method of Stevens' seeking is, from first to last, dialectical—a ceaseless process of antithetical formulation, sublimation, and synthesis—but in his later poetry the nature of this dialectic undergoes a major change. The two poles of the later dialectic are occupied by opposing metaphysical paradigms: on the one hand, the dualism of mind and reality that informs *Harmonium* (1923), and on the other hand, a transcendental unity of the mind and reality within the "mind of minds" (*CP,* 254). From the dualistic perspective, fulfillment consists of a momentary rapprochement with reality; it is thus associated with what Stevens calls the poetry of normal life, that is, a poetry concerned with "the earth" and "men in their earthy implications" (*OP,* 229). One of these earthy implications is that all the parts of the world constitute only an aggregate of discrete particulars; there is no principle of synthesis that would bind these parts into a "poem of the whole" (*CP,* 442). From the transcendental perspective, fulfillment consists of completed figurations of sentient unity. The kind of poetry that is written from this perspective is what, in his later terminology, Stevens calls "pure poetry," and the elaboration of this mode constitutes the quest for a supreme fiction. If "The cancelings, / The negations are never final" (*CP,* 414), there are nonetheless moments of supreme fulfillment within the quest, moments when, as Stevens says in "The Figure of the Youth as Virile Poet" (1943), the poet

2. Helen Regueiro, *The Limits of Imagination: Wordsworth, Yeats, and Stevens* (Ithaca, 1976), 9, 190; Paul A. Bové, *Destructive Poetics: Heidegger and Modern American Poetry* (New York, 1980), 187.

"writes a poem that completely accomplishes his purpose" (*NA*, 53). In its simplest terms, Stevens' purpose is to render himself the medium through which "the central mind" comes to knowledge of itself (*CP*, 524). The hypotheses or "fictive" propositions on which this purpose depends are that the world itself contains a latent principle of spiritual fulfillment, and that this principle can be activated through the fictions of poetry. (Lucy Beckett, Leonora Woodman, and David La Guardia sometimes use spiritual terms to describe Stevens' poetic ambitions, but they adapt these terms to a purely human context. Adalaide Kirby Morris seeks to demonstrate the way in which Stevens assimilates the diction and imagery of Christianity to a humanistic aestheticism.)[3]

Although many of Stevens' critics have recognized that his poetry has some kind of affinity with Romanticism, most would agree with A. Walton Litz that Stevens unequivocally rejects "the mystical transcendence of the old romantic."[4] The transcendental element in Stevens' later poetry has not, however, gone altogether unnoticed. Three of Stevens' most prominent critics—Harold Bloom, Joseph Riddel, and Roy Harvey Pearce—have commented on it, and they offer divergent opinions about its significance in Stevens' work as a whole. Bloom and Riddel both argue that the primary, dominant motive in Stevens' poetry is the "composition of self." (The primacy of "the self" is also a leading theme in James Baird's study of Stevens. Baird maintains that "Stevens will not accept a transcendental reality.") In his analysis of "Notes Toward a Supreme Fiction" (1942), Bloom argues that Stevens' supreme fiction "will turn out not to be poetry or a poem but, as in Emerson and Whitman (and Wordsworth), to be a poet, to be a fiction of the self." However, in reference to a poem of 1948, "Saint John and the Back-Ache," Bloom remarks, "Saint John is the Transcendental element in Stevens himself, the apocalyptic impulse that he has dismissed for so long but that will begin to break in upon his reveries in *An Ordinary Evening in New Haven* and *The Rock* and then will dominate the poems composed from 1952 through

---

3. Lucy Beckett, *Wallace Stevens* (London, 1974); Leonora Woodman, *Stanza My Stone: Wallace Stevens and the Hermetic Tradition* (West Lafayette, Ind., 1983); David M. La Guardia, *Advance on Chaos: The Sanctifying Imagination of Wallace Stevens* (Hanover, N.H., 1983); Adalaide Kirby Morris, *Wallace Stevens: Imagination and Faith* (Princeton, 1974).

4. A. Walton Litz, "Wallace Stevens' Defense of Poetry: *La poésie pure,* the New Romantic, and the Pressure of Reality," in George Bornstein (ed.), *Romantic and Modern: Revaluations of Literary Tradition* (Pittsburgh, 1977), 130. See also Margaret Peterson, *Wallace Stevens and the Idealist Tradition* (Ann Arbor, 1983), 37.

1955."[5] Riddel locates the supposed irruption of transcendentalism somewhat earlier in *The Auroras of Autumn* (1950), a volume that he calls "a questionable poetry even by generous estimate." Segregating this volume from both the preceding and succeeding volumes, he suggests that "critics could dismiss this kind of poetry, for it is not after all what poetry is supposed to be unless that poetry is apocalyptic, or symbolistic; unless, that is, the poetry deals with transcendence rather than, as Stevens claimed, the human." Like Riddel, Roy Harvey Pearce, in his early work on Stevens, felt that the transcendentalism of the later poetry was "a kind of disease.... It is wanting to have God's mind." In a more recent essay, Pearce announces a decided shift in sympathy. "I now see the poems collected in *Transport to Summer* (my notion of an extended 'Notes' among them) as being preparatory for the transcending efforts of the poems collected in *The Auroras of Autumn* (1950) and the transcendent effort of the *Rock* sequence." Pearce stands virtually alone among Stevens' critics in delineating a purposeful, dramatic progression in the development of Stevens' later poetry.[6]

In his pursuit of a visionary fulfillment, Stevens situates himself within a central Romantic tradition. The normative mode of Stevens' visionary poetry is that of the Romantic sublime—both the elegiac sublime associated with Keats, Tennyson, and Whitman, and the sublime of celestial grandeur associated with these three figures and with Wordsworth, Shelley, and Emerson. The influence of George Santayana—poet, philosopher, and Stevens' mentor at Harvard—sometimes mingles with that of the Romantics, but Santayana's philosophy is not fundamentally transcendental; it is a philosophy of skeptical aestheticism. At the beginning of Stevens' career, the Romantic visionary tradition seems already to have exhausted itself. The course of Stevens' career thus inverts the historical progression of Romanticism and describes a cycle

---

5. Riddel, *The Clairvoyant Eye*, 254; James Baird, *The Dome and the Rock: Structure in the Poetry of Wallace Stevens* (Baltimore, 1968), 74; Harold Bloom, *Wallace Stevens: The Poems of Our Climate* (Ithaca, 1976), 206, 298.

6. Riddel, *The Clairvoyant Eye*, 225; Roy Harvey Pearce, "Wallace Stevens: The Last Lesson of Master," *English Literary History,* XXXI (1964), rpr. in Roy Harvey Pearce and J. Hillis Miller (eds.), *The Act of the Mind: Essays on the Poetry of Wallace Stevens* (Baltimore, 1965), 123; Roy Harvey Pearce, "Toward Decreation: Stevens and the 'Theory of Poetry,'" in Frank Doggett and Robert Buttel (eds.), *Wallace Stevens: A Celebration* (Princeton, 1980), 295. George Bornstein, *Transformations of Romanticism in Yeats, Eliot, and Stevens* (Chicago, 1976), 217, remarks that Stevens "continually made notes to arrange" a "mystic marriage of imagination and reality in the mind," but he argues that Stevens' "radical provisionality prevented" the "consummation" of that marriage.

from the repudiation of a visionary tradition to the renewal and continuation of that tradition. In much of his early poetry, Stevens attempts to find what will suffice within the attenuated Romanticism of a *fin de siècle* aestheticism. Most of the poems in *Harmonium* presuppose that the disclosures of sensory perception are all we know on earth and all we need to know. In "Sunday Morning" (1915), Stevens seeks to demonstrate that lyric naturalism may stand in place of the heaven that has been vacated by the Christian God. The failure of this effort reveals itself in "The Comedian as the Letter C" (1922), the first of Stevens' long poems that synthesize a whole era of his imaginative life. Crispin, the comedian, realizes in his poetic progress the logical extreme of Stevens' metaphysical premises in *Harmonium,* and he concludes in silence. Assuming a stance of ironic detachment, Stevens traces his protagonist's gradual absorption into common material reality. Stevens' own silence from about 1923 to about 1930 both gives evidence of his own preoccupation with the common reality of business and family life and also confirms the acuteness of his metaphysical self-diagnosis in "Comedian." Crispin explicitly commits himself to an anti-Romantic ethos, and when Stevens returns to poetry he consciously begins to orient himself to the creation of "a new romanticism" (*LWS,* 350). The term *a new romanticism* becomes essentially equivalent to the term *a supreme fiction*; by describing his visionary goal as a new Romanticism, Stevens both signals the historical lineage of the supreme fiction and also designates the modal, affective range of the themes, images, and poetic structures that constitute this fiction. Through his own articulations of the Romantic sublime, Stevens implicitly offers a sophisticated interpretation of the Romantic visionary tradition.

In his effort to create a new Romanticism, Stevens draws heavily from the major figures of the old Romanticism, but it would be a mistake to call his poetry "derivative." Adopting T. S. Eliot's distinction, we might say that, like all great poets, Stevens does not "borrow" from other writers; he "steals" from them. He makes very free use of his sources—modifying, combining, and adapting them for his own purposes—and one suspects that he was often not fully conscious of how a certain phrase or image may have taken shape in his mind. In Peter Brazeau's oral biography of Stevens, the composer John Gruen reports, "He told me that he didn't know what his poetry meant at times, that he really had to think hard as to what he meant by that image or that phrase or that word, even. He talked something about submersion, about words being submerged and then rising out, that they seemed to have been hidden and then revealed themselves." If Stevens was not always certain about what his poetry meant, he might have been equally uncertain of its derivation. Many of the echoes of Keats, Tennyson, Emerson, and others in Stevens' poetry may well be cases of "submersion," cases in which words "have been hidden and then revealed themselves." At other times, Stevens' allusive echoes seem consciously designed to define his position in relation to that of his predecessors, either to oppose them or to align himself with them. In "Evening Without Angels" (1934), for example, he seems to be directing a conscious polemic against Shelley's "Mont Blanc." In "A Primitive Like an Orb" (1948), his theme, imagery, and diction are so overtly Emersonian that the poem constitutes an implicit avowal of his doctrinal affiliation. (Stevens' mother gave him a twelve-volume set of Emerson while he was a student at Harvard, and this may well have been the most important gift he ever received.[7] Although he never cites Emerson in his prose, in his poetry he alludes to Emerson more often than to any other writer.) Whether consciously or unconsciously constructed, the subtext of allusions in Stevens' work enriches and illuminates the primary text. Like the robe of peace after death in "The Owl in the Sarcophagus" (1947), Stevens' poetry has

> the whole spirit sparkling in its cloth,
> Generations of the imagination piled
> In the manner of its stitchings. (*CP,* 434)

The purposeful creation of the complex set of metaphysical hypotheses, mythic motifs, and dialectical structures that constitutes the supreme fiction begins very gradually in Stevens' work. In *Ideas of Order* (1936), he makes considerable progress toward reconstructing the Romantic sublime; nonetheless, many of his doctrinal declarations in this volume reiterate Crispin's assumption that "his soil is man's intelligence" (*CP,* 36), and in those poems—such as "The Idea of Order at Key West" (1934)—that suggest a transcendental presence, he refrains from explicitly transcendental formulations of doctrine. In "Owl's Clover" (1935–1936), he laboriously articulates the elementary premises of the supreme fiction, and he produces the figure of the "subman," a personification of the subconscious as a source of archetypal images. Although the subman himself disappears after "Owl's Clover," he marks an

---

7. Peter Brazeau, *Parts of a World: Wallace Stevens Remembered* (New York, 1983), 207. On the gift of the set of Emerson, see Milton J. Bates, *Wallace Stevens: A Mythology of Self* (Berkeley, 1985), 3.

important stage in the development of Stevens' theory of pure poetry as a poetry of mythic vision. In "The Irrational Element in Poetry" (1936), an essay written to accompany a reading of "Owl's Clover," Stevens begins to formulate the theoretical propositions that will govern his later development. He elaborates the opposition between pure and normal poetry, and he identifies the motive of pure poetry as the desire "to find the good which, in the Platonic sense, is synonymous with God" (*OP,* 222). In *Parts of a World* (1942), he first fully recognizes and clearly announces the visionary direction his poetry will take.

The fulfillment Stevens seeks is a poetic vision of the supreme spirit creating space and time and manifesting itself in each creative act of human consciousness. Within this spirit, all oppositions—between mind and material reality, here and there, then and now, signifier and signified, and the individual and the whole—are resolved in a "pure principle" of sentient relation (*CP,* 418). The pure principle animates "The essential poem at the centre of things" *(CP,* 440) that generates the appearances both of phenomenal reality and of poetry. To write poetry that figures forth this generative source is to construct a paradoxical mediation between the conditions of conscious human existence—a consciousness that exists only through limitation and distinction—and a perfect universal presence that both embodies and transcends these limitations. Such poetry is, at best, "A difficult apperception" (*CP,* 440), and the moments of fulfillment within this quest can never be preserved in the form of stable doctrinal constructs. They nonetheless constitute touchstones for the spiritual and aesthetic authenticity of Stevens' "new romanticism." It is in the very nature of the supreme fiction that it cannot be "fixed" (*NA,* 34), but, for all that, "it is not / Less real" (*CP,* 418).

In *Parts of a World* and *Transport to Summer* (1947), Stevens both elaborates the mythic motifs that give form to the supreme fiction and also develops the metaphysical dialectic through which it is to be realized. In *Parts* he establishes his visionary goal as the poetic realization of "essential unity" (*CP,* 215), and he opposes this ideal to a pluralistic belief that "'Words are not forms of a single word. / In the sum of the parts, there are only the parts'" (*CP,* 204). Words that are forms of a single word would constitute an intellective structure that contains both the external world and the sub-intellective or "irrational" components of experience. (Although it is presented with no specific reference to Stevens, the general theory of literature that best illuminates the nature of his visionary enterprise is that of Northrop Frye in "Anagogic

Phase: Symbol as Monad." Frye argues that in this phase all symbols are "united in a single infinite and eternal verbal symbol" and that "the anagogic view of criticism . . . leads to the conception of literature as existing in its own universe, no longer a commentary on life or reality, but containing life and reality in a system of verbal relationships.")[8] Many of the motifs that illustrate Stevens' conception of essential unity originate in the earlier poetry, but it is in *Parts* that Stevens decisively undertakes to fashion "The great structure" (*CP*, 502) of the supreme fiction, a structure that is self-referential, self-qualifying, and all-inclusive. The central mythic figure in this structure is the "ancient mother"; she is the archetype of imaginative presence and of life itself, "the never-ceasing source" (*NA*, 28). She appears in various guises throughout the early poetry, and in *Parts*, Stevens definitively establishes her as the interior paramour: "the image at its source, / The abstract, the archaic queen" (*CP*, 223). In *The Auroras of Autumn*, the ancient mother appears as the mythic embodiment of the essential poem.

Most of the poems in *Parts* and *Transport* are in some sense notes toward a supreme fiction. Although many of these notes move "Toward" Stevens' visionary goal chiefly by defining the dialectical adversatives in response to which he articulates his conception of the supreme fiction, the dominant movement is always one of synthesis within the ever-expanding pattern of themes and motifs that culminates in the visionary mythology of *Auroras*. *Transport*, in some respects Stevens' most opulent volume, contains both his finest realizations of the poetry of normal life and also his most advanced preparations for a poetry of mythic vision. In *Transport* he surveys virtually the whole range of his visionary images: for example, the giant, the diamond crown, the archaic queen, white light as the radiance at the "centre of all circles" (*CP*, 366), the circle itself, the book, the stars, music, and the "breath" of the spirit. In "Notes Toward a Supreme Fiction," "Description Without Place" (1945), and other poems, he expounds his theory of "belief" in "The fiction of an absolute" (*CP*, 404).

In three major poems written in 1947 and early 1948—"The Owl in the Sarcophagus," "The Auroras of Autumn," and "A Primitive Like an Orb"— Stevens gathers together the ideas and images of a poetic lifetime, and he fashions these materials into a comprehensive mythology of life, death, and the imagination. It is in these poems, and especially in "The Owl in the

---

8. Northrop Frye, *Anatomy of Criticism: Four Essays* (1957; rpr. New York, 1965), 121, 122.

Sarcophagus," that he penetrates most closely to what he calls "the ultimate intellect" (*CP*, 433), that is, the mind of God. "Owl" has not received much attention from Stevens' critics, in part because of "all of those difficulties" that Harold Bloom says render it "uninterpretable" and "the least accessible of Stevens' major poems."[9] If we consider "Owl" within the context of Stevens' theoretical and poetic development, it should be possible both to render the poem intelligible and to establish its significance as a culminating visionary achievement. "Owl" sets the limit for Stevens' visionary poetry. "The Auroras of Autumn" is placed first in the volume to which it gives the title, but it was written after "Owl," and it attains its climactic visionary moment only by re-creating the mythological figure that dominates "Owl": the mother of the living and the dead. In "A Primitive Like an Orb," Stevens gives a poetic exposition of the propositions that are embodied in the mythological figurations of "Owl" and "Auroras." Together, these three poems give a definitive form to the "new romanticism," and it is in these poems that Stevens most completely integrates all the main voices of the central Romantic tradition within his own visionary constructs.

The resolutions in the major visionary poems of *Auroras* are of necessity provisional and tenuous. They constitute an imaginative achievement of the first order, but they provide no certain refuge from human misery or intellectual need. In his later poetry, Stevens continues to oscillate between the modes of pure and normal poetry, and in his figurations of pure poetry he reflects on and re-creates the resolutions of the major visionary poems. In 1950 he is seventy years old, and he must test these resolutions against the poverty of old age and the anticipation of death. The Romantic sublime constantly threatens to invert itself into nihilistic vacancy, and Stevens must often take refuge in tragic sublimations of Romantic grandeur. He cannot surpass his former achievements, and in the later poems, beginning with "An Ordinary Evening in New Haven" (1949), the necessity of repetition within "a dwindled sphere" (*CP,* 504) becomes a source of passionate frustration for him. Nonetheless, the memory of his visionary fulfillment helps him to sustain the force of his spirit in the last few years of his life.

Stevens' poetry and prose constitute an intellectual drama and a commentary on that drama. The exposition and development of conflict, the climax, and the denouement of his poetic career define themselves internally by

---

9. Bloom, *The Poems of Our Climate,* 292.

means of a dense network of prophecy and allusive retrospection. In the prose of his last two decades, Stevens provides himself with a discursive outline of the propositions and hypotheses that prepare for, justify, and explicate the realization of his visionary purpose. In the first chapter of this study, I shall examine Stevens' prose works in order to establish the theoretical context within which we may understand the development of thought in his poetry. In the succeeding chapters, I shall attempt to map out the course of his visionary enterprise in order to demonstrate both the problematic complexity and the ultimate coherence of his achievement.

It seems likely that a good many readers of Stevens' poetry have been rather startled by the evidence—summarized in Brazeau's oral biography—that a few days before his death, Stevens joined the Catholic church. There are no Catholic poems, so that in one sense Stevens' apparent conversion has no relevance for criticism. It nonetheless offers an occasion for reevaluating Stevens' history of ambivalent veneration for the established church. In the appendix to this study, I shall examine the evidence for Stevens' conversion and, through journals, letters, and poems over a period of about fifty years, trace his declarations on the seductions of churches.

Although most of Stevens' better critics have assumed that his poetry is in some sense "philosophical," the precise weight to be given to the "ideas" in his poetry remains a matter of some perplexity. The nature of this problem may be illustrated by reference to Frank Doggett's first book on Stevens, *Stevens' Poetry of Thought*. On the one hand, Doggett explicitly focuses his discussion on the philosophical content of Stevens' poetry, and on the other hand, he deprecates the intrinsic significance of this content. He warns against any effort to discover "a body of philosophic doctrine" in the poetry, and he argues that "the concepts that emerge from long reading of the poetry of Stevens are so slight and so basic that any elementary course in philosophy or even a few years of interested reading could yield all of them."[10] Even if we concede the justice of these observations, it is still necessary to consider Stevens a serious philosophical poet—I would argue the most important philosophical poet of the twentieth century. His poetry is philosophical not because the metaphysical hypotheses it contains are strikingly original but because they are elemental or, in Doggett's words, "basic" and "elementary." Stevens' poetry subsists within a genuinely philosophical atmosphere, that is,

---

10. Doggett, *Stevens' Poetry of Thought,* x, viii–ix.

an atmosphere in which metaphysical perspective crucially influences the quality of experience. The dualistic and transcendental paradigms are not for Stevens merely hypotheses propounded for the sake of their dialectical potential; they are primary modes of being. While they are susceptible to modification and elaboration, Stevens responds to them, at any given moment, with the kind of immediacy with which he responds to the weather, and indeed, they often find their symbolic correlatives in metaphors of the sky, the air, and the light. For those who can, however guardedly, entertain the hypotheses that the world contains a latent principle of spiritual fulfillment, and that poetry can serve as the medium of this fulfillment, Stevens' work may well seem to define the basic range of spiritual experience that is still open to us.

CHAPTER ONE

The Imagination as Metaphysics

In a letter of 1948, Stevens remarks that "there is nothing that I desire more intensely than to make a contribution to the theory of poetry" (*LWS,* 585). The essays written between 1936 and 1951 answer to this desire, and the theory of poetry that emerges most distinctly from these essays is one of a visionary Romanticism. In the development and exposition of this theory, Stevens is hampered both by occasional lapses in discursive clarity and by difficulties inherent in the theory itself. As in his poetry, he sometimes confuses the dualistic and the transcendental conceptions of the world, and as a result he is not always clear about the metaphysical status of "reality." Moreover, the transcendental conception, even when it is clearly disengaged from the dualistic, cannot be fully articulated within the forms of rational discourse. In "A Collect of Philosophy" (1951), Stevens declares that the function of "cosmic poetry" is to "make us realize that we are creatures, not of a part, which is our everday limitation, but of a whole for which, for the most part, we have as yet no language" (*OP,* 189). Accordingly, as Stevens says in "The Relations Between Poetry and Painting" (1950–1951), "The theory of poetry . . . often seems to become in time a mystical theology" *(NA,* 173). (For Stevens, *mystic* and *mystical* vary in meaning. In a letter of 1942 [*LWS,* 428], he uses *mystical* to connote mere pretentious exoticism. In the essays and poems, the words are often used as synonyms for visionary ambition.) The referent of a supreme fiction is an object that is no object; it is an illimitable presence that contains all other objects, including the poetic representation of it. Consequently, no simply mimetic theory of poetic figuration can account for the problematic interaction between the poetic artifice and the "reality" that is both its source and end. Moreover, the presence to be depicted in this artifice is not a stable set of relations but the very principle of relation itself. Any definition of this principle must acknowledge simultaneously the ceaseless activity of the principle as process and its perfect equilibrium as the continuous unity of all process. That is, every definition must implicitly contain its own paradoxical negative and so suspend itself in an intentional ambiguity. Although Stevens concedes that "we have as yet no language" that would adequately solve these problems, he emphatically rejects the idea "that I get nowhere in particular. . . . I do at least arrive at the end of my logic" (*LWS*, 861). Despite the confusions and difficulties that attend Stevens' visionary enterprise, he does arrive at the end of his logic, and in his essays he identifies the basic terms and principles that constitute this logic. He defines the nature of his modal dialectic; he articulates a coherent theory of mythic figuration; he establishes a complementary relationship between irrational intuition and speculative reason; and he formulates the metaphysical propositions appropriate to a cosmic poetry.

Apart from his undergraduate exercises, Stevens' first sustained effort at expository prose is the 1936 essay "The Irrational Element in Poetry." The main issues that will occupy Stevens' prose are already signaled in this essay, but Stevens' views on these issues have not yet assumed their definitive form. The essay is thus of exceptional interest, for it reveals Stevens' ideas on the nature and function of poetry in a transitional stage. The key to this transition may be found in the definition he enunciates for "pure poetry." The lingering note of hedonistic aestheticism in his definition of this term harks back to the outlook of his earliest work. At the same time, the definition contains suggestions of a religious purpose for poetry, and though these suggestions are as yet tentative and ambiguous, they point to the way ahead. The transition between these two stages is complicated by Stevens' effort to come to terms with another basic issue: the imaginative functions of the subconscious.

Stevens' chief purpose in "The Irrational Element" is to identify the essence of poetry. He establishes his own definition of pure poetry as a modification of the definition given by the Abbé Bremond, a Jesuit theologian who "elucidated a mystical motive" for the writing of poetry (*OP*, 221). "In his opinion, one writes poetry to find God." In contrast to this strictly religious definition, Stevens declares that "pure poetry is a term that has grown to be descriptive of poetry in which not the true subject but the poetry of the subject is paramount" (*OP,* 222). By "the true subject" Stevens probably means the descriptive, narrative, or expository content of a poem. By "the poetry of the subject" he probably means the purely aesthetic effects of sound and imagery. In a letter of 1935, he remarks that "when HARMONIUM was in the making there was a time when I liked the idea of images and images alone, or images and the music of verse together. I then believed in *pure poetry,* as it was called. I still have a distinct liking for that sort of thing" (*LWS,* 228). In the same letter, however, he remarks that the opinion that his poetry is "entirely without ideas" seems "ridiculously wrong." The conflict of tendencies apparent in these remarks may be traced to a survival in Stevens' thinking of the *fin de siècle* opposition between moralism and aestheticism. In another letter of 1935, he contrasts "pure poetry" with "didacticism." Although he declares that "my real danger is not didacticism, but abstraction," he concedes that "abstraction looks very much like didacticism" (*LWS,* 302). More decisively, in one of the first of the Adagia, he contrasts pure poetry with both didacticism and philosophy, and he urges himself to "seek those purposes that are purely the purposes of the pure poet" (this adage is from the early 1930s; *OP,* 157).[1]

In his adage Stevens suggests that the advantage of pure poetry, a poetry of images and music alone, is that it gives "a sense of the freshness or vividness of life." In "The Irrational Element," he places himself among "those who seek for the freshness and strangeness of poetry in fresh and strange places" (*OP,* 228). At the time of this essay, the most accessible resort of freshness and strangeness appears to be the subconscious. Stevens drives toward an exclusive identification of the imagination with the subconscious, and he sets the imagination in radical opposition to the unpoetic conscious intellect. He suggests that "the irrational element is merely poetic energy," and he explains that he is obsessed with the irrational because "we expect the irrational to liberate us from the rational" (*OP,* 219, 226). In "Owl's Clover" itself, Stevens embodies the irrational in the figure of the subman, "The man below the man below the man, / Steeped in night's opium, evading day" (*OP,* 66), and he explicitly elevates this figure above the authority of the conscious intellect:

---

1. See A. Walton Litz's dating of the Adagia in "Particles of Order: The Unpublished *Adagia,*" in Frank Doggett and Robert Buttel (eds.), *Wallace Stevens: A Celebration* (Princeton, 1980). For a helpful summary of the French and American debate over the term *pure poetry* in the 1920s, 1930s, and 1940s, see Litz, "*La poésie pure,*" in *Romantic and Modern.*

> We have grown weary of the man that thinks.
> He thinks and it is not true. The man below
> Imagines and it is true.

Stevens yields authority to the subman because he is the source of archetypal images, the consciousness within an ancestral memory buried in the mind. The subman is "born within us as a second self, / A self of parents who have never died" (*OP,* 67). The most obvious result of Stevens' fascination with the "parents who have never died" is the extensive genealogical research that bears fruit in poems such as "Dutch Graves in Bucks County" (1943) and "The Bed of Old John Zeller" (1944). A more subtle and far-reaching result appears in the passionate evocation of archetypal images of the mother and father in his later poetry.

In canto ten of "Esthétique du Mal" (1944), Stevens will use the Jungian term *anima* to describe "the child of a mother fierce / In his body, fiercer in his mind, merciless / To accomplish the truth in his intelligence" (*CP,* 321). Although Jung's theories seem to have helped Stevens to develop his own ideas, Stevens' basic conception predates that of Jung and appears to have been an original intuition with him. In a letter of 1909, he divulges a new insight into a conception that has "always" been a part of his thought:

Music, stirring something within us, stirs the Memory. I do not mean our personal Memory—the memory of our twenty years and more—but our inherited Memory, the Memory we have derived from those who lived before us in our own race, and in other races, illimitable, in which we resume the whole past life of the world, all the emotions, passions, experiences of the millions and millions of men and women now dead, whose lives have insensibly passed into our own, and compose them.—It is a Memory deep in the mind, without images, so vague that only the vagueness of Music, touching it subtly, vaguely awakens.... While I had always known of this infinite extension of personality, nothing has ever made it so striking as this application of Music to it.... And what one listens to at a concert, if one knew it, is not only the harmony of sounds, but the whispering of innumerable responsive spirits within one, momentarily revived, that stir like the invisible motions of the mind wavering between dreams and sleep. (*LWS,* 136)

(Frank Doggett cites this passage as "evidence of the long consistency in the work of Stevens of such concepts as this one of a collective unconscious memory."[2] Doggett gives a central place to this conception in both of his

---

2. Frank Doggett, *Wallace Stevens: The Making of the Poem* (Baltimore, 1980), 12.

books on Stevens.) Although Stevens will eventually alter his belief that this memory subsists "without images," music remains a fundamental element of his visionary experience. His application of music to the idea of an ancestral memory may have been suggested to him in part by Emerson's discussion of inherited genetic characteristics as fate: "In different hours a man represents each of several of his ancestors, as if there were seven or eight of us rolled up in each man's skin,—seven or eight ancestors at least; and they constitute the variety of notes for that new piece of music which his life is" (*RWE*, VI, 10). The post-Darwinian, proto-Jungian twist Stevens gives to this idea of a living ancestral memory is to extend it from the personal or private ancestors to the collective subconscious of the whole race. In his commentary on "Sombre Figuration," Stevens declares that "the future must bear within it every past, not least the pasts that have become submerged in the sub-conscious, things in the experience of races" (*LWS*, 373).

In "The Irrational Element," Stevens' preoccupation with the imaginative functions of the subconscious begins to merge with his aestheticism and to give it new depth. At the same time, this preoccupation complicates the conflict between his aestheticism and his tendency toward the abstractive or "didactic." While his conception of the subconscious as the source of mythic images continues to exert a potent influence on his poetry, in his later work the influence of "the man below" is reunited with that of the conscious, reflective intellect. In his letter of 1940 commenting on "Sombre Figuration," Stevens remarks that in this poem the imagination "is treated as an activity of the sub-conscious: the imagination is the sub-conscious" (*LWS*, 373). Later, in 1945 and 1946, he will declare that "if people are to become dependent on poetry for any of the fundamental satisfactions, poetry must have an increasingly intellectual scope and power" and, further, that "supreme poetry can be produced only on the highest possible level of the cognitive" (*LWS*, 526, 500).

Self-contradictory confusion is no virtue in a theorist, but in "The Irrational Element" it saves Stevens from a sterile extremism. The tendency to abstraction he had earlier mentioned as a danger converges with the aestheticism to which it was formerly opposed, and the result is a makeshift form of Platonism that holds the balance against his exaggerated irrationalism. "While it can lie in the temperament of very few of us to write poetry in order to find God, it is probably the purpose of each of us to write poetry to find the good which, in the Platonic sense, is synonymous with God. One writes poetry, then, in order to approach the good in what is harmonious and orderly" (*OP*, 222). The words *harmonious* and *orderly* evoke the aesthetic ethos of *Harmonium* and *Ideas of Order*. While Stevens' idea of God will never be very similar to that of the Jesuit theoretician Bremond, it does eventually come to possess a content considerably more substantial than that which is suggested by these two adjectives. Four years after "The Irrational Element," in a memorandum on poetry to Henry Church, Stevens is already more definite about the religious objective of his poetry, but he remains equivocal about the form it will take. "The major poetic idea in the world is and always has been the idea of God. One of the visible movements of the modern imagination is the movement away from the idea of God. The poetry that created the idea of God will either adapt it to our different intelligence, or create a substitute for it, or make it unnecessary. These alternatives probably mean the same thing" (*LWS*, 378). These alternatives mean the same thing for Stevens himself in that by adapting the idea of God to our different intelligence, he provides a substitute for the traditional idea and thus renders it unnecessary.

If, in 1936, Stevens has not yet clearly formulated the propositions on which his visionary poetry depends, he has at least established the two poles between which these propositions will have to be compounded. At one pole there is the Platonic impulse toward intellectual order, and at the other the Romantic impulse toward the vital mystery of nature. Both extremes draw toward a common center of mystical sublimity. The "good" of harmony and order is synonymous with God, and the mystery of nature, only temporarily limited to the subconscious, also leads to God. Stevens remarks that "life is mysterious; and if it is mysterious at all, I suppose that it is cosmically mysterious" (*OP*, 226). In 1909, Stevens had written to his wife that "in some form or other" everyone admits the existence of God. "The thought makes the world sweeter—even if God be no more than the mystery of life" (*LWS*, 140).

Once Stevens recognizes the central point toward which his poetry is to be directed, he drops the dichotomy between pure poetry and didacticism and he redefines the ideal of pure poetry by setting it in contrast to the poetry of normal life. The distinction between pure and normal poetry implies a difference of rank, but it is by no means so invidious as was the earlier distinction between "pure" and "impure" (didactic, philosophic) poetry (*OP*, 157). While it does not imply any radical opposition among the faculties, it does imply a difference in the range of sensibility operative in any given poem, and this difference may be closely associated with a basic difference in metaphysical perspective. The poetry of normal life, a poetry of sensual immediacy, flourishes within a dualistic view of the world. In the celebratory phase of normal poetry, as for example in "Credences of Summer" (1946), the opposition between the mind and reality results in a shock of satisfied recognition; the external world is a rock, "the visible rock, the audible, / The brilliant mercy of a sure repose" (*CP,* 375). Pure poetry, in contrast, presupposes and articulates a transcendent principle of pure sentient relation that comprehends both the mind and reality within the unity of "the central mind" (*CP,* 524). Insofar as there is a difference of subject matter in pure and normal poetry, one might say that in normal poetry there is more concern for personality and for the relation of the self to the social and political world. In "Of Modern Poetry" (1940), Stevens says of poetry that

> It has to be living, to learn the speech of the place.
> It has to face the men of the time and to meet
> The women of the time. It has to think about war. (*CP,* 240)

(It should be noted that even at its most commonplace, Stevens' poetry tends to represent other men and women only as abstract points of reference.) Pure poetry subsumes but does not directly concern itself with the specific interests of normal poetry. It takes as its subject "the forms of thought" that are also the forms of phenomenal reality (*CP,* 432). The ultimate purpose of pure poetry is to give figurative form to the generative principle of phenomenal and poetic images, that is, to "The essential poem at the centre of things" (*CP,* 440). In many of his major longer poems, Stevens not only alternates between these two modes but also mingles their generic, tonal affects. One can nonetheless identify the dominant tonality of each mode in its relatively pure form. The dominant tonality of normal poetry is that of a robust delight in the physical world, and the dominant tonality of pure poetry is that of a passionate absorption in the Romantic sublime. Stevens frequently reformulates this modal polarity in his prose, and the dialectical interplay between these two modes provides the main thematic structure for all of the later volumes of poetry—from *Parts of a World* through *The Rock* and the final poems of *Opus Posthumous.*

In "The Irrational Element," Stevens' conceptions of pure and normal poetry are undergoing a metamorphosis. The older dichotomy, that between pure and didactic poetry, is at work when Stevens poses this rhetorical question: "When we find in poetry that which gives us a momentary existence on an exquisite plane, is it necessary to ask the meaning of the poem?" (*OP*, 223). The new dichotomy begins to emerge in the conclusion to the essay. Although Stevens sustains the association between imaginative energy and the irrational, he does not oppose this sort of pure poetry to didacticism or abstraction; he opposes it to the poetry of normal life. "The poet cannot profess the irrational as the priest professes the unknown. The poet's role is broader, because he must be possessed, along with everything else, by the earth and by men in their earthy implications. For the poet, the irrational is elemental; but neither poetry nor life is commonly at its dynamic utmost" (*OP*, 229). In an address to the Poetry Society of America in 1951, in which he reiterates the distinction between pure and normal poetry, the definition of pure poetry has changed. "In one direction [poetry] moves toward the ultimate things of pure poetry; in the other it speaks to great numbers of people of themselves, making extraordinary texts and memorable music out of what they feel and know" (*OP*, 240). What Stevens means by "the ultimate things of pure poetry" he discloses in "A Collect of Philosophy," also written in 1951. "If the idea of God is the ultimate poetic idea, then the idea of the ascent into heaven is only a little below it" (*OP*, 193).

The equivocal manner of Stevens' enunciations of purpose in "The Irrational Element" stands in striking contrast to the confidence with which he articulates the spiritual role of the poet in "A Collect of Philosophy." These two essays are separated by a period of fifteen years, and the tonal and doctrinal contrasts between them can be measured out in stages through the essays written in the interim. Stevens' next two prose works are "The Noble Rider and the Sound of Words" (1941) and "The Figure of the Youth as Virile Poet" (1943). In both of these essays, Stevens is already preparing the ground for the "supreme effort" that—as he says of the Canon Aspirin in a letter concerning "Notes Toward a Supreme Fiction" (1942)—it is "inevitable that he should make" (*LWS*, 445).

In "The Noble Rider," Stevens' affirmations remain intentionally obscure; they consist of little more than hints about his goal and remarks on the difficulty of attaining it. He speaks of a "nobility which is our spiritual height and depth," but he declares that "nothing could be more evasive and inaccessible" (*NA*, 33–34). After a series of declarations about what he is *not* thinking of, he openly avows that he is "evading a definition. If it is defined, it will be fixed and it must not be fixed" (*NA*, 34). In "Virile Poet," though he swaddles his objective in an elaborately cautious syntax, he is far more explicit about what constitutes our spiritual height and depth. He introduces his topic by remarking on the "sense of liberation" a poet feels when he writes a poem that "completely accomplishes the purpose of the poet" *(NA,* 50). To describe this feeling, he edges up to a "state of elevation" by means of a series of conditional hypotheses: "If . . . we speak of liberation . . . of justification . . . of purification . . . the experience of the poet is of no less a degree than the experience of the mystic" (*NA,* 50–51). In defining the quasi-mystical quality of this experience, Stevens again resorts to a conditional sentence structure, and he takes further precautions by juggling the mood and tense of his verbs. "If we say that the idea of God is merely a poetic idea, even if the supreme poetic idea . . . the feeling . . . of a perfection touched . . . if we say these things and if we are able to see the poet who achieved God and placed Him in His seat in heaven in all His glory, the poet himself . . . would have seemed . . . a man who needed what he had created, uttering the hymns of joy that followed his creation" (*NA,* 51). In his conclusion (the *then* clause of the *if . . . then* construction), Stevens abandons the present general form of the conditional with which he begins the sentence and replaces it with a past subjunctive, "would have seemed." The effect of the anacoluthon in tense and mood is to shift the logical ground from the syntax of factual statement to the syntax of hypothetical possibility. Stevens is not yet himself a poet who has completely accomplished his purpose, and both facts—that he distinctly envisions his purpose, and that its achievement is still in question—determine the shape of this extraordinary sentence.

After he has announced his purpose, Stevens describes in a much more direct way the program he has undertaken to enable himself to achieve it. "Having elected to exercise his power to the full and at its height . . . he may begin its exercise by studying it in exercise and proceed little by little, as he becomes his own master, to those violences which are the maturity of his desires" (*NA,* 63–64). "Notes Toward a Supreme Fiction," written the year before "Virile Poet," is one such exercise, not one of the acts of violence that are the maturity of his desires but a preparation for those acts. In a letter of 1946, three years after this essay, Stevens writes that "this is a time for the highest poetry" (*LWS,* 526), a sentiment he corroborates and expands in "Of Ideal Time and Choice," the third section of "Three Academic Pieces" (1946–1947). In two of the essays of this period, the prose segment of "Three Academic Pieces" and "Effects of Analogy" (1948), Stevens is primarily concerned with a theory of poetic meaning on a fairly technical level. Although he struggles with the constraints of a dualistic terminology, he nonetheless affirms that "the ideal itself remains alive with an enormous life" (*NA*, 82). The major visionary poems soon follow this declaration, and in his subsequent essays Stevens' tone changes from one of cautious prophecy to one of firm exposition.

Stevens' greatest poetry involves both the human and the divine, and it simultaneously employs metaphysical abstraction and archetypal symbolism. These combinations result in a philosophical mythology that is dominated by the image of life itself as the "ancient mother" (*NA*, 28). In an essay of 1948, "Imagination as Value," Stevens seeks once again to define the essence of poetry, and the definition he gives implicitly provides a rationale for the major visionary poems of 1947 and 1948. He suggests that "the life of the imagination . . . the life of the faculty itself" consists in the effort "to satisfy, say, the universal mind, which, in the case of a poet, would be the imagination that tries to penetrate to basic images, basic emotions, and so to compose a fundamental poetry even older than the ancient world" (*NA*, 144, 145). In "Two or Three Ideas" (1951), one of his most compelling essays, Stevens offers an evocative analysis of mythology, and he explains how a poetry of mythic vision enables the poet to fulfill "a spiritual role" in the modern world (*OP*, 206). He proposes to discuss the kind of response one must feel at the death of the gods, and he professes, for the sake of simplicity, to "speak only of the ancient and the foreign gods" (*OP*, 205). In fact, what he describes is the "experience of annihilation" at the death of his own gods—the Christian pantheon (*OP*, 207). If Stevens' true subject in this essay were only the death of the Mediterranean gods, the historical accuracy of his account of their demise would be patently defective. "To see the gods dispelled in mid-air and dissolve like clouds is one of the great human experiences. It is not as if they had gone over the horizon to disappear for a time; nor as if they had been overcome by other gods of greater power and profounder knowledge. It is simply that they came to nothing" (*OP*, 206). The ancient gods were, in fact, overcome by other and greater gods. Even more telling than this flaw in historical objectivity is the subjective response. Because Stevens could never have entertained any belief in the substantial existence of the ancient gods, he could never have witnessed them being "dispelled in mid-air."

By merging his own gods with those of the ancient world, Stevens can generalize easily about the recurrent experience of lost faith; and by distancing himself with the pretext of discussing a remote calamity, he can illustrate, in a manner at once dispassionate and poignant, the experience he refers to with more reticence in a letter of 1940: "My trouble, and the trouble of a great many people, is the loss of belief in the sort of God in Whom we were all brought up to believe. Humanism would be the natural substitute, but the more I see of humanism the less I like it" (*LWS,* 348). The cause Stevens assigns for the death of the gods is the emergence of "a different aesthetic" in which "the difference was that of an intenser humanity" (*OP,* 212–13). The result of this change was, first, that "it left us feeling dispossessed and alone in a solitude, like children without parents," so that each man had "to resolve life and the world in his own terms" (*OP,* 207). In "Sunday Morning" (1915), Stevens had declared that we live in an "island solitude, unsponsored, free" (*CP,* 70), and within this solitude the terms of resolution he had proposed were those of an intenser humanity. "Divinity must live within herself: / Passions of rain, or moods in falling snow" (*CP,* 67). The course of Stevens' poetic development confirms that the more he saw of this kind of humanism the less he liked it. In "Asides on the Oboe" (1940), he declares that "It is a question, now, / Of final belief" and that "It is time to choose" (*CP,* 250). The choice he makes is not to renounce all gods but to fashion new ones. In "Two or Three Ideas," he seeks to explain and justify this choice. He argues that if the old gods have proven themselves by their death to be nothing more than "a definition of perfection in ideal creatures," then the poet retains as their legacy the capacity for making new definitions of perfection in ideal creatures of his own imagining (*OP,* 212). "There are always available to us the faculties of the past, but always vitally new and strong, as the sources of perfection today and tomorrow" (*OP,* 216). The gods are the "personae of a peremptory elevation and glory"; they are those companions we create because "if not superficially explicative" they are "at least, assumed to be full of the secret of things" and "in any event bear in themselves even, if they do not always wear it, the peculiar majesty of mankind's sense of worth" (*OP,* 206, 208).

So long as Stevens was content to define pure poetry in purely aesthetic terms (music and images), he had no pressing need to reflect on the relations between poetry and philosophy. Once he begins to redefine pure poetry as a spiritual quest, he must directly confront the issue of conceptual content and defend the claims of poetry, as against those of philosophy, for cognitive supremacy. His method for accomplishing these purposes is, on the one hand, to form a rapprochement between poetry and philosophy by establishing their community of metaphysical interests and, on the other hand, to elevate poetry as a more complete form of knowledge. In "Virile Poet," Stevens sets philosophy and poetry on an equal footing. They both seek "truth," and both imagination and reason are necessary complements of any "complete" idea *(NA,* 42). Having established this equation of aim and complementarity of function, Stevens goes a step further and designates poetry as "superior" (*NA,* 43), but he has not yet found any cogent way of validating this claim. He says that the pleasure of the imagination is "the pleasure of powers that create a truth that cannot be arrived at by the reason alone, a truth that the poet recognizes by sensation" (*NA,* 58).

The degree to which Stevens himself felt the feebleness of his resort to sensationalism may be measured by the violence with which, in "Imagination as Value," he swings back the other way. He quotes Ernst Cassirer's characterization of Schelling's Romantic theory of the imagination. "'*The true poem is not the work of the individual artist; it is the universe itself, the one work of art which is forever perfecting itself*'" (*NA,* 136). Stevens wholeheartedly endorses this view of the imagination, which he dubs "the imagination as metaphysics" (*NA,* 138), and he singles out as its essential feature the drive to abstraction. "The imagination is the only genius. It is intrepid and eager and the extreme of its achievement lies in abstraction" (*NA,* 139). The greatest threat to this achievement is "the romantic," which subsists in "minor wish-fulfillments" and "is incapable of abstraction."

At first sight, Stevens' designation of his nemesis as "the romantic" is confusing, for its opposite, the imagination as metaphysics, is what Cassirer calls "'*romantic thought*'" (*NA,* 136). The clue to this puzzle may be found in Stevens' early definition of pure poetry. In the letter in which he recalls identifying "*pure poetry*" with "images and the music of verse," he implicitly concedes that such poetry could be designated "decorative" (*LWS,* 288). In one of the Adagia, he says that "romanticism is to poetry what the decorative is to painting" (*OP,* 169). When, therefore, in "Imagination as Value," he indicts the romantic because it "belittles" the imagination, he is implicitly repudiating his former association with an attenuated form of Romanticism. By the same token, when in "Two or Three Ideas" he says that "the whole effort of the imagination is toward the production of the romantic" (*OP,* 215), he is not contradicting the position he had taken in "Imagination as Value"; he is adapting his terminology to that of Cassirer. His confirmation of the romantic therein may be taken as essentially synonymous with the proclamation of another of the Adagia: "The momentum of the mind is all toward abstraction" (*OP,* 179). (A. Walton Litz dates the composition of this adage late in Stevens' career.)³ What has happened in these last two quotations is that the romantic has been redefined as "the imagination as metaphysics."

If the Paterian sensationalism of "Virile Poet" generates the abstractionist reaction of "Imagination as Value," this reaction does not itself resolve the problem of defining the relative positions of imagination and speculative reason. In "A Collect of Philosophy," Stevens returns to "the question of supremacy as between philosophy and poetry" (*OP,* 200). He acknowledges that "it is not always easy to say whether one is thinking or feeling or doing both at the same time" (*OP,* 197), and he declares that philosophical reason serves as a platform upon which imagination—characterized not by sensation but by "intuition"—rises to the idea of God, "this world's capital idea" (*OP,* 200). Imagination is thus superior to reason, but only insofar as it makes use of reason. At the same time, philosophers are granted a degree of poetic status in that "their ideas are often triumphs of the imagination." The conclusion, then, is not that either reason or imagination alone is supreme, but that "when they act in concert they are supreme" together (*OP,* 201). In "The Irrational Element," Stevens had implied that "meaning" is inessential in poetry. In "A Collect" he declares "that the wing of poetry should also be the rushing wing of meaning seems to be an extreme aesthetic good" (*OP,* 187). In 1955, commenting on a fellowship applicant he had been asked to evaluate, Stevens remarks, "The combination of imagination and intelligence seems to make for something that matures more slowly than either single faculty alone without the other" (*LWS,* 869). This observation undoubtedly reflects his own personal experience.

In conceiving of poetry as committed to meaningful statement, Stevens unavoidably involves himself in the question of poetic belief. In dealing with this question, he consistently assumes that absolute belief, that is, a belief in the absolute validity of any proposition, is obsolete. He believes that the single most distinctive feature of the modern mind is its recognition that all propositions are hypothetical, approximative, conjectural. (This idea is of course all-pervasive in the twentieth century, but two formulations of it to which Stevens may have been particularly attentive are those by James and San-

---

3. Litz, "Particles of Order," in *Wallace Stevens: A Celebration,* 65, 77.

tayana. Margaret Peterson gives a helpful summary of these two versions of hypothetical belief.)[4] In a letter of 1940, Stevens remarks that "the history of belief will show that it has always been in a fiction" (*LWS*, 370). Belief has always been an adherence to fictional constructs, but it is only in the modern world that this fact has been recognized. It is to the older, naïve form of belief that Stevens is referring when (in contrasting poetry and the Bible) he says that "poetry does not address itself to beliefs" (*NA*, 144). Poetry does not pretend to give an incontrovertible, factual account of supreme beings and supreme truths, but it does seek to figure forth man's own experience of striving toward and apprehending the divine spirit. It is in this sense that though poetry is fictive, "the incredible is not a part of poetic truth. On the contrary, what concerns us in poetry, as in everything else, is the belief of credible people in credible things" (*NA*, 53). Stevens' distinction between the two kinds of belief is at work beneath the seemingly paradoxical definition of modern man with which he concludes "A Collect": "It is as if in a study of modern man we predicated the greatness of poetry as the final measure of his stature, as if his willingness to believe beyond belief was what had made him modern and was always certain to keep him so" (*OP*, 202). To believe beyond belief is to employ poetry as the medium of a provisional knowledge of an ultimate spiritual reality. The existence of any such reality is not itself subject to logical proof. It is a poetic hypothesis, and its value as a hypothesis can be measured only by its effect. For Stevens, "the idea of God is the ultimate poetic idea" (*OP*, 193) because it most fully satisfies the poetic need for a complete figurative synthesis. It is, as Stevens often says, a product of "desire," and the mythic figurations through which it is realized are "The children of a desire that is the will" (*CP*, 436). Although these figurations are "full of the secret of things," they can never invest their secret with the status of a belief that is "final" in the sense of a fixed, dogmatic conviction in theoretical principles.

In a letter of 1945, Stevens declares that "for me the most important thing is to realize poetry," and he defines this need as "the desire to contain the world wholly within one's own perception of it" (*LWS*, 501). Short of solipsism, the only way in which Stevens can contain the world within a poetic construct is to conceive of both external reality and the individual mind as dependent elements of "the universal mind." Stevens' supreme fiction is a

---

4. Peterson, *The Idealist Tradition*, 76–79.

closing of the circle of creation. The poem that fashions an image of God—"the central mind"—validates this image by attributing it to the creative agency of God himself. As Stevens puts it, in one of the Adagia, "The mind that in heaven created the earth and the mind that on earth created heaven were, as it happened, one" (*OP,* 176).

The fulfillment that Stevens proposes to himself in his supreme fiction is to become the medium through which God achieves knowledge of himself. Stevens begins to draw toward this conclusion in "Virile Poet," where he declares that "an idea of God," if it satisfied both reason and imagination, "would establish a divine beginning and end for us" (*NA,* 42). It is in this essay, also, that he identifies his quest as a determination to find "a center of poetry, a *vis* or *noeud vital*" (*NA,* 44). At this point, in 1943, Stevens already apprehends the most extreme implications of this quest. He explains the source of "that sense of the possibility of a remote, a mystical *vis* or *noeud vital*" by describing "the way a poet feels when he is writing. . . . To describe it by exaggerating it, he shares the transformation, not to say apotheosis, accomplished by the poem" (*NA,* 49). In one of the Adagia, he is less diffident:

Proposita: 1. God and the imagination are one. 2. The thing imagined is the imaginer.
The second equals the thing imagined and the imaginer are one. Hence, I suppose, the imaginer is God. (*OP,* 178)

Stevens' formulations of these principles probably draw support from similar formulations in Emerson. In "Nature," Emerson defines "Ideas" as "immortal necessary uncreated natures," and he argues that "no man touches these divine natures, without becoming, in some degree, himself divine" (*RWE,* I, 56, 57). The hedging phrase "in some degree" would have found a responsive ear in Stevens. In "The Over-Soul," Emerson is more direct. "The simplest person who in his integrity worships God, becomes God" (*RWE,* II, 292). For Stevens, "the imaginer is God" because in writing poetry the poet shares in the sentient principle that creates the world and that achieves self-recognition in human thought. This is the idea that Stevens in "Imagination as Value" adopts under the title "the imagination as metaphysics," the idea that "the true work of art, whatever it may be, is not the work of the individual artist. It is time and it is place, as these perfect themselves" (*NA,* 139–40). These are the terms Stevens uses in "The Owl in the Sarcophagus" to describe the mythological embodiments of the supreme fiction: "The pure perfections of parental space" (*CP*, 436). The poet is both creator and created, the child of his own images. He brings these images to birth, but they are begotten in him by the parental space in which he resides. Within this space there is an active principle of sentient generation which is the will to perfection. In "The Auroras of Autumn," Stevens says that "There is or may be a time of innocence / As pure principle. Its nature is its end" (*CP*, 418). In "A Primitive Like an Orb," he speaks of

> A vis, a principle, or, it may be,
> The meditation of a principle,
> Or else an inherent order active to be
> Itself. (*CP*, 442)

The supreme figure in Stevens' mythology, the ancient mother, gives visible form to this principle. In "Owl," Stevens calls this figure "The earthly mother and the mother of / The dead," and he merges her with "the ultimate intellect" (*CP*, 432, 433). In "Auroras" he calls her "the innocent mother" and represents her as creating "the time and place in which we breathed" (*CP*, 419).

As Stevens himself knew and readily acknowledged, he was "not a philosopher" (*OP*, 195). His essays, though intended as a general contribution to the theory of poetry, primarily serve as a means for clarifying to himself the purposes and assumptions of his own poetry. In a letter of 1951, he declared that he liked to do his papers "'because they clear my mind and make it necessary to take a good look at ideas that otherwise would drift about vaguely, with no place to go.'" When Louis Martz suggested that Stevens publish "Effects of Analogy," he responded, "'Oh, do you think anybody would be interested in reading it? You know these prose things, just thinking out loud. It's really not . . . Do you think people would be interested?'"[5] People have been interested, but less for the intrinsic merit of the prose than for the light it sheds on the poetry. In "A Collect," Stevens conjures images of both "the philosopher and the poet as raised to their highest exponents," and he asks what such men would compose "by way of fulfilling not only themselves but also by way of fulfilling the aims of their creator?" (*OP*, 199). By turning to the poetry, we may find an answer to half of the question Stevens asks.

5. Brazeau, *Wallace Stevens Remembered*, 162, 174.

CHAPTER TWO

Evanescent Symmetries

The whole body of Stevens' poetry, from *Harmonium* to *The Rock* and the later poems of *Opus Posthumous,* presents a deceptive continuity of surface. It is generally recognized that there is a gradual drift toward a more abstract diction and a more meditative tone, but it is possible to regard this drift as simply the effect of advancing age on a mind that remains fixed in its basic attitudes. For many of Stevens' readers, the same symbolic images and the same themes seem to recur with a monotony that is enlivened only by the ingenuity with which they are reformulated. J. V. Cunningham's view on Stevens' lack of development is fairly representative of the early responses to his work. Cunningham declares that once Stevens had stated his basic theme—"the intuition of a bare reality behind conventional appearance"— "there was nothing more to be done with it, except to say it over again in another place. This he has repeatedly done, though with a prodigality of invention in phrasing that is astounding." Yvor Winters, taking a moralistic view of Stevens' "hedonism," assigns it as the chief cause in the "rapid and tragic decay of the poet's style." In an influential essay, Louis Martz maintains that "Winters has made a brilliant diagnosis of the malady; but he underestimated the patient's will to live." Martz argues that though the hedonistic sensuality of *Harmonium* gives place in the later poetry to a more meditative style, the metaphysical orientation remains the same. "Stevensian meditation becomes: attentive thinking about concrete things with the aim of developing an affectionate understanding of how good it is to be alive." Helen Vendler, emphasizing death over life as a source of poetic energy, attributes to some of Stevens' bleaker late poems a unique strength and authenticity. Nonetheless, she also says of *Harmonium* that "all of Stevens is in it, and not in embryo either." Joseph Riddel rightly observes that "the question of Stevens' development is indeed crucial. To deny him that, it seems to me, is to deny his greatness." He holds that the poetry did in fact "develop and mature" but adds that "the evidence of this development lies in neither his ideas as such nor in basic stylistic changes as such, but in the inner life of a changing and aging sensibility." Riddel, like Martz, believes that "his ideas in the abstract were fully formed (if not clearly refined) in the early poems, and fully in-form them." It would be difficult to conceive of a "sensibility" without ideas or style, and Riddel himself reverts to style as the key term in his analysis of Stevens' development. "His development is manifest in an evolution of style, and thus of the self it expresses." Michel Benamou, protesting against the common opinion that changes in Stevens' poetry "were only stylistic," offers a scheme for the "psycho-symbolic evolution of Stevens' poetry." Benamou's basically psychoanalytic scheme does not concern itself much with Stevens' metaphysical orientation. Alan Perlis is largely correct in his contention that those critics "who mark significant changes in the poems from *Harmonium* (1923) to *The Rock* (1955) insist that these changes concern emphasis and impact rather than a radical shift of ideas." Perlis himself concurs with this view. In his most recent book on Stevens, Frank Doggett reformulates and reaffirms the opinion that "the real effect of his later intentions in poetry were a modulation of tone and language." He gives a sympathetic description of the later style—"the aphoristic air, the discursive tone, the theoretical implications, the suggestion of logical form"—but he also maintains that "the normal was still the center that he sought."[1]

If we look more closely, beneath the apparent repetitions in Stevens' work, we see that his recurrent images do not have fixed symbolic meanings. These

---

1. J. V. Cunningham, "Tradition and Modernity: Wallace Stevens," *Poetry*, LXXV (December, 1949), rev. and rpr. in *The Collected Essays of J. V. Cunningham* (Chicago, 1976), 234; Yvor Winters, "Wallace Stevens or the Hedonist's Progress," in *The Anatomy of Nonsense* (Norfolk, Conn., 1943), rpr. in *In Defense of Reason* (Chicago, 1947), 433; Louis L. Martz, "Wallace Stevens: The World as Meditation," in M. H. Abrams (ed.), *Literature and Belief: The English Institute Essays for 1957* (New York, 1958), rpr. in Marie Borroff (ed.), *Wallace Stevens: A Collection of Critical Essays* (Englewood Cliffs, 1963), 136, 147; Helen Hennessy Vendler, *On Extended Wings: Wallace Stevens' Longer Poems* (Cambridge, Mass., 1969), 65; Riddel, *The Clairvoyant Eye*, 4, 5; Michel Benamou, *Wallace Stevens and the Symbolist Imagination* (Princeton, 1972), 117–18; Alan Perlis, *Wallace Stevens: A World of Transforming Shapes* (Lewisburg, Pa., 1976), 21; Doggett, *The Making of the Poem*, 125, 117, 125.

images can provide us with points of reference through which we may trace profound changes in the framework of his thought. Moreover, the images that in *Harmonium* sometimes appear either casual or decorative gradually develop into motifs that relate to one another in increasingly elaborate and meaningful ways. Stevens' work forms a whole, not of repetition and variation but of continuously evolving structure. In "Sketch of the Ultimate Politician" (1947), Stevens describes his visionary enterprise, as he often does, from a third-person point of view; he affirms the coherence and unity of his work, but he also implicitly denies that this work has already assumed a settled form: "He is the final builder of the total building, / The final dreamer of the total dream, / Or will be" (*CP*, 335). (These declarations may be correlated with Northrop Frye's remarks that from the "anagogic" or spiritual perspective, "literature is a total form" that "imitates the total dream of man.")[2] "Sketch of the Ultimate Politician" is one of those notes toward a supreme fiction that in *Parts of a World* and *Transport to Summer* explicitly declare Stevens' ambition and help to define its qualities. In the poems of *Harmonium,* though Stevens is already orienting himself, as by an instinctive necessity, to the fabrication of a great structure, he is still far from envisioning the metaphysical and aesthetic character this structure will ultimately assume.

A supreme fiction is a figurative synthesis that provides a sense of cosmic unity. The degree to which Stevens succeeds in achieving this sort of synthesis manifests itself in the quiet sublimity of a poem written in 1950, "Final Soliloquy of the Interior Paramour":

> Here, now, we forget each other and ourselves.
> We feel the obscurity of an order, a whole,
> A knowledge, that which arranged the rendezvous.
>
> Within its vital boundary, in the mind.
> We say God and the imagination are one . . .
> How high that highest candle lights the dark. (*CP*, 524)

The sense of purpose in the world belongs not only to the individual mind but also to "the central mind," that is, to a universal spiritual presence. The meeting that this presence has arranged between itself and the mind of the poet consists simply of a momentary recognition. The poet's recognition entails no ritual, no professions of doctrinal conformity, no commitments to a

---

2. Frye, *Anatomy of Criticism,* 118, 119.

given form of behavior, and no quasi-contractual obligations or rewards. The only reward is the achieved sense of a cosmic unity that is a perfected order.

For Stevens, "the major poetic idea in the world is and always has been the idea of God" (*LWS*, 378), but the forms with which Stevens invests his intuitions of divinity change radically in the course of his life. In a letter of 1951, he says, "I am not an atheist although I do not believe to-day in the same God in whom I believed when I was a boy" (*LWS*, 735). After he has abandoned the orthodox beliefs of his boyhood, Stevens seeks to sustain his intuitions of divinity by articulating them within the idiom of Romantic poetry. By the time he is a young man and has begun keeping his journals, it is already "an old argument" with him "that the true religious force in the world is not the church but the world itself: the mysterious callings of Nature and our responses" (*LWS*, 58). He still feels the pathos of traditional religious worship, but the poet in him responds more powerfully to the divinity in nature, where he sees "every leaf and blade of grass revealing or rather betokening the Invisible" (*LWS*, 59). In *Harmonium* and *Ideas of Order*, this sort of Wordsworthian and Whitmanian natural supernaturalism subsists for Stevens only as an intellectually amorphous sentiment. He is unable to integrate it within a complete cosmological structure, and as a result "the Invisible" often reduces itself to the insubstantial, the unreal, or the merely absent. One of the most comprehensive and succinct of Stevens' early cosmological figurations is that of "Negation" (1917), and in this poem Stevens rationalizes his failure to achieve metaphysical closure by attributing this failure to a deficiency that is inherent in the structure of the cosmos:

> Hi! The creator too is blind,
> Struggling toward his harmonious whole,
> Rejecting intermediate parts,
> Horrors and falsities and wrongs;
> Incapable master of all force,
> Too vague idealist, overwhelmed
> By an afflatus that persists.
> For this, then, we endure brief lives,
> The evanescent symmetries
> From that meticulous potter's thumb. (*CP*, 97–98)

The exuberance of this poem is edged with bitterness. God is an "idealist" because he is driven by the need for synthesis, and he is an "Incapable master" because he cannot formulate the principles that would enable him fully to satisfy this need. He is merely the summary term of natural force, and he is himself subject to the irrepressible impulsion of his own inadequacy. As he struggles helplessly toward an unattainable unity, he succeeds only in creating moments of local aesthetic congruence. The "evanescent symmetries" of nature are the objective equivalent of what, in "The Irrational Element in Poetry," Stevens calls "a momentary existence on an exquisite plane" (*OP,* 223). The poet is God's counterpart, and, by mocking the futility of God's blind drive, Stevens threatens to undercut the dynamic impulse that enables him to achieve such moments of partial consummation in his own poetry. Ultimately, despite his mocking tone, Stevens too will be overwhelmed by "an afflatus that persists." He will continue to invent cosmic hypotheses and to test these hypotheses against the norm of a "harmonious whole." Through this process he will gradually correct the vagueness of the creator's idealism, and, by correcting it, he will transform the "Incapable master of all force" into "the central mind."

In *Harmonium,* Stevens' metaphysical vision restricts itself, for the most part, to a simple opposition between the mind and the external world. Given this limitation, the only way in which Stevens can satisfy his need for unity and wholeness is to collapse one pole of his dichotomy into the other: to figure the mind as a reflex of the external world, or to figure the world as a projection of the mind. "Anecdote of Men by the Thousand" (1918) illustrates one such form of reductive resolution. "The soul, he said, is composed / Of the external world" (*CP,* 51). Poetry, even if it is an expression of the soul, is also a reflex of place. It is like "the cackle of toucans / In the place of toucans." At the opposite extreme, represented by "Tea at the Palaz of Hoon" (1921), the soul becomes the only generative term, and the external world is composed of the soul:

> I was the world in which I walked, and what I saw
> Or heard or felt came not but from myself;
> And there I found myself more truly and more strange. (*CP,* 65)

These contrasting forms of reductivism offer contrasting forms of aesthetic satisfaction. The reduction of experience to a reflex of place yields a sensation of the "natural," and the reduction of place to a reflex of the self yields a sensation of the peculiar or "strange."

Dorothea Steiner points out that the first two lines in the final stanza of "Hoon" (just quoted) echo these lines from book three of *The Prelude*: "I had a world about me—'twas my own; / I made it, for it only lived to me" (ll. 144–45).³ Stevens' selective use of this passage provides a good example of the censorship to which he submits the Romantic influence in his early poetry. In his later poetry, he will be more receptive to the whole context of Wordsworth's assertion:

> To every natural form, rock, fruit or flower,
> Even the loose stones that cover the high way,
> I gave a moral life: I saw them feel,
> Or linked them to some feeling: the great mass
> Lay bedded in a quickening soul, and all
> That I beheld respired with inward meaning.
> . . . .
> I had a world about me—'twas my own;
> I made it, for it only lived to me,
> And to the God who sees into the heart. (ll. 130–35, 144–46)

For Wordsworth the "life" of nature—and consequently the sentient relation between man and nature—derives from the transcendental "soul" that he identifies with "the God who sees into the heart." In "Hoon," Stevens excises this enabling condition, and the result is solipsism.

The solipsism of "Hoon" is a form of theoretical extravagance that will not long bear the light of common day; moreover, it stands in conflict with Stevens' powerful need for a sense of a solid reality outside himself. It is this need to which Stevens gives blunt utterance in his address to the "ancient star" in "Nuances of a Theme by Williams" (1918). He asks that the star "Shine alone" so that it "reflects neither my face nor any inner part / of my being" (*CP*, 18). "Intelligence" and naked matter, represented by the star, are to remain utterly alien and distinct. The very forcefulness with which Stevens formulates this dualistic vision reveals its problematic character. "Lend no part to any humanity that suffuses / you in its own light." By affirming the total segregation of subject and object, Stevens discloses the origin of the impulse that drives him, paradoxically, to the solipsism of "Hoon." Light is the medium of visual perception, and in these two lines Stevens attributes this light to the perceiving subject alone. A star that lends no part to humanity

---

3. Dorothea Steiner, "Wallace Stevens: Romantic Traits in Modern Poetic Theory," in James Hogg (ed.), *On Poets and Poetry: A Symposium from the Department of English at the University of Salzburg* (Salzburg, Austria, 1974), 71.

would not be an object of perception; it would not exist within the same cosmos as humanity.

In "Nuances" the paradoxicality of Stevens' desire to participate consciously in a non-sentient nature remains latent. In "The Snow Man" (1921), this paradox constitutes the very structure of the poem. "The Snow Man," like "Nuances," presents itself as a purification of perception. The process of purification advances in two stages: from imagistic brilliance to nothingness. In the first stage, comprising the first three stanzas, the speaker supposes a hypothetical perceptual agent, presumably a human being, who identifies so intimately with the inanimate objects of his perception that he ceases to project his own human feelings onto them. He hears no "misery in the sound of the wind" because his own feelings have been numbed (*CP,* 10). He has been "cold a long time." This sacrifice of the pathetic fallacy still leaves room for a residual Romantic animism on a mental level. By dehumanizing oneself, one may come to think as winter thinks. To have "a mind of winter" is to "behold" the winter landscape with a nonprojective perceptual clarity. In the second stage of purification, the perceptual agent transfers his own cognitive activity, by way of the wind, to the snow man. By means of this transference, Stevens suspends perception in a paradoxical interplay of presence and absence. Perception remains present as pure activity but is detached from a perceptual agent and purified of objective content. The snow man, though "nothing himself," "listens" and "beholds"; what he beholds is "nothing." The mind of winter, as nonentity, continues to perceive, and what is perceived is the absence of mind. By embracing paradox, Stevens manages to escape dualism without falling into the solipsistic reductivism of "Hoon," but he falls instead into the nihilistic asceticism of the "anti-master-man" (*CP,* 241). When in his later poems Stevens employs the technique of paradoxical suspension, he does so in order to evoke a sense of a universal spiritual presence, not to resolve his dialectical oppositions in nothingness.

Poems such as "Tea at the Palaz of Hoon" and "Anecdote of Men by the Thousand" establish doctrinal extremes. The middle ground is held by those poems in which the dichotomy between the mind and nature is not strained to the breaking point but instead provides an arena for imaginative activity. In this middle ground, the mind seeks to encompass, dominate, and give order to an external world of concrete objects, an effort that may or may not, on any given occasion, be successful. If the effort fails and "The squirming facts exceed the squamous mind" (*CP,* 215), it may still be possible to depict poetically the mind's futile engagement with the external world. "Metaphors of a Magnifico" (1918) may serve as a paradigm for this situation, for the poem is a dramatic representation of an attempted formulation that is never realized. The image at the beginning of the poem—"Twenty men crossing a bridge, / Into a village"—is put forth as material for conceptualization, but "the meaning escapes" and the effort of conceptualization dissolves in the ellipsis points that conclude the poem (*CP,* 19). "Anecdote of the Jar" (1919), in contrast, celebrates a moment of aesthetic triumph. Stevens achieves this triumph by means of a tactic similar to that of "The Snow Man"; he transfers his own imaginative activity to an inhuman medium. The effect of this tactic in "Anecdote of the Jar" is to represent the conflict between the mind and external reality as an impersonal play of aesthetic forces:

> I placed a jar in Tennessee,
> And round it was, upon a hill.
> It made the slovenly wilderness
> Surround that hill. (*CP,* 76)

The three stanzas of the poem move in a circling pattern, repeating first elements in a jubilant manner and gradually coming closer to the concentrated focus of the third stanza: "The jar was gray and bare." The jar serves as an extension of the poet's own drive to order, but it achieves dominion over the chaotic wilderness precisely because it is inanimate. "It did not give of bird or bush." The jar does not itself move or change; it merely sheds influence. The source of its power is its perfection of empty form. It is "of a port in air," stately and imposing but also vacant, a mere circular opening in the air. The dominion of the jar is evoked on the level of sound and image by the repetition of the word *round*. The jar is round upon a rounded piece of ground, a hill, and the image of roundness is picked up again, phonetically, in the word *ground*: "The jar was round upon the ground." Stevens catches the assimilation of chaos to order in the moment of transformation. The wilderness, though "slovenly," surrounds the hill, and though it sprawls, it sprawls "around." The transformation to controlled pattern is reflected even in the metrical structure of the poem. The smoothness of contour in the short, tight iambic lines is broken only once, by "slovenly wilderness," and at this point the wilderness is already being rounded up. The word *slovenly* is a backward glance at irregularity. Whatever potential form or roundness there may be in the wilderness answers to the realized form of the jar. The jar simply is round, and because it is round, the wilderness moves to surround it.

The jar in Tennessee represents a purely formal principle of order, and this kind of order cannot satisfy the deepest needs of Stevens' imagination. He ultimately seeks not only to impose order on the external world but to integrate the mind and the world within a sentient unity of being. As long as he remains fixed within a dualistic conception of the world, this fulfillment will elude him. In "Jasmine's Beautiful Thoughts Underneath the Willow" (1923), he professes a "vivid apprehension" of "bliss submerged beneath appearance," but he locates this bliss "In an interior ocean's rocking" (*CP*, 79). That is, to penetrate beneath the surface of things, he has recourse to an intensive subjectivism. He can resolve the opposition of interior and exterior only by coloring the interior with a metaphor of the exterior (the ocean). The apprehension of bliss is no doubt genuine, but the resolution of conflict remains superficial.

Within a dualistic cosmos, the metaphoric mingling of the mind and nature represents the kind of Romanticism that Stevens says subsists in "minor wish-fulfillments" (*NA*, 139). In order to escape from this limited imaginative range, Stevens will have to locate the drive to sentient unity outside the individual mind, and in one early poem, "To the Roaring Wind" (1917), he begins to move in this direction:

> What syllable are you seeking,
> Vocalissimus,
> In the distances of sleep?
> Speak it. (*CP*, 113)

"To the Roaring Wind" is a very slight but, for Stevens, very important poem. He signals this importance by placing it last in *Harmonium,* a decision that reflects an impulse similar to that which tempted him to entitle his first volume "The Grand Poem: Preliminary Minutiae" (*LWS,* 237). "To the Roaring Wind" is a cryptic prefiguration of the supreme fiction. "Vocalissimus" is the wind, and the wind embodies an inhuman force that seeks to achieve conscious expression in human utterance. This is the kind of Romanticism that Stevens calls "the imagination as metaphysics" (*NA,* 138), and in his later poetry Stevens will elaborate the images of this poem. At the climax of "Montrachet-Le-Jardin" (1942), the wind will again appear as the medium of mystic speech, and in both "The Auroras of Autumn" and "The Owl in the Sarcophagus" the wind will be combined with other natural images of the sublime: mountains, vast distances, and the stars. The "syllable" sought in the distances of sleep becomes an emblem of pure experience. In "Owl" the mother of the living and the dead is "she that in the syllable between life / And death cries quickly, in a flash of voice" (*CP*, 432).

At the time of *Harmonium*, Stevens has not yet formulated his dichotomy between the poetry of normal life and pure poetry as a mode of visionary revelation. He has, however, already established a distinction between the consciousness of day and that of night. In "Hymn from a Watermelon Pavilion" (1922), he asks:

> Of the two dreams, night and day,
> What lover, what dreamer, would choose
> The one obscured by sleep? (*CP*, 89)

The answer is that Stevens himself will often choose the dreams of night, and these are the dreams that will dominate his poetic ambitions. In "Owl," at the very apex of his visionary drive, Stevens proclaims that "Sleep realized / Was the whiteness that is the ultimate intellect" (*CP*, 433). The reason that sleep serves for Stevens as the medium of visionary revelation discloses itself in "Effects of Analogy." In this essay, Stevens defines "two theories" of poetry. One concerns itself with ordinary experience, and the other derives from the poet's feeling "that his imagination is not wholly his own but that it may be part of a much larger, much more potent imagination, which it is his affair to try to get at" (*NA*, 115). A poet who feels this way will try to live "on the verge of consciousness." In most of the poems of *Harmonium*, Stevens presupposes that his imagination is "wholly his own." He has nonetheless already begun to cultivate his capacity for living "on the verge of consciousness." Sleep is the natural condition for this "subliminal" state (*NA*, 115), and in "The Curtains in the House of the Metaphysician" (1919), Stevens depicts a drift into sleep that culminates in a glimpse into some shadowy absolute.

"Curtains" exemplifies two techniques that Stevens will continue to employ in his mature visionary poetry: the collapsing of phenomenal categories through paradox, and the ascent to visionary climax through a series of sublime images loosely associated as metaphor or simile. The content of Stevens' vision will develop far beyond that of "Curtains":

> It comes about that the drifting of these curtains
> Is full of long motions; as the ponderous
> Deflations of distance; or as clouds
> Inseparable from their afternoons;
> Or the changing of light, the dropping
> Of the silence, wide sleep and solitude
> Of night, in which all motion
> Is beyond us, as the firmament,
> Up-rising and down-falling, bares
> The last largeness, bold to see. (*CP,* 62)

The designation "these curtains" makes it clear that the speaker represents himself as describing his perceptions and the transformations of these perceptions as they occur. The transformations are rendered in a series of similes, all of which formally refer to the "long motions," an image that is itself an imaginative distortion of the primary object of perception. After "the changing of the light," there is a paradoxical shift from "motions" to the stillness of sleep and solitude. The musings over distances and drifting shapes have become metaphorically equivalent to the passive perception of dream vision, a state in which "all motion / Is beyond us." The up-rising and down-falling of the firmament, though it may vaguely suggest the opening of theater curtains on a stage, is not, strictly speaking, an image that can be visually conceived. Like "the ponderous / Deflations of distance," it merely collapses the categories of three-dimensional perception in order to intimate some form of perception not limited to the ordinary restrictions of space. The "last largeness" beyond the firmament is thus a purely mental, abstract entity. Even "largeness," a stark term of physical magnitude, must be regarded as a metaphor for the substratum or essence of things beyond any physical "accidents" or qualities. The final phrase, "bold to see," conveys the sense of exhilaration afforded the speaker by his glimpse into this substratum.

The notion of a substratum suggests a form of primitive empiricism that harks back to the metaphysics of Locke. In *An Essay Concerning Human Understanding,* Locke defines "substance" as "the supposed, but unknown, support of those qualities we find existing." Although he concedes that we cannot imagine things existing without such a support, he also declares that it is "certain we have no clear or distinct idea of that thing we suppose a support."⁴ The naïvely problematic character of this idea reappears in Stevens' own probing beneath the surface of appearances. The last largeness, though it seems to subsist beneath the phenomenal surface, is itself imaginable only as a colorless surface. It has no metaphoric qualities other than finality and dimension, and the images by which it is approached are vague, dreamy abstractions. Most important, it is static, and though it is featureless, it subsists imaginatively as an externalized object of perception, something "bold to see." Consequently, all Stevens has accomplished in this figuration of the absolute is to have situated the dichotomy between the mind and reality at one remove from the common light of day. He has as yet found no way to conceive and to realize poetically a sentient unity of phenomenal process.

The notion of a substratum, though it is hardly susceptible to elaborate poetic figuration, appears as a spiritual refuge in one of Stevens' most personal and troubled early poems, "Le Monocle de Mon Oncle" (1918). "Monocle" is Stevens' first major poem after "Sunday Morning" (1915), and in "Monocle" he has recourse to "The basic slate, the universal hue" (*CP,* 15) to vindicate the continuing vitality of his creative effort. The pivotal significance of Stevens' reference to the basic slate will become clear once we have identified the themes and analyzed the structure of the poem. The suppression of explicit thematic links between most of the stanzas, the frequent radical shifts in symbolic imagery, and the complex ambiguity of tone render "Monocle" one of Stevens' most difficult, self-consciously modernist poems.⁵ One can nonetheless discern a coherent formal order in the progression of the stanzas.

In a letter of 1928, Stevens gives a typically bland, understated description of the poem. "I had in mind simply a man fairly well along in life, looking back and talking in a more or less personal way about life" (*LWS,* 251). In the poem itself, he suggests much more specifically the occasion that gives rise to this meditation:

> Anguishing hour!
> Last night, we sat beside a pool of pink,
> Clippered with lilies scudding the bright chromes,
> Keen to the point of starlight, while a frog
> Boomed from his very belly odious chords. (*CP,* 17)

---

4. John Locke, *An Essay Concerning Human Understanding,* ed. Alexander Campbell Fraser (New York, 1959), I, 392, 395.

5. For comments on the relation between Stevens' poem and Donald Evans' "En Mono-

The "we" of "Monocle" represents two persons, the speaker and a woman, presumably his wife. The questions and statements directed to "you" suggest an intimate colloquy, but there are no responses recorded from the woman. The recollection of their "Anguishing hour" comes at the very end of the meditative sequence. The one remaining stanza of the poem serves as an allegorical, biographical coda, and it is written at a level of aesthetic tension lower than that of the preceding stanzas. Stevens reveals the immediate stimulus for his meditation only after he has worked through the problem and reached his conclusion. "If sex were all, then every trembling hand / Could make us squeak, like dolls, the wished-for words." The anxiety that has given rise to the poem is that sex might indeed be all. One likely source for this anxiety may be located in the early work of George Santayana. In *The Sense of Beauty* (1896), Santayana argues that "for man all nature is a secondary object of sexual passion" and that "to this fact the beauty of nature is largely due." In several of the essays in *Interpretations of Poetry and Religion* (1900), Santayana applies the idea of sexual sublimation directly to literature.[6] If, as Santayana suggests, sex were the mainspring of imaginative passion, a poet approaching forty could anticipate a gradual decline of his creative drive. The booming of the frog connotes a raw sexual energy that implicitly mocks the meditative sublime connoted by starlight.

Stevens begins his meditative sequence by assuming what he most fears, that youth and sexual energy are the only genuine sources for imaginative vitality. In this way he assimilates the mockery implied in the "odious chords" from the frog's belly:

> "Mother of heaven, regina of the clouds,
> O sceptre of the sun, crown of the moon,
> There is not nothing, no, no, never nothing,
> Like the clashed edges of two words that kill."
> And so I mocked her in magnificent measure.
> Or was it that I mocked myself alone?
> I wish that I might be a thinking stone.

---

cle," see Robert Buttel, *Wallace Stevens: The Making of "Harmonium"* (Princeton, 1967), 92; and Glen G. Macleod, *Wallace Stevens and Company: The "Harmonium" Years, 1913–1923* (Ann Arbor, 1983), 70–75.

6. George Santayana, *The Sense of Beauty: Being the Outlines of Aesthetic Theory* (New York, 1896), 62; George Santayana, *Interpretations of Poetry and Religion* (New York, 1900).

> The sea of spuming thought foists up again
> The radiant bubble that she was. And then
> A deep up-pouring from some saltier well
> Within me, bursts its watery syllable.

Stevens glosses the "clashed edges" by remarking that "in addition to the excitement of suave sounds, there is an excitement, an insistent provocation in the strange cacophonies of words" (*LWS,* 250). The provocation in these words derives not only from the clash of sounds but also from the clash of meanings. It seems likely that these lines are inspired by a recollection from Tennyson's late visionary poem "The Ancient Sage" (1885). "The Ancient Sage" consists of a dialogue between a skeptical hedonist and a mystic seer. The two voices in the poem correspond roughly to the two main tendencies in Stevens' later poetry, and echoes of "The Ancient Sage" may be heard in several of Stevens' late poems. In the passage relevant to the first stanza of "Monocle," the ancient sage is describing a personified Faith. "She reels not in the storm of warring words, / She brightens at the clash of 'Yes' and 'No.'" Yes and no are emblems of affirmation and denial. If we apply these words to Stevens' lines, we may conjecture that there is never nothing because every negation is dialectically suspended with a counterposing affirmation. By placing the first four lines in quotation marks and identifying them as mockery, Stevens implies that he is skeptical about the possibility of a poetry sustained only by a dialectical interplay. His skepticism, it will become apparent, depends on an as yet unexamined assumption that the "verve of earth" (*CP,* 14) derives exclusively from sexual love.

In the letter just cited, Stevens says that "the Mother of Heaven was merely somebody to swear by" and that "the reference was not symbolic" (*LWS,* 251). By "symbolic," Stevens seems to mean a very specific, quasi-allegorical reference such as that to the pigeons and rabbis in the last stanza. The Mother of heaven is not symbolic in this sense; she serves instead as a generalized mythic embodiment of the sublime. If we identify her with "The radiant bubble that she was," and in turn identify the radiant bubble with the female companion to whom these remarks are addressed, we may conclude that this companion has heretofore served as an image of poetic inspiration—in short, a muse. R. D. Ackerman aptly cites a letter that in February, 1909, Stevens wrote to the woman he would marry in September of that year. "Sometimes I am terribly jangled, full of clashing things. But, always, the first harmony comes from something I cannot just say to you at the moment—the touch of you organizing me again—to put it so. . . . You are my—you know what I want to say—what in the fairy tales is called the genius—the thing that comes in smoke a-building marble palaces—thing for the mystery of it" (*LWS*, 131).[7] The language in which Stevens addresses the woman he mocks in "Monocle" is strikingly similar to that with which he will invoke his muse in "To the One of Fictive Music" (1922): "Sister and mother and diviner love, . . . And queen" (*CP*, 87). Stevens' mockery in "Monocle" is an expression of disillusionment. As her youth and beauty fade, the woman he married must gradually cease to be an adequate object for imaginative exaltation. The canceled stanzas for "Monocle" that are published in *Opus Posthumous* render Stevens' disillusionment with crude clarity.

> "*Oh, lissomeness turned lagging ligaments!*"
> Eheu! Eheu! With what a weedy face
> Black fact emerges from her swishing dreams. (*OP*, 19)

The contorted obliquity of Stevens' address in the published poem may be partly attributed to his need to detach his poetic rhetoric from the embarrassingly personal and to purify it of naturalistic grotesquerie.

If in stanza one the direction of Stevens' mockery is unclear even to himself, in stanza two he segregates himself from the illusory idealism of his companion and attacks her belated naïveté:

> These choirs of welcome choir for me farewell.
> No spring can follow past meridian.
> Yet you persist with anecdotal bliss
> To make believe a starry *connaissance*.

In stanzas three and four, Stevens opposes this starry *connaissance* with two elaborate tropes. The first trope suggests the ineluctable ascendancy of erotic reality over any imaginative transformations of this reality:

> You know the mountainous coiffures of Bath.
> Alas! have all the barbers lived in vain

---

7. R. D. Ackerman, "Desire, Distance, Death: Stevens' Meditative Beginnings," *Texas Studies in Literature and Language*, XXV (1983), 621. For other discussions of Elsie Kachel's role as Stevens' muse, see Milton J. Bates, "Stevens in Love: The Woman Won, the Woman Lost," *English Literary History*, XLVIII (1981), 231–55; and Brazeau, *Wallace Stevens Remembered*, 260–61.

> That not one curl in nature has survived?
> Why, without pity on these studious ghosts,
> Do you come dripping in your hair from sleep?

The direct address of the last two lines again locates the source of Stevens' disillusionment in his own intimate relations with his companion. In the next stanza Stevens elevates his personal plight by casting his disillusionment in mythic, biblical terms as a fall from innocence into the knowledge of corruption:

> This luscious and impeccable fruit of life
> Falls, it appears, of its own weight to earth.
> When you were Eve, its acrid juice was sweet,
> Untasted, in its heavenly, orchard air.

The fruit of the tree of knowledge has now been tasted, and in stanza five, Stevens formulates this knowledge in a direct statement of thesis: "The measure of the intensity of love / Is measure, also, of the verve of earth." The verve of earth is poetic inspiration. By thus isolating and clarifying his thesis, Stevens brings himself to the point, in stanza six, where it is possible to counter this thesis:

> If men at forty will be painting lakes
> The ephemeral blues must merge for them in one,
> The basic slate, the universal hue.
> There is a substance in us that prevails.
> But in our amours amorists discern
> Such fluctuations that their scrivening
> Is breathless to attend each quirky turn.

The basic slate is a substratum of experience that stands as the subjective equivalent of "The last largeness." It is featureless, beyond change, and is thus impervious to the decline of sexual verve. Heretofore Stevens has himself taken the side of the "amorists." In this stanza he manages to extricate himself from their position and to turn the mockery back against them. The "ephemeral blues" are the fluctuations of erotic experience that must be subordinated to the substance that prevails.

Once Stevens has confronted and overcome his apprehension, he seeks to reinstitute or reinvent the imagery of the sublime he began by ridiculing. The first movement in this process of reinvention, in stanza seven, places the main thematic opposition on a new footing. By juxtaposing an effete angelicism with an image of brutal mundane reality, Stevens redefines the conflict in nonsexual terms; at the same time, the parodic extremes in this figuration of the conflict create a new tension that must still be resolved:

> The mules that angels ride come slowly down
> The blazing passes, from beyond the sun.
> Descensions of their tinkling bells arrive.
> These muleteers are dainty of their way.
> Meantime, centurions guffaw and beat
> Their shrilling tankards on the table-boards.
> This parable, in sense, amounts to this:
> The honey of heaven may or may not come,
> But that of earth both comes and goes at once.
> Suppose these couriers brought amid their train
> A damsel heightened by eternal bloom.

The last two lines of this stanza propose the possibility of a revelation invested in a mythic image that would replace the "radiant bubble" of merely human origin. The damsel heightened by eternal bloom would be imaginatively equivalent to the "'Mother of heaven, regina of the clouds,'" but she would derive her power and significance from a source more enduring than the quirky turns of human passion. In a letter of 1944, Stevens himself gives a helpful gloss on this stanza. "The honey of heaven may or may not come, but that of the earth both comes and goes at once. But would the honey of heaven be so uncertain if the mules that angels ride brought a damsel heightened by eternal bloom, that is to say, brought a specifically divine revelation, not merely angelic transformations of ourselves. The trouble with the idea of heaven is that it is merely an idea of the earth. To imagine a heaven that is what heaven ineffectually strives to be" (*LWS,* 464). The suspended, incomplete syntax in the last period of Stevens' gloss echoes the reticence in the last two lines of the stanza. The mild imperative "Suppose" translates in the gloss into the infinitival noun phrase "to imagine." These formulations stop short of any definitive declaration of intent—for example, I will try to imagine— but they leave open a prospect of such imagining.

The tentative supposition at the end of stanza seven calls forth a counterposing recognition of human mortality. Any divine revelation such as Stevens hypothesizes must not be confused with or falsified by delusions of angelic transformation:

> We hang like warty squashes, streaked and rayed,
> The laughing sky will see the two of us
> Washed into rinds by rotting winter rains.

The grim gusto in Stevens' prevision of his own fleshly corruption gives evidence of the detachment he has been able to achieve. The "bloom" of love is gone, but poetic inspiration remains unimpaired. Stevens has still not entirely overcome his uneasiness at his own stylistic pretensions to the sublime, and when in stanza nine he calls on himself to reassume the high diction ironically portrayed in the first lines of the poem, his tone retains an ambiguous note of self-mockery:

> In verses wild with motion, full of din,
> Loudened by cries, by clashes, quick and sure
> As the deadly thought of men accomplishing
> Their curious fates in war, come, celebrate
> The faith of forty, ward of Cupido.
> Most venerable heart, the lustiest conceit
> Is not too lusty for your broadening.

The ward of Cupido has come of age, but Stevens is acutely sensitive to the threat of fatuousness in any unguarded exaltation of the faith of forty. His self-conscious irony forestalls the comic potential in the resolution of a mid-life crisis. The tonal ambiguity of Stevens' self-exhortation devolves in the next stanza into a satiric externalization of his anxiety about mystic pretentiousness. Stanza ten responds directly to the question posed at the end of stanza nine, "Where shall I find / Bravura adequate to this great hymn?":

> The fops of fancy in their poems leave
> Memorabilia of the mystic spouts,
> Spontaneously watering their gritty soils.
> I am a yeoman, as such fellows go.
> I know no magic trees, no balmy boughs,
> No silver-ruddy, gold-vermilion fruits.
> But, after all, I know a tree that bears
> A semblance to the thing I have in mind.
> It stands gigantic, with a certain tip
> To which all birds come sometime in their time.
> But when they go that tip still tips the tree.

Through the dialectical progression of images in this stanza, Stevens resolves the conflicting attitudes that have generated his poetic meditation. The "mystic spouts" of a vapid Romanticism stand in contrast to the "deep up-pouring from some saltier well" that bursts the "radiant bubble" of Romantic fancy. Similarly, the "gold-vermilion fruits" of the magic trees appear as a falsely inflated transformation of the "fruit" of love—the "warty squashes, streaked and rayed." Both images test themselves against an image in stanza four, that of the "luscious and impeccable fruit of life" that "like skulls, comes rotting back to ground." By modifying and purifying the image of the magic trees, Stevens enables himself to affirm his own capacity for creative magic without exposing himself to the satiric deflation he has been practicing. The affirmation following the adversative pivot "But, after all" is the climax of the poem. In the spare, restrained sublimity of the gigantic tree, Stevens achieves the tonal poise he has been seeking.

That tonal poise prepares Stevens for the explicit repudiation of his original thesis and the revelation of his "Anguishing hour" as the immediate occasion of the poem. In the final stanza, as in the final lines of "Sunday Morning," the flight of pigeons serves as an image of poetic closure. The blue pigeon that "circles the blue sky" recalls "The ephemeral blues" of stanza six. The white pigeon that "flutters to the ground" signifies that a process of purification has been completed. In his concluding statement—"until now I never knew / That fluttering things have so distinct a shade"—Stevens affirms that in working out his problem, he has gained a new sense of the substantial presence of imaginative forms.

Although Stevens manages to overcome his fear that the verve of earth depends on a power that diminishes steadily throughout later life, his vindication of the nonsexual sublime has as yet no solid doctrinal foundation. The assertion that "There is a substance in us that prevails" leaves the "substance" undefined. The "damsel heightened by eternal bloom" suggests the possibility of a transcendental basis for the sublime, but this possibility is presented only as a supposition, and it is not developed further within the poem. The moment of climactic resolution in stanza ten occurs on a level of "*pure poetry*" where image and tone operate in isolation from ideas. The image of the gigantic tree has no specific doctrinal reference. The tentative transcendental supposition in stanza seven discloses Stevens' imaginative need for some kind of religious construct, and the recourse to a poetry of images and the music of verse alone reveals his incapacity, at this point in his life, to satisfy that need.

The unsettled state of Stevens' early religious views manifests itself most clearly in one of the most seemingly self-assured of his early poems. In "Sunday Morning," Stevens depicts an exchange between himself and a female companion, presumably his wife. The subject of this exchange is religious need, and in responding to his companion's expressions of need, Stevens both directs a polemic against the Christian myth and attempts to provide an alternative to this myth in his own lyric utterance. The climactic moments of lyric expression in the poem do not constitute a unified vision, but they do establish important points of departure for Stevens' visionary enterprise.

The argument of "Sunday Morning" is framed by the image of "water without sound" in the first and last stanzas. In the first stanza, Stevens' companion drifts into a reverie on Christian pathos:

> The day is like wide water, without sound,
> Stilled for the passing of her dreaming feet,
> Over the seas, to silent Palestine,
> Dominion of the blood and sepulchre. (*CP,* 67)

The woman's reverie challenges Stevens to find in his own poetic resources some form of pathos capable of supplanting the power and passion evoked in the "Dominion of the blood and sepulchre." The final stanza suggests that he has succeeded in this effort:

> She hears, upon that water without sound,
> A voice that cries, "The tomb in Palestine
> Is not the porch of spirits lingering.
> It is the grave of Jesus, where he lay."

In the body of the poem, Stevens offers three substitutes for the myth he discredits: a spiritually attenuated form of Wordsworthian natural sentiment; a transposition of mystical passion into the elegiac sublime; and a celebration of the purely physical world couched in biblical diction. Within this sequence of quasi-religious poetic forms, Stevens constructs a dialectical progression of mood and tone. The basic elements of this dialectic are given in the first stanza. The "Complacencies of the peignoir, and late / Coffee and oranges in a sunny chair" represent sensual pleasures that contrast with "The holy hush of ancient sacrifice."[8] The awe that attends this sacrifice derives part of its power from the idea of death, and in the second stanza, Stevens undermines this power by treating death as merely a negative quantity—the absence of life.

> Why should she give her bounty to the dead?
> What is divinity if it can come
> Only in silent shadows and in dreams?

In stanzas five and six, after he has distracted his companion from the silent shadows of Palestine, Stevens appropriates the pathos of death for his own argument.

> Death is the mother of beauty; hence from her,
> Alone, shall come fulfillment to our dreams
> And our desires.

The seventh, penultimate stanza constitutes a tonal synthesis between the "comforts of the sun" and the pathos of "our perishing earth." This dialectical progression provides a measure of formal unity for the poem, but the transition from the first to the second phase of the progression entails a dislocation in the terms of Stevens' argument, and the "chant of paradise" in stanza seven is elaborately meretricious. Despite its dialectical structure, the poem remains something of a pastiche, and despite its apparent persuasiveness, its implicit claim to have solved the problem it poses is premature.

Stevens repudiates the divinity that comes "Only in silent shadows and in dreams," but he is unwilling to exclude divinity from the world altogether. At first he attempts to preserve it by restricting it to the scope of common human feelings stimulated by nature:

> Divinity must live within herself:
> Passions of rain, or moods in falling snow;
> Grievings in loneliness, or unsubdued
> Elations when the forest blooms.

J. V. Cunningham comments on the Wordsworthian character of this passage, and he cites a parallel passage from *The Recluse*:[9]

---

8. For a discussion of Santayana's influence on the diction and sentiment of "Sunday Morning," see Daniel Fuchs, "Wallace Stevens and Santayana," in Marston LaFrance (ed.), *Patterns of Commitment in American Literature* (Toronto, 1967), 139–44.

9. Cunningham, "Tradition and Modernity," in *The Collected Essays of J. V. Cunningham,* 239.

> What want we? have we not perpetual streams,
> Warm woods, and sunny hills, and fresh green fields,
> And mountains not less green, and flocks and herds,
> And thickets of songsters, and the voice
> Of lordly birds, an unexpected sound
> Heard now and then from morn to latest eve,
> Admonishing the man who walks below
> Of solitude and silence in the sky? (ll. 126–33)

Stevens draws on a Wordsworthian range of sensibility but detaches this sensibility from its transcendental base. A divinity that is indistinguishable from human moods and passions is a pleonastic affect, and Stevens will not be able to sustain this rhetorical inflation of sentiment. The mountains, flocks, and herds from *The Recluse* appear in the last stanza of "Sunday Morning," and though they retain their function as emblems of pastoral closure, the note of resolution echoes with ambiguous irony against the "solitude and silence in the sky"—the "island solitude" within "the isolation of the sky." This ironic echoing will sound even more sharply in "Anatomy of Monotony" (1930), where the isolation of the sky metamorphoses into "that fatal and that barer sky" (*CP*, 108). Eventually, "the man who walks below" in Wordsworth will evolve into the visionary protagonist of "The Owl in the Sarcophagus"—"one day / A man walked living among the forms of thought" (*CP*, 432)—but that day is yet far off.

The problematic character of Stevens' new "divinity" already makes itself felt in the third stanza. He depicts the birth of Christ as a "commingling" of "our blood" with heaven, and the emphatic, assured tone of the preceding stanza gives place to an uneasy questioning that is followed by wistful prophecy:

> Shall our blood fail? Or shall it come to be
> The blood of paradise? And shall the earth
> Seem all of paradise that we shall know?
> The sky will be much friendlier then than now,
> A part of labor and a part of pain,
> And next in glory to enduring love,
> Not this dividing and indifferent blue.

Stevens' evocation of a "friendlier" sky hovers uncertainly on the verge of a Wordsworthian affirmation. He suggests that by repudiating the false paradise of Christianity and accepting the limitations of an earthly paradise, we shall gain a new sense of intimacy with our world. This intimacy would perhaps be a sufficient substitute for the "enduring love" of "Jove in the clouds." At present, however, the vanishing of the old gods has left a sense of desolation, and there is no quickening soul in the world that would enable us to feel that the sky participates in human labor and human pain.

In the fourth stanza, Stevens gains a new polemical impetus from his companion's yearning for a paradise that will endure beyond the "sweet questionings" of the "wakened birds." Again drawing on Wordsworth (*The Recluse,* ll. 800–808), he disparages all fantastic forms of paradise.[10] Slipping past the "dividing and indifferent blue," he answers his companion's yearning with an image of exquisite lyricism: "June and evening, tipped / By the consummation of the swallow's wings." Like the image of the "tip" that still tips the tree" (*CP,* 17), this image establishes lyric fulfillment as a norm that takes precedence over doctrinal stance; it provides an authoritative point of aesthetic reference to which doctrine must ultimately adapt itself. In a poem of 1952, "Looking Across the Fields and Watching the Birds Fly," Stevens will allude to this image as one of those definitive moments in his poetic development. The "transparency through which the swallow weaves" (*CP,* 518) serves as a pivotal image in his depiction of the evolution of lyric grace into mythic vision.

Stevens' lyricism lures his companion away from the pathos of the blood and sepulcher and reduces her religious yearning to "'The need of some imperishable bliss.'" The reduction of paradise to an ideal of permanent pleasure gives the occasion for Stevens' dialectical countermovement into the elegiac sublime. In juxtaposing "'Imperishable bliss'" and death as the mother of beauty, Stevens subtly modifies the frame of reference for his lyric argument. The argument of the first four stanzas is governed by an opposition between Christian mythology and an equivocally Wordsworthian norm of an earthly paradise. The argument of stanzas five and six is governed by the opposing poles of Keatsian idealism. In stanza six, Stevens sardonically elaborates the idea of an imperishable bliss, and this elaboration, as Price Caldwell notes, constitutes "a kind of ironic 'Grecian Urn.'"[11] The opposite

10. Cited *ibid.,* 240. See also Buttel, *The Making of "Harmonium,"* 223.
11. Price Caldwell, "'Sunday Morning': Stevens' Makeshift Romantic Lyric," *Southern Review,* n.s., XV (1979), 947.

pole is defined by the kind of elegiac passion that informs "Ode on Melancholy" and "The Fall of Hyperion: A Dream":

> Is there no change of death in paradise?
> Does ripe fruit never fall? Or do the boughs
> Hang always heavy in that perfect sky?
> Unchanging, yet so like our perishing earth?
> . . . .
> Death is the mother of beauty, mystical,
> Within whose burning bosom we devise
> Our earthly mothers waiting, sleeplessly.

In these last three lines, Stevens assimilates the elegiac passion of the Christian myth and transposes it from the realm of shadows to the realm of actual experience. At the same time, through the word *mystical,* he implicitly shifts the locus of "divinity" from the "moods" and "passions" of the individual to a region of experience that transcends individual consciousness. This is the region of myth, and the imagery of these lines forms the nucleus for "the mythology of modern death" in "The Owl in the Sarcophagus." The three figures in this mythology—sleep realized, peace after death, and the mother of the living and the dead—comprise "the forms of thought," and the third figure embodies a transcendental memory that holds men in their death.

To devise earthly mothers within the bosom of death is to preserve the memory of one's own mother within the mythic images of visionary elegy. In her memoir *Souvenirs and Prophecies,* Holly Stevens draws attention to two journal entries of 1912 in which Stevens describes his visits home to see his ▓▓▓▓ther.[12] The development of death as the mother of beauty into the ▓▓▓▓ the living and the dead probably has its deepest roots in the pathos ▓▓▓▓perience. Stevens' descriptions of his mother on these visits are among his most moving pieces of prose, and the memory of his grief remains with him late in his life. "But what his mother was returns and cries on his breast" (*CP,* 453). This speech of the mother who "says good-by" in "Owl" consists of "inventions of farewell" (*CP,* 435, 432). In 1912, Stevens' own mother had shown him the peace and dignity that could be achieved through finding the right inventions of farewell. "Dr. Blackburn, who had given her communion on Saturday morning . . . had told her how his thought had

---

12. Holly Stevens, *Souvenirs and Prophecies: The Young Wallace Stevens* (New York, 1977), 253–55.

turned to the verse, 'I will lift up mine eyes unto the hills whence cometh my strength.' She thought this very 'sweet.' She quoted 'The Lord preserveth all them that love him'; and this I believe is her favorite text. . . . She kissed me when I went (as I did her) and her last words, full of affection, were 'Goodbye!'" (*LWS*, 173–74; Psalms 121.1 and 145.20). Stevens remembers these psalms when he writes stanza seven of "Sunday Morning," and just as he has attempted to assimilate his mother's death to the elegiac sublime, so will he seek to assimilate her religious heritage to "the heavenly fellowship / Of men that perish and of summer morn."

In stanza six, Stevens' visionary impulse does not lead him beyond the word *mystical*. Although at this point the word has little denotative content, it does at least recall the note of brooding melancholy in the evocation of Christian meditation in stanza one. In contrast, the orotund primitivism of stanza seven achieves a more complete articulation, but it succeeds only in supplanting spiritual intensity with muscular enthusiasm:

> Supple and turbulent, a ring of men
> Shall chant in orgy on a summer morn
> Their boisterous devotion to the sun,
> Not as a god, but as a god might be,
> Naked among them, like a savage source.
> Their chant shall be a chant of paradise,
> Out of their blood, returning to the sky.

The orgy of stanza seven seeks to fulfill the prophecy of stanza three, but in order to render the sky "friendlier," Stevens must exploit the religious rhetoric he has sought to disavow:

> And in their chant shall enter, voice by voice,
> The windy lake wherein their lord delights,
> The trees, like serafin, and echoing hills,
> That choir among themselves long afterward.
> They shall know well the heavenly fellowship
> Of men that perish and of summer morn.
> And whence they came and whither they shall go
> The dew upon their feet shall manifest.

In a letter of 1928, Stevens remarks that "Sunday Morning" is "simply an expression of paganism, although, of course, I did not think that I was expressing paganism when I wrote it" (*LWS*, 250). Stevens may have known more when he wrote the poem than when he later interpreted it, for the men in his heavenly fellowship, though supple and turbulent, are hardly rude pagans. They are post-Victorians imbued with the equivocal subtlety necessary to retain the poetic affects of Christianity while discarding the doctrinal content of these affects. Their chant is a lyric adaptation of the psalms from which Stevens' mother had derived comfort. "I will lift up mine eyes unto the hills, from whence cometh my help. . . . The Lord shall preserve thy going out and thy coming in from this time forth, and even for evermore" (121.1, 8).[13] Nothing shall preserve these "men that perish." Their "god" exists only as a metaphoric similitude, but he still enjoys the pomp of his nominal sovereignty. This kind of quasi god can provide no substantial spiritual fulfillment. Stevens interprets the last two lines of this stanza: "Life is as meaningless as dew" (*LWS,* 250).

Stanza seven fails to effect a definitive synthesis of Stevens' lyric insights. The existential heroism he seeks to express does not rise above the level of bravado, and in attempting to close the gap between spiritual passion and a "devotion" to sensual pleasure, he comes very close to self-parody. The lyricism of the final stanza, in contrast, is genuine and compelling, but it succeeds only by renouncing the ambition of complete resolution and adopting a tone that reflects the ambiguity of Stevens' previous affirmations. After his companion hears, and presumably heeds, the voice that proclaims the mortality of Christ, Stevens himself proclaims that we live in an "island solitude, unsponsored, free, / Of that wide water, inescapable." Our freedom is a spiritual confinement, but in this confinement we may participate in the momentary consummations of the natural world:

> Deer walk upon our mountains, and the quail
> Whistle about us their spontaneous cries;
> Sweet berries ripen in the wilderness;
> And, in the isolation of the sky,
> At evening, casual flocks of pigeons make
> Ambiguous undulations as they sink,
> Downward to darkness, on extended wings.

The serenity of this conclusion seems scarcely ruffled by the ambiguous undulations of the pigeon's wings, but "the isolation of the sky," recalling the

---

13. I am indebted to Jim Clark for alerting me to the connection between the last verse and the final two lines of stanza seven.

"dividing and indifferent blue," strikes a note almost imperceptibly more ominous than that of "island solitude." The hint of spiritual emptiness in these phrases later expands into another of Stevens' succinct cosmologies, "Anatomy of Monotony" (included in the second edition of *Harmonium*).

In "Sunday Morning," Stevens represents the sky both as a medium of lyric fulfillment and as an atmosphere of spiritual alienation. In "Anatomy of Monotony," he finds a figurative correlative for this conceptual ambiguity. Assuming a stance of cosmic detachment, he depicts two skies, one contained within the other. The earth is a mortal mother, and "over the bare spaces of our skies / She sees a barer sky that does not bend" (*CP,* 107). The sky that bends is the sky that encircles our island solitude and fosters "The bough of summer and the winter branch" (*CP,* 67). The barer sky is the infinite expanse of spiritual vacancy beyond the plenitude of earth. The division between these two skies corresponds to the division between body and spirit, and in the second of the two stanzas in "Monotony," Stevens discloses the physical reductivism latent in his chant of paradise. Reverting to the idea against which he contends in "Monocle," he suggests that the impulsion to creative effort comes solely from "The body" that "walks forth naked in the sun." The "phantasy" of sexual pleasure sublimates itself as a yearning for the "still finer, more implacable chords" of art, and because the fantasies of the body subsist within a spiritual vacuum, there can be no ideal culmination of desire:

> Yet the spaciousness and light
> In which the body walks and is deceived,
> Falls from that fatal and that barer sky,
> And this the spirit sees and is aggrieved.

The spirit stands apart. It cannot validate the ideal origin of human fulfillment, and it is reduced to a passive observation of its own futility. In a letter of 1944, Stevens declares, "I write poetry because it is part of my piety" (*LWS,* 473). Stevens' piety manifests itself as a need to find a grounding or "sanction" (*NA,* 43) for experience in an ultimate reality. The ultimate reality depicted in "Monotony" is sheer nothingness, and it sanctions only a grief tinged by irony.

The severe expression of nihilistic renunciation in "Monotony" finds a comic complement in the sardonic humor of "A High-Toned Old Christian Woman" (1922). Taking the old Christian woman's elevated earnestness as a foil for his own skeptical hedonism, he suggests that both "the moral law" and "The opposing law"—associated with "bawdiness"—serve equally as means for the indulgence of our theatrical impulses (*CP,* 59). On the basis of the first law, we may "build haunted heaven," and on the basis of the opposing law, we may "project a masque / Beyond the planets." The two types of imaginative construction are both merely forms of entertainment, and "Poetry is the supreme fiction" only because it recognizes its own fictive status. The imputation that religious vision derives from a sublimated hedonistic aestheticism would, no doubt, "make widows wince," and Stevens amuses himself at the spectacle of their supposed perturbation. "But fictive things / Wink as they will. Wink most when widows wince."

Stevens' amusement at the widows' winking suggests a stance of urbane detachment. But what if fictive things cease to wink at all? The seven-year gap between *Harmonium* and the gradual resumption of poetry in 1930 has always troubled Stevens' critics.[14] The apparent reasons for this hiatus—Stevens' preoccupation with domestic and business affairs and his disappointment at the lukewarm reception of *Harmonium*—seem to cast a shadow of suspicion over the seriousness of his poetic vocation; and since the poems themselves seem to offer incontrovertible evidence of this seriousness, the cessation of poetry has remained something of an enigma. Part of the solution to this enigma can be found in stanza seven of "Sunday Morning." A life that is as meaningless as dew offers no basis for poetry.

Stevens himself foresaw and predicted the antipoetic consequences of his "devotion to the sun." "The Comedian as the Letter C" (1922) constitutes a parable of a doctrinal course that leads away from the writing of poetry. Crispin, the protagonist, sets out from Bordeaux, the Old World, goes thence to Yucatán, a land of "Green barbarism" (*CP,* 31), and settles finally in Carolina, a moderate zone where he plans to cultivate a regionalist sort of poetic realism. Instead, his voyage ends in creative sterility. After all his elemental adventures, the world remains for Crispin "The same insoluble lump" (*CP,* 45), and he slips into bemused silence. The cause of his failure lies in the kind of metaphysical assumptions he makes and the conclusions he draws from these assumptions. Stevens himself will ultimately elude the fate of his protagonist, but the hypotheses that govern the course of Crispin's

14. Sidney Feshbach gives a detailed discussion of this issue in "Poetic and Human Anxieties in the Early Poetry of Wallace Stevens," *Wallace Stevens Journal,* II (1978), 43–49. See also Brazeau, *Wallace Stevens Remembered,* 244–45.

adventure comprehend the full range of doctrinal alternatives available to Stevens in his early poetry.[15]

Crispin's point of departure is the assumption that the human spirit has a privileged status in relation to the external world:

> Nota: man is the intelligence of his soil,
> The sovereign ghost. As such, the Socrates
> Of snails, musician of pears, principium
> And lex.

The mingling of grand, Latinate diction with images of triviality indicates that the dignity man accords himself has lost its grounding in significant experience and has degenerated into self-parody. Crispin comes at the decadent end of a noble tradition. Like Jasmine scorning the "paper souvenirs of rapture," Crispin submits himself to "an interior ocean's rocking" so that he may revitalize his imagination (*CP*, 79). The turning point in his adventure can be located in the revision of his initial proposition at the beginning of section four: "Nota: his soil is man's intelligence. / That's better. That's worth crossing seas to find" (*CP*, 36). In "The Transcendentalist," Emerson gives a concise formulation of the difference between these two propositions: "In the order of thought, the materialist takes his departure from the external world, and esteems man as one product of that. The idealist takes his departure from his consciousness, and reckons the world an appearance" (*RWE*, I, 332–33). Stevens' revised proposition seems better to him because it decisively excludes the possibility of a ghostly, that is, a transcendental origin for the human spirit. By defining the soil (material reality) as the source of "intelligence," Crispin escapes from the shadow world of spiritual illusion. The substantial world into which he escapes proves to be barren of imagination.

Crispin's voyage leads him through the phases of Stevens' own effort to grasp some essential reality beyond any "mythology of self" (*CP*, 28) such as that so voluptuously celebrated in "Tea at the Palaz of Hoon." Like the speaker in "The Snow Man," Crispin dissolves his own identity until he is at

---

15. For information about the diverse sources Stevens may have used in depicting Crispin, see Buttel, *The Making of "Harmonium*," 195–96; A. Walton Litz, *Introspective Voyager: The Poetic Development of Wallace Stevens* (New York, 1972), 122–23; Louis L. Martz, "'From the Journal of Crispin': An Early Version of 'The Comedian as the Letter C,'" in Frank Doggett and Robert Buttel (eds.), *Wallace Stevens: A Celebration* (Princeton, 1980), 7–18; Eleanor Cook, "Wallace Stevens: 'The Comedian as the Letter C,'" *American Literature*, XLIX (1977), 195; Brazeau, *Wallace Stevens Remembered*, 101; and Peterson, *The Idealist Tradition*, 123–26.

one with the bare place in which he stands—a "starker, barer self / In a starker, barer world" (*CP,* 29). Through this dissolution of self, he achieves an illusion of pure, transparent perception. In "Nuances of a Theme by Williams," the contradictions inherent in this illusion remain implicit. In "Comedian" they are brought to the fore in a dizzying paradox. Crispin beholds "the veritable ding an sich, at last," and he is thus made "free / From the unavoidable shadow of himself / That lay elsewhere around him" (*CP,* 29–30). Once the unavoidable shadow has been pushed to the side, Crispin temporarily achieves the self-renewal he has sought:

> Crispin beheld and Crispin was made new.
> The imagination, here, could not evade,
> In poems of plums, the strict austerity
> Of one vast, subjugating, final tone.

The "final tone" is an aural equivalent of "the last largeness," and, as in "Monocle," access to this universal substance enables the protagonist to reintegrate his own sensibility.

> It was caparison of wind and cloud
> And something given to make whole among
> The ruses that were shattered by the large.

The first phase of Crispin's journey appears to be an unmitigated success. Although he yields momentarily to the terror of a thunderstorm in Yucatán—"He knelt in the cathedral with the rest" (*CP,* 32)—he recovers himself and experiences a serene exaltation both more expansive and less ambiguous than that in the final stanza of "Sunday Morning." "His mind was free / And more than free, elate, intent, profound" (*CP,* 33). At this point Crispin's sense of himself is entirely free from the ironic perplexity of diction that in Bordeaux had marked him as a clown. This perfect possession of himself constitutes the apex of his imaginative adventure.

In the first two sections of "Comedian," the narrator remains very close to Crispin's own immediate sensations, paraphrasing and echoing his thoughts about his quest. At the beginning of section three, "*Approaching Carolina,*" there is a shift of narrative perspective. The narrator takes a step back and addresses the reader in the manner of a Victorian novelist asking for indulgence toward one of his characters. In this address the narrator presages Crispin's failure as a poet and suggests the reason for that failure:

> The book of moonlight is not written yet
> Nor half begun, but, when it is, leave room
> For Crispin, fagot in the lunar fire,
> Who, in the hubbub of his pilgrimage
> Through sweating changes, never could forget
> That wakefulness or meditating sleep,
> In which the sulky strophes willingly
> Bore up, in time, the somnolent, deep songs.

The mental moonlight is the life of the imagination, the spirit's abode. The form of the narrator's appeal implies that though Crispin will not himself write the book of moonlight, he deserves a place in this book because he remains haunted by the recollection of the imaginative realm from which he exiles himself. In an essay on "Comedian" that Stevens called "not only correct but keen" (*LWS*, 350), Hi Simons remarks that apart from one instance in which the moonlight is literal, "everywhere else in this poem it stands for the 'romantic' imagination, in antithesis to the sun that represents matter-of-fact realism."[16] Tacitly qualifying some of Simon's main conclusions, Stevens expounds the general significance of Crispin's adventures.

I suppose that the way of all mind is from romanticism to realism, to fatalism and then to indifferentism, unless the cycle re-commences and the thing goes from indifferentism back to romanticism all over again. No doubt one could demonstrate that the history of the thing is the history of a cycle. At the moment, the world in general is passing from the fatalism stage to an indifferent stage: a stage in which the primary sense is a sense of helplessness. But, as the world is a good deal more vigorous than most of the individuals in it, what the world looks forward to is a new romanticism, a new belief. (*LWS*, 350)

Stevens wrote this letter in 1940, after he had already begun constructing a new Romanticism and had left his tragicomic protagonist behind him.

Among the many possible antecedents to Stevens' use of the moon as a symbol of the Romantic imagination, perhaps the most thematically impressive is the Mount Snowdon passage in book fourteen of *The Prelude*. As he reflects on this scene Wordsworth interprets the moon as "the emblem

---

16. Hi Simons, "'The Comedian as the Letter C': Its Sense and Significance," *Southern Review*, n.s., V (1940), rpr. in Ashley Brown and Robert S. Haller (eds.), *The Achievement of Wallace Stevens* (Philadelphia, 1962), 102.

of a mind / That feeds upon infinity" and that is "sustained / By recognitions of transcendent power, / In sense conducting to ideal form" (ll. 70-71, 74-76). Tonally, however, Crispin's "sweating changes" set him at a far remove from Wordsworth's manner of solemn declamation. As a "fagot in the lunar fire," Crispin seems more nearly the double of Keats's Endymion. In two journal entries for 1899, Stevens discloses the potent effect Keats's poem has on his imagination. In the entry for July 19, he says he had been reading *Endymion* the previous evening, and, after describing the sunset from an unmistakably Keatsian perspective, he remarks, "The moon was very fine. Coming over the field toward the bridge I turned to see it hanging in the dark east. I felt a thrill at the mystery of the thing and perhaps a little touch of fear. When home I began the third canto of 'Endymion' which opens with O moon! and Cynthia! and that sort of thing. It was intoxicating. After glancing at the stars and that queen again from the garden I went to bed" (*LWS*, 29). Stevens feels Keats along his pulses, but, for Keats as for Wordsworth, immediate sensory impressions are recognitions that conduct in sense to ideal form. *Endymion* concludes in a union of the human and the divine, and for Stevens, the image of the "queen"—detached from the moon—eventually becomes the emblem of a mind that is sustained by recognitions of transcendent power. In "The Candle a Saint" (1939), he represents the night as an archetypal feminine image that is the source of all images:

> The noble figure, the essential shadow,
> Moving and being, the image at its source,
> The abstract, the archaic queen. (*CP*, 223)

While the moon will continue to serve Stevens as a symbol for the Romantic imagination (as, for example, in "Esthétique du Mal," *CP*, 320), in his greatest visionary poetry the stars become a more vital embodiment of that "high romance" Keats never lived to trace. In "The Auroras of Autumn," the "imagination that sits enthroned" is "crystalled and luminous, sitting / In highest night" (*CP*, 417).

The narrator tells us that Crispin conceived of his voyaging as an alternation "between two elements, / A fluctuating between sun and moon" (*CP*, 35), but of the two elements only the sun receives any detailed exposition. The mental moonlight appears only in retrospective epitome as "a Carolina of old time, / A little juvenile, an ancient whim." When, at the beginning of section four, Crispin revises his initial proposition and declares that "his soil is man's intelligence," he ceases to fluctuate even to this limited extent and comes to live in the sun alone. "Exit the mental moonlight, exit lex, / Rex and principium, exit the whole / Shebang" (*CP*, 36–37). Crispin seeks the authentic, and he conceives of the moonlit world as a region of "backward lapses" into the "indulgences" of spiritual illusion (*CP*, 35). "Moonlight was an evasion, or, if not, / A minor meeting, facile, delicate." Consequently, he has no choice but to grip "the essential prose / As being, in a world so falsified, / The one integrity for him" (*CP*, 36).

Crispin's decision to grip the essential prose is not a conscious renunciation of poetry; it is a misguided attempt to revitalize poetry by setting it on a solid, realistic footing. He still hopes that what begins as prose might "wear a poem's guise at last" (*CP*, 36). In "*The Idea of a Colony*," he announces his plans "To make a new intelligence prevail" (*CP*, 37). He bases his colonizing enterprise on the same premise that governs "Anecdote of Men by the Thousand," the idea that "The soul . . . is composed / Of the external world" (*CP*, 51). He declares that "The natives of the rain are rainy men" and that "in their music showering sounds intone" (*CP*, 37). Poetry is to serve as a reflex of place in the most elementary sense. "The man in Georgia waking among pines / Should be pine-spokesman" (*CP*, 38); South Americans "Should make the intricate Sierra scan"; and so on. Poetry written in accordance with Crispin's manifesto would be a natural growth of the soil and would thus be falsified neither by outmoded generic conventions nor by transcendental illusion.

Crispin's grand scheme for a poetic colony comes to nothing because he is a purist of the immediate; all poetic transformation of a primary reality, he perceives, is "Related in romance to backward flights" (*CP*, 39). Even the poetry of the rainy men would thus be implicated in "the reproach / That first drove Crispin to his wandering." He therefore abandons his plans and submits himself still further to a formless reality of immediate sensation. "Preferring text to gloss, he humbly served / Grotesque apprenticeship to chance event." In a letter of 1935, Stevens remarks that "in THE COMEDIAN AS THE LETTER C, Crispin was regarded as a 'profitless philosopher'. Life, for him, was not a straight course; it was picking his way in a haphazard manner through a mass of irrelevancies. Under such circumstances, life would mean nothing to him, however pleasant it might be" (*LWS*, 293).

The consequences of Crispin's materialist doctrine baffle Crispin himself, but they have a certain inevitability. If the intelligence has its origin in material reality, it is only natural that Crispin's interest should gradually limit itself "To things within his actual eye" (*CP*, 40). It is also natural that in comparing poetry and "reality," he should find poetry a superfluous complication. "The words of things entangle and confuse," so Crispin "hasped on the surviving form, / For him, of shall or ought to be in is" (*CP*, 41). Crispin's final reduction to "is," the present indicative, does not deprive him of the capacity for enjoying the pleasures of normal life—the "humped return" of his marriage and the "chromatics in hilarious dark" of his four daughters (*CP*, 43, 45)—but it does definitively annul his poetic ambition.

The "doctrine" that Crispin concocts from the "rout" of his poetic ambition is fatalism, the philosophy of resignation to defeat. When he first acknowledges his defeat, Crispin staunchly refuses to "Scrawl a tragedian's testament" and instead takes refuge in indifferentism. "What is one man among so many men? / What are so many men in such a world?" (*CP*, 41). After the hubbub of his domestic life has filled the place left vacant by the cessation of his poetic activity, Crispin reviews his life and sees in the fulfillment of his destiny a certain fittingness not without grandeur: "Seraphic proclamations of the pure / Delivered with a deluging onwardness" (*CP*, 45). The narrator suggests, in contrast, that despite his energy and courage, Crispin ends as a "profitless / Philosopher, beginning with green brag, / Concluding fadedly" (*CP*, 45–46).

Stevens' own history ends differently. His theory of Romantic cycles implies that the imagination, as a power in the world greater than "most of the individuals" in the world, possesses an irrepressible capacity for self-regeneration. In a postscript to the letter in which he expounds this theory, Stevens speaks of its application to his own work. "About the time when I, personally, began to feel round for a new romanticism, I might naturally have been expected to start on a new cycle. Instead of doing so, I began to feel that I was on the edge: that I wanted to get to the center: that I was isolated, and that I wanted to share the common life" (*LWS*, 352). Unlike Crispin, Stevens never stops fluctuating between the sun and moon, and the tension between these two modes complicates and enriches both of them. Nonetheless, in the volumes that follow *Harmonium*, it is the effort to construct a new Romanticism that gives shape and direction to the development of his poetic powers.

CHAPTER THREE

That Slight Transcendence

The early and middle part of the 1930s are difficult years for Stevens. In "Anatomy of Monotony," one of the first poems that herald his resumption of poetry, Stevens constructs a cosmology in which the spirit has no place, and many of the poems in *Ideas of Order,* "Owl's Clover," and "The Man with the Blue Guitar" (1937) explore the nuances of this spiritual vacancy. The cosmological grief to which Stevens gives voice in "Anatomy" and other poems is exacerbated by a consciousness both of his own debilitated imaginative powers and of the troubled state of American society. In *Ideas of Order,* Stevens' struggle first to regain and then to sustain his imaginative vitality costs him an effort greater and more painful than that of any other period. In "Le Monocle de Mon Oncle," he explores his anxiety about imaginative exhaustion with a compacted intensity of tropic invention that itself suffices to allay the anxiety. Similarly, in "The Comedian as the Letter C" the "deluging onwardness" of highly wrought poetic rhetoric counterpoints and almost contradicts the parable of poetic failure. In "The Sun This March" (1930), Stevens' complaint about a loss of vitality confirms itself in the formal surface of the poem. The enfeeblement illustrated by "The Sun This March" manifests itself in the thinness, both literal and figurative, of *Ideas of Order.* Most of the poems in this volume are short, the rhetoric is spare and direct, and the imagery is less richly varied than that of either *Harmonium* or *Parts of a World.* The major exceptions are "The Idea of Order at Key West" (1934) and "Like Decorations in a Nigger Cemetery" (1935). "Key West" is anything but direct, and the rhetoric is dense, but there is a vagueness in the intellectual substructure of the poem that goes a long way toward explaining the slightness of so many of its companion pieces. "Decorations" contains a wonderful variety of suggestive tropes, but it has no substructure at all, and though "invisible currents clearly circulate," aesthetic meaning reduces itself to the lowest level, that of local affect (*CP,* 156).

If Stevens is to escape Crispin's fate, he must ultimately establish a doctrinal basis for a new Romanticism. In the poems of the middle 1930s, he begins "to feel round for a new romanticism" (*LWS,* 352), but the doctrinal orientation of many of these poems is either explicitly antitranscendental or equivocal and inconclusive. Even in those poems, such as "Sailing After Lunch" (1935) and "Key West," that have a transcendental orientation, Stevens' affirmations scarcely rise above the level of vague gesture. For the most part, the Romantic impulse manifests itself only through implication in the imagery of the sublime, and Stevens himself is not always certain about the significance of this imagery. At the same time, Stevens' faith in the self-regenerating power of the imagination finds confirmation in the way confusion and fatigue themselves contribute to his gradual construction of a new Romanticism. Some of the strongest poems in *Ideas of Order* are elegiac, and the elegiac mode, though it may originate in a sense of personal loss, ultimately becomes the main generic vehicle for that "universal poetry" (*NA,* 160) Stevens will seek to create.

Although the conflicts Stevens must resolve if he is to give substantial form to his Romantic impulse are primarily philosophical in nature, they are complicated and sometimes obscured by the conditions of the time. The increasing "pressure of reality" (*NA,* 22) caused by the depression already makes itself felt in some of the short poems of *Ideas of Order,* and in the two long poems that follow this volume, "Owl's Clover" and "The Man with the Blue Guitar," this pressure compels Stevens to set up a dialogue between his own poetic preoccupations and the concerns of society at large. The need for social relevance does not, finally, alter the course of Stevens' thinking, for if "what the world looks forward to is a new romanticism," the most socially useful thing the poet can do is to satisfy that expectation. The common life, as Stevens depicts it in both poems, is a life of baffled longing for spiritual fulfillment. Consequently, the main struggle for Stevens remains that between his own spiritual needs and his resistance to any meretricious satisfaction of those needs.

When Stevens returns to poetry in 1930, his first need is to come to terms with himself about the enfeebled state of his imaginative life. In "The Sun

This March," he speaks of himself with a directness that is not typical of him and that betrays a special urgency in this need:

> The exceeding brightness of this early sun
> Makes me conceive how dark I have become,
> And re-illumines things that used to turn
> To gold in broadest blue, and be a part
> Of a turning spirit in an earlier self.
> That, too, returns from out the winter's air,
> Like an hallucination come to daze
> The corner of the eye. (*CP*, 133–34)

The flinching from brightness, the dazed recollection of once vivid impressions, and the tone of melancholy reminiscence all make this seem like a poem of old age—but not Stevens' old age. Although the spare simplicity of phrasing in this profession prefigures that of some of Stevens' latest poems, these late poems are distinguished by a grim vigor and acuity that is entirely distinct from the convalescent quality of "The Sun This March." Withdrawing from the painful confusion of this condition, Stevens seeks a manifestation of power through a reflexive dialectical gesture. The gesture does not carry him beyond one couplet, and he concludes in a plea for help:

> Cold is our element and winter's air
> Brings voices as of lions coming down.
> Oh! Rabbi, rabbi, fend my soul for me
> And true savant of this dark nature be.

The sense of power presumably intended to be evoked by the "voices as of lions" has no context and is not realized in the sound of the verse. The very weakness of this gesture lends force to the fervent plea for preservation. The figure of the rabbi appears frequently in Stevens' later poetry as a symbol of the wise man—for example, in canto ten of "Auroras" and canto five of "Things of August" (1949). In a letter of 1953 to his Italian translator Renato Poggioli, Stevens says that the rabbi in "The Sun This March" "is a rhetorical rabbi. Frankly, the figure of the rabbi has always been an exceedingly attractive one to me because it is the figure of a man devoted in the extreme to scholarship and at the same time to making some use of it for human purposes" (*LWS*, 786). Harold Bloom aptly notes that "Stevens' 'rabbi' is the same as Emerson's 'scholar.' Stevens uses the two words interchangeably, and like Emerson he uses 'scholar' to mean 'poet.'"¹ If we compare "The Sun This March" with "Anglais Mort à Florence" (1935), it is tempting to identify the rabbi in the earlier poem with Brahms, whom Stevens as the posthumous, Jamesian Englishman calls "His dark familiar" (*CP,* 148).

"Anglais Mort à Florence," like "The Sun This March," is a poem of complaint about the loss of youthful vitality. In the five years that separate these two poems, Stevens' poetic powers have recuperated considerably from his lapse from creativity in the 1920s. The later poem possesses both a greater intensity of elegiac lyricism and a greater complexity of formal structure. In "Anglais Mort à Florence," Stevens does not employ the first person singular, but as in many of his poems the objectified, anecdotal manner seems only a distancing device for personal revelation. For the "him" of "Anglais," as for the "I" of "The Sun This March," spring is the cruelest season:

> A little less returned for him each spring.
> Music began to fail him. Brahms, although
> His dark familiar, often walked apart.
>
> His spirit grew uncertain of delight,
> Certain of its uncertainty, in which
> That dark companion left him unconsoled
>
> For a self returning mostly memory. (*CP,* 148)

Like Crispin, the protagonist of "Anglais" is haunted by his memory of the moon. This memory has no present validity because, like Crispin, he fails to give it any definite intellectual form. It recurs now in memory merely as "the pale coherences of moon and mood / when he was young." At the end of the poem there is a shift from "mood" to perceptual vividness. Youth was a time "When to be and delight to be seemed to be one, / Before the colors deepened and grew small." In this context, "deepened" probably signifies not that the colors have become more rich and intense, but rather that they have become more remote. Stevens' formulation of this complaint, unlike that in "The Sun This March," implicitly contains its own consolation. The power of evoking such concentrated images of experiential loss seems a fair exchange for a youthful vitality stamped by a Pre-Raphaelite aestheticism that limits itself to pale moods and large sensations.

Given the failure of a delight dependent on mood and sensation, the

---

1. Bloom, *The Poems of Our Climate,* 89.

Englishman has reluctantly called upon his other faculties and has abandoned his youthful independence of spirit. Although he appears bitter about the necessity of his contrivances, they have succeeded in preserving him:

> He used his reason, exercised his will,
> Turning in time to Brahms as alternate
> In speech. He was that music and himself.
> They were particles of order, a single majesty:
> But he remembered the time when he stood alone.
> He stood at last by God's help and the police;
> But he remembered the time when he stood alone.
> He yielded himself to that single majesty.

The music of Brahms gives Stevens access to the transcendent principle of order suggested by "God's help" and "that single majesty." Brahms is himself one of the "particles of order"; he is a policeman because Stevens relies on him to sustain his sense of this order. In his commentary on this poem, Stevens explains, "Most people stand by the aid of philosophy, religion and one thing or another, but a strong spirit (Anglais, etc.) stands by its own strength. Even such a spirit is subject to degeneration. I suppose we have to consider new faiths with reference to states of helplessness or states of degeneration. If men have nothing external to them on which to rely, then, in the event of a collapse of their own spirit, they must naturally turn to the spirit of others. I don't mean conventions: police" (*LWS,* 348). The way in which Stevens describes his new faith appears to have been influenced by one of Emerson's declarations in "The Over-Soul": "We live in succession, in division, in parts, in particles. Meantime within man is the soul of the whole; the wise silence; the universal beauty, to which every part and particle is equally related; the eternal ONE" (*RWE,* II, 269). For Stevens, in contrast to Emerson, faith is never a fixed belief so much as an imaginative process that culminates in an affirmation of the Romantic sublime. Although he declares that he has "yielded himself to that single majesty," Stevens has not yet developed the visionary power that would give force and substance to this affirmation. In the final stanza of "A Primitive Like an Orb," he will again make use of this passage from "The Over-Soul," and he will articulate its significance without any wistful glances back to the time when he stood alone.

Throughout *Ideas of Order,* Stevens is preoccupied with the process of Romantic renewal, and in one poem, "Sailing After Lunch," he attempts to depict this process in paradigmatic form. Almost no one would consider "Sailing After Lunch" one of Stevens' major short poems. Although Stevens himself thought well enough of it to place it first in the Alcestis Press edition of *Ideas of Order,* he concedes that "perhaps it means more to me than it should" *(LWS,* 277). The poem recommends itself to a place of primacy not for its intrinsic merit but for the light it sheds on the other poems in the volume. Stevens explains that "the thing is an abridgment of at least a temporary theory of poetry." The theory illustrated by "Sailing After Lunch" is that "poetry is essentially romantic, only the romantic of poetry must be something constantly new and, therefore, just the opposite of what is spoken of as the romantic."[2] Accordingly, in the poem itself, Stevens repudiates the "heavy historical sail" of established Romantic imagery and concentrates on the actual images before him (*CP,* 120). The result is that he is able "to give / That slight transcendence to the dirty sail." The problem with this resolution is that "transcendence" has no thematic content. It is defined only in terms of mood and attitude, and it has no more substance than does a moment of evanescent sensory clarity—"the way one feels, sharp white." In his gloss, Stevens remarks that "what one is always doing is keeping the romantic pure: eliminating from it what people speak of as the romantic." By so thoroughly eliminating what people speak of as the Romantic, Stevens restricts himself to a purity that consists only of images and the music of verse.

The purified "romantic" of "Sailing After Lunch" enables Stevens to "rush brightly through the summer air," but this kind of purity can provide no stay against the "Fears of life and fears of death" ("The Brave Man" [1933]; *CP,* 138). In "A Fading of the Sun" (1933), Stevens acknowledges the limitations of unreflective, transitory states of well-being:

> Who can think of the sun costuming clouds
> When all people are shaken
> Or of night endazzled, proud,
> When people awaken
> And cry and cry for help? (*CP,* 139)[3]

---

2. On the idea of Romanticism as a form of perpetual renewal, see Santayana, *The Sense of Beauty,* 150.
3. In the 1936 trade edition of *Ideas of Order,* the last line of the third stanza reads "And will not cry for help." There is a period at the end of the line. In *The Man with the Blue Guitar Including Ideas of Order* (1952), the last line of the stanza becomes "And cry and cry for help?"

Stevens' answer to the distress he depicts is to appeal to some inner source of strength. "If joy shall be without a book / It lies, themselves within themselves." Both in depicting his distress and in responding to it, Stevens appears to have been inspired by Coleridge. In "Dejection: An Ode," Coleridge speaks for all Romantics, old and new, who have lost the "shaping spirit of Imagination." Like Stevens, he evokes the sublime imagery in which he can no longer participate: "A light, a glory, a fair luminous cloud / Enveloping the Earth." Again like Stevens, he locates the source of this glory in his own inner strength:

> Joy, Lady! is the spirit and the power,
> Which wedding Nature to us gives in dower
> A new Earth and new Heaven.

In Wordsworth, Coleridge finds an embodiment of "The passion and the life, whose fountains are within." Since he cannot imitate Wordsworth's creative vitality, he determines "to be still and patient" and to take refuge in "abstruse research." Coleridge himself foresees the failure of this recourse, and the warning provided by his example may well have influenced Stevens' presupposition that "joy shall be without a book." If to be patient and to study will not serve to regenerate the passion and the life, to what source of inner strength may Stevens appeal? In "A Fading of the Sun," he can do no better than entertain a willful illusion. The question that provokes his Coleridgean declaration of self-reliance is "How can the world so old be so mad / That the people die?" The reassurance that follows his declaration is that "they will not die."

Joy "without a book" is a spontaneous exaltation that takes no definite intellectual form. Most of the poems in this period are recitations without book; they are explorations of the empty air. The tone of these explorations, determined by the quality of light and the mood of the moment, ranges from delight to despair. "Botanist on Alp (No. 1)" (1934) defines this situation and, because the mood of the moment is favorable, postpones doing something about it. The poem begins with what seems to be a complaint that the contemporary preoccupation with social ideology has obstructed the poet's

---

This version makes no sense, but *The Collected Poems* reproduces it. It seems likely that the later version is a printer's error and that the last line of stanza three has been inadvertently replaced with the last line of the first stanza.

normal preoccupation with natural beauty. "Marx has ruined Nature, / For the moment" (*CP,* 134; see also *LWS,* 350–51). This initial gesture is a false start. In the body of the poem, Stevens does not complain about a lost simplicity of lyric vision; he complains of a lost capacity for intellectual construction:

> For myself, I live by leaves,
> So that corridors of clouds,
> Corridors of cloudy thoughts,
> Seem pretty much one:
> I don't know what.

To live by leaves is to live by the changing seasons, to live in fact as the speaker in "Sunday Morning" counsels his companion to live. "The bough of summer and the winter branch. / These are the measures destined for her soul" (*CP,* 67). In "Sunday Morning," lyric expansiveness covers a deficiency of intellectual signification. In the first "Botanist," both sensual perception and intellectual activity have reduced themselves to indifferent vapor. Stevens evokes the poverty of his own spiritual condition by contrasting it to the intimations of transcendent unity in the composition of Claude Lorrain:

> But in Claude how near one was
> (In a world that was resting on pillars,
> That was seen through arches)
> To the central composition,
> The essential theme.
>
> What composition is there in all this:
> Stockholm slender in a slender light,
> An Adriatic *riva* rising,
> Statues and stars,
> Without a theme?

In time Stevens will himself compose a new context for "The essential theme." Meanwhile, he must make do with slender images. Standing in the rubble of an outmoded Romanticism, he reverts to pure perception, cleansed even of "cloudy thoughts":

> The pillars are prostrate, the arches are haggard,
> The hotel is boarded and bare.
> Yet the panorama of despair

> Cannot be the specialty
> Of this ecstatic air.

The reversal from elegy to ecstasy in the last three lines has a tone of wondering surprise, as if the ecstatic air unexpectedly opens up new possibilities that release Stevens from the necessity of any "central composition."

In "Evening Without Angels" (1934), Stevens attempts to give ideological content to the ecstatic air and to make a positive norm of it by setting it in opposition to a fairy-tale form of angelicism composed of both Christian and Romantic elements. This simple opposition leads him very quickly through a complete cycle, beginning with the negation of the Romantic and concluding with a visionary resurgence that prefigures the imagery of "The Auroras of Autumn." Stevens' most obvious Romantic antecedents in "Evening Without Angels" are Shelley and Wordsworth. The first two stanzas of Stevens' poem constitute a disavowal of the Romantic faith implicitly expressed in the opening lines of "Mont Blanc":

> The everlasting universe of things
> Flows through the mind, and rolls its rapid waves,
> Now dark—now glittering—now reflecting gloom—
> Now lending splendour, where from secret springs
> The source of human thought its tribute brings
> Of waters.

The grammatical antecedent of "where" appears to be "splendour," but it might also be "the mind" or even "The everlasting universe of things." Like Wordsworth's equivocal affirmations in book fourteen of *The Prelude*, Shelley's declaration suggests obscure intimations of transcendent power within a sublime scene. Wordsworth takes the scene at Snowdon as the "express / Resemblance of that glorious faculty / That higher minds bear with them as their own" (ll. 88–90). Those who exercise this power are "Like angels stopped upon the wing by sound / Of harmony from Heaven's remotest spheres" (ll. 98–99). Stevens may have recalled this evocation of the angels, and he may also have recalled Matthew Arnold's characterization of Shelley as a "beautiful and ineffectual angel, beating in the void his luminous wings in vain."[4] In any case, he repudiates the angels, and he interprets Shelley's glittering splendor as an intimation of spiritual vacancy:

---

4. Matthew Arnold, *English Literature and Irish Politics* (Ann Arbor, 1973), 237, vol. IX of *The Complete Prose Works of Matthew Arnold,* ed. R. H. Super.

> Why seraphim like lutanists arranged
> Above the trees? And why the poet as
> Eternal *chef d'orchestre?*
>
>   Air is air,
> Its vacancy glitters round us everywhere.
> Its sounds are not angelic syllables
> But our unfashioned spirits realized
> More sharply in more furious selves. (*CP*, 136–37)

The keen clarity of this glittering vacancy recalls that of "The Snow Man," a poem in which Stevens achieves the illusion of perfect transparency by reducing the observer to nothing. In "Evening Without Angels," Stevens tries to fill the glittering vacancy with frenetic self-agitation and achieves only violence without power. It is but a short step from this energetic but futile assertiveness to "The American Sublime" (1935), where

>   the sublime comes down
> To the spirit itself,
>
> The spirit and space,
> The empty spirit
> In vacant space. (*CP*, 131)

"Evening Without Angels" is an explicitly doctrinal poem. Its doctrine consists of a negation of dialectic through tautology: air is air. In "Re-Statement of Romance" (1935), Stevens employs this doctrinal tactic to create a static image of a self that, though it is surrounded by air, interchanges nothing with it. "The night knows nothing of the chants of night. / It is what it is as I am what I am" (*CP*, 146). This is the mode of the realist, and it implicitly segregates itself from the Wordsworthian and Shelleyan assumption of a vital interchange between the mind and an animate, sentient nature. Wordsworth says of the "higher minds" that "They from their native selves can send abroad / Kindred mutations" and that "in a world of life they live" (ll. 93–94, 105). It is by means of these mutations that "all affections" are "by communion raised / From earth to heaven, from human to divine" (ll. 117–18). Shelley, gazing on Mont Blanc, situates his meditation within a similar aesthetic and doctrinal framework:

> I seem as in a trance sublime and strange
> To muse on my own separate phantasy,
> My own, my human mind, which passively

> Now renders and receives fast influencings,
> Holding an unremitting interchange
> With the clear universe of things around. (ll. 35–40)

In "Evening Without Angels," Stevens' unwillingness to tolerate the obscurity of this order signals itself in a shorthand notation of familiar symbols. "Let this be clear that we are men of sun / And men of day and never of pointed night." From this position, there are only two possible directions for Stevens to take: the path to the silence into which Crispin disappears, or the inversion of negation in a renewal of the Romantic sublime. Stevens will take first one path and then the other:

> Light, too, encrusts us making visible
> The motions of the mind and giving form
> To moodiest nothings, as, desire for day
> Accomplished in the immensely flashing East,
> Desire for rest, in that descending sea
> Of dark, which in its very darkening
> Is rest and silence spreading into sleep.

"Mont Blanc" concludes in a rhetorical question, and Stevens' firm lyric declaration, echoing the diction and rhythm of Shelley's poem, gives an answer contrary to the intent of this question:

> In the calm darkness of the moonless nights,
> In the lone glare of day, the snows descend
> Upon that Mountain.
> . . . .
> And what were thou, and earth, and stars, and sea,
> If to the human mind's imaginings
> Silence and solitude were vacancy? (ll. 130–32, 142–44)

In Stevens' response to this question, the "motions of the mind" are reduced to reflections of the natural cycles of light and dark; the content of poetic form reduces itself to a vacancy suffused with mood; and despite the grand scale of the imagery, we are not far from the indifferentism in which corridors of clouds and corridors of cloudy thoughts "Seem pretty much one: / I don't know what."

The descent into darkness recalls the conclusion to "Sunday Morning," but Stevens then shifts into a different key:

> . . . Evening, when the measure skips a beat
> And then another, one by one, and all
> To a seething minor swiftly modulate.
> Bare night is best. Bare earth is best. Bare, bare,
> Except for our own houses, huddled low
> Beneath the arches and their spangled air,
> Beneath the rhapsodies of fire and fire,
> Where the voice that is great within us rises up,
> As we stand gazing at the rounded moon.

The measures of glittering vacancy "swiftly modulate" on the turn of a single adversative "Except" and become spangled arches, thus reverting to the kind of "central composition" in which the world is "seen through arches." The ineffectual fury of self-assertion in the first stanza—punching holes in nothingness—modulates into awe and reverence. The angels who are absent, "seraphim" with wings and lyres and trailing robes, are negligible in comparison with those who are present, those who compose the celestial choir that sings the rhapsodies of fire and fire. If Stevens' initial negations have been directed toward Shelley, so also—in compensation—does Shelley form part of the new celestial choir. The skylark that pours forth "a flood of rapture so divine" springs from earth "Like a cloud of fire":

> All the earth and air
>   With thy voice is loud,
> As when night is bare
>   From one lonely cloud
> The moon rains out her beams, and Heaven is overflowed.

Shelley's angelicism is beautiful but ineffectual because his experience remains divided between his sense of the world as a place "vacant and desolate" and the inconstant visitations of Intellectual Beauty. As Stevens works toward the creation of his new Romanticism, he will seek to transcend this kind of extreme opposition. Like Wordsworth and like Keats—in their very different ways—he will make a continuous effort toward a reconciliation between the mundane and the rhapsodic.

The visionary resurgence at the end of "Evening Without Angels" has no doctrinal foundation. Like the renewal of the sublime in "Sailing After Lunch," it is an exercise in tone and imagery. The main poem of this period in which Stevens attempts to go beyond such exercises is "The Idea of Order at

Key West" (1934). Contrasting "Key West" to "The Comedian as the Letter C," Stevens remarks that in the later poem "life has ceased to be a matter of chance. It may be that every man introduces his own order into the life about him" (*LWS,* 293). The order that Stevens introduces into this poem is actually a series of questions, both direct and implied, about the origin of the human spirit. Although none of these questions receives a decisive answer, they suggest a transcendental source, and by remaining inconclusive, they leave the way open to the Romantic resolutions of Stevens' later poetry. Stevens' syntactic method in "Key West" puts to systematic use the kind of rhapsodic obscurity to be found in "Mont Blanc" and the visionary segments of *The Prelude.* In a manner that foreshadows the technique of his major visionary poems, Stevens leaves his syntactic relations suspended in an intentional ambiguity that suggests complex but logically obscure arrangements among the elements of the poem.[5]

"Key West" opens with a simple assertion of the division between the mind and external reality; however, this assertion almost immediately becomes problematic:

> She sang beyond the genius of the sea.
> The water never formed to mind or voice,
> Like a body wholly body, fluttering
> Its empty sleeves; and yet its mimic motion
> Made constant cry, caused constantly a cry,
> That was not ours although we understood,
> Inhuman, of the veritable ocean. (*CP,* 128)

Apart from the singer and the listeners (later identified as the speaker and Ramon Fernandez), there are two agents in this stanza: the sea that is "wholly body" and "the veritable ocean." The phrase "of the veritable ocean" seems most nearly identifiable as the genitival object of "constant cry." It may also be the object of "mimic motion." The mindless water makes no sound, but it mimics the veritable ocean, presumably a spiritual force, and this mimicry either paradoxically constitutes a cry or causes a cry from the veritable ocean. Finally, "of the veritable ocean" may be a descriptive genitive modifying the

---

5. For a shrewd commentary on the syntactic method of "Key West," see Helen Vendler, "The Qualified Assertions of Wallace Stevens," in Roy Harvey Pearce and J. Hillis Miller (eds.), *The Act of the Mind: Essays on the Poetry of Wallace Stevens* (Baltimore, 1965), 175. See also Bornstein, *Transformations of Romanticism,* 197–202.

"we" of "we understood." All these syntactic possibilities seem to merge in such a way that the cry, associated with mind, takes on a separate, transcendental identity while at the same time it vaguely influences or animates the sea, the singer, and the listeners. In other words, there is a spiritual presence distinct from yet somehow diffused through all the concrete elements in the scene that is being described. The cry, originating in the veritable ocean, is what in stanza two the woman hears and translates into her own song: "What she sang was what she heard."

Harold Bloom maintains that in Stevens' poetry the imagery of the ocean "belongs to Whitman, the Whitman of *The Sleepers* and the *Sea-Drift* pieces." Thus, "to sing beyond the genius of the sea is to defy the poetics of Whitman, who found the muse his mother to be his oceanic sense and who identified his father with the shore."[6] Bloom is right to associate Stevens' oceanic imagery with that of Whitman, but the conclusion he draws from this association is misleading. In "Out of the Cradle Endlessly Rocking," Whitman describes the ocean's moaning as an "undertone, the savage old mother incessantly crying," and in "As I Ebb'd with the Ocean of Life" he identifies the ocean as a place where "the fierce old mother endlessly cries for her castaways." In the first stanza of "Key West," Stevens does not "defy the poetics of Whitman"; he contrasts the veritable ocean—Whitman's ocean—with the water "never formed to mind or voice."

As Bloom rightly argues, "Key West" "affirms a transcendental poetic spirit yet cannot locate it."[7] If Stevens' problem were only to distinguish sea and singer—not to relate both of them to the veritable ocean—the poem could end with the second stanza. The "grinding water" inspires the woman's song, but she is herself the primary origin of that song: "it was she and not the sea we heard." The first three lines of stanza three draw out this separation still more sharply, so that we are brought back to where we began in line one. The singer makes her own song and the sea is merely "a place by which she walked to sing." At this point, Stevens states the main issue of the poem and shows that nothing has yet been solved. "Whose spirit is this? we said, because we knew / It was the spirit that we sought." We know from the previous stanzas that it is not the sea speaking through the woman, not the dumb force of the elements forming to mind and voice. We also know that though the

6. Bloom, *The Poems of Our Climate*, 72, 98.
7. *Ibid.*, 104.

woman is "the maker of the song she sang," she is not the sole force responsible for her song. Stevens does not give a specific answer to his question. All he can tell us is that "it was more than that," more than the voice of the sea and "more even than her voice and ours, among / The meaningless plungings of water and the wind." The song imposes meaning, but the source of meaning is something else. The rest of stanza four (after the paragraph break) gives itself over to a celebration of the Orphic autonomy of the singer. Her song masters the brute elements and assimilates them by transforming them into aesthetic meaning. The complex of forces narrows to a single point of creative freedom—the singer's.

The singer seems complete unto herself. There is no world for her beyond that of her own making, and the question "Whose spirit is this?" appears to have been set aside. In the fifth stanza, however, the question reemerges, for the world does not become spiritually empty when the singer leaves:

> Ramon Fernandez, tell me, if you know,
> Why, when the singing ended and we turned
> Toward the town, tell why the glassy lights,
> The lights in the fishing boats at anchor there,
> As the night descended, tilting in the air,
> Mastered the night and portioned out the sea,
> Fixing emblazoned zones and fiery poles,
> Arranging, deepening, enchanting night.[8]

Stevens had momentarily quelled his wonder by attributing sole mastery to "the single artificer." This mastery continues after the singing stops, again implying the presence of a spiritual force greater than the water and wind or the singer. It is this force that inspires her song and that deploys itself also in the perceptions of those who are walking among the lights of the fishing boats. That the force is an objective presence, something "not ours," is made evident in the externalization of these perceptions. It is the glassy lights and not the two men who master the night and the sea.

Stevens only dimly apprehends the nature of the enchantment he has experienced. No conclusion is reached, and the last stanza, an extended apostrophe with no main verb, abjures the form of proposition altogether:

8. In his letters, Stevens makes it clear that the Ramon Fernandez he addresses here is a fictive figure and is not to be identified with Ramon Fernandez the critic. Stevens merely "chose two everyday Spanish names" (*LWS,* 798; and see *LWS,* 823). Ramon Fernandez is the Spanish equivalent of John Smith.

> Oh! Blessed rage for order, pale Ramon,
> The maker's rage to order words of the sea,
> Words of the fragrant portals, dimly-starred,
> And of ourselves and of our origins,
> In ghostlier demarcations, keener sounds.

Because the rage to order concerns "ourselves" and "our origins," it refers to the speaker as much as to the singer. The order toward which the speaker strives is not, ironically, such as lends itself to any unequivocal precision of statement. The predicates of the phrase "words of" are grouped in no distinct order. The sea and the fragrant portals could be taken as separate entities; alternatively, *portals* could be taken as an appositive of *sea*. Neither the sea nor the portals stand in any clearly defined relationship to "our origins." The preposition "of" in "words of" may mean either about or from. It probably means both, and if so this dual meaning catches up the ambiguity of spiritual location that permeates the poem. The words to be ordered are about the sea, the portals, and our origins, and also from them. The fragrant portals are entranceways that have no spatial location. They are dimly starred as if they were remote passages in the night sky, but they are intended to evoke no concrete setting. They are simply the portals of mystic vision, perhaps vision into "our origins." These origins, in turn, if they are the origins of the spirit, are themselves the portals of vision.

"Key West" is a *tour de force* of paradoxical intimation and evocative equivocation. There is no definite proposition in the poem that asserts the existence of a transcendental spirit. Nonetheless, the spirit that is present—first in song and in the sea and then in the glassy lights—sheds its influence all around the men who are seeking it. Their associations and questions are themselves the "ghostlier demarcations" of the poem. The principle of order suspends itself between their ambiguous demarcations and the "keener sounds" that lend these demarcations an appearance of vivid precision.

The conclusions of both "Evening Without Angels" and "Key West" represent the positive sublime of celestial grandeur. The complementary side of Stevens' visionary poetry is the elegiac sublime, a mode in which loss or absence transmutes itself into pathos and power. Stevens has already tapped this generic source in "Sunday Morning," and in *Ideas of Order,* his probings of spiritual grief lead to a significant growth of lyric articulation in the elegiac mode. Most of the elegies in *Ideas of Order* have reference to some specific, personal type of loss, but in the first two stanzas of "Waving Adieu, Adieu,

Adieu" (1935), Stevens rises above the personally specific and defines the elegiac as a form of pure experience:

> That would be waving and that would be crying,
> Crying and shouting and meaning farewell,
> Farewell in the eyes and farewell at the centre,
> Just to stand still without moving a hand.
>
> In a world without heaven to follow, the stops
> Would be endings, more poignant than partings, profounder,
> And that would be saying farewell, repeating farewell,
> Just to be there and just to behold. (*CP,* 127)

The sweeping dactylic rhythm captures the image of waving farewell and counterpoints the image of passive stillness. The tension between movement and stillness gives a concentrated, almost visual sensation of time flowing past the speaker. As in "Sunday Morning," Stevens arrives at this elegiac sublimity by opposing the idea of a static paradise. As Stevens' title indicates, "Waving Adieu" is directly inspired by Keats's Melancholy, who "dwells with Beauty— Beauty that must die; / And Joy, whose hand is ever at his lips / Bidding adieu." Keats's Melancholy is more than a mood. It is an intuitive apprehension of a divine power that manifests itself in the mingling of life and death, being constantly passing away into nothingness, or, more precisely, the mediation of being and nothingness at the still point of sentient becoming. Death is the mother of beauty, and Stevens' own Melancholy is

>   she that says
> Good-by in the darkness, speaking quietly there,
> To those that cannot say good-by themselves.
> . . . .
> The earthly mother and the mother of
> The dead. (*CP,* 431–32)

Keats's evocation of the Melancholy as an elegiac symbol of pure aesthetic experience merges in its influence on Stevens with the depiction of Moneta in the second "Hyperion," "The Fall of Hyperion: A Dream." In this depiction, Keats shifts from the mode of the epic to a mode of mystical lyricism, that is, to a visionary mode. As Moneta parts the veils covering her face she becomes a mythic emblem of a suprahuman consciousness. Like the earthly mother and the mother of the dead in "Owl," she is "a self that knew, an inner thing" (*CP,* 435):

> But for her eyes I should have fled away.
> They held me back, with a benignant light,
> Soft-mitigated by divinest lids
> Half closed, and visionless entire they seem'd
> Of all external things—they saw me not,
> But in blank splendour beam'd like the mild moon,
> Who comforts those she sees not, who knows not
> What eyes are upward cast. (canto one, ll. 264–71)

In this description the image of the goddess is static, but if we associate her with the veiled figure of "Ode on Melancholy," it becomes clear how Stevens may have compounded elements from both these images in the earthly mother and the mother of the dead.[9] Moneta replaces the Mnemosyne of the first "Hyperion"; she is the mother of the muses, and the poet addresses her as "'Shade of Memory.'" The ancient mother in "Owl" calls out to the dying, "Keep you, keep you, I am gone, oh keep you as / My memory" (*CP*, 432). She moved

> With a sad splendor, beyond artifice,
> Impassioned by the knowledge that she had,
> There on the edges of oblivion. (*CP*, 435)

Keats's Melancholy and Stevens' ancient mother may both be associated with the apotheosis of Apollo in the first "Hyperion." By dying into life, Apollo experiences both life and death at once. In the second "Hyperion," Moneta tells the poet, "'Thou hast felt / What 'tis to die and live again before / Thy fated hour'" (canto one, ll. 141–43). As a reward, he is allowed to worship at the shrine of an inhuman spirit and "To see as a God sees" (canto one, l. 304). This is also the kind of vision Stevens ascribes to the protagonist of "Owl," where "one day / A man walked living among the forms of thought / To see their lustre truly as it is" (*CP*, 432).

In "Owl," Stevens commingles the elegiac voice of Keats with that of Tennyson, who also draws directly on Keats. (For Stevens' early response to Tennyson, see *LWS*, 26, 92.) "Waving Adieu" represents the first important step in this process of assimilation. The sweep of Stevens' verse, gathering power through repetition, recalls this stanza from section 57 of *In Memoriam*:

---

9. For an illuminating comparison of Moneta and the figure of the mother in "Owl," see Beckett, *Wallace Stevens*, 15.

> I hear it now, and o'er and o'er,
>   Eternal greetings to the dead;
>   And 'Ave, Ave, Ave,' said,
> 'Adieu, adieu' for evermore.

In section 123, Tennyson declares that "though my lips may breathe adieu, / I cannot think the thing farewell." Tennyson's "Eternal greetings to the dead" gradually convert themselves into a means for preserving the dead within a visionary construct. In "Owl," Stevens' own "inventions of farewell" (*CP*, 432) serve to sustain the dead within the mythic memory of the ancient mother.

Stevens' assimilation of the elegiac sublime is perhaps the single most important factor in his eventual realization of a visionary mythology that figures forth a sentient origin for the world, "a divine beginning and end for us" (*NA*, 42). The generation of consciousness through the mediation of being and nothingness becomes the "essential theme" of his visionary poetry. In "A Primitive Like an Orb," he depicts the universe as a "giant of nothingness" that is "ever changing, living in change," and he defines the governing principle of this universe as "The essential poem at the centre of things" (*CP*, 443, 440). In *Ideas of Order*, he is not yet capable of any sustained or complete realization of this vision, but in "The Reader" (1935), one of the finest short poems in the volume, he rises to a partial prefiguration of it:

> All night I sat reading a book,
> Sat reading as if in a book
> Of sombre pages.
>
> It was autumn and falling stars
> Covered the shrivelled forms
> Crouched in the moonlight.
>
> No lamp was burning as I read,
> A voice was mumbling, "Everything
> Falls back to coldness,
>
> Even the musky muscadines,
> The melons, the vermilion pears
> Of the leafless garden."
>
> The sombre pages bore no print
> Except the trace of burning stars
> In the frosty heaven. (*CP*, 146–47)

In the eighth stanza of "Monocle," Stevens uses the decaying form of vegetables as a metaphor for the two human figures in the poem:

> We hang like warty squashes, streaked and rayed,
> The laughing sky will see the two of us
> Washed into rinds by rotting winter rains. (*CP*, 16)

In "The Reader" this "trivial trope" becomes a figuration within a tropic structure. The world itself is a book, a composition of signs pregnant with meaning, and thus a form for the spirit. The voice that interprets the "trace" of signification left by the burning stars may be Stevens' own voice, but it is more probably a voice, like that of the ancient mother, speaking through him. Although this poem is little more than a fragment, in both the cosmic scope of its vision and the tonal mingling of the "sombre" and the brilliantly intense it strikes the note of Stevens' greatest poetry. In the seventh canto of "Auroras," Stevens envisions "an imagination that sits enthroned / As grim as it is benevolent" (*CP*, 417), and in describing the action of this high imagination, he confirms the fateful character of the message traced by the burning stars:

> It leaps through us, through all our heavens leaps,
> Extinguishing our planets, one by one,
> Leaving, of where we were and looked, of where
>
> We knew each other and of each other thought,
> A shivering residue, chilled and foregone,
> Except for that crown and mystical cabala.

In the ninth canto, the imagination that sits enthroned modulates into the figure of "the innocent mother," another incarnation of the mother who says farewell to the dying in "Owl." The innocent mother stands as the subject within a hypothetical figuration of mythic resolution. The destructive power of the high imagination yields to the maternal principle as origin and medium of sentient process; it is as if she "Created the time and place in which we breathed" (*CP*, 419).

The path to the mythological figuration of sentient process leads through the elegiac intuitions of "Waving Adieu" and "The Reader." At this point in his life, Stevens has developed no theoretical framework within which to elaborate these intuitions. After its initial burst of lyric magnificence, "Waving Adieu" lapses into an invocation of the "singular self" and an anomalous appeal to "the ever-jubilant weather." It concludes fadedly in a baffled interrogative:

> One likes to practice the thing. They practice,
> Enough for heaven. Ever-jubilant,
> What is there here but weather, what spirit
> Have I except it comes from the sun?

In "Hymn of Apollo," Shelley's sun god asserts that "Whatever lamps on Earth or Heaven may shine / Are portions of one power, which is mine." In Shelley's poem the sun serves as a metaphor for a power that transcends the merely physical, and in "The Greenest Continent," the third poem of "Owl's Clover," Stevens will appropriate the full signification of this visionary metaphor. In the final stanza of "Waving Adieu," his designation of the sun as a spiritual source remains on the level of the literal and the materialistic. He remarks in a letter that "the 'ever-jubilant weather' is not a symbol. We are physical beings in a physical world; the weather is one of the things that we enjoy, one of the unphilosophical realities. The state of the weather soon becomes a state of mind" (*LWS*, 348–49). Despite this disclaimer of philosophical significance, there is a close connection between the enfeebled conclusion of "Waving Adieu" and the declension to the empty spirit in vacant space. As Stevens says in "The American Sublime," "One grows used to the weather, / The landscape and that" (*CP*, 131).

Stevens' delight in "unphilosophical realities" defines one boundary of his imaginative life. The opposing boundary defines itself as the need for a "central composition." Ultimately, these impulses are dialectically interdependent, but in the mid-1930s the satisfactions to be derived from unphilosophical realities are more readily accessible than those from any prospective realization of a central composition. "Like Decorations in a Nigger Cemetery" (1935) is the longest poem or group of poems in *Ideas of Order,* and in this poem the absence of connection among the fifty disparate sections provides a structural correlative for Stevens' thematic perplexity. The poem is merely a collection of tropes, and it is perhaps for this reason that Stevens designates Walt Whitman as its patron saint. Stevens' evocation of Whitman in section one answers to what in a letter of 1955 he calls "the elan of the essential Whitman" (*LWS*, 871)—an expansiveness that invests the world of sensuous particulars with eternal presence:

> In the far South the sun of autumn is passing
> Like Walt Whitman walking along a ruddy shore.
> He is singing and chanting the things that are part of him,
> The worlds that were and will be, death and day.

> Nothing is final, he chants. No man shall see the end.
> His beard is of fire and his staff is a leaping flame. (*CP,* 150)

(This evocation appears to draw most directly on sections two and three of "Song of Myself.") In his letter, Stevens remarks that for many people, the poems in which Whitman "collects large numbers of concrete things" must seem "all opulence and elan. For others, I imagine that what was once opulent begins to look a little threadbare." The aesthetic and philosophical leveling that accompanies Whitman's celebration of all the things that are part of himself is antithetical to the articulation of complex thematic and structural hierarchies. As "the final builder of the total building," Stevens can make use of materials from Whitman; for drawing up the designs, however, Whitman's example can be of little help.

The sun-drenched vitalism of the Whitmanian strain sets one tonal extreme for "Decorations." The opposing extreme can be located in the elegiac and tragic strains of sections ten and twelve. As Harold Bloom suggests, Whitman, through his representations of death and the mother, enters also into Stevens' elegiac range.[10] Nonetheless, Stevens' primary ancestors within this range are Keats and Tennyson. In section ten, Stevens adds another notation to his study of the Keatsian and Tennysonian "farewell." In section twelve he offers a preliminary sketch both for the sinister serpent-god and for the grimly triumphant Ananke of "The Greenest Continent":

> Between farewell and the absence of farewell,
> The final mercy and the final loss,
> The wind and the sudden falling of the wind.
>
> The sense of the serpent in you, Ananke,
> And your averted stride
> Add nothing to the horror of the frost
> That glistens on your face and hair.

(Stevens borrows his illustration of the space between "The final mercy and the final loss" from a 1917 poem, "The Death of a Soldier.") The space or moment between the final mercy and the final loss becomes one of the most important subjects of meditation in Stevens' visionary poetry. In "The Owl in

---

10. Bloom, *The Poems of Our Climate,* 14, 33, 72. See also Diane Middlebrook, *Walt Whitman and Wallace Stevens* (Ithaca, 1974), 164.

the Sarcophagus," the mother of the living and the dead says farewell to the dying, and as they recede into oblivion she is "reddened and resolved / From sight, in the silence that follows her last word" (*CP,* 435). Within the final moment of life the cry of farewell vanishes into the darkness. The "frost" of Ananke is the chill insensibility of death, Necessity or Fate as oblivion.

Stevens' horror before the frost renders him susceptible, in section thirty-six, to the kind of consolatory fantasy represented by Whitman's "Whispers of Heavenly Death." In "Song of Myself" (section six), Whitman declares that "All goes onward and outward, nothing collapses, / And to die is different from what any one supposed, and luckier." To die can be luckier than to live only if death is actually a rebirth to a fuller life. Whitman assures us it is so, but Stevens seldom expresses any such hope. In both "Sunday Morning" and "Evening Without Angels," he establishes his own standard of ontological and lyrical validity by means of a polemic against the insipid paradise of traditional Christian mythology. Notwithstanding these intimations of mortality, in section thirty-six of "Decorations" he depicts a celestial transumption:

> The children will be crying on the stair,
> Half-way to bed, when the phrase will be spoken,
> The starry voluptuary will be born.

In a letter to Hi Simons, Stevens explains, "Death is like this. A child will die halfway to bed. The phrase is *voice of death*; the *voluptuary* is the child in heaven" (*LWS,* 349). In light of this section, Stevens' deathbed conversion to Catholicism may be considered a regression or rejuvenation antecedent to a celestial rebirth.

The starry voluptuary, like all the tropes in "Decorations," is an experimental poetic proposition; it does not represent a fixed belief in the immortality of the soul. And indeed, the only fixed form of idealism to which Stevens binds himself is that which is suggested in section five, the indeterminate search:

> If ever the search for a tranquil belief should end,
> The future might stop emerging out of the past,
> Out of what is full of us; yet the search
> And the future emerging out of us seem to be one.

A tranquil belief would be a poetic realization in which the tranquillity of a central unity would be reconciled with the infinite variety and infinite mutability of the phenomenal world. In "Owl," Stevens represents the locus of visionary resolution as a point

> colored from distances, central
> Where luminous agitations come to rest,
> In an ever-changing, calmest unity. (*CP,* 433)

In "The Rock" (1950), he reconstructs this visionary resolution in the image of the rock as an abstract locus for "the habitation of the whole":

> It is the rock where tranquil must adduce
> Its tranquil self, the main of things, the mind,
> The starting point of the human and the end,
> That in which space itself is contained. (*CP,* 528)

In "Owl" and "The Rock," as in section five of "Decorations," Stevens subordinates the phenomenal world (time and space) to "the main of things, the mind."

In "Decorations," Stevens is prepared to give no more than prophetic hints about his search for a tranquil belief. The self-exhortation of section eight discloses his intention to relocate religious worship from the obsolete religious institutions to personal poetic utterance, a determination he will reaffirm as late as 1952 in "St. Armorer's Church from the Outside":

> Out of the spirit of the holy temples,
> Empty and grandiose, let us make hymns
> And sing them in secrecy as lovers do.

Stevens' self-exhortation prefigures what in "The Man with the Blue Guitar" his interlocutors will demand of him, that he compose a "Poetry / Exceeding music" that will "take the place / Of empty heaven and its hymns" (*CP,* 167). Stevens' culminating response to these spiritual injunctions will be to propound the apotheosis of poetry itself as the medium of "essential imagination" (*LWS,* 370). Accordingly, in section forty-eight of "Decorations," where he resumes his musical metaphor for poetry, he takes as the subject of his visionary prophecy not the musician but the musical medium:

> Music is not yet written but is to be.
> The preparation is long and of long intent
> For the time when sound shall be subtler than we ourselves.

This is the sort of music Stevens has in mind in "The Noble Rider and the Sound of Words" (1941), where he speaks of searching the sound of words "for a finality, a perfection, an unalterable vibration, which it is only within the power of the acutest poet to give them" (*NA,* 32). In "Montrachet-Le-Jardin" (1942), he declaims:

> The cocks crow and the birds cry and
> The sun expands, like a repetition on
> One string, an absolute, not varying,
> Toward an inaccessible, pure sound. (*CP,* 263)

In "Montrachet" the subtle music of the pure sound joins with the clarion call of the birds, an aural image that echoes the cry of the cockerel in section thirty of "Decorations."

Section forty-eight of "Decorations" is a quiet but definite intimation of visionary intent. In his explanation of this section, Stevens implies a conflict between the kind of creative ideal represented by the subtle music he projects and the pressures of reality that will retard and complicate its realization. "In music we hear ourselves most definitely, but most crudely. It is easy enough to look forward to a time when crudely will be less crudely, and then subtler: in the long run, why not subtler than ourselves? What is true of music is obviously, not to say violently true of poetry. These arts which are so often regarded as exhausted are only in their inception. What keeps one alive is the fury of the desire to get somewhere with all this, in the midst of all the other things that one has to do" (*LWS,* 350).

The generic and tonal affects with which Stevens occupies himself in "Decorations" have no particular social or political orientation. Nonetheless, in the mid-1930s, Stevens feels a need to define the place of his own imaginative quest within the context of a disturbed social order. In "Farewell to Florida" (1936), he bravely renounces the tropical indulgences of his past and commits himself, however reluctantly, to the contemporary social world:

> My North is leafless and lies in a wintry slime
> Both of men and clouds, a slime of men in crowds.
> . . . .
> To be free again, to return to the violent mind
> That is their mind, these men, and that will bind
> Me round, carry me, misty deck, carry me
> To the cold, go on, high ship, go on, plunge on. (*CP,* 118)

To regard a fascination with exotic escapism as a form of enslavement is possible perhaps only within the peculiar context in which being bound to the violent mind of men in crowds appears as a form of freedom.

"Farewell to Florida" is the first poem in the trade edition of *Ideas of Order,* but the poem serves less as an introduction to that volume than as a presage of the next, *The Man with the Blue Guitar,* which originally included "Owl's Clover." In both "Sad Strains of a Gay Waltz" (1935) and "Mozart, 1935," Stevens evokes the "angry fear" and "besieging pain" of the collective mind; but the pressure of this distress does not disturb the movement of his own lyric elegance (*CP,* 132). In "Mozart, 1935" his invocation of the musician implies that the anguish of a world in which "the streets are full of cries" can be sublimated into exquisite artistic form and resolved in the Romantic sublime:

> Be thou that wintry sound
> As of the great wind howling,
> By which sorrow is released,
> Dismissed, absolved
> In a starry placating. (*CP,* 132)

There is nothing here of the choppy laboriousness in the last two lines of "Farewell to Florida." The effects of the constraint to which Stevens commits himself in "Florida" do not make themselves strongly felt in *Ideas of Order.* In "Owl's Clover" they become fully apparent.

The group of five poems that make up "Owl's Clover" is one of Stevens' least successful efforts in extended composition. By addressing himself to specific social issues—the depression, the adaptation to social change, the white man in Africa, socialism, and the "portent" of world war—he attempts to define the relation of high poetry to society at large, and in doing so he falls into an unhappy stylistic blend, at once allegorical and oblique, rhetorical and obscure. The stylistic defects of "Owl's Clover" may be attributed in part to Stevens' choice of the statue as a structuring device linking up the five poems. The statue has the vices without the virtues of an allegorical image. Stevens says that "the choice of the statue as the central image in OWL'S CLOVER was deliberate," in contrast to another image that was "instinctive" (*LWS,* 319). Although "deliberate," the symbol is also "variable." In one of the detailed explanatory notes Stevens wrote for the poem, he remarks that "part of your difficulty arises, very likely, from the fact that the symbol: the statue, is not always the symbol for the same thing. In one poem it is a symbol for art; in another for society, etc." (*LWS,* 355). The statue is both arbitrary, an object posed for the intellect to analyze, and also unstable in reference. The combination of deliberateness and instability results in verse that is often both flat and opaque.

Although the results of Stevens' effort in "Owl's Clover" are poetically infelicitous, the effort itself was necessary to his development as a poet. He derives from it both a strengthened sense of the vital role of poetry in modern life and a clarified sense of the purpose and direction of his own poetry. In section three of "Sombre Figuration," the last of the five poems, the imagination emerges triumphantly as lord of past and future:

> And memory's lord is the lord of prophecy
> And steps forth, priestly in severity,
> Yet lord, a mask of flame, the sprawling form
> A wandering orb upon a path grown clear. (*OP,* 70)

The course of Stevens' wandering through these five poems is determined not by their specific social themes but by the motifs of the Romantic sublime. His aesthetic and philosophical bent is so strongly marked that social topics, however sincerely he may be interested in them, inevitably come to serve as occasions for the reformulation of the problems that have preoccupied him in *Harmonium* and *Ideas of Order.* This reformulation is by no means complete, but in the process of composition Stevens identifies for himself principles that are of fundamental importance for a supreme fiction.

As Stevens himself suggests, the ostensible subject of "Owl's Clover," the relation of art to society, is only a special instance of the broader dichotomy between imagination and reality. He remarks that though "The Old Woman and the Statue," the first of the five poems, "deals specifically with the status of art in a period of depression, it is, when generalized, one more confrontation of reality (the depression) and the imagination (art). A larger expression than confrontation is: a phase of the universal intercourse. There is a flow to and fro between reality and the imagination" (*LWS,* 368). At a deeper level, beneath this obdurate dichotomy, the real subject of the poem is the nature and function of the spirit in the modern world. This subject appears in section four of "The Old Woman" and again in section three of "The Greenest Continent" in the guise of "transparence." In the first three sections of "The Old Woman," Stevens merely juxtaposes the images of the statue, symbol of art, and the destitute old woman, symbol of the disfranchised and alienated individual. In section four he executes a visionary reconciliation between these two images:

> If the sky that followed, smaller than the night,
> Still eked out luminous wrinklings on the leaves,
> Whitened, again, forms formless in the dark,
> It was as if transparence touched her mind. (*OP,* 45)

In the passage that follows this sudden moment of illumination, the old woman serves as little more than a mask for a purely Stevensian meditation that in its convoluted form recalls the coda of "Key West." The statue becomes the mind and the mind becomes the night, itself a "sovereign shape" containing both the mind and the night. The word *transparence* thus signals the dissolution of phenomenal categories through a transcendent principle of sentient unity.

The motif of transparence will remain a major transcendental trope for Stevens. It may well have been suggested to him by Emerson's "Nature." Emerson declares that "if a man would be alone, let him look at the stars. The rays that come from those heavenly worlds will separate between him and what he touches. One might think the atmosphere was made transparent with this design, to give man, in the heavenly bodies, the perpetual presence of the sublime" (*RWE,* I, 7). The words *transparent* and *transparence* occur several times in the essay and refer, as they do in Stevens, to a spiritual atmosphere. At one point, Emerson describes a moment of sudden illumination like that which comes to the old woman. "Crossing a bare common, in snow puddles, at twilight, under a clouded sky, without having in my thoughts any occurrence of special good fortune, I have enjoyed a perfect exhilaration. I am glad to the brink of fear.... Standing on the bare ground,—my head bathed by the blithe air and uplifted into infinite space,— all mean egotism vanishes. I become a transparent eyeball; I am nothing; I see all; the currents of the Universal Being circulate through me; I am part or parcel of God" (*RWE,* I, 9–10).

The old woman has probably never heard of Emerson, and she is only dimly aware of the spiritual experience Stevens attributes to her. While she is "Thinking of heaven and earth and of herself," she feels the touch of transparence, she does not "know" it. Stevens himself, however, is fully conscious of the philosophical implications of her experience. Transparence, in both Emerson and Stevens, denotes a self-reflexive transcendental teleology, in short, a recognition of God as the origin of the individual spirit. In "The Greenest Continent," Stevens delineates this Romantic conception in opposition to a vulgar, institutionalized form of religion. "The heaven of Europe is empty, like a Schloss / Abandoned because of taxes" (*OP*, 53). The heaven to which Stevens contrasts this abandoned Schloss is that of the Romantic sublime. Stevens constructs this second heaven by integrating the Emersonian motif of transparence with images from Shelley's "Hymn of Apollo." Shelley himself has already adapted the ancient myth of the sun god to the central Romantic premise of a self-reflexive spiritual recognition:

> Then I arise, and climbing Heaven's blue dome,
>   I walk over the mountains and the waves.
>
> . . . .
>
> And the pure stars in their eternal bowers
>   Are cinctured with my power as with a robe;
> Whatever lamps on Earth or Heaven may shine
>   Are portions of one power, which is mine.
>
> . . . .
>
> I am the eye with which the Universe
>   Beholds itself, and knows itself divine.

In implicit acknowledgment of Shelley's transcendental displacement of this myth, Stevens subordinates his own solar imagery to the emblem of transparence. His response to Emerson and Shelley elevates his verse above the ordinary level of the rhetoric in "Owl's Clover," and his depiction of a noble solitude—"Like a solitude of the sun"—achieves true grandeur:

> There was a heaven once,
> But not that Salzburg of the skies. It was
> The spirit's episcopate, hallowed and high,
> To which the spirit ascended, to increase
> Itself, beyond the utmost increase.
> . . . .
>   There each man,
> Through long cloud-cloister-porches, walked alone,
> Noble within perfecting solitude,

> Like a solitude of the sun, in which the mind
> Acquired transparence and beheld itself
> And beheld the source from which transparence came.
> . . . .
> There, too, he saw, since he must see, the domes
> Of azure round an upper dome, brightest
> Because it rose above them all, stippled
> By waverings of stars, the joy of day
> And its immaculate fire, the middle dome,
> The temple of the altar where each man
> Beheld the truth and knew it to be true. (*OP,* 53-54)

"The source from which transparence came" is what Stevens calls "pure poetry" or "essential imagination." He also calls this source "God," but in his commentary on "The Greenest Continent" he makes a distinction between God as a fixed, traditional image—the erstwhile inhabitant of the abandoned Schloss in Salzburg—and the self-renewing power of pure poetry. "The idea of God is a thing of the imagination. We no longer think that God was, but was imagined. The idea of pure poetry, essential imagination, as the highest objective of the poet, appears to be, at least potentially, as great as the idea of God, and, for that matter, greater, if the idea of God is only one of the things of the imagination" (*LWS,* 369). When, in "Final Soliloquy of the Interior Paramour," Stevens declares that "God and the imagination are one," the God to whom he refers is not a thing but a process. As "The essential poem at the centre of things," God is not only a fiction; he is himself the originative fictionalizing principle.

The problem Stevens poses for himself in "The Greenest Continent" is that of coming to terms with a world that has never known either the traditional heaven of Europe or its reconfigurations within the Romantic sublime. "That was never the heaven of Africa, which had / No heaven, had death without a heaven" (*OP,* 54). In attempting to reconcile his vision of this savage world with the aspirations of pure poetry, Stevens compromises these aspirations. He abandons the motif of transparence and proposes an allegorical emblem of necessity as the supreme force. By raising Ananke ($\dot{\alpha}\nu\dot{\alpha}\gamma\kappa\eta$) to the status of a pagan idol, he temporarily situates himself in the fatalistic stage of the Romantic cycle:

> Fateful Ananke is the final god.
> . . . .

> Lord without any deviation, lord
> And origin and resplendent end of law,
> Sultan of African sultans, starless crown. (*OP,* 59–60)

Ananke is a provisional experimental figure; in the fourth and fifth poems of "Owl's Clover," Stevens will already be seeking some embodiment of pure poetry more vital than the figure of Ananke. In his explication of this passage in "The Greenest Continent," written in 1940, Stevens concedes the almost perfunctory character of his invention. "If one no longer believes in God (as truth), it is not possible merely to disbelieve; it becomes necessary to believe in something else. Logically, I ought to believe in essential imagination, but that has its difficulties. It is easier to believe in a thing created by the imagination. A good deal of my poetry lately has concerned an identity for that thing. While Ananke may have been an improvisation, or an importation from Italy, still it was, at the time the poem was written, that thing" (*LWS,* 370).[11] In 1940, Stevens' recent efforts to create a substitute for the idea of God have begun to involve themselves seriously with the "difficulties" of giving figurative form to "essential imagination." Because this figuration is "logically" consequent, it is both necessary and unavoidable for Stevens. In the major visionary poems of 1947 and 1948, the idea of fatality is closely intertwined with the figurations of the Romantic sublime, but brute necessity never stands alone as God. Ananke himself appears only two other times in Stevens' work: in section twelve of "Decorations" and in a canceled stanza for "Examination of the Hero in a Time of War" (1942; *OP,* 83).

In the second poem of "Owl's Clover," "Mr. Burnshaw and the Statue," Stevens identifies a characteristic that must distinguish a modern supreme fiction from its traditional European forms. The modern manifestations of "transparence" must not represent "spirit" as something distinct from the world of physical nature. Stevens' way to this disclosure lies through a rhetorically inflated juxtaposition of the statue—here a symbol for a rigidified and irrelevant form of civilization (*LWS,* 366)—and the "celestial paramours" who represent the vital activity of the spirit. On the level of social allegory, the celestial paramours serves as agents of reconciliation to inevi-

---

11. For information on Stevens' sources for the figure of Ananke, see Woodman, *Stanza My Stone,* 165*n*4; and Peter Brazeau, "Wallace Stevens at the University of Massachusetts: Checklist of an Archive," *Wallace Stevens Journal,* II (1978), 50 (cited in Woodman, *Stanza My Stone,* 166*n*11).

table social change. On another level, they serve as emblems for the kind of poetic inspiration necessary for the construction of a new Romanticism. Stevens' commentary on this section suggests the close connection between this poem and "The Comedian as the Letter C." "It is impossible to be truly reconciled, if one romanticizes the past (ploughmen, peacocks, doves). Nor is one a part of the oncoming future, if one enters it with indifference (fatalism), traceable to a sense of its impermanence (the temple is never quite composed). What is necessary is to recognize change as constant" (*LWS*, 367). The problem for Stevens is to find that precise point of view from which constant change may be reconciled with a sense of divine presence. The celestial paramours represent a pluralized version of the "damsel heightened by eternal bloom" (*CP*, 15) indecisively invoked in "Le Monocle de Mon Oncle":

> Come, all celestial paramours,
> Whether in-dwelling haughty clouds, frigid
> And crisply musical, or holy caverns temple-toned.
> . . . .
> Then, while the music makes you, make, yourselves,
> Long autumn sheens and pittering sounds like sounds
> On pattering leaves and suddenly with lights,
> Astral and Shelleyan, diffuse new day. (*OP*, 47)

The necessary step forward, beyond Crispin's "realism," is to relocate the divine within the natural world, to merge the celestial and the earthly in such a way that man may be the intelligence of his soil. The celestial paramours—"all the things in our nature that are celestial" (*LWS*, 367)—derive from and give access to a permanent spiritual reality: "The radiant disclosures that you make / Are of an eternal vista" (*OP*, 48). At the same time, with seeming paradox, their influence "composes" change and raises chaos into momentary aesthetic order. At the end of his invocation, Stevens focuses this paradox and suggests the manner in which it is ultimately to be resolved. The paramours, "Speaking and strutting broadly, fair and bloomed," are to be "No longer of air but of the breathing earth, / Impassioned seducers and seduced" (*OP*, 52). The shift of tone in Stevens' invocation mimics the kind of transformation he propounds. In calling the celestial paramours out of the holy caverns, Stevens leaves behind the "frigid / And crisply musical" modality of the temples and appropriates for his hymns the seductions of a breathing earth.

In the fourth poem, "A Duck for Dinner," Stevens sketches a description of the poet who will achieve the transformation he has envisioned in "Mr. Burnshaw and the Statue." At this point, in section five, the statue becomes a symbol for high poetry, "something pure and something lofty" (*LWS,* 372), and Stevens represents this symbol as supplying something of which, in the first "Botanist," he could only lament the absence: "the centre-point of the composition." The artist who achieves this central composition becomes the savior of his civilization:

> Exceeding sex, he touched another race,
> Above our race, yet of ourselves transformed,
> Don Juan turned furious divinity,
> Ethereal compounder, pater patriae,
> Great mud-ancestor, oozer and Abraham,
> Progenitor wearing the diamond crown of crowns,
> He from whose beard the future springs, elect. (*OP,* 64)

Stevens explains that "exceeding sex means surpassing it, having progeny by the spirit," and he identifies the diamond crown as "the crown of life, as compared with the starless crown with which THE GREENEST CONTINENT concluded" (*LWS,* 372). *Life* thus becomes the mediating term between the ethereal and the physical. If the celestial is to be conjoined with the earthly, the aspirations of poetry must be directed away from a heaven that is conceived as a place of bliss distinct from the world of nature. (A strong variation on this opposition appears as late as 1949, in canto ten of "An Ordinary Evening in New Haven," where Stevens repudiates a Yeatsian heaven of magical artifice.) Stevens' provisional solution for this problem in "A Duck for Dinner" reveals yet again his descent from Victorian ideology. He speaks of the duty of the poet as "the diverting of the dream / Of heaven from heaven to the future, as a god" (*OP,* 65). This idea—the apotheosis of the social future—will reappear in "The Sail of Ulysses" (1954), where it again associates itself with an inflated rhetorical mode that is alien to the genius of Stevens' finest visionary poetry.

"Owl's Clover," though it falls below the level of supreme poetry, provides material for that poetry. The "mud-ancestor" reappears as an archetypal source for the "first idea" in "Notes Toward a Supreme Fiction":

> There was a muddy centre before we breathed.
> There was a myth before the myth began,
> Venerable and articulate and complete. (*CP,* 383)

The "diamond crown of crowns" will become one of the main symbols in Stevens' mythic elaboration of the first idea. It appears in "Notes" as "the spirit's diamond coronal" (*CP*, 396) and in "The Auroras of Autumn" as a "crown and diamond cabala" in the sky (*CP*, 417). By combining the images of the mud-ancestor with that of the diamond crown, Stevens effects a symbolic linkage between the primordial source of mythic images and the transcendental consciousness, that is, the "imagination that sits enthroned" (*CP*, 417).

Leonora Woodman suggests one possible source for the image of the crown in Stevens' poetry. She explains that the "return to the Divine Idea is often identified in mystical literature as a return to the region of 'Nothing'—the absolute Void. In Kabbalistic speculation, it is proposed as the first stage in the manifestation of the *En-Sof*, itself an unknowable divine essence. The highest *Sefirah* in a series of emanations symbolizing God's gradual unfolding, 'Nothing' is the *kether*, the divine crown considered by many mystics 'infinitely more real than all other reality.' Its symbol is the point in the center of the circle."[12] To my knowledge, the source and extent of Stevens' familiarity with the Cabala have not yet been disclosed, but the allusion in "Auroras," along with Stevens' repeated invocations of the rabbi, lend credibility to Woodman's suggestion. The mystical "nothingness" appears in the final stanza of "A Primitive Like an Orb" and is thus associated with the center and the circle; it reappears in the first strophe of "The Rock," where it again signifies the generative center of all phenomena. Another possible source for the image of the crown discloses itself in "The Figure of the Youth as Virile Poet." Stevens structures his commentary in this essay around fragmentary evocations of Ariadne, half sister of the Minotaur. At the end of the essay, he addresses Ariadne in terms that link her with "the one of fictive music": "*Inexplicable sister of the Minotaur, enigma and mask, although I am part of what is real, hear me and recognize me as part of the unreal*" (*NA*, 67). In one common tradition, Ariadne was deserted by Theseus in Naxos, where Dionysus found and married her. Bulfinch gives the essential information. "As Ariadne sat lamenting her fate, Bacchus found her, consoled her, and made her his wife. As a marriage present he gave her a golden crown, enriched with gems, and when she died, he took her crown and threw it up into the sky. As it mounted the gems grew brighter and were turned into stars, and preserving its form

---

12. Woodman, *Stanza My Stone*, 57.

Ariadne's crown remains fixed in the heavens as a constellation, between the kneeling Hercules and the man who holds the serpent."[13] Stevens' description of the night sky in the first stanza of "Auroras" suggests a similar association of images.

> This is where the serpent lives, the bodiless.
> His head is air. Beneath his tip at night
> Eyes open and fix on us in every sky. (*CP*, 411)

The eyes that "open and fix on us in every sky" are the stars, and in canto seven of "Auroras" these stars become the "crown and diamond cabala," a phrase Stevens reformulates as "that crown and mystical cabala" (*CP*, 417). In canto nine, these traditional sources merge with the imagery of the stars that derive from the Romantic tradition. All these sources may already contribute to the image of "the diamond crown of crowns" in "A Duck for Dinner."

In the fifth poem of "Owl's Clover," "Sombre Figuration," Stevens breaks away from the resolutions of the former poems by introducing a new thematic conflict. The poetic hero as "Great mud-ancestor, oozer and Abraham" evolves into the figure of the subman, an allegorical emblem of the subconscious. By reducing poetic inspiration to the promptings of the subconscious, Stevens creates an exaggerated opposition between the conscious and subconscious parts of the mind. The conscious mind "thinks and it is not true. The man below / Imagines and it is true" (*OP*, 66). This opposition between the conscious and the subconscious sets in motion a dialectical process that culminates, theoretically and poetically, in a visionary mythology. The immediate purpose of the subman in "Sombre Figuration" is twofold. On the one hand, it modifies the purely intellectual ideal of religious vision depicted in the images of transparence and of the celestial paramours, and on the other hand, it qualifies the apotheosis of the social future announced in the fourth poem. By means of the subman, Stevens replaces this ideal with an image of the poet as spokesman for the whole, continuous consciousness of his race. The subman presides over "shapes / That are dissembled in vague memory," and he generates a mythic image, a "sprawling portent" that is at once the specter of world war and a secular displacement of the spirit from the empty heaven of Europe:

---

13. Thomas Bulfinch, *The Age of Fable*, in *Bulfinch's Mythology* (New York, 1934), 135. I am indebted to Rachel Matheis for drawing my attention to this version of the myth.

>   It is the form
>   Of a generation that does not know itself,
>   . . . .
>   A mass overtaken by the blackest sky,
>   Each one as part of the total wrath, obscure
>   In slaughter; or if to match its furious wit
>   Against the sleepers to re-create for them,
>   Out of their wilderness, a special fane,
>   Midmost in its design. (*OP,* 68–69)

"We" cannot "see" the portent, that is, give him a distinct form in the consciousness, but the image nonetheless subsists within or below the mind: "The man below beholds the portent poised, / An image of his making." What the man below beholds, though it is a somber figuration, reconciles the conflicting claims of past and future to provide the mythic locus of visionary fulfillment.

>   The future must bear within it every past.
>   . . . .
>   The portent may itself be memory;
>   And memory may itself be time to come. (*OP,* 70)

Historically, the alternative implications of the portent—"slaughter" and "a special fane"—are both realized, and in many of the poems written during the Second World War, Stevens will seek a resolution of grief for the men that are falling in the visionary sublimations of an archetypal memory. In 1936 the significance of the portent remains shrouded in mystery, but the image nonetheless serves to allay the most serious anxiety of Stevens' middle phase: the anxiety over whether he can himself continue to create strong images. The portent has "supporting arms" that "Reach from the horizons, rim to rim," and it breathes "immense intent." As "A wandering orb on a path grown clear," this image of the giant will ultimately evolve into the central image of one of Stevens' strongest visionary poems. In "A Primitive Like an Orb," Stevens collects his multifarious motifs into one mythic image: "a giant, on the horizon, glistening" (*CP,* 442).

For the "realist" the world consists of solid objects extended in space (*NA,* 31), a world that for Crispin remains "The same insoluble lump." One of the most important theoretical advances Stevens makes in his poetic life is the recognition that reality is not "a solid" (*CP,* 489) but rather an infinite set of dynamic relations. In "Sombre Figuration," Stevens intuitively prefigures this idea and in doing so he foreshadows a reconciliation between "The man below" and "the man that thinks." The scene of this reconciliation is the visionary night renounced by Crispin:

> The solid was an age, a period
> With appropriate, largely English, furniture.
> . . . .
>   Summer night,
> Night gold, and winter night, night silver, these
> Were the fluid, the cat-eyed atmosphere, in which
> The man and the man below were reconciled. (*OP,* 68)

In the conclusion to the poem, as in the conclusion to "The Irrational Element," Stevens returns to the normal world, "Without imagination, without past / And without future, a present time," but he has firmly established for himself a locus for future inspiration, a locus he identifies once again in the last line of the poem—"Night and the imagination being one" (*OP,* 71).

Between "Owl's Clover" and "The Man with the Blue Guitar," Stevens wrote two shorter poems, "A Thought Revolved" (1936) and "The Men That Are Falling" (1936), both of which are concerned with diverting the dream of heaven to earthly things. "A Thought Revolved" merely reworks the old theme of a contrast between a delusory heaven and a solid natural world. The poet-protagonist sings "hero-hymns" that are "Happy rather than holy but happy-high, / Day hymns instead of constellated rhymes" (*CP,* 185). Having rejected "the mystic garden," the poet seeks "an earthly leader" who is "With all his attributes no god but man / Of men whose heaven is in themselves" (*CP,* 185, 186). "The Men That Are Falling," like "A Thought Revolved," contrasts earth and heaven, but Stevens in "Falling" constructs a more ambiguous and dramatically interesting relation between the terms. In "A Thought Revolved" the adherents of celestial illusion are represented with rather mean-spirited mockery:

> A lady dying of diabetes
> Listened to the radio,
> Catching the lesser dithyrambs.
> So heaven collects its bleating lambs. (*CP,* 184)

"The Men That Are Falling," in contrast, begins by representing the poet himself in a state of religious quiescence. What disturbs this state is the poet's own need for some more intense and immediate spiritual fulfillment:

> God and all angels sing the world to sleep,
> Now that the moon is rising in the heat
>
> And crickets are loud again in the grass. The moon
> Burns in the mind on lost remembrances.
>
> He lies down and the night wind blows upon him here.
> The bells grow longer. This is not sleep. This is desire. (*CP,* 187)

The protagonist of "A Thought Revolved" complacently illustrates a settled doctrine. The protagonist of "The Men That Are Falling" is not so easily satisfied. "What is it he desires? / But this he cannot know, the man that thinks." Since the man that thinks is baffled by his own need, Stevens submits himself to the influence of the man below. The result is hallucination. He sees

> a head upon the pillow in the dark,
> More than sudarium, speaking the speech
>
> Of absolutes, bodiless, a head
> Thick-lipped from riot and rebellious cries,
>
> The head of one of the men that are falling, placed
> Upon the pillow to repose and speak,
>
> Speak and say the immaculate syllables
> That he spoke only by doing what he did.
>
> God and all angels, this was his desire,
> Whose head lies blurring here, for this he died.

In a letter of 1953, Stevens remarked that he had "the Spanish Republicans in mind when I wrote *The Men That Are Falling*" (*LWS,* 798). It seems reasonable to suppose that the head on the pillow is that of one of the fallen republicans. He represents an extreme form of purification through noble, self-sacrificing action. His commitment to a life-and-death struggle has placed his action within the realm of "absolutes," an earthly equivalent to "God and all angels." Following upon the hallucinatory intensity of this vision, Stevens' conclusion, though apt enough, seems disappointingly pat and overly explicit. "This man loved earth, not heaven, enough to die."

In 1939, Stevens sent his friend Henry Church a copy of *The Man with the Blue Guitar,* including "Owl's Clover." He remarked that "while it bores me in spots," it "is a very much better book than IDEAS OF ORDER" *(LWS,* 338). Presumably the boring spots were primarily in "Owl's Clover," since Stevens excluded this poem from his *Collected Poems.* The critical judgment implied by this exclusion was no doubt correct, but "Blue Guitar," though poetically superior to "Owl's Clover," may be considered, in a doctrinal sense, as an appendage to it. Or, to phrase the matter differently, "Owl's Clover" serves as a necessary preparation for "Blue Guitar." In "Owl's Clover," Stevens laboriously defines the basic problems and themes for the poetically more exhilarating acrobatics of "Blue Guitar." The comparative virtues of "Blue Guitar" lie on the surface: a greater freedom of movement and spontaneity of invention, pithier diction, and a more dynamic phrasing. And indeed, these virtues are so striking as possibly to distract critical attention from the limitations of the poem: the lack of deep structure, the inconclusive circling around main themes, the too-ready willingness to confuse felicitous local effects with "final solutions" (*CP,* 177).[14]

In a letter to the Italian translator of "Blue Guitar," Stevens says that the interrelations between reality and imagination form the subject of the poem (*LWS,* 788). This is true enough, but only if one takes this dichotomy as the starting point for a deeper concern, the problem of transcendence. In strophe five, Stevens' interlocutors, representatives of the mass of men, demand in effect that he become the poet-savior described in "Owl's Clover":

> Do not speak to us of the greatness of poetry,
> Of the torches wisping in the underground,
>
> Of the structure of vaults upon a point of light.
> There are no shadows in our sun,
>
> Day is desire and night is sleep.
> There are no shadows anywhere.
>
> The earth, for us, is flat and bare.
> There are no shadows. Poetry
>
> Exceeding music must take the place
> Of empty heaven and its hymns,
>
> Ourselves in poetry must take their place,
> Even in the chattering of your guitar. (*CP,* 167)

14. For a purely invidious comparison of "Owl's Clover" and "Blue Guitar," see Martz, "The World as Meditation," in *Wallace Stevens: A Collection of Critical Essays,* 142. For a good statement on the development from the one poem to the other, see Riddel, *The Clairvoyant Eye,* 136.

The "structure of vaults upon a point of light" is a compressed allusion to Stevens' brilliant evocation of "the source from which transparence came" in "The Greenest Continent" (*OP,* 54). The declaration "Day is desire and night is sleep" recalls the passage in "Evening Without Angels" where the darkness "Is rest and silence spreading into sleep" (*CP,* 137). What in "Evening Without Angels" appears to be a boast of unillusioned self-sufficiency is in "Blue Guitar" unquestionably a spiritual complaint. Desire and sleep are animal activities, and a world without shadows is a positivistic world in which the spirit has no place. In "The Noble Rider and the Sound of Words," Stevens gives us an important clue to the philosophical character of the shadowless world:

If we go back to the collection of solid, static objects extended in space, which Dr. Joad posited, and if we say that the space is blank space, nowhere, without color, and that the objects, though solid, have no shadows and, though static, exert a mournful power, and, without elaborating this complete poverty, if suddenly we hear a different and familiar description of the place . . . if we have this experience, we know how poets help people to live their lives. . . . he gives to life the supreme fictions without which we are unable to conceive of it. (*NA,* 31)

The "familiar description" Stevens quotes is Wordsworth's description of early-morning London seen from Westminster Bridge. Even without these allusions, internal and external, the nature of the complaint is perfectly clear, and the solution, as Stevens' interlocutors present it, is equally clear. They require a poetry that is

> Perceived in a final atmosphere;
> For a moment final, in the way
> The thinking of art seems final when
> The thinking of god is smoky dew. (*CP,* 168)

Art achieves finality when the spirit becomes substantial reality, and the spirit becomes substantial reality when the material world is perceived as an emanation of a divine intelligence. Stevens is prepared to formulate these transcendental hypotheses, but he is not yet prepared to embrace them. The "thinking of god" still seems to him a too purely intellectual world, and in the next strophe of the poem he retreats to the common daylight. "It is the sun that shares our works. / The moon shares nothing." The strings grow cold on the blue guitar, and Stevens lapses into a vacillating exchange between reality and the imagination.

In strophes seventeen through twenty-two, Stevens reapproaches the task he has evaded and attempts to resolve the problem without transcending the terms of his initial dichotomy. He begins in strophe seventeen by defining the spirit in purely naturalistic terms. "The angelic ones / Speak of the soul, the mind. It is / An animal" (*CP,* 174). Given this definition, the problem that presents itself is to find "A dream (to call it a dream) in which / I can believe." The difficulty of this task manifests itself, in strophe nineteen, through the awkward heaping up of qualifications and rephrasings:

> That I may reduce the monster to
> Myself, and then may be myself
>
> In face of the monster, be more than part
> Of it, more than the monstrous player of
>
> One of its monstrous lutes, not be
> Alone, but reduce the monster and be,
>
> Two things, the two together as one,
> And play of the monster and of myself,
>
> Or better not of myself at all,
> But of that as its intelligence,
>
> Being the lion in the lute
> Before the lion locked in stone.

The monster is an allegorical emblem for nature (*LWS,* 790). In the phrase "of that as its intelligence," Stevens comes close to the Romantic conception of nature he later propounds in "Imagination as Value" (*NA,* 136). The logical irreconcilability of this conception with a static opposition between imagination and reality finds a poetic correlative in the visually unrealizable images of the last two lines. The words are strong, but the imagination merely boggles at their combination.

Stevens is not himself deceived by the appearance of strong statement at the conclusion of strophe nineteen. In strophe twenty he drifts into yearning reverie:

> Is it ideas that I believe?
> Good air, my only friend, believe,

> Believe would be a brother full
> Of love, believe would be a friend,
>
> Friendlier than my only friend,
> Good air. Poor pale, poor pale guitar . . .

At this point we are back to the submerged bafflement of "Sunday Morning"—"The sky will be much friendlier then than now" (*CP,* 68)—with the difference that here the bafflement has emerged to the surface.

After the ellipsis with which strophe twenty concludes, Stevens restates the central issue of the poem: "A substitute for all the gods: / This self, not that gold self aloft." A substitute, but at the same time something that in no way approximates the spiritual qualities of the gods: "Without shadows, without magnificence, / The flesh, the bone, the dirt, the stone." Once he has rejected the transcendental spirit, Stevens can claim for poetry only a negative existence as "An absence in reality," and he is saved from negation only by means of interrogative equivocation:

> But are these separate? Is it
> An absence for the poem, which acquires
>
> Its true appearances there, sun's green,
> Cloud's red, earth feeling, sky that thinks?
>
> From these it takes. Perhaps it gives,
> In the universal intercourse. (*CP,* 177)

The "true appearances" of poetry, like those of "Westminster Bridge," are fundamentally dependent on animistic perception, that is, the pathetic fallacy ("And all that mighty heart is lying still!"). Stevens' commentary on this passage from "Blue Guitar" is very similar in phrasing to the passage from "The Noble Rider" quoted earlier, and these passages together disclose what is at stake here: the validity of poetic perception, operating within an animistic atmosphere, as an alternative to the positivistic world without shadows. "The purpose of writing poetry is to attain pure poetry. The validity of the poet as a figure of prestige to which he is entitled, is wholly a matter of this, that he adds to life that without which life cannot be lived, or is not worth living, or is without savor, or, in any case, would be altogether different from what it is today" (*LWS,* 363–64).

The "Perhaps" in "Perhaps it gives" must bear the whole weight of conclusion in this inconclusive sequence. In the following strophe, Stevens announces, by sheer fiat, a resolution, or "A few final solutions." Although he is left divided between two voices, one "in the clouds" and the other "on earth," and between two irreconcilable elements, "The imagined and the real, thought / And the truth," he nonetheless holds "all / Confusion solved." The remaining strophes of the poem contain several superb vignettes, but there is no further attempt to penetrate the essential metaphysical issues that are the occasion for the poem. The last lines of the poem call back up the images of night and day from strophe five, and they substitute the jingle of rhyme for a resolution of thought:

>   and we shall sleep by night.
> We shall forget by day, except
> The moments when we choose to play
> The imagined pine, the imagined jay.

The significance of this "play" remains fundamentally problematic. Even so, Stevens has learned something about poetic exploration, and he has received distinct intimations of what the end of his exploring will be. By means of the labor he has undertaken in "Owl's Clover," he has fully recovered from the compositional enervation of *Ideas of Order,* and "Blue Guitar," if it does not convincingly represent any final solutions, does give evidence of a renewed imaginative verve without which these solutions would be impossible.

CHAPTER FOUR

The Pure Idea

Parts of a World is Stevens' freshest, most vigorous and inventive volume between *Harmonium* and *Transport to Summer*. If it does not contain such famous showpieces as those in *Harmonium*, it has in compensation a more coherent sense of intellectual purpose, and it sustains its arguments with a consistently high standard of poetic excellence. Stevens himself remarked in 1944 that "there is always a disposition to select from a man's first book, which in my case was HARMONIUM. Personally, I think that the best things that I have done are in the last two books: PARTS OF A WORLD and NOTES, etc." (*LWS*, 475). And again, responding in 1945 to Knopf's premature wish to publish a Collected Poems: "I thought that PARTS OF A WORLD, the last book of mine that you published, was by far the best thing that I have done. Since not many people seem to have been interested in it, I should like to try again before getting round to a collection" (*LWS*, 501). As this last comment suggests, though Stevens was himself pleased with the merit of *Parts*, he was disappointed at its reception. In a letter of 1942, he identifies the precise character of this disappointment. "But I think I am right in saying that in not a single review of PARTS OF A WORLD was there even so much as a suggestion that the book gave the man who read it any pleasure" (*LWS*, 430). (Stevens' concern for this problem will bear didactic fruit in part three of "Notes Toward a Supreme Fiction": "It Must Give Pleasure.") After more than forty years, *Parts of a World* has still seldom excited the kind of attention that has been bestowed on *Harmonium*, "Notes," or *The Rock*, and only one of Stevens' many critics attributes any sort of definitive significance to *Parts*. Thomas Hines argues that in several of the poems in *Parts*, Stevens achieves a Heideggerian vision of "Being" that enables him to close "the gap between subject and object." Harold Bloom, who has done much to illuminate the "persistence and diversity of strength" in Stevens' later poetry, calls *Parts* "Stevens' most underrated book," and—if we leave *The Auroras of Autumn* out of account—this judgment seems just.[1]

In *Parts of a World*, the earlier opposition between a sun-drenched "realism" and a vaguely angelic Romanticism develops into a philosophically more sophisticated opposition between what—adapting William James's terms—we may call pluralistic empiricism and monistic idealism. In *A Pluralistic Universe*, James rejects both the "cynical materialism" that defines the world "so as to leave man's soul upon it as a sort of outside passenger or alien" and also the traditional, Christian view of God as an "external creator." He argues that once these views have been excluded, there are two basic ways of thinking and feeling about the universe. Both monism and pluralism fall within the

> general scope of what may roughly be called the pantheistic field of vision, the vision of God as the indwelling divine. . . . Both identify human substance with the divine substance. But whereas absolutism thinks that the said substance becomes fully divine only in the form of totality, and is not its real self in any form but the *all*-form, the pluralistic view which I prefer to adopt is willing to believe that there may ultimately never be an all-form at all, that the substance of reality may never get totally collected, that some of it may remain outside of the largest combination of it ever made.[2]

Stevens' own expositions of a pluralistic vision range between the "cynical materialism" James repudiates and the pantheistic but "distributive" form of reality he accepts.

There are many explicitly doctrinal poems in *Parts,* and while they by no means embody a consistent ideology of poetic knowledge, they certainly do establish the conflicting terms of a coherent epistemological and metaphysical debate. This debate is carried on between the opposing personas who occupy

---

1. Thomas J. Hines, *The Later Poetry of Wallace Stevens: Phenomenological Parallels with Husserl and Heidegger* (Lewisburg, Pa., 1976), 27; Bloom, *The Poems of Our Climate,* 89, 136.
2. William James, *A Pluralistic Universe: Hibbert Lectures at Manchester College on the Present Situation in Philosophy* (New York, 1909), 23, 30, 34. For an incisive exposition of the opposition between pluralism and monism in Coleridge and Wordsworth, see M. H. Abrams, "Structure and Style in the Greater Romantic Lyric," in Frederick W. Hilles and Harold Bloom (eds.), *From Sensibility to Romanticism: Essays Presented to Frederick A. Pottle* (London, 1965), 544–47.

the poles of Stevens' dialectical universe. At the one pole, Stevens declares that the highest possible form of "truth" is an awareness of the multiplicity of concrete phenomena in the world. At the other pole, he declares that an imaginative unity of all phenomena within poetic perception is both possible and necessary. In *Parts* this latter pole already begins to dominate Stevens' poetic ambitions. Whereas the metaphysical paradigm for *Harmonium* is a primitive empiricism that presupposes a "last largeness" or substratum to all phenomena—a substratum that either absorbs and cancels the mind or leaves it "as a sort of outside passenger or alien"—the governing idea of *Parts* is something very similar to Kant's description, in the *Critique of Pure Reason,* of the three necessary principles or regulative tendencies of pure reason. We must of course substitute Stevens' term *essential imagination* for Kant's term *pure reason.* These three matrix principles are homogeneity (or, in Stevens' terms, *similarity*), variety or multiplicity (*parts*), and a third principle that mediates between these two: continuity (*relation*).[3] In various ways, Stevens attempts to strike a balance between his devotion to the multiplicity of things in the world and his ever-increasing desire for a central unifying principle of imaginative vision. Throughout all his dialectical taking of stances and counterstances, Stevens is electing "to exercise his power to the full and at its height," so that he may "proceed little by little, as he becomes his own master, to those violences which are the maturity of his desires" (*NA,* 63–64).

To my knowledge, there is no evidence that Stevens ever read either Kant's *Critique* or James's metaphysical works, *A Pluralistic Universe* and *Essays in Radical Empiricism.* He was, however, clearly affected by the philosophical ferment at Harvard during his student years. Margaret Peterson summarizes the situation in philosophy at Harvard around the turn of the century. "The Harvard department of philosophy was dominated by two rival factions. Under Josiah Royce, who was at Harvard from 1882 to 1913, Harvard became the center of the resurgence of German transcendentalism known as Neo-Hegelianism or Absolute Idealism. Santayana at the time was a distinguished young disciple of Royce. The opposing faction was led by an iconoclast named William James, Professor in Philosophy from 1880 to 1907." In Peter Brazeau's oral biography of Stevens, Richard Wilbur recalls a conversation with Stevens after one of his readings at Harvard. "He talked at great length

---

3. Immanuel Kant, *Critique of Pure Reason,* trans. J. M. D. Meiklejohn (New York, 1934), 381.

about the Harvard of his days, about Royce and Santayana.... Those were the people he talked about, and we went out feeling *that's* what happened. Not the publication of a few poems in the *Advocate*, but his philosophy courses." Actually, Robert Buttel's list of Stevens' undergraduate courses indicates that Stevens never officially enrolled in a philosophy course, but the poetry of his later years confirms Wilbur's impression that Stevens was profoundly interested in the themes that were discussed in these courses.[4] Moreover, his personal relationship with Santayana would have given him a particularly acute sense of the poetic implications of these themes. In a letter of 1945, Stevens recalls his visits with Santayana and remarks, "I always came away from my visits to him feeling that he made up in the most genuine way for many things that I needed. He was then still definitely a poet" (*LWS*, 482).

The level of philosophical abstraction in *Parts of a World* is much higher than that in either *Harmonium* or *Ideas of Order*, but the poetic passion and the fertility of invention that accompany these abstractions give them high dramatic relief. There are very few poems in *Parts* that recall either the laboriousness of "Owl's Clover" or the evasive obliquity of "Blue Guitar." The religious element in Stevens' thought, already apparent in *Harmonium*, emerges in a more significant fashion than it ever has before, and for Stevens any revelation of divinity is suffused with pathos and power. The Romantic impulse gains strength steadily, and in two longer poems, "Extracts from Addresses to the Academy of Fine Ideas" (1940) and "Montrachet-Le-Jardin" (1942), Stevens decisively announces his intention to achieve a mystical unity of vision. The emotional and intellectual fulfillment this achievement would effect manifests itself in Stevens' passionate depiction of the female figure who is largely to embody this vision. Images of the female as muse or goddess or earth mother appear in some of the earliest poems in *Harmonium*, and Stevens in *Ideas of Order* and "Owl's Clover" continues to develop these images. In *Parts of a World*, the "ancient mother" (*NA*, 28) assumes a preeminent place in Stevens' poetic preoccupations. In several of the shorter poems in *Parts*, he describes this figure and expresses his yearning for consummation with her. In the long poems "Extracts" and "Montrachet," he articulates the relations between this figure and the mystical ideal of intellectual unity within a self-reflexive spiritual presence.

4. Peterson, *The Idealist Tradition*, 73; Brazeau, *Wallace Stevens Remembered*, 169; Buttel, *The Making of "Harmonium,"* 251.

The elementary terms within the dichotomy of monistic idealism and pluralistic empiricism consist in an opposition between the unitary and the plural—that is, wholeness and "difference"—and the intellective and the sub-intellective components of experience. (The sub-intellective includes both sensory perception and the irrational element.) The dynamic interplay between these larger paired oppositions derives part of its impetus from Stevens' repeated efforts to circumvent intellectual perplexity and achieve resolution by associating the idea of wholeness with sub-intellective forms of experience—a short-circuiting that results in what we might call monistic empiricism. "The Latest Freed Man" (1938) exemplifies this effort to absolutize the condition of "being" prior to "knowing." Although the poem proclaims a temporary victory, it radically undercuts itself, thus giving occasion for a renewal of the conflict on a higher dialectical level. The protagonist of the poem sits in the sun, a physical world, and repudiates "doctrine," which he identifies with "description." Together, these two terms comprehend all intellective and linguistic formulation. As he revels in what he supposes to be purely sensual experience, Stevens situates himself in the paradoxical position of describing in great metaphoric detail what it is like "To be without a description of to be" (*CP*, 205). The articulation of a consciousness prior to interpretation subverts itself, and the escape from doctrine necessarily involves itself in problematic doctrinal implications. The doctrinal basis of the experience related in the poem is a dualism that has been partially suspended by being situated in an incipiently transcendental atmosphere of sentient relation. This incipient transcendentalism manifests itself in the pathetic fallacy. Like the poet, the sun is a "strong man," and he "bathes in the mist / Like a man without a doctrine." By attributing the world of phenomena to the "works" of this strong man, Stevens reapproaches the mode of religious sublimation practiced in stanza seven of "Sunday Morning." To be without a description of to be is

> To know that the change and that the ox-like struggle
> Come from the strength that is the strength of the sun,
> Whether it comes directly or from the sun.

The access of power may come from the sun—not as a god but as a god might be—or it may come "directly" to both the sun and the poet. If it does come directly, its origin remains unspecified. In the climax of the poem, Stevens' equivocation about the source of power resolves itself in a paradoxical figuration of doctrinal perspective:

> It was everything being more real, himself
> At the centre of reality, seeing it.
> It was everything bulging and blazing and big in itself.

The self—objectified as "himself"—is both part of reality and apart from it. Although "At the centre of reality," the percipient retains the distance necessary to "see" that which as object stands apart from him; that is, he simultaneously cancels and exploits the distinction between himself and the external world. The problematic character of this resolution veils itself in exclamatory description. The word *everything* subsumes all difference within the physical magnitude of its modifiers, and the phrase "in itself" surreptitiously reaffirms the integrity of an external world that is ostensibly independent of a perceiving subject. In the last two lines of the poem, Stevens gives a list of particular objects that stand as appositives for things that are big in themselves: "The blue of the rug, the portrait of Vidal, / *Qui fait fi des joliesses banales,* the chairs." (Vidal was Stevens' bookseller and general supplier in Paris. His portrait hung in Stevens' bedroom.)[5] The self-conscious preciosity of the French phrase suggests a sly stylistic recognition of irony. One of the objects listed is a portrait, itself an artistic image or "description," and it evokes a literary response, a description, from an "ox" with a taste for fine phrases.

Stevens' proclamation of resolution in "The Latest Freed Man" entails a willful naïveté, and in "The Sense of the Sleight-of-Hand Man" (1939) and "Dezembrum" (1942), he formulates the opposition between being and knowing at a higher level of doctrinal self-consciousness. In "Sleight-of-Hand," he declares,

> It may be that the ignorant man, alone,
> Has any chance to mate his life with life
> That is the sensual, pearly spouse. (*CP,* 222)

This declaration appears to echo a phrase from Matthew Arnold's *Empedocles on Etna.* Empedocles fears that because "mind" and "thought" have become his "master part," his "ineffable longing for the life of life" will be "baffled for ever" (Act II, ll. 345–46, 357–58). The life of life implies a sub-intellective,

---

5. See Brazeau, *Wallace Stevens Remembered,* 27n.

Wordsworthian animism that extends throughout nature; life becomes the singular term that resolves the opposition between the soul and the external world, but this resolution establishes a new conflict between nature and the conscious intelligence. In "Dezembrum," Stevens formulates this secondary conflict as an opposition between "reason" and "desire." Reason figures in Stevens' prose as a metonymy for "philosophy" and is often opposed to the imagination, the subconscious, and poetry. Desire and "need" appear throughout *Parts of a World* and *Transport to Summer* in association with anticipations of the mythic vision that will be realized in *The Auroras of Autumn*. In "Dezembrum," Stevens personifies the stars as objects of poetic desire:

> Tonight the stars are like a crowd of faces
> Moving round the sky and singing
> And laughing, a crowd of men,
> Whose singing is a mode of laughter,
> IV
> Never angels, nothing of the dead,
> Faces to people night's brilliancy,
> Laughing and singing and being happy,
> Filling the imagination's need. (*CP*, 218)

"Never angels" recalls us to "Evening Without Angels" and invites the comparison of stars that are laughing, happy men, and the glittering vacancy of air. "Evening Without Angels" begins in a grim repudiation of illusory fancy. "Dezembrum" frankly embraces the pathetic fallacy and identifies it as a primary imaginative need. In the fulfillment of this need, reason, if not a hindrance, is entirely irrelevant. "The reason can give nothing at all / Like the response to desire." The basis for this poetic fulfillment is religious. The stars may be invested with spirit because Stevens has made allowance for a supreme spirit that pervades the whole nonhuman world:

> Over and over again you have said,
> This great world, it divides itself in two,
> One part is man, the other god:
> Imagined man, the monkish mask, the face.

In this poem, the divine spirit, though it may be mated with the poetic imagination, cannot be related to the conscious intellect or "reason." In the prose and poetry of the next decade, one of Stevens' main purposes will be to integrate the idea of a pervasive spiritual presence with the idea of an "ultimate intellect" (*CP,* 433).

The negation of reason and the elevation of ignorance are only the first movement in a dialectical process. The question whether the mind is to be "satisfied" forms a main thread connecting the poems of *Parts,* and in the majority of cases the answer Stevens gives is affirmative. In "The Poems of Our Climate" (1938), he poses this question by resuming, in a more elegant form, the image of the jar in Tennessee. His response to the cold, round porcelain bowl reveals that he can no longer be satisfied with any purely formal kind of aesthetic order:

> Clear water in a brilliant bowl,
> Pink and white carnations. . . .
> . . . .
> Pink and white carnations—one desires
> So much more than that. The day itself
> Is simplified: a bowl of white,
> Cold, a cold porcelain, low and round,
> With nothing more than the carnations there.
>   II
> Say even that this complete simplicity
> Stripped one of all one's torments, concealed
> The evilly compounded, vital I
> And made it fresh in a world of white,
> A world of clear water, brilliant-edged,
> Still one would want more, one would need more,
> More than a world of white and snowy scents. (*CP,* 193–94)

The cold, composed, concrete image of order allays what Stevens once called "The torments of confusion" (*CP,* 27). These torments include the distracting and frustrating drives, the vanities and ambitions, of the individual personality. Pure sensory perception, and the imagistic or impressionistic art that restricts itself to this perception, may provide a temporary release from such torments, but the composure thus attained is superficial and cannot long appease the blessed rage to order.

The "evilly compounded, vital I" is a negative incarnation of the solipsistic self lauded in "Tea at the Palaz of Hoon." In "Prelude to Objects" (1938), a companion piece to "Our Climate," Stevens firmly asserts

> That the guerilla I should be booked
> And bound. Its nigger mystics should change
> Foolscap for wigs. Academies
> As of a tragic science should rise. (*CP*, 195)

The "guerilla I" may be identified with the perspective that governs "The Greenest Continent." After describing the heaven that once was, Stevens declares, "That was never the heaven of Africa, which had / No heaven, had death without a heaven" (*OP*, 54), and he describes this aboriginal state as the absence of any transfiguring, "mystic" vision:

> No god rules over Africa, no throne,
> Single, of burly ivory, inched of gold,
> Disposed upon the central of what we see,
> That purges the wrack or makes the jungle shine,
> As brilliant as mystic, as mystic as single. (*OP*, 55)

Stevens cannot long endure the thought of such complete spiritual poverty, for when "Death, only, sits upon the serpent throne... Each fretful fern drops down a fear like dew." In response to this fear, Stevens will assume a missionary function, but he cannot immediately traverse the distance between the condition he has depicted and that which he will imagine in "Blue Guitar," an ideal state in which "The thinking of god is smoky dew" (*CP*, 168). As a transitional stage between the fretful ferns and the thinking of god, a pagan idol occupies the throne where only death has sat. "Fatal Ananke is the common god," and since Ananke knows "Each look and each necessitous cry," he also "sees the angel in the nigger's mind" (*OP*, 59). Ananke "knows" but "he does not care," and his indifference casts his worshipers back on what Stevens sometimes calls "humanism," that is, the exaltation of the individual human mind as the only form of sentient teleology that remains after the old gods have vanished into air. In "Prelude to Objects," when he repudiates the "nigger mystics" of the "guerilla I," Stevens also implicitly proclaims the necessity of a metaphysical vision in which the highest principle of intellectual and aesthetic order transcends the claims and assertions of a renegade egoism. He will himself seek to satisfy this need; the "Academies / As of a tragic science" will take form in "the academy of fine ideas" that will listen to his "addresses."

Stevens himself has always had strong promptings from the renegade egoism of Hoon. In a letter of 1936 to Ronald Lane Latimer—a vaguely Faustian figure who elicited the Mephistophelian side of Stevens' personality—Stevens declares, "The truth is that egotism is at the bottom of everything everybody does, and that, if some really acute observer made as much of egotism as Freud has made of sex, people would forget a good deal about sex and find the explanation for everything in egotism" (*LWS*, 305–306). In this declaration, Stevens confirms his implicit answer to the rhetorical question he poses about Crispin's motives for seeking to found a colony. After the exit of the mental moonlight, the narrator of "Comedian" asks,

> What was the purpose of his pilgrimage,
> Whatever shape it took in Crispin's mind,
> If not, when all is said, to drive away
> The shadow of his fellows from the skies,
> And, from their stale intelligence released,
> To make a new intelligence prevail? (*CP*, 37)

Stevens' alternating affirmations and repudiations of the "guerilla I" provide the grounds for a basic difference of critical opinion. Among the many critics who argue for the primacy of the individual ego in Stevens' work, Harold Bloom is perhaps the most prominent. Bloom advances his thesis into the very ranks of the opposition in Stevens himself. Despite Stevens' revulsion before "the evilly compounded, vital I," Bloom maintains that Stevens' purpose in "The Poems of Our Climate" is to arrive "back at a fresh version of the Whitmanian 'me myself.' Where Keats deprecated 'identity' or the 'sole self,' Whitman and Stevens quest for the powerful press of themselves."[6] I would suggest, on the contrary, that Whitman's exaggerated emphasis on his own poetic persona is what renders him least attractive to Stevens. In a letter of 1942, Stevens declares that "you must know without my telling you how one struggles to suppress the merely personal" (*LWS*, 413). Objecting to the image of poets as "human curiosities," he remarks that "the conception of the figure of the poet has changed and is changing every day. It was only a few years ago when Joaquin Miller or Walt Whitman were considered to be approximations of a typical image. But were they? Weren't they recognized by people of any sense at all as, personally, poseurs? They belong in the same category of eccentrics to which queer looking actors belong" (*LWS*, 414). Stevens' response to Whitman is considerably more complex than this contemptuous dismissal would suggest, but it is precisely the quality of histrionic egotism in Whitman that excites Stevens' repugnance and drives him to a

---

6. Bloom, *The Poems of Our Climate*, 141–42.

one-sided characterization. Stevens, like Keats, can never escape for long from the preoccupations of the sole self, but the highest mythic symbols in their visionary poetry represent principles that transcend the urges and appetites of personality.

After the "guerilla I" has been booked and bound, what is left that might provide a stimulus and goal for poetry? In the third stanza of "Our Climate," Stevens attempts to give an answer:

> There would still remain the never-resting mind,
> So that one would want to escape, come back
> To what had been so long composed.
> The imperfect is our paradise.
> Note that, in this bitterness, delight,
> Since the imperfect is so hot in us,
> Lies in flawed words and stubborn sounds.

In "Crude Foyer" (1947), Stevens will describe "paradise" as "A foyer of the spirit in a landscape / Of the mind," and he will set this paradise in opposition to the plain reality of the senses, "a landscape only of the eye" (*CP*, 305). In "Our Climate" the mind escapes from the bondage of the senses, but the mental realm into which it escapes fails of that "complete simplicity" that renders this bondage so seductive. The mental realm comprises the generic antecedents of the old Romanticism—the "legendary moonlight" that Crispin "never could forget" (*CP*, 33)—and the problematic oppositions that motivate Stevens' quest and that give new life to "what had been so long composed." A paradise so constituted is necessarily "imperfect." In his early address to the muse, "To the One of Fictive Music" (1922), Stevens had declared that no music "Gives motion to perfection more serene / Than yours, out of our imperfections wrought" (*CP*, 87). The polished rhetorical surface of this poem betrays a facile opposition between the imperfect world of reality and the paradise of art. It seems one of Stevens' most finished early poems—too finished, too much a superficial reflex of what had been so long composed. In "Our Climate," Stevens' rhetorical motions are far from serene, and the idea of paradise is no longer an idea of "that perfect sky" beneath which we "pick the strings of our insipid lutes" (*CP*, 69). The angelic melodies Stevens repudiates in "Sunday Morning" have given place to "flawed words and stubborn sounds." The ambiguous tonal mingling of "bitterness" and "delight" captures the accent of "our unfinished spirits," and Stevens' own "angelic syllables" now sound the vital note of human passion (*CP*, 137). Through his confrontations with Romanticism in *Ideas of Order,* he has come to recognize that what had been so long composed was itself a speech of unfinished spirits and might thus be a part of what "is so hot in us." In "Notes Toward a Supreme Fiction," he will describe his visionary persona, the "major man," as a "foundling of the infected past," and he will also declare that "The hot of him is purest in the heart" (*CP*, 388).

Imperfection is a necessary stimulus to visionary ambition—"And not to have is the beginning of desire" (*CP*, 382)—but if Stevens is to sustain this ambition there must also be a prospect of having. In one of his most vivid shorter poems, "Of Bright and Blue Birds and the Gala Sun" (1940), the dynamic interplay of having and not having results in a complex and paradoxical development of what has been so long composed:

> Some things, niño, some things are like this,
> That instantly and in themselves they are gay
> And you and I are such things, O most miserable . . .
>
> For a moment they are gay and are a part
> Of an element, the exactest element for us,
> In which we pronounce joy like a word of our own.
>
> It is there, being imperfect, and with these things
> And erudite in happiness, with nothing learned,
> That we are joyously ourselves and we think
>
> Without the labor of thought, in that element,
> And we feel, in a way apart, for a moment, as if
> There was a bright *scienza* outside of ourselves,
>
> A gaiety that is being, not merely knowing,
> The will to be and to be total in belief,
> Provoking a laughter, an agreement, by surprise. (*CP*, 248)

By addressing himself in Spanish to a little boy, Stevens gives us a clue to the provenance of his instant gaiety. In *Scepticism and Animal Faith,* Santayana remarks, "At first, as we see in children, spirit is carried away by the joy of doing or seeing anything . . . it is innocently happy in accepting any task and watching any world."[7] The adult can expect to enjoy this kind of spontaneous

---

7. George Santayana, *Scepticism and Animal Faith: Introduction to a System of Philosophy* (New York, 1923), 214–15.

gaiety only "For a moment"; after this moment, knowing and being ineluctably diverge, and in order to be "erudite in happiness," Stevens must have recourse to those elaborate "stratagems / Of the spirit" by means of which "what is possible / Replaces what is not" (*CP*, 376). Stevens' reconstruction of a childlike spontaneity and joy is itself one such stratagem. Although he declares that "you and I are such things," his self-reflexive apostrophe "O most miserable" implicitly concedes that his identification with the little boy is fictitious and incomplete. In the self-transforming sentence of the last three stanzas, the opposition between being and knowing serves as a platform on which Stevens erects his third, synthetic term: "to be total in belief." In "Description Without Place" (1945), he will reformulate the ideal of total belief as a state in which

> observing is completing and we are content,
> In a world that shrinks to an immediate whole,
> That we do not need to understand, complete
> Without secret arrangements of it in the mind. (*CP*, 341)

Stevens will achieve moments of completion and wholeness, but he will never escape the necessity of making secret arrangements of it in the mind. The supreme fiction contains an unresolvable residuum of the problematic, and Stevens will never fully satisfy, for himself, "The will to be and to be total in belief." It is no doubt his frustration with this state of things that prompts him, in his elegy for Santayana, to suspend all sense of the problematic and to attribute to Santayana what he cannot achieve for himself: "It is a kind of total grandeur at the end, . . . Total grandeur of a total edifice" (*CP*, 510).

Stevens' thought characteristically drives toward a culmination, an absolute or condition of totality, and it spontaneously seeks out mythic representations for this absolute. "Country Words" (1937), one of the earliest of Stevens' mythic prophecies of apocalyptic illumination, diverges from the main line of Stevens' mythic poetry in that it derives the personae of the poem from preestablished mythic personages, an anomaly that perhaps influences the semicomic tone and the unusual use of rhyme:

> I sang a canto in a canton,
> Cunning-coo, O, cuckoo cock,
> In a canton of Belshazzar
> To Belshazzar, putrid rock,

The Pure Idea / 119

> Pillar of a putrid people,
> Underneath a willow there
> I stood and sang and filled the air. (*CP,* 207)

In Daniel 5, Belshazzar is the son of Nebuchadnezzar and the last king of Babylon. It is he, putrid pillar of a putrid people, who sees his doom written on the wall ("MENE, MENE, TEKEL, UPHARSIN"). If we extend the biblical parallel, the "I" who "stood and sang" appears to be a latter-day Daniel, a prophet and interpreter of visions. In stanzas two and three, Belshazzar himself becomes a visionary prophet and merges with Daniel. (If Stevens is, as I am assuming, working from a biblical source, he may have merged the names Belshazzar and Bel-te-shazzar, as Daniel was called by the Babylonians.)

> It was an old rebellious song,
> An edge of song that never clears;
> But if it did . . . If the cloud that hangs
> Upon the heart and round the mind
> Cleared from the north and in that height
> The sun appeared and reddened great
> Belshazzar's brow, O, ruler, rude
> With rubies then, attend me now.

The temporal position of the speaker is ambiguously suspended between the "then" of Belshazzar's time and the "now" of the moment of composition. What he sings is not a fully assured prophetic vision like the biblical Daniel's. It is, rather, a clouded apprehension of some possible visionary fulfillment. The projection of fulfillment is represented as a clearing of the sun that illuminates Belshazzar, now become something like an awe-inspiring pagan idol. The sprung sequence of tenses within the conditional sentence structure operates a sleight of hand whereby the future conditional implications of the protasis—"If the cloud . . . Cleared" and "The sun appeared"—become the basis for the invocational imperative in the apodosis, "attend me now." What was to be comes to be what has occurred; Belshazzar was illuminated and can thus illuminate in turn. At the conclusion to "Description Without Place," Stevens alludes to and further expounds the technique of poetic self-validation explored in the second stanza of "Country Words." He declares that "description" must "Be alive with its own seemings, seeming to be / Like rubies reddened by rubies reddening" (*CP,* 346). Belshazzar is a ruler "rude" with rubies that are part of his barbarian splendor. In "Description Without Place," the rubies remain as a memory of a moment of poetic realization that can and does inspire other such realizations.

In the third stanza, Belshazzar becomes the prophet and interpreter of Hermetic texts. The symbol of spiritual illumination with which Stevens invests him, "the diamond pivot bright," has appeared in "Owl's Clover" as "the diamond crown of crowns" that is worn by the "Great mud-ancestor, oozer and Abraham" (*OP*, 64):

> What is it that my feeling seeks?
> I know from all the things it touched
> And left beside and left behind.
> It wants the diamond pivot bright.
> It wants Belshazzar reading right
> The luminous pages on his knee,
> Of being, more than birth or death.
> It wants words virile with his breath.

Although Belshazzar himself never reappears in Stevens' poetry, the symbols associated with him—crown, luminous page, breath—continue to develop in *Parts* and *Transport to Summer*; in *Auroras*, they will form part of the regalia for the mythic pantheon of the supreme fiction. In "The Owl in the Sarcophagus," the "deep atmosphere / Of sleep, the accomplished, the fulfilling air" gives access to "the whiteness that is the ultimate intellect, / A diamond jubilance beyond the fire" (*CP*, 433). In "The Auroras of Autumn," the diamond jubilance metamorphoses into a "crown and diamond cabala" (*CP*, 417). When, in "Things of August" (1949), Stevens as rabbi takes a synoptic review of his visionary symbols, he recalls "A crown within him of crispest diamonds" and "A hand of light to turn the page" (*CP*, 492).

Stevens' dialectical sallies into the sub-intellective physical world make it clear that the negation of description contains its own contrary and that the repudiation of doctrinal order inescapably imposes a new order. His sallies into pluralistic empiricism will make it equally clear that all doctrine has an inherent tendency toward a unity of principle. The dialectical starting point for this process may be located in "On the Road Home" (1938), a poem that establishes one doctrinal extreme for *Parts of a World*: the rejection of any final mentalistic unity and the affirmation of a pluralistic material reality. "On the Road Home" consists of a dialogue between like-minded people; both of them have been freed from the bondage of monistic superstition and have bravely adopted a world view in which the highest moments of experience derive not from intellectual or spiritual satisfactions but from the intensity of sensory awareness:

> It was when I said,
> "There is no such thing as the truth,"
> That the grapes seemed fatter.
> The fox ran out of his hole. (*CP,* 203)

The second speaker slightly qualifies this assertion. "'There are many truths, / But they are not parts of a truth.'" The qualified proposition implies that "truth" is a matter of local concurrences between the mind and the disparate parts of the world. For Stevens, this philosophical issue is closely bound to a fundamental religious issue. "We said we stood alone." The negation of unitary truth associates itself in Stevens' mind with the negation of any form of knowledge superior to the human percipient's. In other words, there is no god that sustains the unity of the world within his own perception. In the fourth stanza, Stevens explicitly denies that there is any single unifying design accessible to human cognition.

> "Words are not forms of a single word.
> In the sum of the parts, there are only the parts.
> The world must be measured by eye."

In this poem the repudiation of intellectual and spiritual unity entails no frustration. The reduction of reality to sensual particulars rewards itself through a superlative magnification of these particulars. "It was at that time, that the silence was largest / And longest, the night was roundest." As in "The Latest Freed Man," everything here is bulging and big in itself. The superlatives provide closure on a purely grammatical scale, and there is no need, for the moment, to probe the ground for the intimacy between the mind and the world.

"Connoisseur of Chaos" (1938) sets out from the same premises that govern "On the Road Home," and it demonstrates the inherent instability of these premises. The dialectical structure of this poem adapts itself to a tone of relaxed rumination. The first two sections juxtapose contrary theses. The first thesis (both "A" and "B" in section one) is that any principle of intellectual unity is an arbitrary imposition:

>   A. A violent order is disorder; and
>   B. A great disorder is an order. These
>   Two things are one. (Pages of illustrations.) (*CP*, 215)

In the second section, Stevens proposes an idea of order that is not at all violent but is, indeed, "as pleasant as port." The idea is that things going on in an orderly way depend on "a law of inherent opposites" that is appositionally equated with a law "of essential unity."[8] The facility of this appositional equation is deceptive; the unity beneath the inherent opposites is merely assumed, and in the next section the arbitrariness of this assumption generates its negation. The first two lines make a show of offering logical support for the law of essential unity, then the third line—"At least that was the theory"—simply shrugs off the law as an obsolete idea. The sentence beginning "And yet" in the sixth line executes another adversative turnabout:

> After all the pretty contrast of life and death
> Proves that these opposite things partake of one,
> At least that was the theory, when bishops' books
> Resolved the world. We cannot go back to that.
> The squirming facts exceed the squamous mind,
> If one may say so. And yet relation appears,
> A small relation expanding like the shade
> Of a cloud on sand, a shape on the side of a hill.

"Relation" is the incipient impulse to the continuity between multiplicity and unity that motivates the squamous mind.

The fourth section of "Connoisseur" also has a tripartite movement, but it begins and ends at a pole opposite to that at which section three begins and ends. The first movement of section four (proposition "A") qualifies and reasserts the pluralism in "A" of section one. Proposition "B" of section four starts off as if illustrating proposition "B" of section one, but then, as by an instinctive tendency, the order within disorder drifts into the principle of essential unity:

>   A. Well, an old order is a violent one.
>   This proves nothing. Just one more truth, one more

---

8. The inherent opposites that pervade Stevens' poetry probably owe something to Emerson's declaration, in "Compensation," that "an inevitable dualism bisects nature, so that each thing is a half, and suggests another thing to make it whole; as, spirit, matter; man, woman; odd, even; subjective, objective; in, out; upper, under; motion, rest; yea, nay" (*RWE*, II, 97).

>   Element in the immense disorder of truths.
>   B. It is April as I write. The wind
>   Is blowing after days of constant rain.
>   All this, of course, will come to summer soon.
>   But suppose the disorder of truths should ever come
>   To an order, most Plantagenet, most fixed . . .

The wistful supposition dissolves into meditative ellipsis points, and in the next line Stevens pulls himself back to his pluralistic doctrine. "A great disorder is an order." Despite the reversion, by depicting the drift of his thoughts, Stevens has suggested that if the mind loves order, it will be drawn by its own nature to the idea of a unitary order, "most Plantagenet, most fixed." The couplet that is the fifth and final section of the poem poses the eagle's eye as a metaphor for a unifying perspective: "The pensive man . . . He sees that eagle float / For which the intricate Alps are a single nest."

The elaborate dialectical structure of "Connoisseur" is so clear in outline that it may be diagrammed by section:

> Section one: Pluralistic ("great disorder")
> Section two: Monistic ("essential unity")
> Section three: Monistic ("partake of one")
>   Pluralistic ("squirming facts")
>   Monistic ("relation")
> Section four: Pluralistic ("disorder of truths")
>   Monistic ("an order, most Plantagenet")
>   Pluralistic ("great disorder")
> Section five: Monistic ("a single nest")

The extraordinary rigor of formal order within the relaxed, ruminative mode of "Connoisseur" marks an important advance toward the compositional mastery that distinguishes Stevens' greatest poetry. The sophisticated thematic and symbolic constructions of the later poetry evolve from the simpler, more elementary patterns of the earlier poetry. In *Parts,* Stevens is concerned with the precise articulation of the basic themes that will govern the visionary poetry. For example, the image of the eagle's nest as a simple emblem of the monistic universe provides a foundation for the far more complex and problematic image of the serpent's nest in canto one of "Auroras" and in "Saint John and the Back-Ache" (1948). In these two later poems, the nest also serves as an image of essential unity, but it operates on the paradoxical verge of consciousness where all propositions constantly threaten to invert or cancel themselves.

In "Landscape with Boat" (1940), Stevens again employs a diagrammatically distinct dialectical structure. "Landscape" is a satirical portrait, one of the finest in a series that begins with the Doctor of Geneva and includes Crispin, Mrs. Alfred Uruguay, and the Canon Aspirin's sister ("Notes"). Through his portrayal of his hypothetical antagonist, "An anti-master-man, floribund ascetic," Stevens establishes two metaphysical extremes: the pluralistic sensualism the floribund ascetic scorns, and the reductive, negative absolutism he embraces. In the second major movement of "Landscape"—beginning "He never supposed"—Stevens offers a third, synthetic term as a resolution of the opposition established by the floribund ascetic.

Stevens' description of his antagonist is given in the third person, and it is clear from the tone of mockery that the man being described is not simply another mask for Stevens himself. He is an ascetic who has made a fundamental mistake in his conception of the world. This mistake corresponds closely to—and may well have been influenced by—the mistake Santayana derides in his depiction of the "mystical" temperament:

> The way of true wisdom, therefore, if true wisdom is to deal with the Absolute, can only lie in abstention: neither the senses nor the common understanding, and much less the superstructure raised upon these by imagination, logic, or tradition, must delude us: we must keep our thoughts fixed upon the inanity of all this in comparison with the unthinkable truth, with the undivided and unimaginable reality. Everything, says the mystic, is nothing, in comparison with the One. . . . The end of his purification is the atrophy of his whole nature, the emptying of his whole heart and mind to make room, as he thinks, for God.

Stevens' two chief modes of poetic experience are the mode of the senses and the common understanding and the mode of visionary exaltation. Neither of these modes has any essential affinity with asceticism. Through both modes, though in different ways, Stevens seeks the fullest possible realization of life.[9] Both are modes of affirmation, and the anti-master-man, like Santayana's mystic, is a spirit for whom all affirmation inverts itself into denial:

---

9. Santayana, *Interpretations of Poetry and Religion,* 14, 225–26. For a sharply contrasting view of Stevens' basic orientation, see Vendler, *On Extended Wings,* 93.

> He brushed away the thunder, then the clouds,
> Then the colossal illusion of heaven. Yet still
> The sky was blue. He wanted imperceptible air.
> . . . .
>   Nabob
> Of bones, he rejected, he denied, to arrive
> At the neutral centre, the ominous element,
> The single-colored, colorless primitive. (*CP,* 241–42)

The "neutral centre, the ominous element" without "Any azure under-side or after-color" recalls in ironic inversion the pivotal assertion in stanza six of "Monocle":

> If men at forty will be painting lakes
> The ephemeral blues must merge for them in one,
> The basic slate, the universal hue. (*CP,* 15)

The nabob of bones represents one direction Stevens might have taken but did not. By reformulating the dichotomy between surface and substance into a dichotomy between pluralism and essential unity, Stevens has saved himself from following the degeneration of the universal hue into "The single-colored, colorless primitive."

 Lest we have any doubt that Stevens now entirely dissociates himself from the anti-master-man, he breaks from his satiric stance for the space of two lines in which he stands back and directly criticizes his doctrinal antagonist. "It was not as if the truth lay where he thought, / Like a phantom, in an uncreated night." This break foreshadows the *propria persona* speech in the second major movement. For the remainder of this movement, Stevens shifts back to satirically objective portraiture. The succession of negative suppositions builds a castle in the air that subsists only on the condition of its disconnection from any perceptible or conceivable reality:

>   its place had to be supposed,
> Itself had to be supposed, a thing supposed
> In a place supposed, a thing that he reached
> In a place that he reached, by rejecting what he saw
> And denying what he heard. He would arrive.
> He had only not to live, to walk in the dark,
> To be projected by one void into
> Another.

Here we have, indeed, the "flow to and fro between reality and the imagination" that is "a phase of the universal intercourse" (*LWS*, 368), but both reality and imagination have been stripped of all content and have been reduced to negative categories. The universal intercourse subsists only as pure activity between two negative infinities.

As in "Connoisseur" and several other poems of this period, the conflict of pluralistic and monistic doctrines entails a concern for the nature of truth and belief. The anti-master-man supposes a truth but fatally disables it by requiring that it be beyond any knowable truth:

> It was his nature to suppose,
> To receive what others had supposed, without
> Accepting. He received what he denied.
> But as a truth to be accepted, he supposed
> A truth beyond all truths.

The phrases "a truth" and "all truths" are distinguished from each other only by plurality and singularity and by the segregative spatial metaphor "beyond." The effect of this metaphor is to expel from "a truth" all the positive criteria of knowledge that can be extrapolated from "all" particular "truths." The one, absolute truth is "to be accepted," but the imperative force of the gerundive is left suspended in the negative space, the pure nothingness, of what is to be accepted.

In the second major movement of "Landscape," Stevens counters the anti-master-man by suggesting in his own voice what the "truth" actually is:

>   He never supposed divine
> Things might not look divine, nor that if nothing
> Was divine then all things were, the world itself,
> And that if nothing was the truth, then all
> Things were the truth, the world itself was the truth.

Simply through inverting the negative—"nothing" becomes "all things"—Stevens effects a synthesis in which the parts of the world are no longer merely disparate parts; they are parts of "the truth." Since man himself is part of the world, he is also part of the truth, and the truth, the enabling condition of this synthesis, is the comprehensive, intellective being of divinity.

The third and final movement of "Landscape" hypothetically describes what the anti-master-man might have been, had he thought the way Stevens does in the preceding movement. The transformation of the external world into a "celestial pantomime" is accompanied by delighted perceptual metaphors of the finely realized setting:

> Had he been better able to suppose:
> He might sit on a sofa on a balcony
> Above the Mediterranean, emerald
> Becoming emeralds. He might watch the palms
> Flap green ears in the heat. He might observe
> A yellow wine and follow a steamer's track
> And say, "The thing I hum appears to be
> The rhythm of this celestial pantomime."

In the Mediterranean benignity of this closing movement, Stevens composes a harmony between the robustly Epicurean tone of normal poetry and the rarefied sublime of pure poetry. Of these two tonal elements, the Epicurean is dominant, for humming, even in rhythm to a celestial pantomime, expresses cheerful quiescence in a general sense of well-being. This sense appears to depend more on the immediate situation—yellow wine and a splendid view—than on religious rapture. Moreover, in the very moment of closure, the doctrine of the poem begins to slip away from the idea of pantheistic unity espoused in the second movement and to generate a new, implied dichotomy: that between heaven as real essence and the world as approximation or reflection ("pantomime") of this real essence.

If Santayana contributes to Stevens' satirical portrait of the anti-master-man, he may also influence both the conception of a pantheistic alternative and the incipient regression of this alternative into a quasi-Platonic idealism. In *Scepticism and Animal Faith*, Santayana propounds a theory of "essences" that he associates with but distinguishes from the Platonic theory:

This recognition that the data of experience are essences is Platonic, but it is a corrective to all that is sentimental in Platonism, curing it as it were homeopathically. The realm of essence is not peopled by choice forms or magic powers. It is simply the unwritten catalogue, prosaic and infinite, of all the characters possessed by such things as happen to exist, together with the characters which all different things would possess if they existed.... In themselves all the points of space-time are equally central and palpitating, and every phase of every psyche is a focus for actual readjustments to the whole universe.

Although the "things" in Santayana's cosmic catalog "happen to exist," Santayana also argues that "existence" cannot be attributed to "essence," so that he concludes in a peculiarly detached contemplation of idealized phenomenological "data" that are unrelated either to objects or to perceiving subjects. Any given image is to be "taken neither for the manifestation of a substance nor for an idea in a mind nor for an event in a world," but merely for what it is in itself, an image: "a color for that color . . . music for that music . . . a face for that face."[10] Stevens' early conception of pure poetry as music and images alone skirts this sort of radical, Paterian aestheticism, but Stevens never settles into it as Santayana does. In "A Collect of Philosophy," Stevens says that "the exquisite and memorable way in which [Santayana] has always said things has given so much delight that we accept what he says as we accept our own civilization" (*OP*, 187). The way in which we accept our own civilization often entails a tacit but fundamental modification of its premises, and in "To an Old Philosopher in Rome" (1952), Stevens will reformulate Santayana's distinction between existence and essence as a distinction between the ordinary world and the world of ideal vision, that is, between normal and pure poetry.

The kind of pantheistic unity Stevens espouses in the second movement of "Landscape," though it advances on the extreme pluralism of "On the Road Home," remains little more than a shapeless supposition—a profession, as it were, of undiscriminating liberality. In experiential practice, there is little to choose between a total negation of an ultimate truth and a dissipation of this ultimate into multitudinous particularity. As Stevens remarks about "Notes Toward a Supreme Fiction," "In trying to create something as valid as the idea of God has been, and for that matter remains, the first necessity seems to be breadth. It is true that the thing would never amount to much until there is no breadth or, rather, until it has all come to a point" (*LWS*, 435). It is this, the coming to a point, that Stevens lacks in "Landscape." In "Extracts from Addresses to the Academy of Fine Ideas," among other poems, he will acknowledge and attempt to correct this defect.

The dialectic between negation and belief links a series of five poems in *Parts*: "Landscape," "Mrs. Alfred Uruguay," "Asides on the Oboe," "Extracts," and "The Well Dressed Man with a Beard." In the last three of these

---

10. Santayana, *Scepticism and Animal Faith*, 77, 165, 74.

poems, Stevens emphatically declares for the positive, though he still wavers as to the doctrinal form his affirmation will take. In "Mrs. Alfred Uruguay" (1940), as in "Landscape," Stevens creates a satirical contrast between those who deny and those who affirm both the world and the imagination. The anti-master-man "brushed away the thunder," and Mrs. Uruguay declares, "'I have wiped away moonlight like mud'" (*CP,* 249). Whereas the anti-master-man seeks "A truth beyond all truths," Mrs. Uruguay appears to seek only a purified dualism. She seeks "'to get at myself'" and to approach "the real." In this context, the moonlight serves as an object of sensory perception and as a symbol for the imagination. By wiping it away and saying "'no / To everything,'" Mrs. Uruguay leaves no point of reference either for the real or for the self. Both of these concepts, as in "Landscape," reduce themselves to facing voids, so that her absolute, the infinitive "To be," is a blank. "Her no and no made yes impossible."

The figure Stevens opposes to Mrs. Uruguay is less successfully realized than is Mrs. Uruguay herself. He is a "figure of capable imagination," but his capabilities are rather crudely represented, and his thematic significance can scarcely be derived either from his physical description or from his somewhat simpleminded adherence to the imagination in contrast to "the real." He is "a rider intent on the sun, / A youth, a lover with phosphorescent hair," who recalls the poet of "Kubla Khan"—"His flashing eyes, his floating hair." Phosphorescence seems a dubious enhancement of "floating," and the effect of this image, out of the Coleridgean context of hallucinatory exaltation, seems almost ludicrous. Still, whatever self-conscious comedy Stevens may intend, it is clear that the youth is, in fact, an imaginatively potent figure. He is an "Eventual victor" who "out of the martyrs' bones" creates "The ultimate elegance: the imagined land." The virile youth of "Mrs. Alfred Uruguay" is a transitional figure in Stevens' work. In his gaudiness and in the hint of a solipsistic retreat from the real, the youth represents something of a regression to the voluptuous subjectivism of "Tea at the Palaz of Hoon." At the same time, he anticipates the poet-hero in many of Stevens' later poems. In "Montrachet," Stevens celebrates "The naked man, the naked man as last / And tallest hero and plus gaudiest vir" (*CP,* 262). Both the virile youth and the tallest hero are gaudy, but gaudiness is not finally the essential quality of the poet who composes a supreme fiction. Stevens' later heroes are more somber men. The virile youth's imagination feeds itself on the stuff of the high serious ("the martyrs' bones"), but his goal, "elegance," is the same as Mrs. Alfred Uruguay's, except for the superlative modifier "ultimate." The poet-hero will gain in dignity as his vision increases in scope and power.

In "Asides on the Oboe" (1940), Stevens creates yet another figure of capable imagination, the "philosophers' man," and though he assigns to this figure the task of creating a supreme fiction, he loses sight of this purpose in his preoccupation with the more pressing concerns of normal poetry: the function of the poet in a time of war. (This preoccupation is given more extended treatment in "Examination of the Hero in a Time of War" [1942].) The point of intersection between these metaphysically different modes may be found in the image of diamonds and/or crystals as symbols of poetic realization. "Asides" begins with a premature assertion that the critical moment for the realization of pure poetry has now arrived:

> The prologues are over. It is a question, now,
> Of final belief. So, say that final belief
> Must be in a fiction. It is time to choose. (*CP*, 250)

The climactic period of Stevens' visionary drive, 1947–1948, is still seven years away. This preliminary announcement may help to orient Stevens to the course his poetry is to take, but "Asides on the Oboe" does not, in the main body of the poem, align itself philosophically with pure poetry. The poet-hero of "Asides," unlike the virile youth of "Mrs. Alfred Uruguay," does not flee from the real; he operates within the imagery of the sublime, but he also reflects the real world and humanity around him. His frankly paradoxical mode of existence—"The impossible possible philosophers' man"—links him with the mode of thought embodied in the mythological figures of *Transport* and *Auroras,* but he also participates in the poetry of normal life, and as philosopher he seeks no higher than a comprehensive pluralistic empiricism. The diamonds that have already appeared as a crown of consciousness in "Owl's Clover" and "Country Words"—"the diamond pivot bright"—appear here as the multitudinous crystallizations of consciousness. The philosophers' man is "the man of glass, / Who in a million diamonds sums us up," and in his poems "we find peace." The kind of peace Stevens has in mind here is apparently a resolution of grief for the men who have fallen:

> One year, death and war prevented the jasmine scent
> And the jasmine islands were bloody martyrdoms.
> . . . .

> It was not as if the jasmine ever returned.
> But we and the diamond globe at last were one.
> We had always been partly one. It was as we came
> To see him, that we were wholly one, as we heard
> Him chanting for those buried in their blood,
> In the jasmine haunted forests, that we knew
> The glass man, without external reference.

Unity ("wholly one") and comprehensive inclusiveness ("without external reference") are attributes of pure poetry. In "Asides," Stevens borrows these attributes in order to invest the pathos of martial heroism with the quality of an absolute. In other words, "Asides" raises normal poetry, temporarily, to the level of a "final belief."

In "Extracts from Addresses to the Academy of Fine Ideas" (1940), Stevens reviews his position as it has developed through the proliferation of fine ideas in his recent poems. "Extracts," like "Comedian," includes the full range of doctrinal alternatives available to Stevens at the time of its composition. The speaker in "Extracts" does not, like the narrator of "Comedian," detach himself from a fateful sequence of doctrinal decisions. He does place an ironic distance between himself and the extreme range of his antidoctrinal doctrines, but by doing so he enables himself to isolate the main points of doctrinal conflict in his poetic vision and to prophesy a resolution of them. In "Extracts," Stevens says yes not only to life and the imagination but also to the concept of spiritual and intellectual unity, and he continues to develop the phrases, ideas, and images that are the materials of his supreme fiction.

Canto one of "Extracts" reaffirms the extreme antidoctrinalism represented by "The Latest Freed Man"; that is, the poem begins at the beginning of the dialectical progression that constitutes the thematic structure of *Parts of a World*. The world has become encrusted with descriptions of the world and cannot be perceived through the literary transformations of it:

> It is an artificial world. The rose
> Of paper is of the nature of its world.
> The sea is so many written words; the sky
> Is blue, clear, cloudy, high, dark, wide and round;
> The mountains inscribe themselves upon the walls.
> And, otherwise, the rainy rose belongs
> To naked men, to women naked as rain. (*CP*, 252)

The "rainy rose" or "blood-rose living in its smell" has already been contrasted to the "false roses" of paper that symbolize lifeless imitation. To be "naked" is to be "Naked of hindrance" (*CP*, 279), that is, to have unmediated contact with the natural world. Stevens asks not only that he be freed from the constraints of words used by others but also that he be totally absorbed in a reality altogether alien to the mind. This wish reaches back beyond "The Latest Freed Man" to "Comedian." Crispin too sets out from an old world that is overgrown with trope, and he seeks a poetic in which mind is completely encompassed in landscape. "The natives of the rain are rainy men. . . . And in their music showering sounds intone" (*CP*, 37). In canto one of "Extracts," Stevens presses the opposition between mind and the external world to its extreme limit:

> And in what covert may we, naked, be
> Beyond the knowlege of nakedness, as part
> Of reality, beyond the knowledge of what
> Is real, part of a land beyond the mind?

In this interrogatory vision of an Edenic innocence, Stevens once again reduces the concept of "reality" to a quality that inheres in external objects alone. The result is that the mind is relegated to a negative existence as the opposite of reality. It is the "unreal."

In the first three stanzas of "Extracts," Stevens plays out the anti-intellective impulses of the latest freed man. At the beginning of stanza four (the last of canto one) and in canto two, he executes one of those dialectical shifts at which he has become so expert in poems such as "Connoisseur of Chaos" and "Landscape with Boat." He suddenly rejects the rain, with all its doctrinal associations, and he repudiates the epistemology of "On the Road Home." In this reversal, Stevens places the spirit beyond the tyranny of a world that "must be measured by eye" (*CP*, 204). The sun is "A shapener of shapes for only the eye," and "The spirit laughs to see the eye believe / And its communion take." The spirit does not, as in "Waving Adieu," come from the sun, which is only the medium of sensory perception. The immediacy of sensory perception creates a deceptive appearance of wholeness, and the spirit sees through this illusion. The degree of Stevens' spiritual progress from 1930 to 1940 can be measured by comparing the difference between the spirit's response to sensory illusion in "Anatomy of Monotony" and in "Extracts." In the earlier poem the spirit "is aggrieved" at its own helplessness. In "Extracts" the spirit's ironic laughter gives evidence of a detached confidence that implies the prospect of its own fulfillment.

The remainder of canto two drops down from the level of pure metaphysical meditation and attempts to incorporate, or at least juxtapose, this meditation with a meditation on the nature of evil. In the letter of 1940 in which Stevens declares that "the extreme poet will produce a poem equivalent to the idea of God," he broadens the concept of a supreme fiction so as to comprehend moral experience. "The extreme poet will be as concerned with a knowledge of man as people are now concerned with a knowledge of God. The knowledge of man is the knowledge of good and evil; the extreme poet has knowledge of good and evil" (*LWS,* 369–70). Stevens' first major efforts in this direction appear in "Owl's Clover," where the level of engagement with specific social issues is too high to admit of an adequate poetic sublimation of the materials. The problem of evil will form the subject of one of the longer poems in *Transport,* "Esthétique du Mal," and will continue to occupy Stevens to the end of his life. In "Asides on the Oboe" and "Extracts," both written at the beginning of World War II (and in "Examination of the Hero," written in 1942), Stevens limits and focuses the ideas of good and evil by associating them exclusively with the war. In "Asides," Stevens speaks of the year of "death and war" as the time in which "If we found the central evil" we also found "the central good" (*CP,* 251). In "Extracts," Stevens says that "The good is evil's last invention," and he bids the men that have fallen to "Be tranquil in your wounds. It is [a] good death / That puts an end to evil death and dies." (In a correction of proofs for "Extracts," Stevens writes "a good death" [*LWS,* 387].) By dividing death into good and evil types, Stevens masks the more threatening aspect of death as itself the ultimate evil. When he returns to the problem of evil in the last canto of "Extracts," he will take the dissolution of death as also a dissolution of evil, thus leaving both good and evil as only human categories that become irrelevant in death.

In canto three, Stevens defines the nature of the fulfillment he has ironically suggested through the spirit's mocking laughter in canto two. By identifying the principle of intellectual unity as the aim of his poetic effort, by suggesting the embodiment of this objective in two mythological figures, and by identifying the main hindrances to the achievement of this objective, Stevens consciously begins laying foundations for the construction of a supreme fiction. The reformulation of his doctrinal position puts the earlier poems of *Parts* in a new perspective. Stevens sets out from the equivocally dialectical stance of "Connoisseur of Chaos"; he rejects the old Christian doctrine and its attendant priests, and, following Whitman, he asserts the divinity of all things in the profane world. In the 1855 preface to *Leaves of Grass,* Whitman proclaims that "there will soon be no more priests. Their work is done.... A new order shall arise and they shall be the priests of man, and every man shall be his own priest." In a similar vein of new-world assertiveness, Stevens declares, "The lean cats of the arches of the churches, / That's the old world. In the new, all men are priests."[11] In contrast to the doctrine of "The Latest Freed Man," Stevens now concedes that the land and time in which men live are something "To be described." The holy text of the new priests is the principle of essential unity:

> If they could gather their theses into one,
> Collect their thoughts together into one,
> Into a single thought, thus: into a queen,
> An intercessor by innate rapport,
> Or into a dark-blue king, *un roi tonnere,*
> Whose merely being was his valiance,
> Panjandrum and central heart and mind of minds—
> If they could!

While the idea of essential unity has many antecedents, it seems probable that Stevens' formulation in this passage was inspired most directly by Emerson and Whitman. In "Nature," Emerson remarks that the spirit prefers the human form to all others. "In fact, the eye,—the mind,—is always accompanied by these forms, male and female; and these are incomparably the richest informations of the power and order that lie at the heart of things" (*RWE,* I, 45). Stevens' figurations of the ancient mother as "The abstract, the archaic queen" and of the father as "yet the king and yet the crown" (*CP,* 223, 415) imply an emphatic affirmation of Emerson's proposition. It may also be through Emerson's influence that Whitman draws away from pantheistic expansiveness in order to celebrate the power and order that lie at the heart of things. In "Song of the Universal," Whitman provides both the thematic pattern and one of the central phrases for Stevens' passage:

11. Walt Whitman, *Leaves of Grass,* ed. Harold W. Blodgett and Sculley Bradley (New York, 1965), 727. Harold Bloom notes that "section III begins with a variation upon the most central of all Emersonian-Whitmanian figurations, the American poet-prophet as a preacher of what is to be" (*The Poems of Our Climate,* 151).

> In this broad earth of ours,
> Amid the measureless grossness and the slag,
> Enclosed and safe within its central heart
> Nestles the seed perfection.

In Whitman the tension between an all-embracing and all-leveling vitalism and the hierarchical principle implicit in the idea of perfection remains latent or at least static. Stevens, in contrast, gives conscious elaboration to the dialectical relation between the need for "breadth" and the need for a perfected order. He surpasses Whitman in dialectical complexity, but when he includes the knowledge of good and evil within this perfected order, he follows Whitman's tendency toward a mystical theodicy. In "Song of the Universal," Whitman declares that for the soul

> the real to the ideal tends.
> For it the mystic evolution,
> Not the right only justified, what we call evil also justified.

The conclusion to Stevens' suppositional phrase "If they could" hangs in suspense. In the preceding passages, he has touched upon and moved beyond "The Latest Freed Man," "On the Road Home," and "Connoisseur of Chaos." This brings him to the point he has reached in "Landscape with Boat." What was problematic in "Landscape," the diffusion of significance in undifferentiated multitudinousness, now comes to the fore:

> If they could! Or is it the multitude of thoughts,
> Like insects in the depths of the mind, that kill
> The single thought? The multitudes of men
> That kill the single man . . . ?

Stevens will return to the first question in canto five. In both cantos four and five, by describing the meditative action of the solitary man, he implicitly answers yes to the second question.

Canto four stands out in "Extracts" as the one passage of blank-verse narrative in a sequence of "addresses" or doctrinal disquisitions. The first eight lines appear to be purely descriptive, but the eighth line keys in to "The Snow Man," and this allusion provides an occasion for meditating on those occasional moments of sudden revitalization and illumination recorded in poems such as "Martial Cadenza" (1940). The narrative in canto four sets place and time and distances the protagonist from the narrator only by the masculine personal pronoun, what we might call the first-person "he":

> On an early Sunday in April, a feeble day,
> He felt curious about the winter hills
> And wondered about the water in the lake.
> . . . .
> . . . The wind blew in the empty place.

The scene is real, and the allusion is a memory of the wind that in "The Snow Man" "is blowing in the same bare place." In the lines that follow this narrative passage, Stevens elaborates the allusion to "The Snow Man"—snow man becomes "No man" who listens to the wind—and associates it with an allusion to "The Man on the Dump" (1938):

> The winter wind blew in an empty place—
> There was that difference between the and an,
> The difference between himself and no man,
> No man that heard a wind in an empty place.
> It was time to be himself again, to see
> If the place, in spite of its witheredness, was still
> Within the difference.

No man is the nemesis; he is identified by the indefinite article, the grammatical signal for the general, abstract, and hypothetical. The definite article is the particular, both the identity of the particular man and the highly differentiated world of particular objects in which he lives. The protagonist's probing of the difference between the definite and the indefinite article draws on the conclusion of "The Man on the Dump." In the last line, Stevens suggests that the motive force for his exalted, sardonic rhapsody is a search for "the truth," here identified as "The the" (*CP,* 203). Sitting on the dump, locus of discarded images, Stevens "feels the purifying change," and he sounds the note of "belief" that has been echoing in his poetry since "Blue Guitar." "One sits and beats an old tin can, lard pail. / One beats and beats for that which one believes" (*CP,* 202). In canto four of "Extracts," Stevens' search for the truth explicitly declares itself as a breaking of abstraction. The hypothetical revitalization—"would be"—immediately follows in a metaphoric equation with spring:

> If,
> When he looked, the water ran up the air or grew white
> Against the edge of the ice, the abstraction would
> Be broken and winter would be broken and done,
> And being would be being himself again,
> Being become seeing and feeling and self,
> Black water breaking into reality.

"Black water" is an appositive of "abstraction" (= "an") and stands in opposition to "being," which is identified through predicate nominatives as the acute consciousness of self as a center of experience.

The chanting cadence of the conclusion to canto four echoes the rhythm of the more ethereal chant at the end of "Martial Cadenza" (1940). It is one of Stevens' more personal poems, and he uses the first-person pronoun to narrate the incident of the poem, another special moment of revitalization:

> Only this evening I saw again low in the sky
> The evening star, at the beginning of winter, the star
> That in spring will crown every western horizon,
> Again . . . as if it came back, as if life came back. (*CP,* 237)

Already *life* seems a richer word than does *being,* and in the final stanza, as in the major visionary poems, life becomes detached from the personal self and extends into the forms of phenomenal reality:

> The present close, the present realized,
> Not the symbol but that for which the symbol stands,
> The vivid thing in the air that never changes,
> Though the air change. Only this evening I saw it again,
> At the beginning of winter, and I walked and talked
> Again, and lived and was again, and breathed again
> And moved again and flashed again, time flashed again.

"I" becomes "time," itself a synecdochic figure for "The vivid thing in the air," a presence that is clearly antithetical to the "glittering vacancy" of "Evening Without Angels." The evening star thus comes to serve as an emblem for a "life" that includes and transcends the individual consciousness. Like the "crystal-pointed star of morning" in "Chocorua to Its Neighbor" (1943), it is "A fusion of night, its blue of the pole of blue / And of the brooding mind" (*CP,* 296, 297).

The moment of illumination in canto four of "Extracts" is more emphatically concerned with the assertion of the individual self than are the similar moments in "Martial Cadenza" and "Chocorua." Stevens' meditation, though it might seem a detached episode, is actually a response to the question posed in canto three: Is it "The multitudes of men / That kill the single man"? (*CP,* 254). In canto five, Stevens directly confronts the multitudes of men and engages in philosophic warfare:

> Chaos is not
> The mass of meaning. It is three or four
> Ideas or, say, five men or, possibly, six.
>
> In the end, these philosophic assassins pull
> Revolvers and shoot each other. One remains.

(This struggle to emerge from the chaos of conflicting personalities and ideologies replays in semicomic fashion the more brutally direct depiction of the struggle in a poem of 1939, "Thunder by the Musician.") The successful assassin composes a song that is "the music of the mass of meaning," meaning that has consolidated itself within one "pure idea":

> And yet it is a singular romance,
> This warmth in the blood-world for the pure idea,
>
> This inability to find a sound,
> That clings to the mind like that right sound, that song
>
> Of the assassin that remains and sings
> In the high imagination, triumphantly.

This "singular romance" is the "new romanticism," a mode of the sublime "Far, far beyond the putative canzones / Of love and summer" (*CP,* 256).

In isolating sound, Stevens is developing a motif that will be one of the main symbolic elements of the pure idea. Stevens' first published hint in prose about the supreme fiction attaches special importance to sound as the medium through which "perfection" is to be realized. In "The Noble Rider" (1941), he declares that "the deepening need for words to express our thoughts and feelings which, we are sure, are all the truth we shall ever experience, having no illusions, makes us listen to words when we hear them, loving them and feeling them, makes us search the sound of them, for a finality, a perfection, an unalterable vibration" (*NA,* 32). Stevens associates this unalterable vibration with "that nobility which is our spiritual height and depth" (*NA*, 33–34), a spatial metaphor that recalls "the high imagination" of canto five. In "Of Modern Poetry" (1940), he combines the aural and spatial elements in an evocation of

> Sounds passing through sudden rightnesses, wholly
> Containing the mind, below which it cannot descend,
> Beyond which it has no will to rise. (*CP*, 240)

Stevens returns to "The vital music" in the finale of "Extracts," and in "Montrachet" he identifies the absolute as "an inaccessible, pure sound" (*CP*, 263).

The references to "the pure idea" and the "pure sound" in "Extracts" and "Montrachet" are not realizations but projections of fulfillment. What yet stands in the way of fulfillment is the one primary dichotomy, that between the mind and the external world. In canto six, Stevens first affirms the basic assumption of his supreme fiction, then replays in synoptic form the recurrent drift away from this assumption:

> That other one wanted to think his way to life,
> Sure that the ultimate poem was the mind,
> Or of the mind, or of the mind in these
> Elysia, these days, half earth, half mind;
> Half sun, half thinking of the sun; half sky,
> Half desire for indifference about the sky.

Once this drift has been depicted, the problem can be isolated and clearly stated. Intellectual satisfaction depends on a unified cosmology in which mind and sky are but aspects or points of relation within essential imagination:

> And, being unhappy, talk of happiness
> And, talking of happiness, know that it means
> That the mind is the end and must be satisfied.
>
> It cannot be half earth, half mind; half sun,
> Half thinking; until the mind has been satisfied,
> Until, for him, his mind is satisfied.

The mind can be satisfied only by spiritual unity, and the way to this unity is through the "mind of minds" that is the embodiment of the unifying thesis Stevens propounds in canto three. The mind of minds would contain both the sky and the individual mind. The doctrinal problem seems simple enough, but the poetic resolution remains remote:

> Time troubles to produce the redeeming thought.
> Sometimes at sleepy mid-days it succeeds,
> Too vaguely that it be written in character.

After reassuring himself that the redeeming thought is slowly engendering itself in sleep, Stevens again drifts away from the pure idea. In canto seven he depicts both the moment of "turning away" from this idea and the consolatory meditation that immediately follows this turning away:

> To have satisfied the mind and turn to see,
> (That being as much belief as we may have,)
> And turn to look and say there is no more
> Than this, in this alone I may believe.

As in "Waving Adieu," Stevens solaces himself for the sudden lapse of visionary intensity by assuring himself that simple perception of the weather is the highest form of "belief":

> The casual reunions, the long-pondered
> Surrenders, the repeated sayings that
> There is nothing more and that it is enough
> To believe in the weather and in the things and men
> Of the weather and in one's self.

In order to invest simple sensual experience with the quality of an absolute, Stevens juxtaposes it with nothingness. The vehicle for this metaphysical affect is a trip to the moon. The atmosphere of the moon is pure alienation or difference. "One would be drowned in the air of difference, / Incapable of belief, in the difference." After such total anesthetization, the slightest breath of sensory reality would be "the deepest inhalation" and "Would come from that return to the subtle centre." This center, like that of "The Latest Freed Man," is spontaneous sensory vitality, before language.

In canto seven, by returning to his point of departure, Stevens begins the movement toward a formal closure in the dialectical structure of the poem. In canto eight he completes this movement. He first reaffirms that the redeeming thought lies latent beneath the divided, daytime consciousness, and then seeks to include within this sense of metaphysical peace the problem of death and evil broached in canto two:

> We live in a camp . . . Stanzas of final peace
> Lie in the heart's residuum . . . Amen.

> . . . .   If earth dissolves
> Its evil after death, it dissolves it while
> We live. Thence come the final chants, the chants
> Of the brooder seeking the acutest end
> Of speech: to pierce the heart's residuum
> And there to find music for a single line,
> Equal to memory, one line in which
> The vital music formulates the words.

Good and evil are merely human concerns, and the vital music must transcend the merely human. The heart's residuum is that substratum of poetic passion that merges into the "central heart and mind of minds." Death is the mother of beauty, and the music that is "Equal to memory" would contain the dead within the archetypal, transcendental memory of "The earthly mother" (*CP* 432).

Stevens will drop back often from the affirmations of "Extracts." When the fear of losing himself in a world of abstraction comes over him, he re-creates the abrupt juxtaposition of life and "difference" in canto seven of "Extracts." One such moment appears in "The Well Dressed Man with a Beard" (1941). In this poem the clash of yes and no reduces itself to a simple opposition between the oblivion of the night and the physical world of the sun. Within the sun, reality is composed only of the parts of the world, and to emphasize that particularity, Stevens hypothetically strips himself of all the parts except one, "No greater than a cricket's horn" (*CP,* 247). The brief rhapsody that follows this hypothetical reduction draws on the diction and imagery of the sublime—"The aureole above the humming house"—but no firm concept emerges, and the poem remains a fragment composed of elements that are not fully integrated. The failure to achieve integration manifests itself in the final line as a polemical declaration: "It can never be satisfied, the mind, never." This declaration is true in the sense that no poetic absolute ever attains for Stevens the rigid stability of dogma, and no satisfaction ever brings a lasting peace. The supreme fiction does nonetheless come to a point, a pinnacle of vision from which Stevens can perceive a resolution of diversity in a unity of phenomenal process emanating from "The essential poem at the centre of things." In *Parts of a World,* Stevens is still concentrating on the purely human character of the supreme fiction, and he still balks before the idea of a god that may be too close a reflection of the traditional Christian deity. In "Les Plus Belles Pages" (1941), he remarks that Aquinas "spoke, / Kept speaking of God. I changed the word to man" (*CP,* 245). Stevens himself has kept speaking of God, and he will continue to do so, but even if we were to overlook his frequent use of this word, we would still have to recognize that he is preoccupied with the possible poetic realization of an "essential imagination" that is the equivalent of a divine mind. In "Extracts" and "Montrachet," he begins to see his way more clearly toward this realization.

In "Montrachet," Stevens employs the three-line stanza he will use in "Notes," "Owl," "Auroras," "New Haven," and "The Rock," but unlike these poems, "Montrachet" is not divided into cantos or strophes. It attempts, with some success, to support its length by riding the swell of surrealistic verve with which it begins, but the middle of the poem sags a bit into the dogged rhetoric that weighs down much of "Owl's Clover." There is also a hint of the laborious, abstract meticulousness that will limit the effectiveness of some of the later poems—the most egregious example is "The Bouquet" (1948). Still, the poem begins and ends strongly, and it has something important to say. The first eight stanzas pose a question and intimate the kinds of responses appropriate to the alternative answers. The response to the first of the two possible answers is a poetic saturnalia presided over by the precise, menacing measurements of the clock:

> What more is there to love than I have loved?
> And if there be nothing more, O bright, O bright,
> The chick, the chidder-barn and grassy chives
>
> And great moon, cricket-impresario,
> And, hoy, the impopulous purple-plated past,
> Hoy, hoy, the blue bulls kneeling down to rest.
>
> Chome! clicks the clock, if there be nothing more. (*CP,* 260)

The question Stevens poses constitutes a late reprise of the issue that animates "Monocle," that is, the question whether there is to be any fresh source of poetic inspiration. Stevens is a long way beyond the sexual anxieties of "Monocle," but he is by no means beyond the need for some commanding inspiration of the Romantic sublime. Stevens' liturgical response to the images that will embody this sublime, though it is colored by the jocundity of his verve, expresses a sincere and profound reverence:

> But if, but if there be something more to love,
> Something in now a senseless syllable,

> A shadow in the mind, a flourisher,
>
> . . . .
>
> But if there be something more to love, amen,
> Amen to the feelings about familiar things,
> The blessed regal dropped in daggers' dew,
>
> Amen to thought, our singular skeleton,
> Salt-flicker, amen to our accustomed cell,
> The moonlight in the cell, words on the wall.

Toward the end of the poem, the "shadow in the mind" becomes "the auroral creature musing in the mind." The shadow prefigures the mother of the living and the dead in "Owl" and the innocent mother in "Auroras." In "Owl" her "senseless syllable" is a speech of pure experience to those who are passing from life into death. In "Montrachet" this syllable, like the pure idea of "Extracts," is spoken "Too vaguely that it be written in character." Nonetheless, because Stevens says "Amen to thought," the redeeming thought of "Extracts" becomes more accessible:

> To-night, night's undeciphered murmuring
> Comes close to the prisoner's ear, becomes a throat
> The hand can touch, neither green bronze nor marble,
>
> The hero's throat in which the words are spoken,
> From which the chant comes close upon the ear,
> Out of the hero's being, the deliverer
>
> Delivering the prisoner by his words,
> So that the skeleton in the moonlight sings,
> Sings of an heroic world beyond the cell,
>
> No, not believing, but to make the cell
> A hero's world in which he is the hero.
> Man must become the hero of his world.

"Montrachet" celebrates a specific moment ("To-night") of heightened awareness, and it implicitly contrasts the experience of this moment with that in the second strophe of "Blue Guitar," where Stevens complains,

> I cannot bring a world quite round.
>
> . . . .
>
> I sing a hero's head, large eye
> And bearded bronze, but not a man. (*CP,* 165)

The elevation of man to "hero" in "Montrachet" depends on his susceptibility to something more than man, to a "night" that has the power of speech. The poet is both the man held prisoner within the boundaries of the common world and also the hero who chants words of liberation. The hero is human, but he is also the voice of the night, and there is a "rhetoric" that is part of the night, not contained within the human, but accessible through the skeleton of thought. The skeleton sings, "echoing rhetorics more than our own."

The murmuring of night, though still "undeciphered," encourages Stevens to prophecy. The first prophecy will be fulfilled in canto eight of "Auroras." Stevens promises that "in the hero-land to which we go" "The poison in the blood will have been purged." The poison of the cosmic serpent in the first canto of "Auroras" is that we should "disbelieve" that the serpent is "Relentlessly in possession of happiness" (CP, 411). The moment of innocence and belief in canto eight dissolves this poison. Stevens' second prophecy follows a retrospective judgment on the spiritual dissatisfactions of his earlier poetry:

> A little while of Terra Paradise
> I dreamed, of autumn rivers, silvas green,
> Of sanctimonious mountains high in snow,
>
> But in that dream a heavy difference
> Kept waking and a mournful sense sought out,
> In vain, life's season or death's element.
>
> Bastard chateaux and smoky demoiselles,
> No more. I can build towers of my own.

The "heavy difference" may be identified with the spiritual grief in "Anatomy of Monotony." Life's season and death's element are the two modes of "Sunday Morning," idyllic serenity and elegiac sublimity. Stevens now recognizes that if he is ever to realize the full potential of either mode, the Terra Paradise of "Sunday Morning" must give place to a mystical centrality, here figured in pure sound, the wind, and breath:

> Item: The cocks crow and the birds cry and
> The sun expands, like a repetition on
> One string, an absolute, not varying
>
> Toward an inaccessible, pure sound.
> Item: The wind is never rounding O
> And, imageless, it is itself the most,

> Mouthing its constant smatter throughout space.
> Item: The green fish pensive in green reeds
> Is an absolute. Item: The cataracts
>
> As facts fall like rejuvenating rain,
> Fall down through nakedness to nakedness,
> To the auroral creature musing in the mind.
>
> Item: Breathe, breathe upon the centre of
> The breath life's latest, thousand senses.
> But let this one sense be the single main.

Although the sun is itself an "absolute," it can never encompass the "pure sound" that is to be the poet's single main sense. The imperative following the last "Item" assumes the possibility of a fusion between the pluralistic and monistic modes, and this synthetic absolute may give access to the pure sound. The final stanza dramatically illustrates the necessity for constant, renewed meditation:

> And yet what good were yesterday's devotions?
> I affirm and then at midnight the great cat
> Leaps quickly from the fireside and is gone.

The affirmations of belief hold their sole strength in the momentary realizations of poetry.

The "final belief" Stevens projects in "Asides on the Oboe" will be a fiction that figures forth the pure idea as origin and end of reality. It will be, as Stevens calls it in "Contrary Theses (II)" (1942), "An abstract," but one that is different from the ice-locked thought in canto four of "Extracts":

> He wanted and looked for a final refuge,
> From the bombastic intimations of winter
> And the martyrs à la mode. He walked toward
>
> An abstract, of which the sun, the dog, the boy
> Were contours. Cold was chilling the wide-moving swans.
> The leaves were falling like notes from a piano.
>
> The abstract was suddenly there and gone again.
> The negroes were playing football in the park.
> The abstract that he saw, like the locust-leaves, plainly:
>
> The premiss from which all things were conclusions,
> The noble, Alexandrine verve. (*CP,* 270)

The abstract appears suddenly and, like the great cat of "Montrachet," is gone as suddenly. These brief moments of actual illumination are like the flickering of a guiding star that serves to orient Stevens' further poetic development. They give him all the assurance he needs that there is "something more to love" and that the particulars of the world—"the sun, the dog, the boy"—may be contained within the wider sky of the spirit.

The abstract of "Contrary Theses (II)" is the imagination itself, not the individual imagination but the mind of minds. To give poetic substance to this mind, Stevens must embody it in an image, and the image that this idea most frequently assumes is that of the ancient mother. When, in "Extracts," Stevens supposes that he might collect his thoughts into a single image, "into a queen," he is drawing both on a series of his own references to a mythic feminine figure and on the Romantic tradition. In *Harmonium* and *Ideas of Order,* the numinous female figure appears most often as a voluptuous personification of the natural world. In "In the Carolinas" (1917), Stevens figures the earth itself as a "Timeless mother" (*CP,* 5), a trope he will repeat, with important variations, in "Anatomy of Monotony," "World Without Peculiarity" (1948), and "Madame La Fleurie" (1951). In "O Florida, Venereal Soil" (1922) and the second landscape in "Six Significant Landscapes" (1916), he represents the night as an obscure, mysterious woman. Conversely, in "Homunculus et la Belle Etoile" (1919), "Hymn from a Watermelon Pavilion" (1922), "Ghosts as Cocoons" (1936), and "Meditation Celestial and Terrestrial" (1935), the woman embodies summer and the tints of day.

> But what are radiant reason and radiant will
> To warblings early in the hilarious trees
> Of summer, the drunken mother? (*CP,* 124)

These incarnations of the feminine principle, though they are ultimately subsumed by "the auroral creature musing in the mind," lead most directly to the "Fat girl, terrestrial, my summer, my night" of "Notes Toward a Supreme Fiction" (*CP,* 406). They are representations of sensual delight and as such align themselves under the aegis of normal poetry.

The feminine figures who preside over Stevens' pure poetry are of a different character. In "Monocle," Stevens identifies the generic province of his muse even as he appears to be mocking her for having failed to sustain the ideal status with which he has invested her: "'Mother of heaven, regina of the clouds, / O sceptre of the sun, crown of the moon.'" This failure appears to be closely linked with the deterioration of romance in Stevens' marriage. In a series of poems salvaged in *Opus Posthumous*—"Red Loves Kit" (1924), "Good Man, Bad Woman" (1932), and "The Woman Who Blamed Life on a Spaniard" (1932)—and in "Gallant Chateau" (1934), Stevens meditates on this deterioration and detaches his creative spirit from it. As a substitute for the "'Mother of heaven'" in "Monocle," a "damsel heightened by eternal bloom" will be a bearer of divine tidings. Throughout *Harmonium* and *Ideas of Order,* this damsel remains only a faint hypothesis. In his first major depiction of the feminine muse, "To the One of Fictive Music," Stevens attempts to incorporate the celestial damsel with her lustier counterpart, but the result is an image not so much synthetic and "abstract" as merely composite. She partakes of both the "diviner love" and "the arrant spices of the sun" (*CP*, 87, 88), and she emerges, though gorgeously clad in Stevens' rhetoric, with no distinct character at all. In "Owl's Clover," Stevens reverts to the damsel, in the plural, through the "celestial paramours" who give quasi-mythic shape to his reformulation of pure poetry.

The development from these early figurations of the muse to the more potent figurations in the later poetry depends heavily on the assimilation of images from the Romantic tradition. "The Owl in the Sarcophagus" is directly informed by Tennyson's rendering of the myth of Demeter and Persephone, and Stevens refers to the myth again in "Things of August" (*CP,* 491). When Stevens designates life itself as "one's ancient mother" (*NA,* 28), he seems to be recalling a passage from "The Fall of Hyperion." The fragmentary vision avouched to Keats through Moneta begins with an image of the deposed Saturn sleeping on a shore:

> His old right hand lay nerveless, listless, dead,
> Unsceptred; and his realmless eyes were clos'd,
> While his bow'd head seem'd listening to the Earth,
> His antient mother, for some comfort yet. (ll. 323–26)

The earth as mother draws its pathos from the human mother. In "World Without Peculiarity" (1949), Stevens, like Saturn, turns to his ancient mother for some comfort yet, and he explicitly transposes his feeling for his human mother to "the earth itself" (*CP*, 454). His understanding of this transposition probably owes as much to Wordsworth as to anyone else. In book two of *The Prelude,* Wordsworth traces the poet's visionary power to infancy, a time when the child "with his soul / Drinks in the feelings of his Mother's eye" (ll. 236–37). Wordsworth describes the way in which the child's affection for the mother extends itself through the faculties of sense to the objects of perception. The maternal bond becomes a "filial bond / Of nature that connects him with the world" (ll. 243–44). By means of this connection, the poet nurtures his capacity for the "observation of affinities" (l. 364), or, in Stevens' terms, the recognition of "the resemblance between things" (*NA*, 71). (J. V. Cunningham notes that Stevens' "doctrine of metaphor and resemblances . . . is precisely Wordsworth's doctrine of affinities.")[12] Stevens argues that resemblance is the basis of metaphor, and that metaphor is the basis of poetry. "A poetic metaphor—that is to say, a metaphor poetic in a sense more specific than the sense in which poetry and metaphor are one—appears to be poetry at its source" (*NA*, 81). The filial instinct sublimates itself into a desire for figurative synthesis, and the central figure in this synthesis, for Stevens, is the mother herself.

In depicting the queen of "Extracts" and the auroral creature of "Montrachet," Stevens draws most directly on three poems of 1939: "The Candle a Saint," "Bouquet of Belle Sçavoir," and "The Woman That Had More Babies Than That." In "The Candle a Saint," the feminine figure appears first as a personification of the night. "Green is the night, green kindled and apparelled. / It is she that walks among astronomers" (*CP*, 223). The night is the locus of spiritual mystery, and in "The Candle," Stevens gives form and definition to this mystery by embodying it in a mythic figure and depicting it as the archetype of poetry:

> The noble figure, the essential shadow,
> Moving and being, the image at its source,
> The abstract, the archaic queen. Green is the night.

In these few lines, Stevens captures the nature of essential imagination. "Moving" and "being" are adjectives and nouns. As adjectives they testify to the mythic vitality of the "shadow in the mind," and as nouns they identify this shadow as the source of all vitality. The "image at its source" is transcendent, abstract, and imageless. At the same time, this transcendent source of images is itself an image, drawn from the archaic or archetypal images of the

---

12. Cunningham, "Tradition and Modernity," in *The Collected Essays of J. V. Cunningham*, 242. See also Robert Pack, "Wallace Stevens' Sufficient Muse," *Southern Review*, n.s., XI (1975), 769–70.

sublime.[13] In "Phosphor Reading by His Own Light" (1942), Stevens specifies the archetypal character of the shadow as "That elemental parent, the green night, / Teaching a fusky alphabet" (*CP,* 267). From these beginnings Stevens will evolve a visionary mythology that represents "The pure perfections of parental space" (*CP,* 436).[14]

Just as the "abstract" is "The premiss from which all things were conclusions," the elemental parent is the transcendent source of images, both the images of the phenomenal world (sense perceptions) and the images of poetry. Stevens' longing to possess this image is a longing of the "philosophers' man" and of the humanly natural man. It is a need for an ultimate intellectual order and for a sense of perfect union with the parental space of the natural world. In "Bouquet of Belle Sçavoir," Stevens selects one of the particulars of the world as the nearest approach to the creative feminine principle:

> It is she alone that matters.
> She made it. It is easy to say
> The figures of speech, as why she chose
> This dark, particular rose.
> II
> Everything in it is herself.
> Yet the freshness of the leaves, the burn
> Of the colors, are tinsel changes,
> Out of the changes of both light and dew. (*CP,* 231)

The "Yet" in stanza two expresses sudden dissatisfaction. To know the shadow only through its effects is no more satisfying than to know the premiss only by inference from the conclusions. This quiet intrusion of dissatisfaction stimulates a memory of many such abrupt accessions of spiritual need:

---

13. For an interpretation of Stevens' feminine figures that emphasizes their archetypal character but deprecates their transcendental aspect, see Doggett, *Stevens' Poetry of Thought,* 47–48. On the rationale for a personification of the transcendental ideal, see Kant, *Critique of Pure Reason,* 342n. For an interpretation of Stevens' feminine figures in Heideggerian terms, see Hines, *Phenomenological Parallels,* 128–34.

14. For a contrasting view of the meaning and development of Stevens' maternal figures, see R. D. Ackerman, "Death and Fiction: Stevens' Mother of Beauty," *English Literary History,* L (1983), 407.

> How often had he walked
> Beneath summer and the sky
> To receive her shadow into his mind . . .
> Miserable that it was not she.
>
> IV
> The sky is too blue, the earth too wide.
> The thought of her takes her away.
> The form of her in something else
> Is not enough.

The first two lines of stanza four give two reasons why the pure idea remains inaccessible except for those brief glimpses avouched in poems such as "Extracts" and "Contrary Theses (II)." The world as physical absolute overwhelms the mind, and the very efforts to formulate the pure idea inescapably limit and thus negate it. As Stevens says in discussing "that nobility which is our spiritual height and depth," "Nothing could be more evasive and inaccessible. Nothing distorts itself and seeks disguise more quickly. . . . If it is defined, it will be fixed and it must not be fixed" (*NA*, 33–34). In stanza five of "Bouquet of Belle Sçavoir," Stevens' frustration reaches its peak; in stanza six, there is a partial resolution:

> The reflection of her here, and then there,
> Is another shadow, another evasion,
> Another denial. If she is everywhere,
> She is nowhere, to him.
>
> VI
> But this she has made. If it is
> Another image, it is one she has made.
> It is she that he wants, to look at directly,
> Someone before him to see and to know.

The "image" that "she has made" is no longer the rose but the poem itself, and in the poem there is an image of her. Already, here, Stevens has adopted the extreme mystical stance of *Auroras*: he presents his own poetry not as an object created by an individual craftsman but as the medium through which essential imagination or the mind of minds comes to knowledge of itself.

Stevens' yearning "to see and to know" the abstract and archaic queen will be most completely satisfied in *Auroras*. In *Parts of a World,* Stevens' visionary drive operates more in the modes of prophecy and preliminary construction than in the mode of fulfillment. In only two poems does the queen take on a sufficiently substantial form to appease his desire: "The Woman That Had More Babies Than That" and "The Hand as a Being" (1942). "More Babies" was included in the first edition of *Parts* but was dropped from *The Collected Poems*. Stevens does not give his reasons for this decision (see *LWS,* 830); the form of the poem—meditative, quasi-allegorical or symbolical blank verse that is not broken down into stanzas—is like that of both "Owl's Clover" and another poem of this period Stevens drops from *The Collected Poems,* "Life on a Battleship" (1939). Although this is also the form Stevens adopts for all but one of the cantos in "Extracts," it is one in which he is particularly inclined to be rather too ponderously deliberate. Unlike "The Candle a Saint," "Belle Sçavoir," or "The Hand as a Being," "More Babies" is not a dramatic enactment of imaginative need. The speaker takes a detached stance from which he contrasts the sea as part of "the universal machine" to the earth and sky as a "mother." The human subject of the poem is not "he"—the third-person I— but rather "The old men, the philosophers" who "are haunted by that / Maternal voice." The depiction of the sea as machine recalls the sea of "Key West" that "never formed to mind or voice":

> The waves
> Were mechanical, muscular. They never changed,
> They never stopped, a repetition repeated
> Continually. (*OP,* 81)

The woman who has had more babies than the universal machine is the muse who presides over the philosophers' quest "for a thesis, a music constant to move." The mother's children are the "old men and philosophers" who listen in the night for the voice of poetry:

> The self
> Detects the sound of a voice that doubles its own,
> In the images of desire, the forms that speak,
> The ideas that come to it with a sense of speech.
> The old men, the philosophers, are haunted by that
> Maternal voice, the explanation at night.

The maternal voice is the same voice that is the night speaking into the prisoner's ear in "Montrachet." In "More Babies," Stevens describes "night's undeciphered murmuring," and the flatly formulaic quality of his description is perhaps one of the reasons he suppressed the poem:

> She has a supernatural head.
> On her lips familiar words become the words
> Of an elevation, an elixir of the whole.

This climax fails of pathos and power. We do not feel the effect Stevens describes, and the last line of the poem foreshadows the lackluster, inflated abstraction of "The Sail of Ulysses" (1954).

In "The Hand as a Being," Stevens enacts a moment of visionary fulfillment that is dramatically convincing but that is also more limited in doctrinal scope than is "More Babies." The fulfillment depicted in "The Hand as a Being" is one of quasi-erotic feeling, a temporary composure beneath the level of completed knowledge:

> In the first canto of the final canticle,
> Too conscious of too many things at once,
> Our man beheld the naked, nameless dame.
>
> Seized her and wondered: why beneath the tree
> She held her hand before him in the air,
> For him to see, wove round her glittering hair.
>
> . . . .
>
> Of her, of her alone, at last he knew
> And lay beside her underneath the tree. (*CP*, 271)

The multitude of thoughts continue to kill the single thought, and it is just as well. As Stevens says in a letter from which I have already quoted, the first requirement of a supreme fiction is breadth (*LWS*, 435). Stevens will continue to wait and prepare until the moment of inspiration, that is, the moment at which a special need for a comprehensive synthesis will intersect with a perfected capability. He has organized his thoughts and set his course. After *Parts of a World,* the eventual realization of the supreme fiction seems almost inevitable. Stevens postpones the inevitable until it forces itself upon him as "the maturity of his desires."

CHAPTER FIVE

A Landscape of the Mind

Both in length and in tonal and tropic range, *Transport to Summer* is Stevens' most expansive volume of poetry. It is also the volume that, next to *Harmonium,* has met with the most favorable response from Stevens' critics. "Notes Toward a Supreme Fiction" (1942), which was originally published in a small, select edition as a book by itself, has often been nominated Stevens' greatest poem, and the luster it sheds on *Transport* has helped raise the volume to its favored position. Besides "Notes," *Transport* contains more relatively long poems—mythical, theoretical, meditative—than does any volume except *The Auroras of Autumn,* and though none of these poems has ever rivaled "Notes" in critical acclaim, they are generally regarded with, at the least, distant respect. "Esthétique du Mal" (1944) and "Credences of Summer" (1946), especially, have received a good deal of sympathetic critical attention. "Description Without Place" (1945), "The Pure Good of Theory" (1945), and "Chocorua to Its Neighbor" (1943) have assumed a less prominent place in the canon, but they too give evidence that Stevens' imaginative vigor has by no means begun to decline with his advancing age. If they do not recall the "deluging onwardness" of "Comedian" or the ripe lyricism of "Sunday Morning," they are more graceful than "Owl's Clover" and more continuous than "Blue Guitar." Like *Parts of a World, Transport* contains more very good poems of one and two pages than does either *Harmonium* or *Ideas of Order,* and it contains almost none of those slight exercises in "images and the music of verse" (*LWS,* 288) that reflected Stevens' early conception of pure poetry.

The style of *Transport,* as a volume, locates itself somewhere in between the inventive variousness of *Harmonium* and the formal thematic coherence of

Parts of a World. Stevens surveys the full range of his themes and motifs, and he assimilates these tropes to the sophisticated dialectical techniques he has begun to develop in *Parts*. Poems such as "Notes" and "Esthétique" traverse the metaphysical extremes of pluralistic empiricism and transcendental idealism. Other poems such as "Chocorua" and "Credences" situate themselves more decisively in the modes of either pure or normal poetry, but Stevens uses the affects and images of each mode to enrich those of the other. "Credences," Stevens' finest celebration of the poetry of normal life, borrows from his imagery of the Romantic sublime, and "Chocorua," a poem of mythic vision, insists on the organic vitality of the spiritual principle it describes. In both pure and normal poetry, Stevens achieves a new fullness and clarity of symbolic representation.

The dialectical tension that governs *Transport to Summer* may be succinctly represented by "Crude Foyer" (1947). (The fact that "Crude Foyer" was not published separately in a magazine suggests that it was written shortly before *Transport* went to press.) Unlike "Connoisseur of Chaos" and "Esthétique du Mal," "Crude Foyer" does not simply alternate in its doctrinal modes; it simultaneously upholds and repudiates both modes. Few of Stevens' critics have commented on this poem, but in the problematic complexity of its structure, the lucid simplicity of its phrasing, and the subtle, haunting power of its central image, "Crude Foyer" stands high among the best of Stevens' short poems. Its five stanzas are a single sentence; the first four words, before the colon, constitute the thesis that is to be expounded: "Thought is false happiness" (*CP,* 305). This thesis is reiterated in the fourth stanza, and the subordinate clause that follows the restatement—"since we know"— explains the thesis. The first three stanzas define in detail what is meant by "false happiness." At the same time, Stevens establishes within this false happiness an autonomous critical authority that reads and rejects the thesis propounded by the initial speaker of the poem. From one pole of his metaphysical sphere, Stevens as empiricist writes a critique of "paradise" in the "antimythological" tradition of Crispin (*LWS,* 778), and from the other pole, Stevens as idealist reads this critique and calls it the work "Of a comedian":

>Thought is false happiness: the idea
>That merely by thinking one can,
>Or may, penetrate, not may,
>But can, that one is sure to be able—

> That there lies at the end of thought
> A foyer of the spirit in a landscape
> Of the mind, in which we sit
> And wear humanity's bleak crown;
>
> In which we read the critique of paradise
> And say it is the work
> Of a comedian, this critique;
> In which we sit and breathe
>
> An innocence of an absolute,
> False happiness, since we know that we use
> Only the eye as faculty, that the mind
> Is the eye, and that this landscape of the mind
>
> Is a landscape only of the eye; and that
> We are ignorant men incapable
> Of the least, minor, vital metaphor, content,
> At last, there, when it turns out to be here.

The metamorphosis between the initial, anti-intellective thesis and the antithesis that is formulated within paradise itself takes place in the dramatically mimetic speech of the first stanza. What begins as negation modulates through the groping eagerness in the alternations of "can" and "may" until the phrase "that one is sure to be able" breaks free from the critique of paradise and speaks from within the false happiness that is being repudiated. The "landscape / Of the mind" is a landscape that has been wholly assimilated and made subordinate to the poetic imagination. By virtue of its noble simplicity, its effortless grandeur, and its restrained pathos, the second stanza could serve as an Arnoldian touchstone of "high seriousness." To breathe "An innocence of an absolute" is to come very close to the visionary realizations of "The Owl in the Sarcophagus" and "The Auroras of Autumn"; and for this absolute to be, then, "an absolute, / False happiness" reinstates with abrupt incisiveness the ironic ambiguity in the formal structure of the poem. The reason Stevens gives for designating the landscape of the mind a false paradise is that the mind not only does not create reality, it is itself dependent for its content on the passive reception of sense perceptions. This thesis has precedents as far back as "Anecdote of Men by the Thousand" and "The Comedian as the Letter C"—"his soil is man's intelligence"—and Stevens has reformulated the thesis as recently as "On the Road Home." The world in which "the mind / Is the eye" is very similar to the world that "must be measured by eye" (*CP*, 204). The eye as "faculty" is the eye as physical organ receptive within a physical world.

In "Sunday Morning" and "On the Road Home," in parts of "Notes" and "Esthétique," and in "Credences of Summer," Stevens celebrates the world as "a landscape only of the eye," but there is a sense of dissatisfaction latent within the necessary limitations of this celebration, and this dissatisfaction makes itself felt in the tone of stoic renunciation in the last two stanzas of "Crude Foyer." Stevens' renunciation culminates in the first three lines of the last stanza. From the word *content* at the end of the third line, there appears to be another reversal. The final line saturates itself in ambiguity of pronominal reference. We are "content, / At last, there, when it turns out to be here." Where are "there" and "here," and what is "it"? Is "there" paradise? And are we content "here," in the "landscape only of the eye," when "it," that is, "the least, minor, vital metaphor" turns out to be "here"? Is this vital metaphor an incipient metaphor of paradise? If it is, "here" may be paradise after all: the interior of the metaphor that is projected from the landscape of the eye.

In "The Transcendentalist," Emerson defines a perennial philosophical antithesis that may have contributed to Stevens' inspiration in "Crude Foyer." "What is popularly called Transcendentalism among us, is Idealism; Idealism as it appears in 1842. As thinkers, mankind have ever divided into two sects, Materialists and Idealists; the first class founding on experience, the second on consciousness; the first class beginning to think from the data of the senses, the second class perceive that the senses are not final" (*RWE*, I, 329). Here, as in "Nature," Emerson unequivocally aligns himself with the perspective of the idealist. "These two modes of thinking are both natural, but the idealist contends that his way of thinking is in higher nature." The idealist will "affirm facts not affected by the illusions of sense, facts which are of the same nature as the faculty which reports them, and not liable to doubt; facts which in their first appearance to us assume a native superiority to material facts, degrading these into a language by which the first are to be spoken; facts which it only needs a retirement from the senses to discern. Every materialist will be an idealist; but an idealist can never go backward to be a materialist" (*RWE*, I, 330). In affirming that "we use / Only the eye as faculty," Stevens, speaking from the materialist's pole of the poem, seems to be directly controverting Emerson's affirmation of a "faculty" that is independent of "the illusions of sense." From the other pole of the poem, Stevens' figuration of the bleak splendor may owe something to the diction and imagery with which, in the essay "Fate," Emerson describes moments of transcendental illumination. "'T is the majesty into which we have suddenly mounted, the impersonality, the scorn of egotisms, the sphere of laws, that engage us. . . . Just as much intellect as you add, so much organic power. He who sees through the design, presides over it, and must will that which must be. We sit and rule, and, though we sleep, our dream will come to pass" (*RWE,* VI, 26–27). If the reading I have proposed for the final line of "Crude Foyer" is correct, Stevens has given a compacted representation of the process through which the materialist converts into the idealist who sits and rules and finds that his dream has come to pass.

Many of Stevens' later poems are so densely packed with cryptic allusions to his other poems that they would scarcely be intelligible if read in isolation from those poems. "Crude Foyer" could stand alone, but it too answers to a continuous meditation within the whole body of Stevens' work. In "Extracts from Addresses to the Academy of Fine Ideas," Stevens discloses his spiritual need by describing how "That other one wanted to think his way to life" (*CP,* 256). That other one is Stevens himself. He speaks from within the commonplace,

>   these Elysia, these origins,
> This single place in which we are and stay,
> Except for the images we make of it,
> And for it.

As in "Evening Without Angels," the adversative "Except" serves as a modal pivot, for it is within "the images we make of it" that "being unhappy" we

>   talk of happiness
> And, talking of happiness, know that it means
> That the mind is the end and must be satisfied.

The paradise represented in the images of the second stanza of "Crude Foyer" is a symbolic figuration for that "final belief" that "Must be in a fiction" (*CP,* 250). The "end of thought" signifies a fulfilled teleology of human consciousness. The "foyer of the spirit" evokes the transparent architecture of pure presence Stevens described as "The spirit's episcopate" (*OP,* 53). In "The Greenest Continent," he declares, "There was a heaven once," a place "in which the mind / Acquired transparency and beheld itself / And beheld the source from which transparency came." The second stanza of "Crude Foyer" reconstitutes this heaven and at the same time integrates it with the bleak fatalism of Ananke: "lord / And origin and resplendent end of law, / Sultan of African sultans, starless crown" (*OP*, 60). Ananke is a harsh god, an "obdurate ruler"; he is resplendent only in contrast to "the black sublime" of an Africa where "No god rules" and "Death, only, sits upon the serpent throne" (*OP*, 55). He subsumes but does not cancel death; he is majestic because he elevates death into what Emerson calls "the sphere of laws," a sphere within which the intellect can preside. In "Crude Foyer," Stevens compresses the history of this African succession into a single tonal modifier, the word *bleak*, through which he implicitly gives the necessary answer to the question he posed in "Sunday Morning": "Is there no change of death in paradise?" (*CP*, 69). The paradise of "Crude Foyer," like that of "The Poems of Our Climate," is "imperfect" not only because it is bleak but also because those who preside there can reject but cannot altogether suppress the critique that pronounces this paradise false. The conflict between the comedians and the angels manifests itself as a debate about the vitality or ontological validity of metaphor. In "The Pure Good of Theory," Stevens declares, "He woke in a metaphor: this was / A metamorphosis of paradise" (*CP*, 331). In "Esthétique du Mal," he defines "the paradise of meaning" by contrasting it to the condition in which one is able "to see" nothing but "what one sees" and "To hear only what one hears, one meaning alone" (*CP*, 320)—a positivistic state of mind exemplified by Crispin (in his latter days), by Mrs. Alfred Uruguay, and by the Canon Aspirin's dull, prosaic sister ("Notes," *CP*, 402). The crown that is worn within paradise appears in "Notes" as "the spirit's diamond coronal" (*CP*, 396) and in "Description Without Place" as "The crown and week-day coronal" of an archaic, abstract queen (*CP*, 339). In "Chocorua to Its Neighbor," Stevens describes the "shadow" that is the subject of the poem as "of human realizings, rugged roy" (*CP*, 302). This regal designation, like the image of the crown, signifies a teleological principle of thought. Despite its tragic overtones, "humanity's bleak crown" is an "end of thought" that is itself the end or final cause of a transcendental or "essential" imagination. The crown is one of those images we make not only "of it" but also "for it."

"Crude Foyer" dramatically depicts a synchronic opposition between metaphysical doctrines. In "The Bed of Old John Zeller" (1944), Stevens applies this technique of ambiguous suspension to the relations of presence and absence in the life of the past that is held in subconscious memory. As in "Crude Foyer," Stevens states his thesis at the beginning of the poem. "This structure of ideas, these ghostly sequences / Of the mind, result only in disaster" (*CP,* 326). Following the pattern of "Connoisseur of Chaos," he first depicts a drift toward some ideal structure of ideas—"luminous / Sequences, thought of among spheres in the old peak of night"—and then pulls up short and repudiates his meditative yearning as mere wish fulfillment. The "habit of wishing" manifests itself as an imaginative projection of spiritual experience into the lives of one's ancestors. It is "as if one's grandfather lay / In one's heart and wished as he had always wished." Stevens seems to reject the spiritual yearnings of his grandfather and to propose an alternative to this "disaster" a sort of passive positivism. In the final sentence of the poem, he suddenly reverses himself and resolves the opposition between the "structure of ideas" and "the structure / Of things":

> It is more difficult to evade
> That habit of wishing and to accept the structure
> Of things as the structure of ideas. It was the structure
> Of things at least that was thought of in the old peak of night.

What was thought of in the old peak of night was at once a luminous sequence and the structure of things as they are. The reconciliation here is twofold: between ideas and the concrete parts of the world, and between the ghostly past and the living present.

In "Sketch of the Ultimate Politician" (1947), the "casual poet" of "Old John Zeller" presents himself as fully resolved to achieve a poetry that is both a complete structure of ideas and, by virtue of its completeness, a satisfaction of the archetypal needs expressed in the ancestors' ghostly yearnings:

> There is a total building and there is
> A total dream. There are words of this,
> Words, in a storm, that beat around the shapes.
>
> . . . .
>
> There is a building stands in a ruinous storm,
> A dream interrupted out of the past,
> From beside us, from where we have yet to live. (*CP,* 335–36)

The place in which "we have yet to live" is the full mythic consciousness transmitted through the past, constituted partly by the ghosts of the past, and realized objectively in the fulfilled teleology of the "total dream." The "final dreamer of the total dream" is not the last dreamer; he is the dreamer and builder who has achieved closure—the end, the final construction—through the satisfaction of his imaginative desire.

Stevens' most elaborate theoretical effort to isolate a central principle that might serve as a keystone for the total building can be found in "Notes Toward a Supreme Fiction," especially in the first of the three sections, "It Must Be Abstract." "Notes" is not itself the total building; it is a collection of materials for that building. In discussing "Notes" with his correspondents, though Stevens wavers a bit about the degree of systematic development of theory in the poem, he never claims any but the most casual organization for the sequence of individual cantos (of seven stanzas each). Stevens defends the theoretical pretensions of the poem by denying that "theory" needs to be systematic in its exposition of principle. "It is only when you try to systematize the poems in the NOTES that you conclude that it is not the statement of a philosophic theory. A philosopher is never at rest unless he is systematizing: constructing a theory. But these are Notes; the nucleus of the matter is contained in the title. It is implicit in the title that there can be such a thing as a supreme fiction" (*LWS,* 430). In explaining the division of the work into three sections, Stevens fails to connect the thesis of the first section to that of the second, and he collapses the second and third sections into synonyms. "I have no idea of the form that a supreme fiction would take. The NOTES start out with the idea that it would not take any form: that it would be abstract. Of course, in the long run, poetry would be the supreme fiction; the essence of poetry is change and the essence of change is that it gives pleasure." It is on the basis of this rather feeble rationale that Stevens maintains "that, after all, with very little in the NOTES to go by, there is a theory," but he acknowledges that "the NOTES are a miscellany in which it would be difficult to collect the theory latent in them" (*LWS,* 430–31). Finally, Stevens concedes that he consciously sacrificed a continuous thematic development for the sake of other poetic interests. "I very soon found that, if I stuck closely to a development, I should lose all of the qualities that I really wanted to get into the thing, and that I was likely to produce something that did not come off in any sense, not even as poetry" (*LWS,* 431). In some measure, then, "Notes" represents a late, more purposeful reprise of the perceptual and stylistic explorations of *Harmonium.* Apart from the broad cataloging suggested by the division into three subheadings, the work consists of a frequently disjunctive sequence of cantos that are united primarily through their sometimes tenuous relation to the underlying idea of a supreme fiction. "It is a collection of just what I have called it: Notes. Underlying it is the idea that, in the various predicaments of belief, it might be possible to yield, or to try to yield, ourselves to a declared fiction" (*LWS,* 443). The principle of relation to this one underlying idea is nothing more specific than the pantheistic thesis of "Landscape with Boat": "All things were divine." The important truth within this diffusive principle is that a supreme fiction, if it is to be supreme, must be all-comprehending. Although it usually operates within the distinctive stylistic modes of the Romantic sublime, the supreme fiction must assimilate the experience of ordinary life.

The principle of comprehensive inclusiveness that hinders formal unity in "Notes" is itself presented through a neatly balanced dialectical figuration, the Canon Aspirin's nocturnal explorations in section three, "It Must Give Pleasure." The Canon Aspirin goes first to one extreme of the dualistic universe and then to the other: to the "point, / Beyond which fact could not progress as fact" and then to the "point, / Beyond which thought could not progress as thought" (*CP,* 402, 403). In these swift visionary movements, Stevens synoptically depicts and demonstrates the futility of the opposing drives to one or the other form of absolute reductiveness that inform the poems of *Harmonium.* Pure "fact" and pure "thought" both entail stasis in the progressive activity of the mind. Each alone is an absolute, but only in the negative sense of a substratum without "accidents" or distinguishing qualities. Consequently, neither can serve as the base for a supreme fiction. The Canon Aspirin knows that he must seek resolution outside the boundaries of dualism, but he is not yet able to articulate fully the way in which the elements of this dichotomy are to be synthesized:

> He had to choose. But it was not a choice
> Between excluding things. It was not a choice
>
> Between, but of. He chose to include the things
> That in each other are included, the whole,
> The complicate, the amassing harmony.

The "choice" the Canon Aspirin makes is less a positive declaration of thesis than a holding action that leaves open the question of how one is to order the compositional elements of the supreme fiction.

Although the Canon Aspirin repudiates the false absolutes of reductive materialism and mentalism, he does not renounce the possibility of all poetic absolutes. The absolute he still considers resolves the opposition of "fact" and "thought" by defining "the real" as a fiction of an absolute:

> It is possible, possible, possible. It must
> Be possible. It must be that in time
> The real will from its crude compoundings come,
>
> Seeming, at first, a beast disgorged, unlike,
> Warmed by a desperate milk. To find the real,
> To be stripped of every fiction except one,
>
> The fiction of an absolute—Angel,
> Be silent in your luminous cloud and hear
> The luminous melody of proper sound.

The real situates itself here as the last in a series of fictions and also as the primary or matrix fiction. To find the real, Stevens must invest the imagination with absolute ontological status, and the only way to do this is to conceive of essential imagination as a ubiquitous presence.

In his efforts to come to terms with the "difficulties" inherent in the idea of essential imagination (*LWS,* 370), Stevens will often seek assistance from Emerson, and it may be in response to Emerson that he chooses the name for the central principle of the supreme fiction. In "The Over-Soul," Emerson declares that "the heart which abandons itself to the Supreme Mind finds itself related to all its works," and he describes this sense of relation as a "primary and aboriginal sentiment" (*RWE,* II, 276). In "Extracts from Addresses to the Academy of Fine Ideas," Stevens had defined the principle of sentient relation as "the pure idea." In the first section of "Notes," "It Must Be Abstract," the pure idea becomes "The first idea." The concept Stevens delineates under this title is essentially equivalent to that which in "Contrary Theses (II)" he had called "a final refuge." "The abstract" of "Contrary Theses (II)" appears only as the flicker of an intuition. "The abstract was suddenly there and gone again." In "Notes," Stevens does not "walk toward" this abstract as toward a portal through which he can step into a foyer of the spirit. Instead, he circles about it, taking sightings and sketching out preliminary studies. As in "Extracts," the pure idea remains an inaccessible, transcendental source of images—"the image at its source" (*CP,* 223)—and the images Stevens makes of it necessarily fail to "fix" it. "If it is defined, it will be fixed and it must not be fixed" (*NA,* 34).

In his commentary on canto six of "It Must Be Abstract," Stevens defines the supreme fiction through a distinction between "existence" (presumably the mode of being for the particulars of the world) and "immanence" (the mode of being for the source of those particulars). "The abstract does not exist, but it is certainly as immanent: that is to say, the fictive abstract is as immanent in the mind of the poet, as the idea of God is immanent in the mind of the theologian. The poem is a struggle with the inaccessibility of the abstract" (*LWS,* 434). The distinction between "existence" and "immanence" manifests itself poetically as a paradoxical suspension between the perceptible poetic image and the unimageable abstract:

> It must be visible or invisible,
> Invisible or visible or both:
> A seeing and unseeing in the eye.

Within this sort of suspension, the forms of reason can have no bearing, and in canto four, Stevens explicitly exempts the first idea from the authority of reason:

> The first idea was not our own. Adam
> In Eden was the father of Descartes
> And Eve made air the mirror of herself.

Stevens explains that "Descartes is used as a symbol of the reason. But we live in a place that is not our own; we do not live in a land of Descartes; we have imposed the reason; Adam imposed it even in Eden" (*LWS,* 433). What renders the first idea so difficult of access is that it is no specific idea; it is the essence of thought itself. The first idea is a fiction, something which to be realized must be fabricated in poetry, but at the same time it is the ultimate reality from which all fictions derive and to which a supreme fiction must refer.

The first idea must, then, both implicitly concede its own fictive nature and also transcend dependence on the individual human mind, a locus in which pure thought reaches stasis. Thus it is that Stevens opens his poem with a series of seemingly contradictory imperatives. Taking the sun as the object of his meditation, he requires of himself (as "ephebe") that he

> Begin, ephebe, by perceiving the idea
> Of this invention, this invented world,
> The inconceivable idea of the sun.

Although conceiving of the world as "invented," Stevens forbids himself to "suppose an inventing mind as source / Of this idea." Like the latest freed man, he must "see the sun again with an ignorant eye," but he must also "see it clearly in the idea of it." Even though, as he says in canto eight, "The first idea is an imagined thing," the sun may be "seen in its idea" only when it "has expelled us and our images." These paradoxical directives all tend toward one result: they objectify the spirit and render it an autonomous creative agency identical with external reality:

> There was a muddy centre before we breathed.
> There was a myth before the myth began,
> Venerable and articulate and complete. (*CP*, 383)

By propounding the idea that the spirit precedes the human figurations of it, Stevens enables himself to imagine human life as itself contained within a spiritual medium. The name for that which "never could be named" (*CP*, 381) is God, that is, the pathetic fallacy raised to its highest metaphysical exponent. "We live in a place that is not our own and, much more, not ourselves. The first idea, then, was not our own. It is not the individual alone that indulges himself in the pathetic fallacy. It is the race. God is the centre of the pathetic fallacy" (*LWS*, 444). The essence of the pathetic fallacy is the assumption that nature, the world external to man, participates in some form of sentient reflection, that it has a consciousness of its own existence and is thus capable of some form of pathos. In "The Auroras of Autumn," for example, Stevens speaks of "An unhappy people in a happy world" (*CP*, 420).

In *Scepticism and Animal Faith,* Santayana offers a helpful explanation of how it is that one may come to conceive of the external world as a sentient presence. Since the psyche is not "composed of a different sort of substance from the common earth, light, and air out of which she has arisen, and by which she is fed," one might suppose that "all the substance of nature is ready to think, if circumstances allow by presenting something to think about, and creating the appropriate organ."[1] Despite Stevens' declaration that the "myth before the myth began" is "complete," within his fully articulated theory he represents this primary "myth" as existing in a state of mere potentiality until it is made active and completed by the creative effort of the poet. He himself becomes what Santayana calls "the appropriate organ" for the thinking of nature:

> The poem refreshes life so that we share,
> For a moment, the first idea . . . It satisfies
> Belief in an immaculate beginning
>
> And sends us, winged by an unconscious will,
> To an immaculate end. We move between these points:
> From that ever-early candor to its late plural
>
> And the candor of them is the strong exhilaration
> Of what we feel from what we think, of thought
> Beating in the heart, as if blood newly came,
>
> An elixir, an excitation, a pure power.
> The poem, through candor, brings back a power again
> That gives a candid kind to everything. (*CP*, 382)

"The poem" is both the individual poem and "The essential poem at the centre of things" (*CP*, 440) that is the source of all appearances, both phenomenal and poetic. The individual poem fulfills itself in fulfilling the teleological need of the "muddy centre" to achieve a mythic figuration of itself. The nature of the myth is suggested in the imagery of the immaculate beginning and end. The word *immaculate* is a variation on *pure*, which is itself an alternative for *supreme*. In "The Figure of the Youth as Virile Poet" (1943), Stevens meditates on the kind of "complete" idea that would result from a union of the philosophic and poetic powers. "An idea that satisfies both the reason and the imagination, if it happened, for instance, to be an idea of God, would establish a divine beginning and end for us which, at the moment, the reason, singly, at best proposes and on which, at the moment, the imagination, singly, merely meditates" (*NA*, 42). If the immaculate beginning and end can be equated with the "divine beginning and end for us," the first idea can be equated with "an idea of God." At the same time, the images of origin and end in "Notes" also figure the dialectical poetic process that culminates in the

1. Santayana, *Scepticism and Animal Faith,* 250.

supreme fiction. The "every-ready candor" is pure perception, as, for example, a perception of the sun when the sun is seen "in its idea." The word *its* in this phrase might suggest that the sun is to be seen in its own idea, that is, the idea it has of itself. Stevens' use of the pathetic fallacy can extend this far, as it does in "The Latest Freed Man." At its more rarefied levels, however, the "idea" of the sun is not the sun's own idea; it is a cognitive presence that sustains the sun within a field of consciousness. The activation of pathos and power within this consciousness depends on the poem that for a moment participates in the first idea. This participation culminates in the "late plural" of a fully articulated mythic and theoretic representation of the first idea.

In canto one, Stevens concentrates on the sun as the object of an "ever-early candor" of perception. In the fifth and sixth stanzas of canto three, he reverts to the moon as a standard emblem of the Romantic sublime. Beneath the jazzy, "Blue Guitar" manner in Stevens' depiction of the moon as an Arabian astronomer, there is a serious declaration of prophetic anticipation:

> We say: At night an Arabian in my room,
> With his damned hoobla-hoobla-hoobla-how,
> Inscribes a primitive astronomy
>
> Across the unscrawled fores the future casts
> And throws his stars around the floor. By day
> The wood-dove used to chant his hoobla-hoo
>
> And still the grossest iridescence of ocean
> Howls hoo and rises and howls hoo and falls.
> Life's nonsense pierces us with strange relation.

Stevens deciphers this image: "The Arabian is the moon; the undecipherable vagueness of the moonlight is the unscrawled fores: the unformed handwriting" (*LWS*, 433). The new vigor in the representation of the moon as a symbol of the Romantic responds to the repudiation of "stale moonlight and shabby sleep" at the end of canto two. Within these two cantos, Stevens replays the swift transition and renewal in the Romantic cycle that he practiced in poems such as "Sailing After Lunch" and "Evening Without Angels." In the final stanza just quoted, he gives the comic correlative to the elegiac sublime. The strangeness of sentient relation is the main source of marvel and awe in his visionary poetry.

In cantos six through nine of "It Must Be Abstract," Stevens attempts to construct a pluralized figuration in which the poet and his images become integral components of the first idea. The metaphoric vehicle for this figuration is the image of the giant. In "Sombre Figuration," when Stevens had submitted himself to the influence of "the man below," the image that resulted was "a sprawling portent" (*OP,* 68). Although "invisible," this image assumed quasi-mythic form.

> The supporting arms
> Reach from the horizons, rim to rim,
> While the shaggy top collects itself.

Stevens now adopts this image to serve as an emblem for that which must be invisible, visible, or both:

> A seeing and unseeing in the eye.
>
> The weather and the giant of the weather,
> Say the weather, the mere weather, the mere air:
> An abstraction blooded, as a man by thought. (*CP,* 385)

The giant is a spiritual shadow of the weather. Stevens seems at first to resolve this remaining opposition between matter and spirit by canceling spirit; then, in the last line quoted, it becomes apparent that spirit has been absorbed into and identified with the weather. The weather becomes an "abstraction" that is "blooded" by the spirit in the same way that a man is blooded by his thought of the "abstract." In canto eight the giant, as an embodiment of the first idea, merges with "the MacCullough," a representative of major man (canto seven):

> The first idea is an imagined thing.
> The pensive giant prone in violet space
> May be the MacCullough, an expedient,
>
> Logos and logic, crystal hypothesis,
> Incipit and a form to speak the word
> And every latent double in the word.

Stevens explains that "MacCullough is any name, any man" (*LWS,* 434). MacCullough is not only the maker of the word, he is the word; not only the maker of hypotheses, but the incarnation of a "crystal hypothesis." He is at once the artificer of the supreme fiction and an essential component of that fiction.

In the last four stanzas of canto eight, Stevens employs MacCullough as a vehicle for the most cautious form of prophecy, the hypothetical depiction of what "might" happen:

> But the MacCullough is MacCullough.
> It does not follow that major man is man.
> If MacCullough himself lay lounging by the sea,
>
> Drowned in its washes, reading in the sound,
> About the thinker of the first idea,
> He might take habit, whether from wave or phrase,
>
> Or power of the wave, or deepened speech,
> Or a leaner being, moving in on him,
> Of greater aptitude and apprehension,
>
> As if the waves at last were never broken,
> As if the language suddenly, with ease,
> Said things it had laboriously spoken.

There are two types of major men in Stevens' poetry, and the difference between them corresponds to the distinction between pure and normal poetry. That difference is also reflected in two uses for the image of the giant. One type of major man is the soldier as common hero who appears as the giant in "Gigantomachia" (1943) and "Repetitions of a Young Captain" (1944). Stevens remarks that in "Repetitions," "the words major men merely mean the pick of young men, but major men as characters in humanism are different. Since humanism is not enough, it is necessary to piece out its characters fictively" (*LWS,* 489). To say that MacCullough is MacCullough is to concede that he is merely human, but as major man he is other and more than human. "The trouble with humanism is that man as God remains man, but there is an extension of man, the leaner being, in fiction, a possibly more than human human, a composite human. The act of recognizing him is the act of this leaner being moving in on us" (*LWS,* 434). At some point in the fictive process, there is a qualitative leap from an "extension" of the human to the more than human. The leaner being begins as a dependent, fictive entity, but then attains the power of active movement toward the mind by which it is recognized. In the ambiguous suspension between these two "acts," that of recognition and that of movement, Stevens opens a breach in the limitations of the individual human mind. It is apparently to a complication such as this that Stevens refers in the esoteric phrase "every latent double in the word."

This phrase seems to be an echo of the passage in "The Over-Soul" in which Emerson declares that anyone who "worships God, becomes God": "Ineffable is the union of man and God in every act of the soul. . . . [F]or ever and ever the influx of this better and universal self is new and unsearchable. It inspires awe and astonishment. . . . It is the doubling of the heart itself, nay, the infinite enlargement of the heart with a power of growth to a new infinity on every side" (*RWE*, II, 292–93). It is through this "doubling of the heart itself" that both Emerson and Stevens gain access to what Emerson calls "the power and order that lie at the heart of things" (*RWE*, I, 45). In "Extracts from Addresses to the Academy of Fine Ideas," Stevens refers to the pure idea as an equivalent of the "central heart and mind of minds." What Emerson calls "the influx of this better and universal self" Stevens refers to as "this leaner being moving in on us." Stevens minimalizes Emerson's rhetoric while nonetheless implicitly affirming a fundamental affinity both in doctrine and in dialectical method.

Insofar as major man is the MacCullough, and the MacCullough is "The pensive giant prone in violet space," major man participates in divinity. In canto nine, Stevens boldly avows this implication but also qualifies it:

> The romantic intoning, the declaimed clairvoyance
> Are parts of apotheosis, appropriate
> And of its nature, the idiom thereof.
>
> They differ from reason's click-clack, its applied
> Enflashings. But apotheosis is not
> The origin of the major man. He comes,
>
> Compact in invincible foils, from reason,
> Lighted at midnight by the studious eye.

The "romantic intoning" probably refers to the kind of poetry that is exemplified in the last stanza of the previous canto, "As if the waves at last were never broken." Apotheosis, though not the origin, may still be the "end" of the major man, and if it is the end, it becomes, retroactively and paradoxically, also the origin. By attributing the origin to "reason," Stevens again emphasizes the individual poet's constructive function in the realization of the final dream. If we compare this passage with the passage in canto four where Stevens contrasts reason ("Descartes") to the "muddy centre," we appreciate the justice in his denying a systematic development of theory in the poem. At the same time, we should recognize that in attributing the origin of the major man to reason, Stevens is implicitly seeking to correct the imbalance created by his exaggerated emphasis on the subconscious in "Owl's Clover" and his consequent segregation of "reason" from the imagination both in "Owl's Clover" and in "The Irrational Element in Poetry."

Despite Stevens' claim that "reason" is the origin of major man, the governing element in "Notes" is not reason but allusive symbolism, and the principle by which symbols are linked is not logic but tonal and stylistic association. In the last three stanzas of canto nine, Stevens associates the major man with the images and phrases appropriate to the romantic intoning:

> My dame, sing for this person accurate songs.
>
> He is and may be but oh! he is, he is,
> This foundling of the infected past, so bright,
> So moving in the manner of his hand.
>
> Yet look not at his discolored eyes. Give him
> No names. Dismiss him from your images.
> The hot of him is purest in the heart.

In "Extracts" the "Stanzas of final peace" that "Lie in the heart's residuum" refer to "a singular romance, / This warmth in the blood-world for the pure idea." The descriptive phrase "So moving in the manner of his hand" allusively blurs the distinction between the poet and his own mythic constructs. In "The Hand as a Being," it is "Her hand" that "composed him and composed the tree" (*CP*, 271). This blurring has already appeared in canto seven, where the giant himself becomes the "thinker of the first idea." The confidence evident in the exulting phrase "but oh! he is, he is" probably derives some of its strength from Emerson's assurance that "the doubling of the heart itself . . . inspires in man an infallible trust. He has not the conviction, but the sight, that the best is the true, and may in that thought easily dismiss all particular uncertainties and fears, and adjourn to the sure revelation of time the solution of his private riddles. He is sure that his welfare is dear to the heart of being" (*RWE*, II, 292–93). At the end of "It Must Change," Stevens will instruct himself, again echoing Emerson, "Of these beginnings, gay and green, propose / The suitable amours. Time will write them down." Although Emerson would no doubt wince at the more erotic aspects of Stevens' Romantic sublime, the passion of Stevens' ambition finds perpetual renewal in Emerson's visionary ardor.

The "dame" to whom Stevens addresses his appeal can be identified with the "naked, nameless dame" he beholds in "The Hand as a Being." She represents the most comprehensive principles of his poetic inspiration, and her stylistic modes encompass the full range of his visionary poetry. In her more philosophical guise, she is closely associated with the "abstract" of "Contrary Theses (II)." In "Adult Epigram" (1946), Stevens calls her "the diva-dame," and in her attributes he displays the necessary paradoxicality of the abstract as a "premiss from which all things were conclusions":

> The romance of the precise is not the elision
> Of the tired romance of imprecision.
> It is the ever-never-changing same,
> An appearance of Again, the diva-dame. (*CP*, 353)

"The romance of the precise" is an Emersonian romance. In "History," Emerson declares that "Nature is a mutable cloud which is always and never the same. . . . Through the bruteness and toughness of matter, a subtle spirit bends all things to its own will. The adamant streams into soft but precise form before it, and whilst I look at it its outline and texture are changed again" (*RWE*, II, 13). For Stevens as for Emerson, the romance of the precise answers to "the power and order that lie at the heart of things." Although she is "abstract," the naked, nameless dame speaks to the deepest emotional needs of Stevens' poetry. In the invocation to "Notes," she evokes a response far more personal than that which is suggested by the mincing rhyme of the diva-dame. (In the 1947 edition of *Transport*, Stevens was careful to arrange the layout so that the invocation was clearly not addressed to Henry Church, to whom there is a dedication.) Stevens remarked of the invocation that "this poem is the most important thing in the book" (*LWS*, 538):

> And for what, except for you, do I feel love?
> Do I press the extremest book of the wisest man
> Close to me, hidden in me day and night?
> In the uncertain light of single, certain truth,
> Equal in living changingness to the light
> In which I meet you, in which we sit at rest,
> For a moment in the central of our being,
> The vivid transparence that you bring is peace.

As in canto eight of "It Must Be Abstract," the meeting Stevens describes is between two independent entities. The meeting place, "the central of our being," is a locus common to both and is thus the point of intersection between the individual human mind and a transcendental "mind of minds." The temporal stance of this invocation is the present general; Stevens is describing what usually or typically occurs. In canto seven of section two, "It Must Change," Stevens elaborates on this sense of fulfillment and peace by describing one particular occasion on which it occurs:

> Tonight the lilacs magnify
> The easy passion, the every-ready love
> Of the lover that lies within us and we breathe
>
> An odor evoking nothing, absolute.

The "lover that lies within"—the interior paramour—generates a language of subjective description. (Harold Bloom aptly characterizes the manner of this description as "the rhetoric of Transcendentalist eros.")[2] In the following canto, Stevens shifts into the more objective, symbolistic mode of "To the One of Fictive Music." The dame appears as Nanzia Nunzio, and Stevens presents himself or major man in the guise of Ozymandias. In a poem of 1952, "Two Illustrations That the World Is What You Make of It," Stevens will foresee his own fate in terms that derive from Shelley's "king of kings"—"his mastery / Left only the fragments found in the grass" (*CP,* 515). But in 1942 he is still in the full vigor of his pride, and he is a worthy consort for Nanzia Nunzio:

> On her trip around the world, Nanzia Nunzio
> Confronted Ozymandias. She went
> Alone and like a vestal long-prepared.
>
> I am the spouse. She took her necklace off
> And laid it in the sand. As I am, I am
> The spouse. She opened her stone-studded belt.
>
> I am the spouse, divested of bright gold,
> The spouse beyond emerald or amethyst,
> Beyond the burning body that I bear.
>
> I am the woman stripped more nakedly
> Than nakedness, standing before an inflexible
> Order, saying I am the contemplated spouse.

When Nanzia Nunzio opens her stone-studded belt, she is reducing herself to a pure, feminine principle of consciousness. The principle is one of synthesis or relation, symbolized by the diamond crown:

---

2. Bloom, *The Poems of Our Climate,* 198.

> Speak to me that, which spoken, will array me
> In its own only precious ornament.
> Set on me the spirit's diamond coronal.

The "spirit's diamond coronal," as it appears in "Crude Foyer" and "Description Without Place," differs from the crown in "Fictive Music," and this difference is a measure of the progress Stevens has made through "the various predicaments of belief." In "Fictive Music" the crown, though it is "set with fatal stones," gives regal authority to an imagination that remains "Unreal," a mere negative inversion of material reality (*CP*, 88). In "Crude Foyer" the wearer of the crown, in paradise, can at least read and reject the critique of the realist, and in "Description Without Place" the queen who wears the "crown and week-day coronal" is herself the source of all appearances, including those of the "real."

The sense of reality in the image and presence of the naked, nameless dame has already proved itself in the archetypal passion of "Bouquet of Belle Sçavoir," "The Candle a Saint," and "The Hand as a Being." In "Late Hymn from the Myrrh Mountain" (1946), Stevens again records a moment of erotic rapprochement between himself and the dame.

> Take the diamonds from your hair and lay them down.
> The deer-grass is thin. The timothy is brown.
> The shadow of an external world comes near. (*CP*, 350)

The interior paramour is an intellective ideal, but in the complex doubling of Stevens' late poetry she may also serve as the medium through which he regains access to "an external world" that has receded from direct sensory perception. At the same time, she herself remains inaccessible to direct perception. The bride may divest herself of her ornaments, but, as Ozymandias says, she may never appear fully naked. "A fictive covering / Weaves always glistening from the heart and mind" (*CP*, 396). As a mythological embodiment of the first idea, she must be visible and invisible both. Stevens' solution to this problem is to fashion images that contain their own negation of the visible. This technique, which he practices throughout *Transport*, finds its most sophisticated application in the poems of *Auroras*. In "The Owl in the Sarcophagus," for example, the ancient mother "stood tall in self not symbol, quick / And potent, an influence felt instead of seen" (*CP*, 435).

Although Stevens at the time of "Notes" has not yet settled on a definite form for his visionary mythology, the crowned female figure has already clearly assumed the leading place within his preparatory exercises for this mythology. In canto three of section three, "It Must Give Pleasure," Stevens' abortive experiment with a distinctly masculine image of God may suggest some of the reasons for his apparently instinctive choice of a female figure to represent the principle of pure poetry. Although the Belshazzar of "Country Words" never reappears by name, the "face of stone" in canto three clearly derives from him:

> A lasting visage in a lasting bush,
> A face of stone in an unending red,
> Red-emerald, red-slitted-blue, a face of slate,
>
> An ancient forehead hung with heavy hair,
> The channel slots of rain, the red-rose-red
> And weathered and the ruby-water-worn. (*CP*, 400)

Rubies are the ornamental emblems of Belshazzar's power—"O, ruler, rude / With rubies"—and in the final stanzas of this canto, Stevens both reinforces the allusion and also implies his own dissatisfaction with the image:

> Red-in-red repetitions never going
> Away, a little rusty, a little rouged,
> A little roughened and ruder, a crown
>
> The eye could not escape, a red renown
> Blowing itself upon the tedious ear.
> An effulgence faded, dull cornelian
>
> Too venerably used.

"Too venerably used" suggests that the "lasting visage," like the image of Belshazzar, is too well defined and limited for Stevens' purposes. It is an image "the eye could not escape," that is, an image that is incapable of transcending itself through the negation of the visible. In his commentary on this canto, Stevens touches obliquely on the difficulty of forming any image of God. "The first thing one sees of any deity is the face, so that the elementary idea of God is a face: a lasting visage in a lasting bush. Adoration is a form of face to face. . . . We struggle with the face, see it everywhere & try to express the changes. In the depths of concentration, the whole thing disappears" (*LWS*, 438). The problem Stevens attempts to explain is the same problem of which he complains in "Bouquet of Belle Sçavoir": "The thought of her takes her away." The transcendent source of all form and definition cannot be named and defined. Any limiting term is a falsifying term. This source is, consequently, accessible only through paradox. In Stevens' mind, the object of desire that exists within an atmosphere of supra-rational vitality naturally assumes a feminine guise. Neither Belshazzar nor the idol that descends from him answers to the special quality of Stevens' imaginative need.

Stevens' remark at the time of writing "Notes," "I have no idea of the form that a supreme fiction would take" (*LWS,* 430), must be weighed against the overwhelming evidence that he is continuously constructing a "total building" of complexly related themes and motifs. This remark nonetheless finds some measure of corroboration in the structural latitude Stevens allows himself in the poem. Not only does he decline to fabricate a unified mythic structure, he also declines to limit his explorations to the modal range implied in the title of the poem. The marriage between Nanzia Nunzio and Ozymandias takes place within the Romantic sublime, but the marriage in section three, canto four, "Between a great captain and the maiden Bawda" takes place within a very different range of sensibility. Stevens calls this ceremony "a mystic marriage," but it actually celebrates "the earth and . . . men in their earthy implications" (*OP,* 229):

> The great captain loved the ever-hill Catawba
> And therefore married Bawda, whom he found there,
> And Bawda loved the captain as she loved the sun.
>
> They married well because the marriage-place
> Was what they loved. It was neither heaven nor hell.
> They were love's characters come face to face. (*CP,* 401)

The exotic figure who invests Nanzia Nunzio with her crown is a protagonist of pure poetry. His marriage does not involve him in the world of other people. Bawda and the great captain, in contrast, are both real if exemplary human beings, and their marriage confirms their voluntary limitation to a physical world. When, in canto ten of section three, Stevens again invokes a muse, the figure he fashions, in contrast both to Nanzia Nunzio and to the figure (never named) in the poem's invocation, defines itself as the mythical embodiment of normal poetry:

> Fat girl, terrestrial, my summer, my night,
> How is it I find you in difference, see you there
> In a moving contour, a change not quite completed?

> You are familiar yet an aberration.
> Civil, madam, I am, but underneath
> A tree, this unprovoked sensation requires
> That I should name you flatly; waste no words,
> Check your evasions, hold you to yourself.
> . . . .
> That's it: the more than rational distortion,
> The fiction that results from feeling. Yes, that. (*CP,* 406)

"The fat girl is the earth," Stevens tells us (*LWS,* 426); she is the earth of summer celebrated in "Credences." She is also the "night," but she is found "in difference," the medium opposite to that of "relation." She is not "the abstract" but the "moving contour" of differentiation that emanates from the abstract. In "Contrary Theses (II)," Stevens sets the abstract beyond the phenomenal forms that conduct him to it. "He walked toward / An abstract, of which the sun, the dog, the boy / Were contours" (*CP,* 270). As in "The Hand as a Being," Stevens lies "underneath / A tree"—"a man stretched out at his ease, underneath a tree, thinking" (*LWS,* 444). He does not, however, lie with the woman he invokes. In "Notes" the tree is symbolically contrasted to the changing nature of "the earth." "A great tree is a symbol of fixity, permanence, completion, the opposite of 'a moving contour.'" Unlike the naked, nameless dame, the fat girl can be named, and in such a way that the naming captures and fixes its object:

> They will get it straight one day at the Sorbonne.
> We shall return at twilight from the lecture
> Pleased that the irrational is rational,
>
> Until flicked by feeling, in a gildered street,
> I call you by name, my green, my fluent mundo.
> You will have stopped revolving except in crystal.

The crystal globe suspends the revolving earth within the fixity of poetic representation. Despite the future perfect tense, this image provides a sense of limited closure within the suspension of closure implied both in the title of the poem and in Stevens' commentary on the poem. The limited closure with which Stevens concludes "It Must Give Pleasure" does not revoke the transcendental ambitions in the preceding parts of the poem, but it does open the way for those holidays in reality that culminate in "Credences of Summer."

The formal principles of pure and normal poetry suppose one another by negative inference, and there is a continuous dialectical interplay between the developments of the pure idea and the articulation of joy in the parts of the world.

The greater part of Stevens' poetically productive life occurs in an extended period of public crisis. In every volume from *Ideas of Order* to *Transport,* the "pressure of reality" leaves its impress in poems of public concern. In the poems of *Parts* and *Transport* the "men in crowds" who haunt *Ideas of Order,* "Blue Guitar," and "Owl's Clover" metamorphose into columns of soldiers. Stevens eulogizes the men that are falling as early as 1936, and in *Parts* and *Transport* he dedicates a long series of poems to the soldier as common hero. The envoi to "Notes" directly addresses the soldier and lectures him on the affinity between the poetic and the martial hero. "Soldier, there is a war between the mind / And sky" (*CP,* 407). Although this "is a war that never ends," Stevens declares that it "depends" on the soldier's more limited war. The war between the mind and sky in "Extracts" is an imperialistic war waged by thought for complete dominion over the external world. Consequently, despite Stevens' propitiatory concession of dependence, he ultimately attributes definitive authority to the poet's heroism, not the soldier's, and in fact he renders the soldier dependent on poetry to give meaning to both his life and death:

> How simply the fictive hero becomes the real;
> How gladly with proper words the soldier dies,
> If he must, or lives on the bread of faithful speech.

The note of official, consolatory rhetoric in these lines does not appear to be intended as self-undercutting irony. Stevens takes seriously the injunctions in "Of Modern Poetry" concerning the social role of the poet (*CP,* 240). If his consolations seem remote from the actual suffering of individual soldiers, the ennobling myth he creates is without pretentiousness or bombast. And if there seems to be something self-serving in the implicitly invidious contrast between the two types of major men, this contrast gradually fades as the major men who enter the realm of death merge with the "giant" of phenomenal presence that is one incarnation of the supreme fiction.

The path Stevens takes toward a submerging of the war dead in a collective mythic memory leads through his continuing meditation on the nature of good and evil. The Second World War seemed to focus the problem of good and evil in satisfyingly large, simple terms, and Stevens' latent bent for theodicy finds ready lyric form in consolatory war poems from "Asides on the Oboe" (1940) to strophe three of "Description Without Place" (1945). In "Dutch Graves in Bucks County" (1943), he reaffirms the consolatory doctrine of "Asides" and "Extracts." "The armies kill themselves, / And in their blood an ancient evil dies" (*CP*, 292). In canto seven of "Esthétique du Mal," Stevens fashions the dying armies into a single collective being, "The soldier of time grown deathless in great size," situated in a fictive Valhalla, a paradise in which the "mystical convolutions" of the soldiers' "sleep" effect a close communion between the collective being and the lyric presence of the living world:

> the summer breathes for them
> Its fragrance, a heavy somnolence, and for him,
> For the soldier of time, it breathes a summer sleep. (*CP*, 319)

This evocation of a deathless sleep in summer air seems to press further into consolatory fantasy than Stevens ever goes either before or after, but it is a natural extension of the supreme fiction. In "Extracts" the culminating prophetic declaration follows immediately upon a declaration of a cosmic resolution of evil.

> If earth dissolves
> Its evil after death, it dissolves it while
> We live. Thence come the final chants. (*CP*, 259)

In "Flyer's Fall" (1945), Stevens provides a fictive locus or "dimension" for this cosmic resolution, and though he delineates this dimension by negation—"nothingness of human after-death"—he also designates it as the supreme locus of fictive existence; it is a "dimension in which / We believe without belief, beyond belief" (*CP*, 336). The myth of the soldier's deathless rest, like that of the supreme fiction, must function within the confines of a modern, relativistic epistemology. At the end of "A Collect of Philosophy," Stevens suggests that modern man's "willingness to believe beyond belief was what had made him modern and was always certain to keep him so" (*OP*, 202). The locus of a belief beyond belief is the essential poem, the self-sustaining "giant of nothingness" that is "ever changing, living in change" (*CP*, 443). In "Description Without Place," Stevens situates the genre of war elegy within the realm of "potential seemings" that culminate in the supreme fiction:

> There are potential seemings turbulent
> In the death of a soldier, like the utmost will,
>
> The more than human commonplace of blood,
> The breath that gushes upward and is gone,
>
> And another breath emerging out of death,
> That speaks for him such seemings as death gives. (*CP*, 341)

The breath "emerging out of death" is at once the breath that "summer breathes for them," the "one breath" that in "Montrachet" is "the single main," the poet's own voice speaking for the dead, and, finally, the syllable of farewell that in "Owl" is spoken by the ancient mother to those who are passing into "memory" (*CP*, 432).

Stevens' hypothesis of a living mythic memory takes its most concrete form in the evocation of the ghosts of his own ancestors. Stevens' preoccupation with the subconscious as a burial ground of unquiet spirits is already well established by the time of *Harmonium,* and it eventually becomes one of the main sources of pathos in his visionary poetry. In "The Weeping Burgher" (1919), Stevens represents his own ghostly nature as compounded of the ghosts of the past, "the people burning in me still" (*CP*, 61). In "Comedian," Crispin evokes the "dreamers buried in our sleep" (*CP*, 39) only to reject them. Crispin expunges dreamers and dreams so that he may the more fully embrace the ordinary world of things and events. In "Owl's Clover," Stevens corrects Crispin's error through his invention of the subman, "A self of parents who have never died, / Whose lives return, simply, upon our lips" (*OP*, 67). In "Dutch Graves in Bucks County," Stevens first repudiates the ancestors and then, at the end of the poem, as in "Old John Zeller," he reverses himself and affirms their living presence. "Time was not wasted in your subtle temples. / No: nor divergence made too steep to follow down" (*CP*, 293). The subtle temples, like the luminous sequences of thought in "Old John Zeller," are those inspirations of the past that remain active in the dreams of the present.[3]

Within its context of an intersection between the present world of action

---

3. See also "Recitation After Dinner" (1945).

and the mythic memory of a collective subconscious, the envoi to "Notes" illustrates the way in which, at bottom, pure and normal poetry not only imply but involve each other. They are both part of "the things / That in each other are included." Stevens no longer faces the kind of either/or dilemma forced on Crispin by his reductive absolutism. The "giant of nothingness" in "Primitive" is the mythic and metaphysical equivalent of "the whole, / The complicate, the amassing harmony." This kind of "nothingness" is the exact opposite of the two kinds of nothingness the Canon Aspirin discovers at the end of fact and the end of thought. It is not a mere blank or absence, but the state of pure phenomenal potentiality. In "The Motive for Metaphor" (1943) and related poems, Stevens explores the purely physical world of "fact" untransformed by poetic figuration and finds that it is a desert. In these poems the dichotomy between "real" and "unreal" becomes problematic and ironic, for the "real" world of appearances exists only within the contexts of artifice. The pure "real," untinged by imagination, exists only as a hypothetical monstrosity:

> Desiring the exhilarations of changes:
> The motive for metaphor, shrinking from
> The weight of primary noon,
> The A B C of being,
>
> The ruddy temper, the hammer
> Of red and blue, the hard sound—
> Steel against intimation—the sharp flash,
> The vital, arrogant, fatal, dominant X. (*CP,* 288)

As in "The Latest Freed Man," the elaborate poetic rhetoric underlines the paradoxicality of describing that which supposedly transcends description. "Primary noon" is the "point, / Beyond which fact could not progress as fact" (*CP,* 402); the noonday metaphor Stevens chooses to describe this condition draws on the plaint of the multitude in "Blue Guitar." "There are no shadows in our sun" (*CP,* 167). The "dominant X" is a vital force, and it is a necessary, complementary antithesis to the nothingness of pure thought, but it is also, hypothetically, "fatal." No fact comes into human recognition unmediated by the filtering, dissolving, and synthesizing functions of the imagination. The dominance of fact implies the annihilation of the human. As Stevens puts it in "The Figure of the Youth as Virile Poet," "We live in the center of a physical poetry, a geography that would be intolerable except for the non-geography that exists there" (*NA*, 65). In "Somnambulisma" (1943), Stevens figures the poet's imagining the ocean's waves as a "bird that never settles," and he declares that without this bird, "The ocean, falling and falling on the hollow shore, / Would be a geography of the dead" (*CP*, 304). A geography of the dead is a place without description.

In "Credences of Summer" (1946), Stevens returns to the paradoxical moment of "The Latest Freed Man." He exhorts himself to "Trace the gold sun about the whitened sky / Without evasion by a single metaphor" (*CP*, 373). This project is, of course, impossible, and Stevens does not even attempt to carry it out. Nonetheless, in canto seven he formulates his relation to the objective world in a way that yields the illusion of grasping an unmediated, objective reality. As Robert Buttel has suggested, the subject of the first two stanzas—"they"—seems to denote the representatives of a poetic tradition that has receded into an unreal world, the Palace of Art.[4] If so, "they" also serve as surrogates for Stevens' own problematic relation to "the object":

> Far in the woods they sang their unreal songs,
> Secure. It was difficult to sing in face
> Of the object. The singers had to avert themselves
> Or else avert the object. Deep in the woods
> They sang of summer in the common fields.
>
> They sang desiring an object that was near,
> In face of which desire no longer moved,
> Nor made of itself that which it could not find . . .

The singers have retreated from the object only so that they might sing of it, but their strategy has left them suspended in a state of perpetual longing. In the shift of perspective that follows the ellipsis, Stevens attempts to resolve this dilemma by main force:

> Three times the concentred self takes hold, three times
> The thrice concentred self, having possessed
>
> The object, grips it in savage scrutiny,
> Once to make captive, once to subjugate
> Or yield to subjugation, once to proclaim

---

4. Buttel, *The Making of "Harmonium,"* 224. For a deconstructive critique of Stevens' "stratagems" in "Credences," see Joseph N. Riddel, "The Climate of Our Poems," *Wallace Stevens Journal,* VII (1983), 68–75.

> The meaning of the capture, this hard prize,
> Fully made, fully apparent, fully found.

The purpose of these three grippings is to possess the object, and the willfulness in Stevens' proclamation of success reveals itself in the phrase preceding his description of the three stages. The self is represented as already "having possessed / The object" before the three stages ever begin. Within the appositives that describe the result of this process, the essential problem re-emerges; the object is both "fully found," that is, discovered in its pristine state, and also "Fully made," that is, invented out of "desire." The strategy of paradoxical apposition absorbs the problematic implications of a dualistic cosmos into the self-consciously rhetorical declarations of an absolute fulfillment.

In canto eight, Stevens tacitly reflects on the procedure of the preceding canto. The trumpet cry that announces "the more than visible" seeks to restrict itself to the near side of "the invisible," but to do so it must take refuge in the kind of paradoxical equivocation that has enabled Stevens to celebrate his "hard prize":

> The trumpet of morning blows in the clouds and through
> The sky. It is the visible announced,
> It is the more than visible, the more
> Than sharp, illustrious scene. The trumpet cries
> This is the successor of the invisible.
>
> This is its substitute in stratagems
> Of the spirit.

The "invisible" is, presumably, a transcendental presence that would enable the singers to sing in face of the object. Stevens' "substitute" for this presence is not the object itself but the "stratagems" that sustain the object as a fictive construct, a construct that simultaneously upholds the illusion of its integrity as a thing apart from the mind and also acknowledges its own fictive character.

Before "Credences," in "Description Without Place" (1945), Stevens had already established the ontological limits of summer:

> If seeming is description without place,
> The spirit's universe, then a summer's day,
>
> Even the seeming of a summer's day,
> Is description without place. (*CP,* 343)

In this poem Stevens expounds his theory of fictive belief and links this theory with the transcendental ideas he has been developing ever since "Key West." He argues that we live in appearances, perceptual and poetic. In articulating these appearances, we both fulfill our own sense of human purpose and also serve as the medium through which essential imagination realizes itself. In strophe one, Stevens establishes appearance as a universal presence and embodies this presence in the image of the queen:

> It is possible that to seem—it is to be,
> As the sun is something seeming and it is.
>
> . . . .
>
>   It was a queen that made it seem
> By the illustrious nothing of her name.
> Her green mind made the world around her green.
> The queen is an example . . . This green queen
> In the seeming of the summer of her sun
> By her own seeming made the summer change.

In the image of "This green queen," Stevens alludes to a line of color symbolism that extends from "The Candle a Saint" to "Repetitions of a Young Captain." In "The Candle" the green night is also "The abstract, the archaic queen," and this same figure, the "essential shadow," appears in "Phosphor Reading by His Own Light" as "That elemental parent, the green night." In "Chocorua to Its Neighbor," the "prodigious shadow" that is the subject of Chocorua's discourse is said to know that "There were others like him safely under roof" (*CP,* 299). Among these others, Chocorua mentions "the scholar, / Whose green mind bulges with complicated hues" (*CP,* 300). In canto six of "Repetitions of a Young Captain," Stevens opposes pure and normal poetry in the figure of the theater—taken from "Of Modern Poetry"—and he decisively chooses the stage of pure poetry. This choice is signaled by an emphatic repetition of his color symbology.

> The choice is made. Green is the orator
> Of our passionate height. He wears a tufted green,
> And tosses green for those for whom green speaks. (*CP* 309)

The green queen of "Description Without Place"—elsewhere figured as the shadow, the giant, the abstract, and the essential poem—creates appearances but is herself created through her poetic image. "In the golden vacancy she came, and comes, / And seems to be on the saying of her name." Through perceiving the parts of the world, the human mind recognizes itself as the perceptual agent for realizing the total of appearances that constitutes the world of sentient presence. Local perception is

> The lesser seeming original in the blind
> Forward of the eye that, in its backward, sees
> The greater seeming of the major mind. (*CP*, 340)

If passive perception is the starting point of spiritual experience, the end toward which this experience tends, as by an organic necessity, is the articulation of appearances, especially in poetry. The extreme realization of the tendency toward articulation is the supreme fiction, a closing of the perceptual circle:

> There might be, too, a change immenser than
> A poet's metaphors in which being would
> Come true, a point in the fire of music where
> Dazzle yields to a clarity and we observe,
> And observing is completing and we are content,
> In a world that shrinks to an immediate whole. (*CP*, 341)

The "change" Stevens describes seems to place mystical illumination beyond the active manipulations of poetry. In the passage that follows this description, he shifts his attention from the passive aspect of revelation to the dynamic aspect of poetic process. The anaphoral phrase "There might be" indicates that these two passages are not to be set in contrast. They are meant as alternative descriptions of the same thing:

> There might be in the curling-out of spring
> A purple-leaping element that forth
> Would froth the whole heaven with its seeming-so,
> The intentions of a mind as yet unknown,
> The spirit of one dwelling in a seed,
> Itself that seed's ripe, unpredictable fruit.

The spirit of one is the principle of essential unity. The seed is Stevens' own poetry, and the fruit is the supreme fiction: the idea that the universe is a process of divine consciousness realizing itself in a human medium.

Stevens' bold intimations of the monistic and transcendental character of his supreme fiction bring him to the border of paradox surrounding his formally coherent theory of fictive belief. In strophes five through seven of "Description Without Place," he progresses in three stages toward a conclusive affirmation of the ontological supremacy of poetic figuration or "description." The first stage, the acknowledgment that description is artifice, generates the dialectical progression through the positing of "difference":

> It is an expectation, a desire
> A palm that rises up beyond the sea,
> A little different from reality:
> The difference that we make in what we see
> And our memorials of that difference,
> Sprinklings of bright particulars from the sky. (*CP*, 344)

In this context, "difference" is the element of strangeness in artifice. In "Fictive Music," Stevens asks for a poetry close to the sensual world, but he also asks that it be

> not too like, yet not so like to be
> Too near, too clear, saving a little to endow
> Our feigning with the strange unlike, whence springs
> The difference that heavenly pity brings. (*CP*, 88)

The one of fictive music is "Unreal," and in "Holiday in Reality" (1944), Stevens identifies this "strange unlike" as the origin or root of aesthetic sensation. "Intangible arrows quiver and stick in the skin / And I taste at the root of the tongue the unreal of what is real" (*CP*, 313). At this point *unreal* and *real* have become interdependent, and there is already a movement toward an ironic inversion of these terms. The "Sprinklings of bright particulars from the sky" are parts of the world, but they are not physical objects; they are "memorials," that is, fragments of poetic utterance.

In the second stage of Stevens' progression, in strophe six of "Description Without Place," he reaffirms "difference" but also asserts the positive reality of artifice. Although it is "the double of our lives," artifice is not mimesis. "Description is revelation. It is not / The thing described, nor false facsimile." Description has its own laws of self-realization and it assumes a sovereign role as the goal of experience. It is "A text we should be born that we might read." It is "Intenser than any actual life could be," and though there is still an actual life that is "real," artifice is no longer "Unreal." It is an alternative, independent reality that "exists, / In its own seeming, plainly visible."

Once he has attributed an independent reality to description, Stevens advances to the third and final stage of his progression; he attributes primary creative power to the imagination. The world exists for us only in our imaginative constructions of it, and this constructive drive has no rationale beyond the complete realization of itself:

> Thus the theory of description matters most.
> It is the theory of the word for those
>
> For whom the word is the making of the world,
> The buzzing world and lisping firmament.
>
> It is a world of words to the end of it,
> In which nothing solid is its solid self.

A world of solid selves is a world of discrete particulars segregated within an atmosphere of "difference." A world of unsolid substances activated by a teleological principle of speech is a world of relations synthesized in poetic figuration. The "word" makes the world, but only in the sense that the world itself consists of latent speech that is activated in poetry.

Stevens' theory of description implicitly designates his own poetry as a reflex of time and place as these perfect themselves. In keeping with this conception, Stevens must represent his figurative forms as autonomous, self-originating entities. In "Creations of Sound" (1944), he articulates this radically Romantic view of poetry by criticizing an anonymous poet "X." The problem with X's poetry is that it does not come to him "of its own, / Without understanding . . . in sounds not chosen" (*CP*, 310). Stevens is not merely criticizing stiffness or meretricious artificiality; he frankly requires that the poet be the passive instrument of a voice that arises of its own accord, apart from the self of the poet:

> We do not say ourselves like that in poems.
> We say ourselves in syllables that rise
> From the floor, rising in speech we do not speak.

Here the first-person plural serves as a pronominal mask for self-vindication (*I* do not speak myself like that in poems) and as an oblique form of didactic address (none of us *should* speak like that). Moreover, by avoiding the first-person singular, Stevens reinforces the theme of the poem. X remains "a man

/ Too exactly himself," and through his critique of X, Stevens reaffirms his determination "to suppress the merely personal" (*LWS*, 413).

Stevens' determination to speak "in sounds not chosen" answers to his conceptions of the irrational element in poetry and of "the imagination as metaphysics." These conceptions are the deepest sources of his poetic inspiration, but when they fail him, the criterion of spontaneous utterance can result in poetry that is merely disconnected and obscure. This danger is particularly acute in longer poems, and in "Esthétique du Mal" (1944), one of the longest poems in *Transport,* Stevens frequently succumbs to it. Helen Vendler, with understandable harshness, designates "Esthétique" as "at once the most random and the most pretentious of Stevens' long poems."[5] "Esthétique" has a skeletal structure, but this structure does not constitute a truly dialectical progression toward a comprehensive synthesis or climactic moment of resolution. There is a series of temporary, partial resolutions within the alternating modes of pure and normal poetry. Presumably, the residual dissatisfaction of every partial resolution generates a compensatory response, but there is not, as in "Connoisseur of Chaos," a single metaphysical issue that can be defined and logically developed. "Esthétique" is a mélange of meditations on pain, evil, religion, war, ideology, metaphysics, and poetry; and these meditations, though often prosy, are also vague and inconclusive. The climactic moments within the poem are nonetheless generically distinct, defined through well-established motifs such as the sun and moon, the shadow, the fat girl, and summer. Like "Notes," "Esthétique" ends on the note of summer celebration, and as in "Notes," the final statement is not so much a conclusion as a resting place along a path much longer than that which is traversed by either poem in itself.

The first climactic moment in "Esthétique," an appeal to "the honey of common summer" in the last three stanzas of canto three, represents a conclusion to the meditation paraphrased in the first three cantos. The "He" who is the subject of this paraphrase, though he is "at Naples writing letters home," is very close to Stevens himself and, indeed, to Stevens when he is too exactly himself. As he lies "On his balcony at night," he listens to "the accents of / Afflicted sleep," and he fears that these accents will ultimately "communicate / The intelligence of his despair" (*CP,* 314). In "Esthétique," more than in any of his other poems, Stevens concerns himself with the human implications of any possible form of a supreme fiction. In the word *despair,* he touches

5. Vendler, *On Extended Wings,* 206.

on the sinister aspect of a transcendental resolution that absorbs and sublimates both the will and the suffering of the individual. He then turns his attention to the consolatory aspect of the Romantic sublime. The emblem he chooses to represent this sublime is the moon. In strophe seven of "Blue Guitar," the inhuman detachment implied by the moon horrifies Stevens and compels him to abandon the transcendental hypothesis of the preceding strophe ("The thinking of god is smoky dew," *CP,* 168). In canto two of "Esthétique," the remoteness of the noon serves as a means of salvation; it is associated with the "shadow" of "The Candle a Saint," "Montrachet," and "Chocorua":

> The moon rose up as if it had escaped
> His meditation. It evaded his mind.
> It was part of a supremacy always
> Above him. The moon was always free from him,
> As night was free from him. The shadow touched
> Or merely seemed to touch him as he spoke
> A kind of elegy he found in space.

For Stevens, "elegy" is an expression of a detached, lyric sense of perpetual loss. The association between the moon's detachment and elegiac lyricism derives in part from the complex of Keatsian images that first asserts itself in "Sunday Morning" and then again in "Waving Adieu." Moneta's eyes "saw me not, / But, in blank splendour, beamed like the mild moon, / Who comforts those she sees not." Stevens' reading of Keats confirms for him that the ceaseless absorption of the present into the past constitutes pure experience. His effort to fashion a supreme fiction can be seen as in part an attempt to invest this elegiac consciousness with mythic life. Elegy is a mode of resolution, but the conclusion to canto two speaks only of a salvation that could take place were the protagonist not hindered by pain. "It is pain that is indifferent to the sky."

Stevens' meditation on pain's distracting effect stimulates the critique of religion in the first five stanzas of canto three. In Nietzschean fashion, he repudiates the "too, too human god, self-pity's kin."[6] The moon, which appears in canto two as a more nobly detached, inhuman patron, now associ-

---

6. Stevens' reading of Nietzsche in the 1940s was prompted by the interest of his friend Henry Church (see *LWS,* 409, 431–32, 532). The impressions from this reading do not seem to have entered very deeply into Stevens' construction of a supreme fiction (see the brief, dismissive comment on Nietzsche in "A Collect of Philosophy," *OP,* 187).

ates itself, through a submerged allusion, to the too human god, and Stevens reacts to this association by polemically affirming the physical world. The allusion is a perhaps subconscious recollection of "Lunar Paraphrase," a poem of 1917 that was included in the second edition of *Harmonium*:

> When the body of Jesus hangs in a pallor,
> Humanly near, and the figure of Mary,
> Touched on by hoar-frost, shrinks in a shelter
> Made by the leaves, that have rotted and fallen;
> When over the houses, a golden illusion
> Brings back an earlier season of quiet
> And quieting dreams in the sleepers in darkness—
> The moon is the mother of pathos and pity. (*CP*, 107)

"Lunar Paraphrase" is sympathetic to the "golden illusion" it discredits, and even the speaker in "Esthétique" feels the seductive influence of a religion of self-pity. As in "Sunday Morning," Stevens tries to vanquish the "Dominion of the blood and sepulchre" by invoking a pagan ethos of sensual joy:

> It seems
> As if the health of the world might be enough.
> It seems as if the honey of common summer
> Might be enough.

The health of the world is another locus for theodicy, a quasi-transcendental purification of individual suffering through a detached appreciation of life outside oneself. The special character of this theodicy is determined by the word *health*. The honey of common summer is physical experience in its moment of fruition. This moment, though it is paradigmatic for normal poetry, cannot serve as a "final refuge" (*CP*, 270).

The honey of common summer stands in generic contrast to the "elegy he found in space." In order to define the metaphysical dimension of these two generic poles, Stevens in canto four gives a symbolic formulation of the dichotomy between pluralistic empiricism and monistic idealism. Referring to a piano recital, he asks whether what "we heard" was "All sorts of notes" or, rather, "Variations in the tones of a single sound." In the passage that follows this formulation, both poles succumb to the distorting effect of an aesthetic of evil. Stevens calls the pluralistic sensualist a "sentimentalist," and the "genius" with whom he compares the sentimentalist proves equally faulty:

> The genius of misfortune
> Is not a sentimentalist. He is
> That evil, that evil in the self, from which
> In desperate hallow, rugged gesture, fault
> Falls out on everything: the genius of
> The mind, which is our being, wrong and wrong,
> The genius of the body, which is our world,
> Spent in the false engagements of the mind.

This double negation leaves Stevens in limbo, caught between a falsifying, surreptitious animism that infuses the world of particulars with problematic vitality, and a totalizing of evil, that is, difference and alienation.

The negativism with which Stevens concludes canto four retroactively suspends the two previous moments of resolution, that of summer and that of the moon. When, in canto eight, Stevens again approaches to a moment of resolution, he implicitly criticizes the resolution of evil by way of the health of the world:

> The death of Satan was a tragedy
> For the imagination. A capital
> Negation destroyed him in his tenement
> And, with him, many blue phenomena.

Not even the gift of bearing pain with equanimity can compensate for the loss of a mythology that, however grotesque, bore in itself something of the mystery and awe of human experience. In canto eight, Stevens fixes the moment of anomie that precedes the revolution of the cycle back to the Romantic; he now explicitly locates this moment at a specific juncture in the history of belief. The shift to affirmation presents itself in the guise of the "realist" who has denied the old gods but not the imagination that fashioned them:

> How cold the vacancy
> When the phantoms are gone and the shaken realist
> First sees reality. The mortal no
> Has its emptiness and tragic expirations.
> The tragedy, however, may have begun,
> Again, in the imagination's new beginning,
> In the yes of the realist spoken because he must
> Say yes, spoken because under every no
> Lay a passion for yes that had never been broken.

The "tragedy" of which Stevens speaks is the disappearance of the old gods, a play he had presented in "Evening Without Angels" as an antidivine comedy—"Air is air, / Its vacancy glitters round us everywhere" (*CP*, 137). If the tragedy begins again in the imagination's new beginning, it is because the imagination will of necessity fashion new gods.

The yes of the realist seems at first as if it might represent either an affirmation of normal poetry, as it does in "The Well Dressed Man with a Beard"—"Yes is this present sun"—or an affirmation of imagination in general, as it does in "Mrs. Alfred Uruguay." But canto nine defines the yes of canto eight as a preparation for another celebration of the Romantic sublime:

> Effendi, he
> That has lost the folly of the moon becomes
> The prince of the proverbs of pure poverty.
> To lose sensibility, to see what one sees,
> As if sight had not its own miraculous thrift,
> To hear only what one hears, one meaning alone,
> As if the paradise of meaning ceased
> To be paradise, it is this to be destitute.

Both Crispin and Mrs. Uruguay make this mistake, and they are consequently "comedians" who can only write a critique of paradise from sterile, positivistic principles. Stevens opposes this critique not through doctrinal counterassertion but through a sonorous exhibition of an inspiration that overwhelms the tautological perceptions of pure poverty:

> A loud, large water
> Bubbles up in the night and drowns the crickets' sound.
> It is a declaration, a primitive ecstasy,
> Truth's favors sonorously exhibited.

The loud large water is an interior fons similar to that depicted in the first stanza of "Le Monocle de Mon Oncle": "The sea of spuming thought foists up again / The radiant bubble that she was" (*CP*, 13). Both the interior fons and the "indifferent crickets" that "chant / Through our indifferent crises" signal opposing modes without defining the philosophical implications of these modes. Both images nonetheless answer to the critique in canto four. The image of indifferent crickets places the speaker beyond the sentimentalism he has criticized, and the loud large water spontaneously reasserts the vitality of the mind's engagements.

The moon that "was always free from him" and "the health of the world" offer means of escape from the suffering of individual existence. They are regions of "impersonal pain." In canto ten, Stevens repudiates any intellectual detachment that deprives him of a personal life. The "reality" Stevens depicts in the figure of the anima is at once the fat girl, terrestrial, and the ancestral subconscious seeking luminous sequences in the old peak of night:

> He had studied the nostalgias. In these
> He sought the most grossly maternal, the creature
> Who most fecundly assuaged him, the softest
> Woman with a vague moustache and not the mauve
> *Maman.* His anima like its animal
> And liked it unsubjugated, so that home
> Was a return to birth, a being born
> Again in the savagest severity,
> Desiring fiercely, the child of a mother fierce
> In his body, fiercer in his mind, merciless
> To accomplish the truth in his intelligence.

This grossly maternal figure seems very remote from "The Candle a Saint," but it is in fact a necessary emotional deepening of the archetype that is at once lover and mother. She is both an instinct of intelligence and a source of primitive ecstasy.[7] She too serves as a transcendent principle that resolves evil, not through impersonal pain, but through the savage innocence of life and death:

>   The softest woman,
> Because she is as she was, reality,
> The gross, the fecund, proved him against the touch
> Of impersonal pain. Reality explained.
> It was the last nostalgia: that he
> Should understand. That he might suffer or that
> He might die was the innocence of living, if life
> Itself was innocent. To say that it was
> Disentangled him from sleek ensolacings.

As in canto eight of "Extracts," Stevens concludes that personal guilt, the accumulated evil of individual experience, is absolved in the prospect of

---

7. For a commentary on the peculiarly Jungian character of this figure, see Doggett, *Stevens' Poetry of Thought,* 39.

death. Nostalgia is the knowledge of innocence, and "the last nostalgia" is the residuum of Romantic feeling that remains after all sentimentality has been expunged. To integrate innocence with understanding is to effect the highest synthesis of which poetry is capable, and it is this sort of synthesis that Stevens achieves in *The Auroras of Autumn*. The mother of "Owl" and "Auroras" is at once "The abstract, the archaic queen" and "An innocence of the earth" (*CP,* 418).

Like the honey of common summer, reality as "The gross, the fecund" is a selected aspect of "the universal whole." Within his cosmic vision, Stevens accords primacy to "innocence," but innocence implies evil, even if only negatively, and the necessary complement to any divine comedy is a divine tragedy. In canto thirteen of "Esthétique," Stevens redefines tragedy, after the death of Satan, as a modern recognition of fate, "the unalterable necessity / Of being this unalterable animal." In his vision of an impersonal, transumptive "universal whole," Stevens resumes the prophetic strain of "Extracts" but modulates it by recognizing the sinister implications of a fatalistic determinism. "This force of nature in action is the major / Tragedy":

> The assassin discloses himself,
> The force that destroys us is disclosed, within
> This maximum, an adventure to be endured
> With the politest helplessness. Ay-mi!
> One feels its action moving in the blood.

So long as the universal whole remains ecstatic, either as "summer, the drunken mother" (*CP,* 124), or as the folly of the moon, personal pain remains anomalous. Stevens can resolve this difference, here, only by totalizing evil. The supreme fiction will require a final affirmation of the good, but Stevens will never be able fully to reconcile the health of the world with human suffering and death. In canto nine of "Auroras," he envisions his own death "Almost as part of innocence, almost" (*CP,* 420), and the gap left by "almost" appears in canto ten as an imbalance in the final formula he selects to explain the relations between man and the universal whole: "An unhappy people in a happy world."

If "A happy people in a happy world" sounds like one of those "sleek ensolacings" from which Stevens has disentangled himself, "An unhappy people in an unhappy world" (*CP,* 420) is equally arbitrary and limiting. In the final canto of "Esthétique," Stevens escapes formulaic reduction through an appeal to all the parts of the world. This final moment of climactic resolution draws strength from a polemical opposition to the Romantic affirmations in canto nine. Stevens redefines poverty by inverting the norms in "the folly of the moon," and he repudiates "paradise" by reducing it to a negative existence. Thus, Stevens has surreptitiously implicated himself in one last fictional totalization, that of the physical. Once again, the "real" is the physical, and paradise, the unreal, occupies only the negative space of the nonphysical:

> The greatest poverty is not to live
> In a physical world, to feel that one's desire
> Is too difficult to tell from despair. Perhaps,
> After death, the non-physical people, in paradise,
> Itself non-physical, may, by chance, observe
> The green corn gleaming and experience
> The minor of what we feel. The adventurer
> In humanity has not conceived of a race
> Completely physical in a physical world.
> The green corn gleams and the metaphysicals
> Lie sprawling in majors of the August heat,
> The rotund emotions, paradise unknown.
> This is the thesis scrivened in delight,
> The reverberating psalm, the right chorale.

Despite the energy and conviction of this chorale, the doctrinal resolution does not advance beyond that in canto three. The final stanza both concedes the failure of comprehensive resolution and also expresses satisfaction at the creative power that has been displayed in the poem:

> Speech found the ear, for all the evil sound,
> But the dark italics it could not propound.
> And out of what one sees and hears and out
> Of what one feels, who could have thought to make
> So many selves, so many sensuous worlds,
> As if the air, the mid-day air, was swarming
> With the metaphysical changes that occur,
> Merely in living as and where we live.

"Monocle," though it is a more closely focused and conclusive meditation than is "Esthétique," seeks closure through a similar tactic of self-reflexive poetic celebration: "Until now I never knew / That fluttering things have so distinct a shade" (*CP*, 18). In both poems this form of closure, if not meretricious, seems external to the central issues. "Esthétique" turns away from "the dark italics it could not propound" and adopts a stance of all-embracing geniality. The completely physical world does not exclude the things of the mind; it simply reifies them as aesthetic objects among other objects. Stevens always has this option of taking a holiday in "reality," but he cannot live permanently in the sun. There are two types of poverty, and one type, the spiritual poverty in canto nine, represents the converse of this physical affluence. In canto nine, paradise is "the paradise of meaning," and since it is "paradise unknown," the "last nostalgia"—"that he / Should understand"— remains unsatisfied.

At the end of "Esthétique," Stevens poses "the dark italics" as the inaccessible code of full closure within the poem. In "Credences of Summer," he achieves closure through self-conscious limitation within "A land too ripe for enigmas." The first six cantos of "Credences" are all written in majors of the August heat and contain no dark italics. The problematic meditation on reality and artifice in cantos seven and eight complicates but does not impede the celebratory mode. Canto nine—"Fly low, cock bright, and stop on a bean pole"—shifts to a foreboding of autumnal decay, but this sinister parenthesis stands apart from both the preceding and concluding cantos. The note of foreboding appears again only once, in the last stanza—"Free, for a moment, from malice and sudden cry"—where it is enclosed between two declarations of fulfillment.

"Credences" is the richest of all Stevens' celebrations of the physical world. It is specific in its location of time and place—a farming valley in eastern Pennsylvania in the first midsummer after the war—but it absolutizes this spatiotemporal moment through a sophisticated process of exclusion: it excludes mental struggle, extension in time and space, and memory. The absolute present functions as the immediate "end" of space and time; negations become means of affirmation through definition of the actual. Stevens' first negation, of mental trouble, establishes the most important element within the poetic landscape: the state of mind that governs it. The first phase in this purification of perspective is similar to that in the process whereby Stevens isolates the first idea in "It Must Be Abstract." He requires that the mind strip itself of all relations so that he might become an ignorant man again:

> Now in midsummer come and all fools slaughtered
> And spring's infuriations over and a long way
> To the first autumnal inhalations, young broods
> Are in the grass, the roses are heavy with a weight
> Of fragrance and the mind lays by its trouble.
>
> Now the mind lays by its trouble and considers.
> The fidgets of remembrance come to this.
> This is the last day of a certain year
> Beyond which there is nothing left of time.
> It comes to this and the imagination's life.
> There is nothing more inscribed nor thought nor felt. (*CP,* 372)

The "fidgets of remembrance" lead directly to the telos of the present moment. The word *last* is echoed in the second stanza of canto four as an appositive to the language of affirmation—"full" and "pure"—a language that displays its summary term in the next-to-last line of the poem: "Complete in a completed scene." This complete rounding of the scene requires that not only the future but also the past be contained in the present. Stevens accomplishes this restriction in canto five by absorbing time within space:

> The more than casual blue
> Contains the year and other years and hymns
> And people, without souvenir.

The "more than casual blue" is at once the sky over Oley and the ideal point in space where a benign teleology of the physical world fulfills itself:

> Things stop in that direction and since they stop
> The direction stops and we accept what is
> As good. The utmost must be good and is
> And is our fortune and honey hived in the trees
> And mingling of colors at a festival.

This teleology, though it is expressed in objective terms, depends on the discipline of the observer. He must exercise a rigorous exclusion of any movement away from what is sensually given:

> And fill the foliage with arrested peace,
> Joy of such permanence, right ignorance
> Of change still possible. Exile desire

> For what is not. This is the barrenness
> Of the fertile thing that can attain no more.

The reward for this discipline is the vivid precision of the imagery through which Stevens symbolizes his delight in concrete reality:

> It is the visible rock, the audible,
> The brilliant mercy of a sure repose,
> On this present ground, the vividest repose,
> Things certain sustaining us in certainty.
>
> It is the rock of summer, the extreme,
> A mountain luminous half way in bloom
> And then half way in the extremest light
> Of sapphires flashing from the central sky,
> As if twelve princes sat before a king.

This is "the final mountain," and the fulfillment of its potential bears a weight of paradox that generates Stevens' meditation on the problematic character of his artifice in cantos seven and eight. Stevens has exhorted himself to "Trace the gold sun about the whitened sky / Without evasion by a single metaphor," and he reaches the culmination of his celebratory hymn in the region of high artifice. The "sapphires flashing from the central sky" and the mythic emblem of the king are close kin to the imagery with which Stevens gives form to the Romantic sublime.

Although "Credences" remains within the realm of normal poetry, it represents a particularly refined and self-reflexive form of the normal. Stevens' affirmations by way of negations are all "for the moment"; they explicitly concede the transience of their absolutes and implicitly concede the potential infinitude of all the finite designations of space and time that create this limited, fictive absolute. Pure and normal poetry imply each other, and at its highest reach, pure poetry not only implies but also contains normal poetry. As Stevens says, the supreme fiction is "a source of poetry" (*LWS*, 485); "The essential poem at the centre of things" is "something seen and known in lesser poems" (*CP*, 440), including poems such as "Credences."

The hierarchical relation between pure and normal poetry finds a concise symbolic representation in "From the Packet of Anacharsis" (1946). This poem begins as a narrative in the "Credences" mode. Anacharsis himself, who drops out of the poem after the second stanza, may be taken as another incarnation of "the old man standing on the tower" (*CP*, 374) who embodies the perspective of "Credences":

> In his packet Anacharsis found the lines:
> "The farm was fat and the land in which it lay
> Seemed in the morning like a holiday."
>
> He had written them near Athens. The farm was white.
> The buildings were of marble and stood in marble light.
> It was his clarity that made the vista bright. (*CP*, 365–66)

In the third stanza and the first line of the fourth stanza, the narrative perspective shifts from Anacharsis and divides itself polemically between Puvis the painter (1824–1898) and Bloom, a proponent of "the fat, the roseate characters" of summer:

> A subject for Puvis. He would compose
> The scene in his gray-rose with violet rocks.
> And Bloom would see what Puvis did, protest
> And speak of the floridest reality . . .

Bloom's protest implies that the scene Puvis composes is dialectically opposed to "the floridest reality." In the next line the poet speaks out in his own voice and corrects Bloom's error. There is no mutually exclusive opposition between a central composition and all the particulars of reality. Relation contains difference; the pure idea precedes and generates the articulations of definite form:

> In the punctual centre of all circles white
> Stands truly. The circles nearest to it share
>
> Its color, but less as they recede, impinged
> By difference and then by definition
> As a tone defines itself and separates
>
> And the circles quicken and crystal colors come
> And flare and Bloom with his vast accumulation
> Stands and regards and repeats the primitive lines.

The center of the circle is a symbol of closure. The whiteness at the center of all circles functions as a natural metaphoric synonym for the pure idea: "The premiss from which all things were conclusions." (In "Owl" the whiteness that is seen in "the height / Of sleep" becomes "the whiteness that is the ultimate intellect" [*CP,* 433].) Diamonds and crystals have served Stevens as symbols within pure and normal poetry. By designating "white" as the source of "crystal colors," Stevens subordinates the pluralistic usage of crystals to the idea of essential unity. The metaphor of a tone that "defines itself and separates" draws on the "inaccessible, pure sound" in "Montrachet" and the "variations in the tones of a single sound" in "Esthétique." Stevens has synthesized a homogeneous complex of metaphors—of geometric form, color, and sound—to declare the originative, primary status of pure poetry.

Stevens' use of the words *centre* and *central* can be confusing, for there are two separate applications of the metaphor, one adapted to normal poetry and the other to pure poetry. It is the former application Stevens has in mind when, in 1940, he explains why he has delayed in his quest for "a new romanticism." "People say that I live in a world of my own: that sort of thing. Instead of seeking therefore for a 'relentless contact', I have been interested in what might be described as an attempt to achieve the normal, the central. . . . Of course, I don't agree with the people who say that I live in a world of my own; I think that I am perfectly normal, but I see that there is a center. For instance, a photograph of a lot of fat men and women in the woods, drinking beer and singing Hi-li Hi-lo convinces me that there is a normal that I ought to try to achieve" (*LWS,* 352). In "The Glass of Water" (1940), Stevens contrasts the imaginative activity exemplified by his meditation on "the plastic parts of poems" with the contemporary distractions of the normal world: "in the centre of our lives . . . this spring among the politicians" (*CP,* 198). In "Effects of Analogy," Stevens uses the term *a central poetry* as a synonym for the poetry of normal life. He describes "two theories" of poetry. The first is transcendental, and the poet who embraces it seeks to live "on the verge of consciousness" (*NA,* 115). The adherent of the second theory, in contrast, seeks "to have such insights into reality as will make it possible for him to be sufficient as a poet in the very center of consciousness."

The other type of center, "The essential poem at the centre of things," is the "white" source for all other centers. In his prose, Stevens illustrates this concept both with Pascal's "'sphère dont le centre est partout et la circonférence est nulle part'" (*OP,* 194) and with Shelley's "'centre and circumference of knowledge'" (*NA,* 44). In "The Relations Between Poetry and Painting" (1950–1951), Stevens approvingly quotes Klee's description of the "'chosen'" one who "'today comes near to the secret places where original law fosters all evolution. And what artist would not establish himself there where the organic center of all movement in time and space—which he calls the mind or heart of creation—determines every function'" (*NA*, 174). Klee's "'organic center of all movement'" recalls "The organic centre of responses" in "Examination of the Hero" (*CP*, 279), the "muddy centre before we breathed" in "Notes," the "central heart and mind of minds" in "Extracts," and "The centre of transformations that / Transform for transformation's self" in "Human Arrangement" (1946; *CP*, 363). All these metaphors are approximations of what, in "Two Versions of the Same Poem" (1946), Stevens calls *that which cannot be fixed*:

> A beating and a beating in the centre of
> The sea, a strength that tumbles everywhere,
>
> Like more and more becoming less and less,
> Like space dividing its blue and by division
> Being changed from space to the sailor's metier. (*CP*, 354)

In this figuration the blue of space stands in place of the white center as the original essence that precedes differentiation. (In "Owl" the whiteness is "folded into less" [*CP*, 433].) The "sailor's metier," that complex of impressions and responses that constitutes his experience of the sea, stands in place of the "crystal colors" that in "Anacharsis" figure the emergence of definite form from the white center.

Both "Anacharsis" and "Two Versions" contribute to Stevens' complex figurative rationale for the supreme fiction, but neither poem offers any figuration of the dynamic process through which essential unity resolves itself into the world of phenomena and this world, in turn, fashions for itself a fiction of essential unity. Both the white center and space dividing its blue imply some sort of substratum, a stubborn conceptual residuum inherited from "The Curtains in the House of the Metaphysician." Stevens manages to dissolve this residuum only in those poems that subsume the concepts of phenomenal generation and sentient relation within highly pluralized mythopoeic figurations—poems such as "Owl," "Auroras," and "Primitive."

In "Anacharsis," by reducing the idea of pure poetry to the image of the white center, Stevens achieves the effect of definitive revelation. "The Pure Good of Theory" (1945) concludes in a similar fashion, and it situates this conclusion more explicitly in the context of a poetic enterprise. Stevens depicts metaphoric activity as an autonomous force that is motivated by the need for completion:

> The need of its element, the final need
> Of final access to its element—
> Of access like the page of a wiggy book,
>
> Touched suddenly by the universal flare
> For a moment, a moment in which we read and repeat
> The eloquence of light's faculties. (*CP*, 333)

Light, the term of resolution, is yet another metaphoric equivalent for "white" and "undivided space." The repeated words *final* and *element* connect the ideas of telos and essence, and the image of the book defines the intellective character of this teleological essence. The phrase "Touched suddenly" signals a moment of revelation and confirmation within this element.

The metaphor of the book often serves Stevens as a figure of the spiritual life. In "Credences," "the old man standing on the tower" of summer "reads no book" (*CP*, 374), and in "The Good Man Has No Shape" (1946), Stevens uses a variation of this metaphor to satirize the spiritual emptiness of the "good life" (*CP*, 364). "They placed with him in his grave / Sour wine to warm him, an empty book to read." In both "The Reader" and "Phosphor Reading by His Own Light," the night becomes a book, and in "Phosphor" the green night teaches "a fusky alphabet." In the first poem in *Transport*, "God Is Good. It Is a Beautiful Night" (1942), the holy text of pure poetry appears simply as "the book": "the head is speaking. It reads the book. / It becomes the scholar again, seeking celestial / Rendezvous" (*CP*, 285). The kind of rendezvous Stevens has in mind reveals itself in "The House Was Quiet and the World Was Calm" (1945). In this poem the book, a literal book, becomes the focal point for a spiritual meditation in which the scholar and the book merge with the night and become the medium for its self-realization:

> The house was quiet and the world was calm.
> The reader became the book; and summer night
>
> Was like the conscious being of the book.
> The house was quiet and the world was calm.
>
> The words were spoken as if there was no book,
> Except that the reader leaned above the page,
>
> Wanted to lean, wanted much most to be
> The scholar to whom his book is true, to whom
>
> The summer night is like a perfection of thought.
> The house was quiet because it had to be.

> The quiet was part of the meaning, part of the mind:
> The access of perfection to the page. (*CP*, 358)

Within the fictive construct of this meditation, there is no personal and individual origin of thought. The words rise "in speech we do not speak" as a completed telos of "That elemental parent, the green night."

"The House Was Quiet" depicts with fine lyric concision the synthetic process through which the poet and language both become integral components of essential imagination. In "Chocorua to Its Neighbor" (1943), Stevens attempts for the first time an elaborate mythic figuration of this process. In stanzas eight and twelve of "Chocorua," he touches on the elegiac sublime of "Owl" and "Auroras," but the dominant tone of the poem, as in "Primitive," is eulogistic exposition. Like "Owl" and "Auroras," "Chocorua" presents itself as a dramatic narrative, but despite the fairly complicated narrative scheme, the poem has no genuinely dramatic, sequential development, and its mythic subject, a "Cloud-casual, metaphysical metaphor" (*CP*, 301), lacks the substantial identity of the characters in "Owl." "Chocorua" nonetheless constructs or reconstructs one of those special moments of genuine mystical illumination that form the experiential base for the mythological figurations of "Owl" and "Auroras." In these latter poems, Stevens will retain the capacity, exercised in "Chocorua," for an intentionally ambiguous multiplicity of metaphysical reference, but he will deploy this multiplicity within more fully articulated mythic structures.

The speaker in "Chocorua," though a persona for the poet, is not a human being. Chocorua is a mountain in New Hampshire, and the neighbor to whom he speaks is, presumably, a neighboring mountain, though the recipient of Chocorua's address may also be, and is, the reader.[8] The subject of Chocorua's discourse is an epiphany to which he has been witness:

> At the end of night last night a crystal star,
> The crystal-pointed star of morning, rose
> And lit the snow to a light congenial
> To this prodigious shadow, who then came
> In an elemental freedom, sharp and cold. (*CP*, 296–97)

---

8. Roy Harvey Pearce identifies a contributing source for "Chocorua" in Henry James's *The American Scene* (see "The Cry and the Occasion: 'Chocorua to Its Neighbor,'" *Southern Review*, n.s., XV [1979], 777–91). For a good, sympathetic reading of "Chocorua" as an exercise in the sublime, see Bloom, *The Poems of Our Climate*, 222–25.

The words *last night,* which Chocorua twice repeats (stanzas sixteen and twenty-five), function as an adverbial signal of specific historical narrative. These indirect assertions of narrative factuality, linked with the historical past tense, reinforce Chocorua's direct assertions of the real presence of the figure he describes. (Between stanzas nineteen and twenty-four, Chocorua shifts into the present tense of general, descriptive exposition.)

Chocorua's descriptions of the shadow demonstrate the way in which separate but related motifs can fuse themselves into a single mythic organism. In stanza five, Chocorua presents several metaphors to describe the shadow, and in stanza six he synthesizes these terms within a dramatically personified image:

> He was a shell of dark blue glass, or ice,
> Or air collected in a deep essay,
> Or light embodied, or almost, a flash
> On more than muscular shoulders, arms and chest,
> Blue's last transparence as it turned to black,
>
> VI
>
> The glitter of a being, which the eye
> Accepted yet which nothing understood,
> A fusion of night, its blue of the pole of blue
> And of the brooding mind, fixed but for a slight
> Illumination of movement as he breathed.

The metaphors that commingle to fashion this mythic entity draw their connotative power in part from the other poems in which they appear. As a fusion of night and mind, the shadow yields a positive synthesis of the negative polar extremes explored by the Canon Aspirin. The metaphor of breath as a symbol of unification dominates the climax of "Montrachet." The flash connects the image of light to the matrix of time in "Martial Cadenza"—"time flashed again." Like the shadow, time symbolizes that which lives but transcends all individual life: "the ever-living and being, / The ever-breathing and moving, the constant fire" (*CP,* 238). In "The Candle a Saint," the "essential shadow" is "Moving and being." Transparence, associated with light, appears in "Owl's Clover" as an emblem of the spirit, and in "Asides on the Oboe" transparence is attributed to "the man of glass" who "in a million diamonds sums us up." All of these associations converge in the last line of stanza six to fashion a mythic figure that has no concrete form beyond the fluctuations of light that embody the organic breath of the spirit.

The image of breathing becomes the pivotal motif of the poem. Through this motif, Chocorua implicitly delineates the shadow's ambiguous ontological status. In stanzas eight and nine, the phrase "he breathed" introduces an exposition of the shadow's paradoxical mode of existence and an evocation of the generic qualities associated with it. In stanzas twenty-two and twenty-three, the shadow's breath becomes the breath of those for whom he is a living presence, and this transmutation reveals the kind of power he exercises in human experience. As a fusion of night and the brooding mind, the shadow occupies no definite locus within the parts of the world. He is a creature of the night, but only because he is a symbol of the poetic mode that defines itself in opposition to the segregative consciousness of day:

> Upon my top he breathed the pointed dark.
> He was not man yet he was nothing else.
> If in the mind, he vanished, taking there
> The mind's own limits, like a tragic thing
> Without existence, existing everywhere.
>
> IX
>
> He breathed in crystal-pointed change the whole
> Experience of night, as if he breathed
> A consciousness from solitude, inhaled
> A freedom out of silver-shaping size,
> Against the whole experience of day.

The shadow exists in reciprocal dependency with the human. He comes into being by breathing in the "Experience of night," an experience that originates in a human consciousness. In turn, a human being who breathes in his presence achieves the mystical integration that is the object of Stevens' visionary quest:

> Cloud-casual, metaphysical metaphor,
> But resting on me, thinking in my snow,
> Physical if the eye is quick enough,
> So that, where he was, there is an enkindling, where
> He is, the air changes and grows fresh to breathe.
>
> XXIII
>
> The air changes, creates and re-creates, like strength,
> And to breathe is a fulfilling of desire,
> A clearing, a detecting, a completing,

> A largeness lived and not conceived, a space
> That is an instant nature, brilliantly.

In "Of Bright and Blue Birds," Stevens speaks of a similar moment of integration, "A gaiety that is being, not merely knowing" (*CP,* 248), and associates it with the ideal of a total grandeur: "To be and to be total in belief." In "Martial Cadenza" he formulates the idea of "A largeness lived and not conceived" as "the present realized, / Not the symbol but that for which the symbol stands." The shadow is a mythic realization of what Stevens calls "the perfection of thought"; if the shadow is "lived," thought itself has come to life and has ceased to be merely an activity of the individual mind.

Through the shadow, Stevens attempts to give mythic form to what, in his commentary on "Notes," he calls "a possibly more than human human" (*LWS,* 434), and his representation of the shadow involves itself in the equivocations attendant on this formulation. In stanza fourteen he declares that the shadow arises out of a collective human need. "He rose because men wanted him to be":

> They wanted him by day to be, image,
> But not the person, of their power, thought,
> But not the thinker, large in their largeness, beyond
> Their form, beyond their life, yet of themselves,
> Excluding by his largeness their defaults.

The needs the shadow comes to satisfy are the same as those that in "The Man with the Blue Guitar" the mass of men demand be satisfied by poetry; they require "A tune beyond us, yet ourselves" (*CP,* 165). "Thought" must exist independently of "the thinker" and yet must involve the thinker in its own essence. Accordingly, in stanzas ten through twelve, Chocorua quotes the shadow's own speech, and in this speech the shadow presents himself as a transcendent spirit that contains its human creator:

>   He said,
> "The moments of enlargement overlook
> The enlarging of the simplest soldier's cry
> In what I am, as he falls. Of what I am,
>   XI
> The cry is part. My solitaria
> Are the meditations of a central mind.

> I hear the motions of the spirit and the sound
> Of what is secret becomes, for me, a voice
> That is my own voice speaking in my ear."

The voice that is his own voice speaking in his ear recalls the epiphany of "Montrachet-Le-Jardin," in which "To-night, night's undeciphered murmuring / Comes close to the prisoner's ear" (*CP,* 261), and prefigures the epiphany of "The Owl in the Sarcophagus," in which the earthly mother and the mother of the dead "speaks, because the ear repeats, / Without a voice, inventions of farewell" (*CP,* 432). The "central mind" is at once the mind of the poet who stands naked at "The organic centre of responses" and also the "mind of minds" that is identical with "the pure idea" (*CP,* 279, 254, 256).

Because of his paradoxical mode of existence—"like a tragic thing / Without existence, existing everywhere"—the shadow as pure presence constantly threatens to invert himself into pure absence. He is ontologically tenuous, and it is apparently this condition that generates his tragic plaint in stanza twelve:

> "There lies the misery, the coldest coil
> That grips the centre, the actual bite, that life
> Itself is like a poverty in the space of life,
> So that the flapping of wind around me here
> Is something in tatters that I cannot hold."

In "The Sense of the Sleight-of-Hand Man," Stevens had suggested that possibly "the ignorant man, alone, / Has any chance to mate his life with life" (*CP,* 222). The shadow maintains that he is himself "a central mind"—a designation antithetical both to ignorance and to human limitation—and he also implies that he is himself "life." He nonetheless evokes a tragic moment in which the visionary mythology reveals a central emptiness. The startling declaration that "life / Itself is like a poverty in the space of life" comes very close to the bleak metaphysical irony of "The American Sublime," in which the sublime comes down to "The empty spirit / In vacant space" (*CP,* 131). In many of the poems written between 1950 and his death in 1955, Stevens will explore the nuances of a tragic or ironic inversion of the Romantic sublime, but his counterpointing of "The romantic intoning, the declaimed clairvoyance" and the negative sublime is never more pronounced than in "Chocorua."

In "Notes," Stevens says that the candor of the first idea is "An elixir, an excitation, a pure power" that "gives a candid kind to everything" (*CP*, 382). In stanza twenty-two of "Chocorua," the shadow, as a late plural of the first idea, has this effect: "So that, where he was, there is an enkindling, where / He is, the air changes and grows fresh to breathe." The shadow is himself what Stevens calls "this leaner being moving in on us," but he is also a self-conscious intelligence; he falls short of the complete synthesis of being and knowing represented by the earthly mother and the mother of the dead in "Owl." Stevens depicts the earthly mother as "losing in self / The sense of self" (*CP*, 435), but the shadow retains a sense of a distinct self, and, what is worse, a self alienated from the phenomenal world around him.

Chocorua resolutely refuses to elaborate on the nature of the "poverty" he evokes. "In spite of this, the gigantic bulk of him / Grew strong, as if doubt never touched his heart." Echoing the tone and phrasing of Blake's "Tyger," Chocorua asks,

> Of what was this the force? From what desire
> And from what thinking did his radiance come?
> In what new spirit had his body birth?

In stanza nineteen, in order to buttress the shadow's strength, Chocorua repudiates any problematic reference to the transcendental:

> To say more than human things with human voice,
> That cannot be; to say human things with more
> Than human voice, that, also, cannot be;
> To speak humanly from the height or from the depth
> Of human things, that is acutest speech.

In "The Noble Rider," Stevens says that the "inherent nobility" of the imagination "is the natural source of another, which our extremely headstrong generation regards as false and decadent. I mean that nobility which is our spiritual height and depth" (*NA*, 33–34). In the word *false*, Stevens touches on the problematic center of the supreme fiction: the transumptive moment in which the leaner being detaches itself from its human creator. At this moment an abyss opens up between the "extension" and "recognition" of "this leaner being moving in on us," and "the act," the autonomous movement, of this leaner being (*LWS*, 434). By excluding the speech of apotheosis, Stevens evades this central problem, but this reassuring exclusion is deceptive, or at least temporary, for it precedes the stanzas in which the shadow, again as a transcendent presence, serves as the medium in which breathing "is a fulfilling of desire, / A clearing, a detecting, a completing." In stanza twenty-five, Chocorua reiterates the awed description of the shadow's first manifestation of himself in stanza three, and he reaffirms both the shadow's mythic actuality as a real presence and his independent will:

> Last night at the end of night and in the sky,
> The lesser night, the less than morning light,
> Fell on him, high and cold, searching for what
> Was native to him in that height, searching
> The pleasure of his spirit in the cold.

The pleasure of the shadow's spirit is to achieve figurations of itself as the end of thought, the regal telos in the landscape of the mind. In the final stanza of the poem, Chocorua reduces the shadow's mythic stature to a human scale but leaves his ontological status in equivocal suspense:

> How singular he was as man, how large,
> If nothing more than that, for the moment, large
> In my presence, the companion of presences
> Greater than mine, of his demanding, head
> And, of human realizings, rugged roy . . .

That aspect of the shadow that has been depicted as the disembodied, autonomous spirit of poetic realization—a perfecting of thought that is also the self-perfecting of time and space—now appears to merge with the man who is the thinker of the first idea. This man, as "the companion of presences" greater than Chocorua, associates the shadow with those elemental forces that will ultimately evolve into "the forms of thought" in "The Owl in the Sarcophagus." In "The Auroras of Autumn," Stevens' visionary protagonist will seek to occupy the throne of a supreme imagination and will be cast down before the power of this "imagination that sits enthroned" (*CP,* 417). As the "rugged roy" of "human realizings," the shadow of "Chocorua" is a direct ancestor of this primary imagination.

Chocorua's declarations about the merely human character of the shadow correspond to the fourth, unwritten section of "Notes Toward a Supreme Fiction." In a letter of 1954, Stevens says that "for a long time, I have thought of adding other sections to the NOTES and one in particular: *It Must Be Human.* But I think that it would be wrong not to leave well enough alone"

(*LWS*, 863–64). This emphasis on the human must be balanced against and ultimately synthesized with its implied complement: *It Must Be Inhuman*. In "Less and Less Human, O Savage Spirit" (1944), Stevens concedes the necessity of some kind of god and establishes the conditions under which its presence will be tolerable to him:

> If there must be a god in the house, must be,
> Saying things in the rooms and on the stair,
>
> Let him move as the sunlight moves on the floor,
> Or moonlight, silently, as Plato's ghost
>
> Or Aristotle's skeleton. Let him hang out
> His stars on the wall. He must dwell quietly.
>
> He must be incapable of speaking, closed,
> As those are: as light, for all its motion, is;
>
> As color, even the closest to us, is;
> As shapes, though they portend us, are.
>
> It is the human that is the alien,
> The human that has no cousin in the moon. (*CP*, 327–28)

In "Montrachet," Stevens says "Amen to thought, our singular skeleton," and in "Anacharsis" and "Two Versions of the Same Poem" he fleshes out this abstraction in basic perceptual terms of light, color, and shape. By allowing this god to "hang out / His stars on the wall," Stevens identifies it with the night, not here as an elemental parent, but as a cousin in the moon. As in "Blue Guitar" and "Esthétique," the moon remains "apart," alien to the human, but not to poetry.[9]

In "Less and Less Human," Stevens' repudiation of the human and his drive to the abstract receive their most extreme formulation. The problematic one-sidedness of this formulation signals itself in the word *closed*. A completely closed god has no point of contact with the human. Although at first he appears as "Saying things," he quickly becomes incapable both of speech and hearing:

> It is the human that demands his speech
> From beasts or from the incommunicable mass.

---

9. The initial propositions in Thomas Weiskel's discussion of the Romantic sublime situate themselves at a point close to that of "Less and Less Human" (see *The Romantic Sublime: Studies in the Structure and Psychology of Transcendence* [Baltimore, 1976], 3).

> If there must be a god in the house, let him be one
> That will not hear us when we speak: a coolness,
>
> A vermilioned nothingness, any stick of the mass
> Of which we are too distantly a part.

By restricting epiphany to inarticulate sensation, Stevens appears to be excluding his god from the "paradise of meaning," but the designation "A vermilioned nothingness" is no simple negation. In "Primitive" the "skeleton of the ether" is also the "giant of nothingness" that is the generative center of phenomena. In "Owl" the vermilioned nothingness divides itself between the mother, "rosed out of prestiges / Of rose," and peace after death, "An immaculate personage in nothingness." The mother says good-bye to the dying, for whom death is a "motion outward, reddened and resolved / From sight." The mythic figures of "Owl," though they are inhuman, are also the constituents of "parental space." Elemental abstraction and archetypal pathos converge in the realizations of pure poetry.

Almost all the poems in *Transport to Summer* are in one sense or another conscious preparations for the celestial rendezvous Stevens knows he will not fail to keep. In "Of Ideal Time and Choice" (1946–1947), Stevens asks, rhetorically, of what "the final choice" will consist, and in his answer he yields primacy to an autonomous transcendental spirit:

> And what heroic nature of what text
> Shall be the celebration in the words
> Of that oration, the happiest sense in which
>
> A world agrees, thought's compromise, resolved
> At last, the center of resemblance, found
> Under the bones of time's philosophers?
>
> The orator will say that we ourselves
> Stand at the center of ideal time,
> The inhuman making choice of a human self. (*NA*, 89)

The "center of resemblance" is the self-generating field of metaphoric relations. The apposition of "we ourselves" and "The inhuman" locates this center of ideal time at the exact point of intersection between essential imagination and the human self that both creates and is created by this imagination. In *Transport*, Stevens achieves the "breadth" that he says is "the first necessity" of a supreme fiction (*LWS*, 435). The task of *Auroras* will be to synthesize this breadth and to bring all the parts of the world within the closed circle of the transcendental imagination:

> Not merely into a whole, but a poem of
> The whole, the essential compact of the parts,
> The roundness that pulls tight the final ring. (*CP,* 442)

CHAPTER SIX

The Essential Poem

The Forms of Thought

Stevens' declarations that "The prologues are over" and that "It is time to choose" a "final belief" begin as early as 1940 (*CP,* 250). The preparation has been long and of long intent, and by 1947, Stevens has become intensely impatient with the delay of his visionary fulfillment. In "The Ultimate Poem Is Abstract" (1947), which was written after "Of Ideal Time and Choice" and before "The Owl in the Sarcophagus," the frustration to which Stevens gives voice suggests that he is now ready for those violences which are the maturity of his desires:

> If the day writhes, it is not with revelations.
> One goes on asking questions. That, then, is one
> Of the categories. So said, this placid space
>
> Is changed. It is not so blue as we thought. To be blue,
> There must be no questions. It is an intellect
> Of windings round and dodges to and fro,
>
> Writhings in wrong obliques and distances,
> Not an intellect in which we are fleet: present
> Everywhere in space at once, cloud-pole
>
> Of communication. It would be enough
> If we were ever, just once, at the middle, fixed
> In This Beautiful World Of Ours and not as now,
>
> Helplessly at the edge, enough to be
> Complete, because at the middle, if only in sense,
> And in that enormous sense, merely enjoy. (*CP,* 429–30)

The ultimate poem would participate in that instant gaiety that transforms itself into "The will to be and to be total in belief" (*CP*, 248). It would achieve the state Stevens anticipates in "Description Without Place," a state in which "observing is completing and we are content, / In a world that shrinks to an immediate whole" (*CP*, 341). Stevens' hypothetical figuration of the ultimate poem draws on a passage from "The Over-Soul" that has already been partially quoted in reference to "It Must Be Abstract." Emerson declares that "the heart which abandons itself to the Supreme Mind finds itself related to all its works" and that "in ascending to this primary and aboriginal sentiment we have come from our remote station on the circumference instantaneously to the centre of the world, where, as in the closet of God, we see causes, and anticipate the universe, which is but a slow effect" (*RWE*, II, 276).[1] Stevens' "ascent into heaven" has been the work of a lifetime, and his realization of "the ultimate poetic idea" (*OP*, 193) carries the accumulated force of all his preliminary exercises. In "The Owl in the Sarcophagus," "The Auroras of Autumn," and "A Primitive Like an Orb," he finally achieves that enormous sense of completion within "The essential poem at the centre of things."

The climactic phase of Stevens' visionary enterprise begins in April of 1947 with the sudden death of Henry Church. "Notes Toward a Supreme Fiction" had been dedicated to Church, and he was clearly the friend Stevens valued most. Stevens wrote to Church's widow that "The Owl in the Sarcophagus" was "written in the frame of mind that followed Mr. Church's death. While it is not personal, I had thought of inscribing it somehow, below the title, as, for example, Goodbye H.C." (*LWS*, 566). The pathos of Church's sudden death releases Stevens' drive to a definitive mythic formulation of the supreme fiction. "Auroras" and "Primitive," along with some of the shorter poems of the same period, are reflexes of the same impulse that generates "Owl." "Auroras," written later in 1947, recapitulates the whole course of Stevens' visionary enterprise. "Primitive," written early in 1948, fulfills the need for a direct theoretical exposition of the supreme fiction. Together, these three poems answer to Stevens' conception of an imagination "that seeks to satisfy, say, the universal mind" and that "tries to penetrate to basic images, basic emotions, and so to compose a fundamental poetry even older than the ancient world" (*NA*, 145).

1. For a different view on the relation between this passage and "The Ultimate Poem," see La Guardia, *Advance on Chaos*, 111–12.

The transcendental resolutions in the major visionary poems of *Auroras* take place within an "element" outside time. The poems themselves nonetheless appear at a definite moment in Stevens' own life, and the realization of his visionary purpose itself entails a problem for him. In *Parts of a World* and *Transport to Summer,* all Stevens' imaginative efforts are subsumed within a single, overriding purpose, the creation of a supreme fiction. Once that fiction has been given a definitive form, the anticipation of fulfillment must yield to wistful retrospection. The sense of visionary fulfillment can sometimes be revived, but the future still comes to appear as an episode of belatedness, an episode that will conclude in oblivion. Even in his highest moments of visionary realization, Stevens' fear of personal extinction cannot be entirely sublimated within the contemplation of essential unity, and in the poems that follow "Primitive" he becomes almost morbidly sensitive to the sinister implications of his "mythology of modern death" (*CP,* 435). "An Ordinary Evening in New Haven" and "Things of August" (both 1949), the longest of the later poems in *Auroras,* represent Stevens' most exhaustive efforts to come to terms with this new phase of his life. In "New Haven" he struggles without success to free himself from his dependence on the figurations of the past, and in "August" he confirms the definitive significance these figurations must have for him.

"The Owl in the Sarcophagus" represents the fullest articulation and the highest synthesis of Stevens' visionary themes and motifs. It is one of Stevens' most complex and difficult poems, but it is also one of his most passionate. Through the creation of three mythic figures—sleep, peace after death, and the mother of the living and the dead—Stevens fashions a cosmological vision that includes and transcends space and time. The poem attempts to figure forth the imperceptible and the inconceivable, and it is thus necessarily written in a mode charged with ambiguity and paradox. At the same time, it is one of the most carefully constructed of Stevens' visionary poems. The locus of the poem, the place or "element" of its transcendental mythology, is established in the first two strophes. The next three strophes each describe one of the three mythic figures. The final strophe serves as a critical coda that situates the poem within the mythology it has itself created.

The first two stanzas of strophe one are a rhetorical unit, an introduction to the land of the dead and the three figures who inhabit it. The tone of quiet sublimity is established both through simple repetitions and variations of the words *high* and *quiet* and through carefully patterned enjambments and caesuras:

> Two forms move among the dead, high sleep
> Who by his highness quiets them, high peace
> Upon whose shoulders even the heavens rest,
>
> Two brothers. And a third form, she that says
> Good-by in the darkness, speaking quietly there,
> To those that cannot say good-by themselves. (*CP,* 431)

By designating the actions of these figures before giving any explicit definition of their qualities, Stevens removes them from the realm of allegorical abstraction and endows them with mythic life. Sleep and peace "move among the dead." Sleep "quiets" them, and the third form "speaks" to them. The most obviously allegorical designation, peace as "peace after death," is not explicitly made until strophe four, at which point the static abstraction is counterbalanced by a detailed mythic figuration. For the present, the representation of peace emphasizes that he is not just a condition of death but a substantial personage, "Upon whose shoulders even the heavens rest." All three figures are given sexual identity and the first two are further personified through their fraternal relationship. The third figure is not even named in the introduction, and so is presented first not as an idea but as a dynamic living agent. She is set apart from peace and sleep by syntactic grouping, by sex, and by her faculty of speech. These distinctions create a certain suspense, an expectation that Stevens will elaborate on the relations among these characters. Since there will be no direct dramatic interaction, this expectation will be diverted to the association of themes and images among the separate descriptions of each figure.

The next three stanzas form another rhetorical unit, held together by interlocking anaphora, metrical repetition, and pronominal reference:

> These forms are visible to the eye that needs,
> Needs out of the whole necessity of sight.
> The third form speaks, because the ear repeats,
>
> Without a voice, inventions of farewell.
> These forms are not abortive figures, rocks,
> Impenetrable symbols, motionless. They move

About the night. They live without our light,
In an element not the heaviness of time,
In which reality is prodigy.

The two stanzas of introduction have functioned as simple description that conveys an implicit fictional belief in what is described. The next three stanzas shift to assertive explication, the presentation of evidence, and the drawing of conclusions from that evidence. The implication of the statement "These forms are visible to the eye that needs" is that the forms are visible *because* the eye needs to see them. The "whole necessity of sight" can mean either the necessity or urgency one feels to see the figures, or the necessity of seeing that is intrinsic to the faculty of sight itself. The ambiguity here, between necessity as human desire and as the nature of things, is intentional. It suggests that there is no conflict between need and truth, but that there is a human need to discover a necessary order. This ambiguity is developed in the next two lines. These lines could be taken to mean that the ear, in repeating inventions of farewell (variations on *good-by*), compels the third form to speak, that is, that subjective need creates an objective correlative, effect (hearing) precedes cause (speech). The statement could also be taken as a logical deduction: *We know the third form speaks because we hear our own repetitions of her speech, and we know that the ear itself has no voice.* Taken together, these two readings imply that there is a correspondence between need and the order it discovers. The following lines confirm this reading and extend its claim to all three figures. The four negative assertions—"not abortive figures, rocks, / Impenetrable symbols, motionless"—establish the authenticity of the figures. Abortive figures would be freaks of fancy that attain no true life, and so would be motionless. Rocks and impenetrable symbols would be abortive figures when *figures* are taken to mean tropes or figures of speech. The defense of the figures is at the same time a defense of their figuration in the poem. The sentence "They move / About the night" gives the evidence for the figures' authenticity. It draws on the implicit belief in the description in the first two stanzas, where we are told that the forms "move among the dead." Thus, in the space of five stanzas, the poem has established a mode of internal reference and verification. What has already been said in the poem may be used to verify the truth of what is or will be said.

The syntactic parallelism of "They move" and "They live" designates these two sentences as functionally equal; they give evidence for the authenticity of the three forms. The second sentence, however, adds new information about the three figures. Like the first sentence, it draws on the introductory stanzas for support, but instead of merely repeating the information contained in them ("They move"), it draws out implications and establishes conditions not self-evident in the introduction. The "dead" of stanza one might at first appear as a Homeric gathering of shades on some nebulous bank in the underworld. We are now told that the region inhabited by these three figures exists in a nontemporal element alien to human perception. The "night" is not just an earthly night, but the absence of any possibility of light or vision. The information "They live without our light" retroactively renders problematical the assertion that these forms are visible to the eye that needs. *Sight* is distanced from visual perception and thus necessarily becomes *insight* or intellectual perception. The three forms "move" in a region accessible only to thought or intuition.

This same rhetorical technique of variation and development within a series of syntactically equivalent phrases appears again in the three phrases modifying "They live." These three modifiers all seem only to give detailed information, but there is a crucial semantic shift between the two negatives— not light, not time—and the affirmative, "In which reality is prodigy." The first two phrases set off the mythical realm *from* reality as a distinct area. The third phrase suddenly brings reality *into* the seemingly alien realm, includes it and subordinates it. From the perspective of ordinary reality, these three figures appear to be prodigies: extraordinary, marvelous, monstrous. From their own perspective, and that of the poet as owl or bird of wisdom inside the sarcophagus, among the dead, it is ordinary reality, with its space, time, and light, that is prodigious.

The last three stanzas of the first strophe are formed out of two sentences. The last sentence is syntactically disjunctive and can be taken as a commentary on the whole strophe:

> There sleep the brother is the father, too,
> And peace is cousin by a hundred names
> And she that in the syllable between life
>
> And death cries quickly, in a flash of voice,
> Keep you, keep you, I am gone, oh keep you as
> My memory, is the mother of us all,
>
> The earthly mother and the mother of
> The dead. Only the thought of those dark three
> Is dark, thought of the forms of dark desire.

In the sentence beginning "There," we are again given three syntactically equivalent units the third of which displays a significant development in meaning: "There sleep . . . is . . . / And peace is . . . / And she . . . / . . . is." The "she" who is the third form is set off from the other two, as she was in the introductory stanzas, by sex and function. Sleep and peace are given one line each in which their kinship status, in a manner typical of myth, is designated as complex and variable: father, brother, cousin. This designation leaves open the possibility of more specification later, but the immediate effect is to render the figures of peace and sleep less definite, to place them in the background, and so to concentrate our attention on the third figure.

In the second stanza, Stevens has already told us that the mother says "good-by" to the dead. In the expansive relative clause "that in the syllable . . . ," he renders her speech dramatically, with striking prosodic skill, and at the same time he complicates and deepens her mythic significance. The gap between life and death, the moment of transition, is imitated prosodically by the gap between the stanzas, "life / And death," and the effect of this enjambment is reinforced by the departure from prosodic parallelism. The preceding lines, devoted to peace and sleep, have each been end-stopped. The prosodic rapidity gained by the run-on line is further reinforced by the adverb "quickly" and by the phrase "in a flash of voice." The quickness of the cry is established before its content is, but the cry itself slows down prosodically, and the tension thus achieved contributes to the emotional intensity of "Keep you, keep you, I am gone, oh keep you as." This line breaks into four distinct phrases and five pauses, if we read with a pause at "oh." The iambic movement is almost reversed to a trochaic in the first four words, and the balance between metrical expectation and speech emphasis results in a spondaic heaviness and slowness. The "as" at the end of the line dangles and forces a reflective pause before the completion of the run-on phrase "as / My memory." "Keep you" seems complete in itself, a parting salutation equivalent to "farewell," so that the predicate complement "as / My memory" comes unexpectedly. The predicate can be read as a modification of "you." "Keep you" is then hortatory and the whole phrase could be restated: *Preserve yourself for the sake of or in the capacity of my memory*. On the other hand, the predicate can be taken to change the modal emphasis of "keep you," transforming it from exhortation to promise: *I shall preserve you as the components of my memory*. This implication gains force from preceding as well as succeeding phrases in the same sentence. The moment of transition between life and death is designated a "syllable," not just a temporal instant but an instant of speech. If speech is taken as a synecdoche for consciousness itself, the mother, as speaker of the syllable between life and death, becomes the mythical embodiment of consciousness. She is an "earthly mother" because she generates conscious life, and "the mother of / The dead" because she preserves time in her own memory. Consciousness is a human attribute and a process independent of any individual. The ambiguity of "keep you" reflects the earlier ambiguity between necessity as human need and as a necessary order. There is a human need for the preservation of the self, and there is a corresponding transcendent necessity that the experience of time be preserved in a timeless memory. The word *There* at the beginning of stanza six refers to the land of the dead, but we have already been told that this realm contains reality as prodigy. The mother spans both realms, the timeless and the temporal, and extends her noetic function to both.

Stevens' grouping of his three figures as two brothers and a mother (not their mother but the earthly mother) appears to have been inspired most directly by Tennyson's version of the myth in "Demeter and Persephone" (1889) and to have received a secondary modulation from "The Ancient Sage." The crucial passage in "Demeter and Persephone" is that in which Demeter tells Persephone how she found her. The cries of Demeter and of Persephone's shadow in this passage contribute to the mother's poignant cry for the dying in "Owl." Stevens' memory of this passage was probably stimulated by the simile with which it begins. For Stevens, the shade of a dying man who says farewell is Henry Church:

> Last as the likeness of a dying man,
> Without his knowledge, from him flits to warn
> A far-off friendship that he comes no more,
> So he, the God of dreams, who heard my cry,
> Drew from thyself the likeness of thyself
> Without thy knowledge, and thy shadow past
> Before me, crying, "The Bright one in the highest
> Is brother of the Dark one in the lowest,
> And Bright and Dark have sworn that I, the child
> Of thee, the great Earth-Mother, thee, the Power
> That lifts her buried life from gloom to bloom,
> Should be for ever and for evermore
> The Bride of Darkness." (ll. 87–99)

In "Owl" the Bright one in the highest is sleep, the condition of mystic vision; the Dark one in the lowest is peace after death, "The prince of shither-shade and tinsel lights." The great Earth-Mother merges with the whole complex of Keatsian images of the "antient mother"—the Melancholy and Moneta—and with the elegiac voice Tennyson evokes in "The Ancient Sage." In an obviously autobiographical passage, Tennyson's persona describes the elegiac sentiments that have possessed him from early childhood:

> A height, a broken grange, a grove, a flower
> Had murmurs "Lost and gone and lost and gone!"
> A breath, a whisper—some divine farewell—
> Desolate sweetness—far and far away—. (ll. 223–26)

The desolate sweetness of Tennyson's evocation verges on the sentimental. Stevens transposes Tennyson's nostalgic reminiscences into an objectified dramatic present. By investing the divine farewell with the dignity of an impersonal mythic figuration—as Keats does in "Ode on Melancholy" and the second "Hyperion"—Stevens retains all the pathos of the mother's cry while elevating it from sweet sorrow to elegiac grandeur.

The indeterminacy of the kinship relations between peace and sleep may have been inspired in part by another recollection of "The Ancient Sage." The skeptic in the poem complains that "'Night and Shadow rule below / When only Day should reign'" (ll. 243–44). The sage responds that the relations of light and dark are problematic and that the issue of sovereignty admits of no firm settlement:

> And Day and Night are children of the Sun,
> And idle gleams to thee are light to me.
> Some say, the Light was father of the Night,
> And some, the Night was father of the Light.
> No night no day! (ll. 245–49)

Unlike the ancient sage, Stevens does not suspend the question of primacy through direct recourse to undifferentiated unity. Instead he suspends all the elements of his mythic realm within a network of reciprocal dependencies. In the conclusion of "Owl," he subsumes all three figures within a transcendent category by merging them as "The pure perfections of parental space." This "space" is at once the three-dimensional space of the phenomenal world and the imaginative presence that pervades this world. Stevens' three figures, his "monsters of elegy," are "The children of a desire that is the will," and the mind itself "is a child" of the parental space in which it resides.

So far, peace and sleep have been left relatively remote, and their kinship has been explicitly extended only to each other. The mother, however, "is the mother of us all." At this point, it is not yet clear whether peace and sleep are to be taken, by analogy with the mother, as kin not only to each other but also to humanity. They are themselves "brothers," traditionally, because they are both states of passive rest. Yet, sleep is a condition of life and is thus related to the mother as the mother of the living. In the main body of the poem, Stevens will represent the mother and sleep as more accessible to human experience than is death, but in the concluding strophe the words *parental space* include all three figures and even suggest, in context, that death is himself the senior "parent." The progress of the whole poem, first distinguishing and then remerging the three mythic figures, is foreshadowed in the first strophe, where the mother is singled out for dramatic presentation, then returned to the darkness as merely one "of those dark three."

The first strophe begins in quietness and darkness. The mother's cry for the dying contrasts sharply against this setting. The synesthesia of light and sound in "a flash of voice" renders her speech as a flicker of lightning or flame in the dark. The run-on line between stanzas six and seven, "between life / And death cries quickly," seems to catch the very moment of dying. In the last stanza, the run-on line "the mother of / The dead" comes to a full stop with the dead, in their stillness, after the moment of transition. Through its repetitions and syntactic ambiguities, the concluding sentence of this strophe serves to draw the cover of darkness and mystery back over the "element" of the dead.

The syntactical ambiguities of the last sentence of the strophe will continue to operate throughout the poem, especially in the final strophe. They serve to blur distinctions of subject and object, of "thought" as human activity and as autonomous process. The phrase "the thought of those dark three" could mean *my thinking* about *those dark three* (objective genitive), or it could mean *the thought* belonging to *those dark three, their thinking* (subjective genitive). Similarly, "thought of the forms of dark desire" could mean *thought* about *the forms of dark desire* or *the thinking that is done* by *the forms of dark desire*. Allowing for all four possibilities, we could read: *Only the thinking about or by those dark three is dark, the thinking about or by the forms of dark desire*. One way, the three forms are the forms or types of desire about which the poet is thinking. Another way, the dark three themselves think about desire, their own or the poet's. If we allow all these implications to stand, thought is at once the thinking done by the dark forms, and the poet's thinking about them. Desire is both the object and the motive force of thought.

In the first strophe, Stevens has set a scene and described the figures in that scene. The present tense of this strophe is the tense of general truth. "They live," the three figures, not just now, at this moment, but always, in a permanent state outside time. In strophe two, turning his attention to the man who is to perceive the transcendental realm of strophe one, Stevens begins in the simple, historical past tense: "There came." By the end of the second strophe, the import of the past tense has been altered so that strophes three, four, and five, also governed by the past tense, must be understood as actually taking place at a point of intersection between the temporal and the timeless. In the final strophe, Stevens returns to the present tense, but this time a "literary present" or present of critical description. The statement "This is the mythology of modern death" will refer to the entire poem, both the present-tense first strophe and the historical past of the intervening strophes. The "mythology" consists not only of the objectified description of a mythic realm but also of the quest to discover and explore that realm.

The temporal stance of the first and last strophes is relatively straightforward. The stance or situation of the middle strophes constitutes, in contrast, a remarkable act of sustained paradoxical balancing. In strophe two, Stevens creates this balance through a subtle manipulation of verb forms:

> There came a day, there was a day—one day
> A man walked living among the forms of thought
> To see their lustre truly as it is
>
> And in harmonious prodigy to be,
> A while, conceiving his passage as into a time
> That of itself stood still, perennial,
>
> Less time than place, less place than thought of place
> And, if of substance, a likeness of the earth,
> That by resemblance twanged him through and through,
>
> Releasing an abysmal melody,
> A meeting, an emerging in the light,
> A dazzle of remembrance and of sight.

Within the single sentence of this strophe, there appears to be a transition between two points of time in the historical past. Within this transition, the man who is the subject of the sentence becomes the object of a transitive verb. He is the visionary protagonist—Stevens himself. He begins as a seeker after "the forms of thought," and he then becomes the recipient of their force; the perennial moment, as a hypothetical "likeness of the earth," "twanged him through and through." Between "walked" and "twanged," the passage into an eternal moment has already taken place, and the past tense has ceased to function as a historical indicator. This passage is effected through the use of a future-purpose infinitive "To see," an ambiguous infinitive "to be," and the participle "conceiving." What was intended becomes, through the act of conceiving, what is achieved.

The strophe opens, with emphatic repetition, in the daytime, a specific day that contrasts doubly with the perpetual night of strophe one. The man "walked," a definite form of motion contrasting with the vague "moving" of the three forms in strophe one and with the bodiless "emerging" at the end of strophe two. In the first stanza of strophe two, the world is explicitly that of the living; yet, the man walks "among the forms of thought," clearly the three figures of strophe one. Set off in their own element, they have been said to be "dark" to him. But he is now "To see their lustre truly as it is" in itself, a luster distinct from "our light," the light of day. Thus, in the conceptual potential of these ambiguities, the passage from temporal to timeless already begins in stanza one of the second strophe. The "harmonious prodigy" will be, and has begun to be, consciousness of an accord between the prodigy of "reality," the real world of time and space, and the timeless element that comprises "the forms of thought." In stanza two the syntax loosens and dissolves the clear outlines of the historical past. The infinitive "to be" can be taken as an infinitive of purpose, parallel to "To see" but placed in inverted position: *walked in order to see . . . and in order to be in harmonious prodigy.* However, it can also be taken as adjectival, modifying "prodigy": *to see their luster truly as it is and in that harmonious prodigy that will be (is to be).* Finally, "in harmonious prodigy" can be taken as an adverbial phrase modifying "walked," with the effect that the purpose infinitive "To see" describes a present action. All these syntactic possibilities hover over the line, with the result that "to be" becomes almost detached from the other words and stands out as a bold assertion of present existence. The sensation of hovering in a temporal ambiguity is immediately reinforced by the indefinite adverbial "A while." It is from this moment of suspension that the next three strophes will issue, all dependent on the participial phrase "conceiving his passage as into a time / That of itself stood still." The next two stanzas render this perennial moment as an achieved fact, the subject, by appositional extension, of a past-tense verb, "twanged." The use of the historical tense, from this point on, must be considered as a semantic paradox, a necessary distortion for the sake of sequential narrative.

Thought can function with logical consistency only within a context bound by space and time.[2] Infinity is not accessible to strict formulation. In order, then, to describe the element of eternity, Stevens is compelled to use a syntax of hypothesis and approximation. His passage is *as* into a time, like time, but less like time than like place, since "place" can be more easily considered non-sequential. Place is not, however, to be considered as position in space, but rather as *topos,* the place of thought. It is a purely intellectual place: "if" it is considered substantial, it is not a self-dependent substance but exists only as a relation or analogy, a "resemblance" of earth. This resemblance is the point of intersection between reality and the timeless element. The images that signal this intersection or "meeting" are variations on motifs already established. The musical metaphor of a harmony that was "to be" (and that has already assimilated the idea of a prodigy that "is") is carried over and presented as a definite occurrence: "twanged him . . . / . . . Releasing an abysmal melody." The epithet "abysmal" serves both to connote the dreadful or prodigious aspect of a journey to the land of the dead, and also to identify the origin of the melody from within the depths of the mythopoeic subconscious. Here, in the luster provided by the forms of thought, the poet perceives the "dazzle of remembrance" earlier described as a "flash of voice" that is the voice of eternal memory.

Strophes three and four, devoted respectively to sleep and to peace after death, both open with the word *There,* which refers not so much to the *There* in strophe one, stanza six, the timeless element of the dead, as to the point of suspended transition between this element and reality. Strophe five, which describes the mother, does not designate a change of "place" and so can be taken also as "There." It should be remembered, however, that the mother

---

2. For a thorough and convincing demonstration of this proposition, see Kant's analysis of the four antinomies in *Critique of Pure Reason,* 257–81.

bears a parental relation not only to the dead but also to the living. Her mode of being extends itself into the temporal and, as the medium of change, can be considered the element of temporality itself. The relative situations of the three figures within the mythic realm—their kinship relations—are depicted through variations on recurrent themes and motifs: the interplay of presence, absence, and comparison; the contrasts of symbolic figuration with essence or inner nature; and the imagery of color, motion, cloth or robing, fire, precious stones, and light. Some of these themes and motifs have already been presented in the first two strophes. The rest are presented in strophe three, which thus completes the referential grounding for the three final strophes.

In strophe three, sleep is depicted as a mythic figure, a "giant body," and as a state of being experienced by the poet: "Then he breathed deeply the deep atmosphere / Of sleep, the accomplished, the fulfilling air." The "There" that opens the strophe has clearly detached itself from the specific "day" of strophe two, and while it refers to a definite historical moment, a period of sleeping, this period is subsumed in the abstract period ("A while") of mythic vision. Sleep as an accomplished and fulfilling state of being is subsequent to—a conclusion from—"sleep realized," sleep as mythic vision. The accomplishment of this vision is poetically reconstructed in the first five stanzas of the strophe through a series of approximative images leading up to the flatly declarative predicate nominatives: "Sleep realized / Was the whiteness that is the ultimate intellect." "Was" tells us what has been perceived, and "is" designates this perception as a general truth. The vision of sleep begins with an abstraction, the negative comparative "less," which links it to the negative definitions of strophe two, where "less" is a comparative adverb used to abstract the perennial moment from time and place. In strophe three, "less" is changed to a noun; the process of abstract comparison has become a thing in itself, the "substance" that is perceived in the height of sleep: "There he saw well the foldings in the height / Of sleep, the whiteness folded into less." Whiteness as pure color or light is "folded," that is, refined into a nonperceptual noetic quality that can be "seen" ("he saw well") only through the metaphoric figurations in the following stanzas, but that can be defined, finally, as "the ultimate intellect."

The metaphoric figurations of this "whiteness folded into less" are complicated, but the total impression that they make is quite distinct. The apocalyptic images of sublimity—height, depth, massive size, great motion, and distance—are subsumed under images of composure, rest, stillness, and central unity. The images that create this impression are meant only to be suggestive, not to state precise logical relations. The central metaphor of "a moving mountain" is connected to "the whiteness" only by a syntactically vague "as":

> Of sleep, the whiteness folded into less,
> Like many robings, as moving masses are,
>
> As a moving mountain is, moving through day
> And night, colored from distances, central
> Where luminous agitations come to rest,
>
> In an ever-changing, calmest unity,
> The unique composure, harshest streakings joined
> In a vanishing-vanished violet that wraps round
>
> The giant body the meanings of its folds.

Filling in the ellipses in Stevens' syntax, we might read: *the whiteness is folded into less as moving masses and a moving mountain are folded into less.* As the passage progresses this syntactic signification ceases to operate. The moving mountain becomes an equivalent for whiteness, and whiteness becomes equivalent to "less." In the phrase "the meanings of its folds," the folds are folds of color converging into the unity of white. A mountain might be said to move through day and night because it subsists in time, but the central point "Where luminous agitations come to rest" is not part of a mass situated in space and time. The mountain is only a "likeness of the earth," and its movement is a metaphor for an intellective "substance" or activity that pervades and transcends the day and night of earthly time. In depicting this transcendental element, Stevens appears to have drawn on a passage from book four of *The Excursion*. In this passage, an eloquent solitary declares to his auditors that the universe imparts

> "Authentic tidings of invisible things;
> Of ebb and flow, and ever-during power;
> And central peace, subsisting at the heart
> Of endless agitation." (ll. 1144–47)

Stevens' recollection of this passage would have been reinforced by its similarity in theme and diction to Whitman's evocation of the "perfection" that nestles within the "central heart" of the earth.

In the image of "harshest streakings joined / In a vanishing-vanished violet," Stevens refigures the luminous agitations that come to rest within the central mountain. A likely source for this refiguration is "The Ancient Sage." The sage describes the locus of the divine presence in terms that may also have contributed to the "abysmal melody" of the previous strophe:

> The Abysm of all Abysms, beneath, within
> The blue of sky and sea, the green of earth,
> And in the million-millionth of a grain
> Which cleft and cleft again for evermore,
> And ever vanishing, never vanishes. (ll. 40–44)[3]

Stevens' use of the word *violet* may reflect an association between this passage and the image of violets in section 115 of *In Memoriam*:

> Now fades the last long streak of snow,
> Now burgeons every maze of quick
> About the flowering squares, and thick
> By ashen roots the violets blow.
>
> . . . .
>
>   and in my breast
> Spring wakens too; and my regret
> Becomes an April violet,
> And buds and blossoms like the rest.[4]

The agitations of Tennyson's regret ultimately resolve themselves within those "empyreal heights of thought" (section 95) that will constitute the special province of the ancient sage. In similar fashion, it is in the foldings at the height of sleep that Stevens finds a resolution for all earthly sorrow.

Within the metaphorical, paradoxical movement of the mountain that is colored from distances, the real movements of space and time come to rest. This second sort of motion, real motion, is illustrated in a metaphor that stands as an appositive to "the meanings of its folds":

> The giant body the meanings of its folds,
> The weaving and the crinkling and the vex,

---

3. The influence of this passage will make itself felt again in stanza seven of "A Primitive Like an Orb."
4. I am indebted to Rachel Matheis for drawing my attention to this connection.

> As on water of an afternoon in the wind
> After the wind has passed.

The troubled surface of water coming to rest again refigures the central peak where "luminous agitations come to rest" and shifts the metaphoric emphasis from light-color imagery (luminous) to the imagery of motion (agitations).

All these images have amplified the noun phrase "the whiteness folded into less." In the succeeding lines of stanza five and in stanza six, this denotation is reformulated as "the ultimate intellect," and new images are introduced to amplify this new formulation:

> Sleep realized
> Was the whiteness that is the ultimate intellect,
> A diamond jubilance beyond the fire,
>
> That gives its power to the wild-ringed eye.
> Then he breathed deeply the deep atmosphere
> Of sleep, the accomplished, the fulfilling air.

The dim abstraction of "less" is transformed into the brilliant appositive "A diamond jubilance beyond the fire." The light imagery of strophe two is subordinated, with the adjective "diamond" suggesting brilliant light, to the noun of emotion, "jubilance." In the fourth strophe, Stevens will elaborate on the association between jewels and brilliant light, and he will suggest that the image of fire may be identified as the purifying flame of death. "Sleep realized" is "beyond the fire," and its jubilance is independent of the emotional state of any individual. Considered in its other aspect, as a state of being, the condition of being asleep, sleep may be interpreted as the medium of vision through which the poet gains insight into this detached jubilance of the ultimate intellect. This jubilance, in turn, is itself the source of the poet's visionary "power." In his interrogatory invocation of sleep in "Sleep and Poetry," Keats had asked, "But what is higher beyond thought than thee? . . . More strange, more beautiful, more regal?" Stevens too suggests that the vision in the height of sleep bears a regal authority. The most direct antecedent of the diamond jubilance is "the spirit's diamond coronal" Nanzia Nunzio asks of Ozymandias. The crown has passed in succession from the "Great mud-ancestor, oozer and Abraham"—whose "diamond crown of crowns" succeeds to the "starless crown" worn by Ananke—to Belshazzar, Nanzia Nunzio, the green queen who wears "The crown and week-day coronal," the shadow of "Chocorua," and the bleak sovereign of "Crude Foyer." The image of the crown obliquely irradiates the ancient mother in strophe five. "It was not her look, but a knowledge that she had." This knowledge is her crown, and like the spirit's diamond coronal, it illuminates its bearer: "she moved / With a sad splendor."

The collocation of images in the last two stanzas of strophe three—breath, brilliant fire, light—and the word *jubilant* strongly suggest that Stevens' figuration of a joyous spiritual life beyond the fire was directly inspired by a passage in Whitman's "Chanting the Square Deific" from "Whispers of Heavenly Death." Whitman invokes a new and "mightier God" that subsumes all previous gods:

> Santa Spirita, breather, life,
> Beyond the light, lighter than light,
> Beyond the flames of hell, joyous, leaping easily above hell.

The speaker of Whitman's poem is himself the God he invokes—"the mightier God am I"—and in the lines following his address to the Santa Spirita, it becomes clear that this God is to be identified with Whitman himself as "Including all life on earth, touching, including God." In "Owl," Stevens does not follow Whitman this far. With sure tact, he abstracts the apocalyptic imagery from the extravagant egotism of its context. In "Auroras," Stevens' visionary persona, the father, will succumb to the seductive precedent of Whitman's egotistical sublime, and Stevens will have to effect a painful recovery from his angelic excess.

The depiction of sleep has concentrated on images of unity and composure. Strophe four, the depiction of peace after death, opens with an assertion of division and alienation:

> There peace, the godolphin and fellow, estranged, estranged,
> Hewn in their middle as the beam of leaves,
> The prince of shither-shade and tinsel lights,
>
> Stood flourishing the world. The brilliant height
> And hollow of him by its brilliance calmed,
> Its brightness burned the way good solace seethes.
>
> This was peace after death, the brother of sleep,
> The inhuman brother so much like, so near,
> Yet vested in a foreign absolute,

Adorned with cryptic stones and sliding shines,
An immaculate personage in nothingness,
With the whole spirit sparkling in its cloth.

"Hewn in their middle" is a difficult phrase. On the one hand, we might take "their middle" to mean *in the middle of the three forms* or *in the midst of ordinary people*. We could then paraphrase: *sleep is carved or fabricated in their midst as a tree* ("the beam of leaves") *is carved*. On the other hand, though it is a plural adjective, the word *their* in the phrase "Hewn in their middle" could be taken as referring to the singular noun *peace,* and we could paraphrase: *peace is hewn in their/his middle* (split in two) *as a tree is split in two*. This reading corresponds to the wrenching assertion of estrangement. Peace is a divided personage—lustrous from the outside but impenetrably dark within. He is "estranged" because he has no human kinship; he is "The inhuman brother." Thus it is that he presides over a dual kingdom of darkness and glittering light, "shither-shade and tinsel lights." As "An immaculate personage in nothingness," peace remains inaccessible, "vested in a foreign absolute." The tinsel lights are sparkling fantasies which the poetic imagination embroiders in this robe of darkness. The contemporary meaning of *tinsel* is something that glitters like precious metal but has little value. This derogatory connotation contrasts the factitious, artificial splendors of human fancy with the genuine, perceived splendors of sleep realized. The original meaning of *tinsel,* however, is a cloth woven with precious threads of gold or silver. As strophe four progresses this original, laudatory connotation becomes dominant, so that the phrase (in stanza seven) "A thousand begettings of the broken bold" sounds a clear note of heroic elegy, without irony. The tinsel lights become "cryptic stones," a metaphoric derivative from the diamond jubilance of sleep. Similarly, the light imagery that has appeared in strophes two and three here serves to describe the "brightness" paradoxically intuited within the darkness of death. These "tinsel" figurations, metaphoric borrowings, are necessary because death is not accessible to human vision. Peace is "like" sleep, but he has no human kinship. He is the "inhuman brother." The word *shither* is a neologism, probably compounded from slither and shimmer, and it is used to connote the elusive quality of this brother, "so much like," yet impossibly distant.

The robe imagery of strophe three functions metaphorically to approach a vision that may be identified and defined as a self-subsistent entity, an ultimate intellect. In strophe four, in contrast, the robe of peace after death designates a tapestry of metaphors that cannot get beyond themselves to the thing they represent:

> Generations of the imagination piled
> In the manner of its stitchings, of its thread,
> In the weaving round the wonder of its need,
>
> And the first flowers upon it, an alphabet
> By which to spell out holy doom and end,
> A bee for the remembering of happiness.
>
> Peace stood with our last blood adorned, last mind,
> Damasked in the originals of green,
> A thousand begettings of the broken bold.
>
> This is that figure stationed at our end,
> Always, in brilliance, fatal, final, formed
> Out of our lives to keep us in our death,
>
> To watch us in the summer of Cyclops
> Underground, a king as candle by our beds
> In a robe that is our glory as he guards.

Confronting death, the imagination points to nothing external and can only reflect "the wonder of its need," its *own* need. Peace has been created as a "figure" and "stationed at our end" by the elegiac tradition in poetry, the "Generations of the imagination." The word *alphabet* serves as a synecdoche for literature, and in the "bee for the remembering of happiness," Stevens seems to be establishing another link in the genealogy of the imagination. Tennyson suggests the ambiguous nature of the kinship between darkness and light, and in the fourth stanza of "To Night," Shelley suggests a further mythic complication of this relationship:

> Thy brother Death came, and cried
>   Wouldst thou me?
> Thy sweet child Sleep, the filmy-eyed,
> Murmured like a noon tide bee,
> Shall I nestle near thy side?

The happiness Stevens is to remember must include the "holy doom and end" of a visionary eschatology. Death is an essential component of the fiction that "sends us, winged by an unconscious will, / To an immaculate end" (*CP,* 382).

Although death is "vested in a foreign absolute," he is also, paradoxically, one of "the forms of thought," and he shares the mother's function as a medium of mythic memory that can "keep us in our death." The burning brightness of death is a fire that is "fatal" to the individual human consciousness, but it is also closely related, as brilliant light, to the mind of minds that lies beyond the fire. Finally, "green" in the phrase "Damasked in the originals of green" draws on the color symbology of *Parts of a World* and *Transport to Summer* and invests that symbology with a connotation of freshness and youth. The "originals of green" suggest the vital, original character of the individual experience that contributes to the ancient traditions of elegy and also suggest that this originality derives from a source deeper than that of the individual consciousness: "That elemental parent, the green night" (*CP,* 267).

In the progression of this strophe, there is a gradual distancing from the point of visionary immediacy. Strophe one is written entirely from a third-person, narrative viewpoint, used to describe the land of the dead. The viewpoint of strophes two and three is provided by "him," the persona of the poet. Both strophes open and close on the third-person singular pronoun: "A man walked . . . twanged him"; "There he saw . . . Then he breathed." Strophe four, in contrast, focuses on the figure of peace itself, then shifts to a general commentary on humanity, signaled by the first-person plural pronoun: "There peace . . . Stood flourishing. . . . This was peace after death. . . . Peace stood. . . . This is that figure stationed . . . to keep us . . . To watch us." The tense shift from past to present here signals a shift from historical occurrence to habitual or repeated action. The final two stanzas of the strophe describe not what "he" saw but what we, people in general, do throughout our lives. We form images of death and invest them with power so that they become protective idols, "a king as candle." We station such figures "at our end" to guard us against the monstrosity—"summer of Cyclops"—of simple dissolution.

In strophe five the visionary tension tightens again. The "But" that opens the strophe accomplishes this tightening in three different ways:

> But she that says good-by losing in self
> The sense of self, rosed out of prestiges
> Of rose, stood tall in self not symbol, quick
>
> And potent, an influence felt instead of seen.
> She spoke with backward gestures of her hand.
> She held men closely with discovery,

Almost as speed discovers, in the way
Invisible change discovers what is changed,
In the way what was has ceased to be what is.

It was not her look but a knowledge that she had.
She was a self that knew, an inner thing,
Subtler than look's declaiming, although she moved

With a sad splendor, beyond artifice,
Impassioned by the knowledge that she had,
There on the edges of oblivion.

O exhalation, O fling without a sleeve
And motion outward, reddened and resolved
From sight, in the silence that follows her last word—

First, "But" signals the shift from present-tense general commentary back to the past tense of visionary immediacy: the mother "stood tall." Second, it explicitly contrasts the symbolic robe of death, the vestment of nothingness, with the substantial reality of the mother, a "self not symbol" whose gestures are a "fling without a sleeve." (This anti-image reverses a metaphor in "The Idea of Order at Key West," where the sea is "Like a body wholly body, fluttering / Its empty sleeves" [*CP*, 128].) To create an image that is no image, a figure of that which is beyond figuration, Stevens resorts to discursive negations of his own metaphors. The mother, as a mythic personage, "stood tall," a poetic symbol of experience, but "in self not symbol." Similarly, the visual suggestion "although she moved / With a sad splendor" is enclosed between two negations of visual content: "Subtler than look's declaiming" and "beyond artifice." The mother's mode of existence—"losing in self / The sense of self"—absolves her from the limitations of personal identity. In order to depict a mythic personage that transcends these limitations, Stevens seems to draw on the passage from "The Ancient Sage" that follows immediately upon Tennyson's evocation of the "divine farewell." The sage describes a mystical trance:

> more than once when I
> Sat all alone, revolving in myself
> The word that is the symbol of myself,
> The mortal limit of the Self was loosed,
> And past into the Nameless, as a cloud
> Melds into heaven.
> . . . .

>   and through loss of Self
>   The gain of such large life as matched with ours
>   Were Sun to spark—. (ll. 229–38)

If as seems likely Stevens has recalled this passage, he has transferred the mystical experience from the human subject to his own mythic personage. The ancient mother is herself what the sage calls "such large life." She cannot be objectified as image because she is the very quick of being, "an influence felt instead of seen." Like the mythic feminine figure in "The Candle a Saint," she is "Moving and being, the image at its source" (*CP*, 223). In strophe one, Stevens suggests that the mother, as the speaker of "the syllable between life / And death," is the medium of conscious experience. This suggestion is now verified, not as speech but as "discovery." We are told not that men discover in change but that change itself "discovers what is changed." In "Notes," Stevens declares that "to find the real, / To be stripped of every fiction, except one, / The fiction of an absolute," it will be necessary "To discover an order" and "Not to impose" one (*CP*, 403–404). The mother discovers herself. Men know, have knowledge, through her; they participate in her knowledge, but she is herself "a self that knew, an inner thing." Finally, the "But" that begins the strophe reaches back beyond the previous strophe to contrast the mother with sleep. The realization of sleep is calmness, rest, unity. The mother is the antithesis of sleep; she is the agent of change and difference. As breath or "exhalation," she is like the wind that disturbs the calm surface of the water in strophe three. The "diamond jubilance" of sleep is the delight of a self-subsistent, complete being, detached from change and experience. The light-emotion motif reappears, with a reversal of noun-adjective placement, in the phrase describing the mother's movement, "a sad splendor." Her sadness is the human sadness at change and loss.

In the three middle strophes, Stevens has concentrated on distinguishing the three mythic figures, but within these distinctions there have been frequent suggestions of kinship. Each figure partially contains the other two, and there are no ultimately stable hierarchies in their relations. As the principle of change, the mother is subsumed in "an ever-changing, calmest unity." Her gestures, "reddened and resolved / From sight," are the "vanishing-vanished violet" that merges into the "whiteness" at the height of sleep. Yet, as the principle of knowledge, "a self that knew," the mother provides the noetic element to sleep and may herself be identified with "the ultimate intellect." As a figuration of central unity, sleep composes both life and death.

Its knowledge is the mother's knowledge; its calm is the calm of peace after death, which "by its brilliance calmed." The mother also composes life and death, holding men with discovery in life, and keeping them, as memory, in death. She seems, then, to contain death, but it is death, as nothingness, "Upon whose shoulders even the heavens rest" and who "Stood flourishing the world." Sleep is a diamond jubilance beyond the fire of death, and the mother remains on the near side of death, "There on the edges of oblivion." There is a "silence that follows her last word," and death remains within this silence. Paradoxically, the ultimate unity is accessible to intuition through sleep, but one element of this unity, peace after death, remains in impenetrable darkness.

At the end of strophe five, Stevens has accomplished the main purpose of the poem, to bring the three figures out of the darkness and into the light. In the concluding strophe, the three figures reenter the darkness and merge as "monsters of elegy":

> This is the mythology of modern death
> And these, in their mufflings, monsters of elegy,
> Of their own marvel made, of pity made,
>
> Compounded and compounded, life by life,
> These are death's own supremest images,
> The pure perfections of parental space.

The tropes by which they have been distinguished are wrapped together as "mufflings" common to all three. The series of attributive phrases modifying "monsters" recalls aspects of each figure, further compounds them, and reasserts the subject-object ambiguities of strophe one. "Of their own marvel made, of pity made" evokes both the mother's sadness and passion and also the human imagination's "wonder" at its need. "Compounded and compounded, life by life" echoes the phrase "Generations of the imagination," and so links the mother, as memory, to the traditions of elegy. Yet, "These are death's own supremest images," not just the images of elegiac poets. All three figures are part of "the mythology of modern death," and it is to death itself that Stevens now attributes the originative force of the poem. Nonetheless, the phrase "The pure perfections of parental space" concedes equal significance to all three figures: to sleep, as the perfection of calmest unity; to peace after death, as the purifying fire; and to the mother, as the mediator between life and death. In the next stanza, the desire that is the will is both the will of death as "parental space" and the will of "the mind," a human mind. The ambiguity of these phrases can be attributed to the inescapable limitations of consciousness:

> The children of a desire that is the will,
> Even of death, the beings of the mind
> In the light-bound space of the mind, the floreate flare . . .

Within its "light-bound space," the mind can create supreme images, images transcending light and space, only by means of paradox. By using paradox, it can divine the "flash of voice" that is at once its own "floreate flare" and the "dazzle of remembrance" reflected from the forms of thought.

After the ellipsis in stanza three, Stevens seems to break away from the visionary mode of paradox and ambiguity:

> It is a child that sings itself to sleep,
> The mind, among the creatures that it makes,
> The people, those by which it lives and dies.

The mind, quite simply, "makes" its mythic creatures. This appearance of simplicity is deceptive. The mind "is a child," and its "parental space" consists of those very "creatures that it makes." The mind lives and dies by creating myths, but it is itself the creature of those myths. The imagination needs "out of the whole necessity of sight" to create images of its life and death, but it is life and death themselves that form this need. Need and necessity meet in the creation of the modern mythology.

The narrative element in "Owl" is very slight, sufficient only to fix its mythic exposition as the visionary object of the man who "walked" and "saw" the forms of thought. The three middle strophes (three through five) have no dramatic progression. Like most of "Chocorua," they operate at the level of visionary resolution, and the final strophe affirms this resolution. In "The Auroras of Autumn," the proportions of dramatic narrative and mythic exposition are reversed. The first two cantos duplicate the opening movements in the first two strophes of "Owl." After an initial exposition of a cosmic myth, Stevens focuses on a man who "is walking" and who "observes." The initial exposition remains more problematic than that of "Owl," and the main body of "Auroras" enacts the man's struggle to achieve the moment of mythic resolution. This moment occurs in the last three stanzas of canto eight. In canto nine, Stevens takes a retrospective survey of his whole lifetime and attempts to reconcile the conflicting perspectives of ordinary life and the transcendental moment. In the final canto, he seeks a formula that will encapsulate the results of this attempt at reconciliation. In "Owl," Stevens yields himself passively to visionary fulfillment. In "Auroras" he never fully escapes a sense of the contrived quality of this fictive fulfillment. Even in the moment of resolution, he implicitly concedes the inescapable necessity of metaphoric displacement; it is *"As if* the innocent mother sang in the dark" (my italics).

The main structure of "Auroras" discloses itself through Stevens' references in cantos one and eight to the lights of the aurora borealis. In a letter of 1954, Stevens explains that the aurora borealis is something "which we have now and then in Hartford, sometimes quite strong enough to attract attention from indoors. These lights symbolize a tragic and desolate background" (*LWS*, 852). In stanza five of canto one, Stevens designates "These lights" as a symbol of visionary conflict, and he proposes a possible resolution for this conflict:

> These lights may finally attain a pole
> In the midmost midnight and find the serpent there,
>
> In another nest, the master of the maze
> Of body and air and forms and images,
> Relentlessly in possession of happiness. (*CP,* 411)

(Harold Bloom describes a display of the auroras and remarks that the "coilings" of the lights "unmistakably resembled a giant, many-folded serpent, with its head at the zenith.")[5] At two moments of crisis in the poem—the final stanzas of cantos two and six—the auroras represent, as Stevens says, a state of tragic desolation. Then, in stanza six of canto eight, after he has affirmed the existence of a "pure principle" of sentient relation, Stevens uses a double conjunction—"So, then"—to indicate that he has succeeded in the visionary project announced in canto one:

> So, then, these lights are not a spell of light,
> A saying out of a cloud, but innocence.
> An innocence of the earth and no false sign.

The unity of purpose that is implied in Stevens' references to "These lights" is reinforced by an explicit declaration in canto three: "The mother's face, / The

---

5. Bloom, *The Poems of Our Climate,* 255.

purpose of the poem, fills the room." In canto eight the conjunctive signal of conclusion is immediately followed by a realization of this purpose:

> An innocence of the earth and no false sign
> Or symbol of malice. That we partake thereof,
> Lie down like children in this holiness,
> As if, awake, we lay in the quiet of sleep,
>
> As if the innocent mother sang in the dark
> Of the room and on an accordion, half-heard,
> Created the time and place in which we breathed . . .

The innocent mother, a refiguration of the earthly mother and the mother of the dead in "Owl," serves as a mythic embodiment of the pure principle that constitutes the "happiness" of the cosmic serpent.

In his depiction of the serpent in canto one, Stevens discloses the ontological dialectic that emerges from the paradox of a fictive form that transcends all forms:

> This is where the serpent lives, the bodiless.
> His head is air. Beneath his tip at night
> Eyes open and fix on us in every sky.
>
> . . . .
>
> This is form gulping after formlessness,
> Skin flashing to wished-for disappearances
> And the serpent body flashing without the skin.

Stevens' powerful evocation of a cosmic pathetic fallacy—the stars as "Eyes"—strains against the paradox of a bodiless "tip." The phrase "form gulping after formlessness" recalls the "Incapable master of all force" who in "Negation" struggles helplessly toward a "harmonious whole" (*CP*, 97). In stanza two the tension between form and formlessness diverts itself into a dichotomy between the real and the ideal. Stevens evokes Plato as the ancestor of this opposition:

> Or is this another wriggling out of the egg,
> Another image at the end of the cave,
> Another bodiless for the body's slough?

The opposition of ideal and actual forms drops beneath the usual level of Stevens' dialectic, and in the next stanza he seems simply to dismiss it:

> This is where the serpent lives. This is his nest,
> These fields, these hills, these tinted distances,
> And the pines above and along and beside the sea.

The reassertion of an identity between the natural world and the spirit—the doctrine propounded in "Landscape with Boat"—precedes the reformulation of the problem as "form gulping after formlessness," and this reformulation gives rise to another displacement. Stevens' prophecy of a possible resolution—"These lights may finally attain a pole"—locates the serpent "In another nest," not the nest of fields and hills and tinted distances.

The seemingly inescapable doubling within an image intended to represent cosmic unity subverts the "happiness" of the serpent, and in the penultimate stanza, Stevens defines this subversive principle as a "poison" that is inherently a part of the serpent's own nature. In seeking to fashion an antidote, Stevens dissolves the spatiotemporal frame within which objects exist independently in definite locations:

> Relentlessly in possession of happiness.
>
> This is his poison: that we should disbelieve
> Even that. His meditations in the ferns,
> When he moved so slightly to make sure of sun,
>
> Made us no less as sure. We saw in his head,
> Black beaded on the rock, the flecked animal,
> The moving grass, the Indian in his glade.

Here the serpent is at once an actual reptile, "in the ferns," and the bodiless "master of the maze." As an actual reptile, the serpent represents a certainty and unity of being on the level of immediate sensory perception—yet another rendering of the latest freed man. As the master of the maze, he embodies a ubiquitous sentient presence that comprises all the particulars of reality. Each of these particulars is an instance of the serpent's meditation. The prepositional phrase "in his head" can be interpreted simultaneously in two separate ways: (1) *The flecked animal, the grass, and the Indian were in the serpent's head; we saw them there;* (2) *We were in the serpent's head, and there we saw the flecked animal, the moving grass, and the Indian.* Either way, the serpent as actual reptile becomes the focal point for all other particular relations and thus metamorphoses into the cosmic serpent. Stevens' recollection of the serpent's "meditations" counteracts the poison of disbelief, but only on the level of transient intuition. His primary motive in the main body of the poem will be to construct a visionary scheme within which the serpent can be "Relentlessly in possession of happiness."

Cantos two, three, and four all begin with "Farewell to an idea," a phrase that signals a change of scene. These changes constitute strategic responses to the problems that have not been solved in the preceding cantos. The main element of continuity within these changes is provided by the persona of the poet. In canto three the protagonist of canto two, "The man who is walking," becomes one member of a family scene within a house, and in canto four he appears as "The father." Stevens describes the father as "yet the king and yet the crown," the sovereign master of consciousness. Through this persona, Stevens presses his visionary purpose to its extreme limit. The father, as "Of motion the ever-brightening origin," is to be identified with God. In canto five the father gathers his poetic resources: actors, musicians, and dancers. These figures play their parts in a theatrical festival, and though the father disappears from the poem after canto five, Stevens continues to use the theater as a metaphoric vehicle for the elaboration of his visionary power. In canto six the components of the theater are simplified, so that they coalesce into a metaphoric "cloud," running streams of color and shape and feeling. Thus compacted, the imagination luxuriates in autonomous metamorphosis, and because the poet has ceased to direct its transformations in a purposeful way, it collapses in ruin. This collapse symbolizes the failure of the poet's effort, announced in canto four, to become pure imagination and thus to achieve apotheosis. Having been cast down from his sovereign throne, he turns in canto seven to an awe-stricken questioning about the nature of absolute knowledge and absolute power. Apotheosis yields to epiphany, and it is this more limited ambition that governs the climax and denouement of the poem.

Canto one concludes with a recollection of an ambiguous moment of visionary certitude. The difficulty of sustaining this certitude implicitly reveals itself in the second canto, where the protagonist struggles ineffectually to overcome a sensation of spiritual vacancy:

> Farewell to an idea . . . A cabin stands,
> Deserted, on a beach. It is white,
> As by a custom or according to
>
> An ancestral theme or as a consequence
> Of an infinite course. The flowers against the wall
> Are white, a little dried, a kind of mark

> Reminding, trying to remind, of a white
> That was different, something else, last year
> Or before, not the white of an aging afternoon,
>
> Whether fresher or duller, whether of winter cloud
> Or of winter sky, from horizon to horizon.
> The wind is blowing the sand across the floor.

The white cabin and the white flowers are both associative stimuli by means of which Stevens attempts to regenerate his memory of the visionary center, "the whiteness that is the ultimate intellect." The whiteness that Stevens actually perceives is a mere absence of color and distinction, a bleaching out of experience in the dullness of old age. At the same time, by associating itself, though below the level of vivid recall, with "a white / That was different," this present whiteness lays claim to an austere sublimity. The "infinite course" subsumes all possibilities of temporal/causal sequence in a detached acknowledgment of a universal force. Similarly, the phrase "from horizon to horizon" mingles detachment from local perception with an exhilarating expansiveness of vision. In this state of mind, indifferent events—"The wind is blowing the sand across the floor"—reflect at once the observer's blankness and the brooding expectancy beneath this blankness. For the moment, Stevens remains suspended between these tonal extremes, and whiteness reduces itself to a meaningless intensity of presence:

> Here, being visible is being white,
> Is being of the solid of white, the accomplishment
> Of an extremist in an exercise . . .

The "extremist" is whiteness itself, and in the change of "season" that occurs within the ellipsis at the end of the stanza, the spiritual negativity of this presence gathers apocalyptic force:

> The season changes. A cold wind chills the beach.
> The long lines of it grow longer, emptier,
> A darkness gathers though it does not fall
>
> And the whiteness grows less vivid on the wall.
> The man who is walking turns blankly on the sand.
> He observes how the north is always enlarging the change,
>
> With its frigid brilliances, its blue-red sweeps
> And gusts of great enkindlings, its polar green,
> The color of ice and fire and solitude.

The significance of this imagery depends on associative contrasts with Stevens' earlier visionary poetry. The color green is frequently associated with the archetypes of pure poetry, and solitude is a precondition of visionary realization. The "frigid brilliances" of "ice and fire and solitude" recall the "diamond jubilance beyond the fire," but the auroras do not attain to the "unique composure" of "Sleep realized," for they have not yet been subsumed within a metaphysical mythic structure. In "Chocorua" the shadow breathes "A consciousness from solitude," and "where he was, there is an enkindling" (*CP,* 298, 301). But the shadow is a "metaphysical metaphor," and the auroras, here, remain natural images, emblems of an inhuman force that has not been mastered and contained by the power of poetic vision. In cantos three through six, Stevens will attempt to gain dominion over a poetic realm that will encompass the polar region. When at the end of canto six he turns again to the "Arctic effulgence," he quails before the inhuman force it represents, and in expressing his fear, he tacitly concedes the limitations of his visionary power. In order to contain this effulgence within a visionary resolution, he must have recourse to "thought's compromise" (*NA,* 89). It is by means of this compromise that "these lights" become symbols of "An innocence of the earth."

The first movement in Stevens' visionary strategy, in cantos three and four, is to fashion archetypal figures with which he can confront the changes of the north. In canto three he takes refuge from polar solitude in the warmth of a family setting, a setting in which he seeks to evoke the mother's presence:

> Farewell to an idea . . . The mother's face,
> The purpose of the poem, fills the room.
> They are together, here, and it is warm,
>
> With none of the prescience of oncoming dreams,
> It is evening. The house is evening, half dissolved.
> Only the half they can never possess remains,
>
> Still-starred. It is the mother they possess,
> Who gives transparence to their present peace.
> She makes that gentler that can gentle be.

The state of mind depicted here is like that of which Stevens complains in "Extracts," one in which the world appears as "half earth, half mind" (*CP,* 257). The "half they can never possess" is the brute reality outside the mind. This world is "Still-starred" in contrast to the cosmos of canto one, where beneath the serpent's tip "Eyes open and fix on us in every sky." In this initial evocation of the mother, her condition wavers uncertainly between an abstract spiritual principle that can dissolve the solid reality of external objects, and a human creature of pathetic memory. Finally, she remains inside the mind, unable to bridge "the dumbfoundering abyss / Between us and the object, external cause" (*CP,* 437). She invests the human and the ordinary with the affects of pure poetry—"transparence"—but in turn she is herself affected by the transience and fragility of the human:

> And yet she too is dissolved, she is destroyed.
> She gives transparence. But she has grown old.
> The necklace is a carving not a kiss.
>
> The soft hands are a motion not a touch.
> The house will crumble and the books will burn.
> They are at ease in a shelter of the mind
>
> And the house is of the mind and they and time,
> Together, all together.

At this point, the mother achieves full realization in neither her human nor her transcendental aspect. As a creature of memory, she manifests herself only in an inanimate heirloom, the necklace. As a spiritual principle, she hovers over the family as an airy fantasm, too nebulous to touch. She does not, as in "Owl," hold "men closely with discovery" (*CP,* 435). Because of her enfeebled condition, she can provide no protection from the elements of destruction. She is a fiction composed of words; she lives in books, and these books, also, will burn in the arctic fire. While external reality gathers its force for a definitive challenge, she falls asleep, and the darkened rooms are lighted only from the outside, by the aurora borealis:

> Boreal night
> Will look like frost as it approaches them
> And to the mother as she falls asleep
> And as they say good-night, good-night. Upstairs
> The windows will be lighted, not the rooms.
>
> A wind will spread its windy grandeurs round
> And knock like a rifle-butt against the door.
> The wind will command them with invincible sound.

"Good-night" is a version of "Good-by," the mother's salutation to the dying in "Owl," but on a reduced, human scale. The force of inhuman reality manifests itself in the wind. At the end of the next canto, in answer to the challenge of this "invincible sound," Stevens will assemble a "company" that is to "choir it with the naked wind."

Stevens' initial evocation of the mother fails to attain to a transcendental resolution. In canto four, therefore, he adopts the persona of the father and invests him with the emblems of transcendental power. In the first two stanzas of the canto, he sums up the dialectic of yes and no that has been expounded in *Parts of a World, Transport to Summer,* and "The Owl in the Sarcophagus":

> Farewell to an idea . . . The cancelings,
> The negations are never final. The father sits
> In space, wherever he sits, of bleak regard,
>
> As one that is strong in the bushes of his eyes.
> He says no to no and yes to yes. He says yes
> To no; and in saying yes he says farewell.

The father is an incarnation both of the man who sits in paradise and wears "humanity's bleak crown" and of major man depicted in "It Must Be Abstract" (*CP*, 387–88). He says no to the anti-master-man's denial of life, and he says yes to the virile poet's affirmation of the imagination. Finally, he says yes to the principle of negation as the dynamic element of change within the essential poem. The father thus assumes the elegiac functions of the mother. His speech, like hers, consists of "inventions of farewell" (*CP*, 432). As an all-encompassing, Whitmanian figure, the father subsumes the mother, for the time being, and when in canto five she appears as his counterpart, she receives no mythic elaboration.

The father's situation "In space" reestablishes the expansiveness of canto two, but Stevens now transforms the bleakness of this expanse into clairvoyant splendor. Through his elegiac formula, the father assumes the mother's capacity for articulating visionary motion; he too discovers "Almost as speed discovers, in the way / Invisible change discovers what is changed" (*CP*, 435):

> He measures the velocities of change.
> He leaps from heaven to heaven more rapidly
> Than bad angels leap from heaven to hell in flames.
>
> But now he sits in quiet and green-a-day.
> He assumes the great speeds of space and flutters them
> From cloud to cloudless, cloudless to keen clear

> In flights of eye and ear, the highest eye
> And the lowest ear, the deep ear that discerns,
> At evening, things that attend it until it hears
>
> The supernatural preludes of its own,
> At the moment when the angelic eye defines
> Its actors approaching, in company, in their masks.

In "Sleep and Poetry," Keats had thrown out a question that stands as a challenge to all later Romantic poets:

> Is there so small a range
> In the present strength of manhood, that the high
> Imagination cannot freely fly
> As she was wont of old? prepare her steeds,
> Paw up against the light, and do strange deeds
> Upon the clouds? Has she not shewn us all? (ll. 162–67)

In order to answer this challenge, Stevens draws on Whitman's confident assertions of visionary power. Whitman had represented himself as the "mightier God" who leaps "Beyond the flames of hell, joyous, leaping easily above hell." By attributing Whitman's rhetorical velocity to the father, Stevens seeks to situate him above the element of destruction in the polar region. In "It Must Be Abstract," Stevens declares, "The romantic intoning, the declaimed clairvoyance, / Are parts of apotheosis"; he is now to test the limits of Romantic declamation (*CP,* 387).

The doctrine Stevens expounds in "Evening Without Angels"—"Air is air"—has a rhetorical correlative: "Its sounds are not angelic syllables" (*CP,* 137). Through the father, Stevens issues an implicit challenge to this anti-Romantic doctrine. It is with an "angelic eye" that the father beholds his "actors approaching, in company, in their masks." These actors are his own rhetorical figures, and it is by means of these figures that he will attempt to transcend his human limitations. In "It Must Give Pleasure," after he has declared that his purpose is not to impose but to discover "The fiction of an absolute," Stevens asks, "What am I to believe?" He responds to this question by asking a second question:

> What am I to believe? If the angel in his cloud,
> Serenely gazing at the violent abyss,
> Plucks on his strings to pluck abysmal glory,

> Leaps downward through evening's revelations, and
> On his spredden wings, needs nothing but deep space,
> Forgets the gold centre, the golden destiny.
>
> Grows warm in the motionless motion of his flight,
> Am I that imagine this angel less satisfied? (*CP,* 404)

Stevens' response to this second question leaves him suspended in "deep space." He suggests—though in an equivocally interrogatory manner—that he can "forget need's golden hand" and be "satisfied without solacing majesty." The fullness of the rhetoric with which Stevens evokes the golden destiny itself argues that the suspension is temporary; in "Auroras" he yields to the need for a solacing majesty:

> Master O master seated by the fire
> And yet in space and motionless and yet
> Of motion the ever-brightening origin,
>
> Profound, and yet the king and yet the crown,
> Look at this present throne. What company,
> In masks, can choir it with the naked wind?

In *"All the Preludes to Felicity,"* Stevens has imagined "A large-sculptured, platonic person, free from time," and he has suggested that if we "imagine for him the speech he cannot speak, / A form, then, protected from the battering, may / Mature" (*CP,* 330). The father embodies this mature form. His purpose is to satisfy the desire Stevens expresses more directly in "This Solitude of Cataracts" (1948); he is to be "released from destruction" and to draw his breath "at the azury centre of time" (*CP,* 425). It is not enough for Stevens that the father occupy the throne on which he may "sit / And wear humanity's bleak crown" (*CP,* 305). He is to occupy the throne of God. Stevens' interrogatory apostrophe—"Master O master"—implies a dual perspective on this Whitmanian ambition. Although he invokes the father as a godlike figure, he remains sufficiently detached from his persona to suggest the hopelessness of satisfying his ambition.

The father's Whitmanian affiliation disturbs Stevens' visionary poise in two separate ways, first by enticing him into the egotistical sublime, and then by distracting him with the seductions of the earth and of men in their earthy implications. As the father assembles his company in canto five he loses sight of his celestial purpose and becomes absorbed in a celebration of normal poetry. The mother and father appear not as gods but as grand seigneurs, descendants of the great captain and the maiden Bawda. In the first line of the canto, the single word *humanity,* divested of any limiting conditions, strikes a note of earthy geniality that persists through six stanzas:

> The mother invites humanity to her house
> And table. The father fetches tellers of tales
> And musicians who mute much, muse much, on the tales.
>
> The father fetches negresses to dance,
> Among the children, like curious ripenesses
> Of pattern in the dance's ripening.
>
> For these the musicians make insidious tones,
> Clawing the sing-song of their instruments.
> The children laugh and jangle a tinny time.
>
> The father fetches pageants out of air,
> Scenes of the theatre, vistas and blocks of woods
> And curtains like a naive pretence of sleep.
>
> Among these the musicians strike the instinctive poem.
> The father fetches his unherded herds,
> Of barbarous tongue, slavered and panting halves
>
> Of breath, obedient to his trumpet's touch.
> This then is Chatillon or as you please.
> We stand in the tumult of a festival.

The tellers of tales, musicians, dancers, and children are all personifications of elements within Stevens' own prosody. The events in which they participate are woven into an almost parodically dense texture of alliteration, assonance, and consonance. The audacious alliteration of "father fetches tellers of tales" is overshadowed by the alternation of short and long vowels in the repetition of *mu.* In stanza two the "ripenesses / Of pattern" in the dance are figured in the close patterning of sound. "Negresses" rhymes with "ripenesses," which also has a frontal rhyme with "ripening." There is an internal hudibrastic with fetch*es* and negr*esses*; the combination of *ren* is varied through neg*re*sses, child*ren*, ripe*ne*sses, patt*ern*, and ripe*ni*ng. "Ripenesses" links with "pattern" through *p, n,* and *r,* and the short *a* of "pattern" rings with that of "dance." In the first two lines of the third stanza, the insidious tones of the musicians make themselves heard in the interweaving of sibilants and nasals separated by short *i*: For the*s*e the mu*s*ician*s* make *insi*diou*s* tones, / Claw*i*ng the *sing-song* of their *ins*truments. The laughter of the children echoes through the assonance of short *a* in "laugh" and "jangle"; and "jangle," catching up the *ng* of Claw*ing* the *sing-song*, backs up the musicians' sing-song with the tinny rattle of tambourines. All these tonal effects are themselves the "insidious tones" of the musicians. The theater in which the musicians play is pulled out of the air, and the festival that is described turns back on itself to become a festival of description. The anaphoral phrase "The father fetches" is a clarion call announcing new acts, and it finally announces itself, the father's trumpet. The musicians are themselves "slavered and panting halves" of the father's breath.

The curtains of the father's theater hark back to "The Curtains in the House of the Metaphysician," and they obliquely suggest those "foldings in the height / Of sleep" that in "Owl" form the starting point for Stevens' evocation of the ultimate intellect. By describing these curtains as "a naive pretence of sleep," Stevens doubles back on his self-conscious earthiness and casts doubt on the spontaneity of "the instinctive poem." This doubt may be reflected again in the reference to Chatillon. Harold Bloom informs us that Chatillon "was a sixteenth-century Huguenot humanist, a doctor expelled from Geneva for heresies from Calvinism, heresies exalting the will, and whose passion for yes led him to translate the Hebrew Bible into Latin and French."[6] If Bloom is correct, Stevens may intend us to understand that the supposedly instinctive poem is actually a product of the will. It is not Stevens but his persona who "fetches pageants out of air," and it is not the father but the father's musicians who "strike the instinctive poem." Stevens is thus, as Bloom suggests, a translator, and he stands at two removes from the original, divinely inspired text of the instinctive poem. The scenes of his theater represent an abortive effort "To compound the imagination's Latin with / The lingua franca et jocundissima" (*CP*, 397).

The father's boisterous display of prosodic virtuosity has submerged his angelic pretensions in comic gusto, and in the last two stanzas of the canto, Stevens disrupts the festival and scatters its participants:

> What festival? This loud, disordered mooch?
> These hospitaliers? These brute-like guests?
> These musicians dubbing at a tragedy,

---

6. *Ibid.*, 268.

> A-dub, a-dub, which is made up of this:
> That there are no lines to speak? There is no play.
> Or, the persons act one merely by being here.

In "Experience," Emerson declares that "inevitably does the universe wear our color, and every object fall successively into the subject itself." On the basis of this principle, he asks, "How long before our masquerade will end its music of tambourines, laughter and shouting, and we shall find it was a solitary performance?" (*RWE,* III, 79, 80). Stevens' masquerade has lasted for just six stanzas. All his poetry, even that in which he celebrates normal life, is lyric meditation. His characters do not take on an independent life and enter into dramatic conflicts with one another. There is no play because there is only one actor, the poet himself. The "tragedy" he has constructed for himself—the hopeless effort to identify himself with pure imagination—will play itself out in solitude. He must himself become the large-sculptured person and through some "latent double in the word" (*CP,* 387) imagine for him the speech he cannot speak.

Although Stevens dismisses the father's company, he retains the father's theater as a scene of poetic metamorphoses. The materials of these metamorphoses recall the imagery of the sublime in strophe three of "Owl"—moving masses, brilliant light, vast spaces—but these images are not subsumed within "an ever-changing calmest unity." There is no central point from which the images originate and to which they return:

> It is a theatre floating through the clouds,
> Itself a cloud, although of misted rock
> And mountains running like water, wave on wave,
>
> Through waves of light. It is of cloud transformed
> To cloud transformed again, idly, the way
> A season changes color to no end,
>
> Except the lavishing of itself in change,
> As light changes yellow into gold and gold
> To its opal elements and fire's delight,
>
> Splashed wide-wise because it likes magnificence
> And the solemn pleasures of magnificent space.
> The cloud drifts idly through half-thought-of forms.

The father's imaginative reverie has opened itself to a recollection of *In Memoriam,* section 123:

> O earth, what changes hast thou seen!
>   There where the long street roars, hath been
> The stillness of the central sea.
> The hills are shadows, and they flow
>   From form to form, and nothing stands;
>   They melt like mist, the solid lands,
> Like clouds they shape themselves and go.

Tennyson's lines give a dramatically concentrated image of geological time, as if a time-lapse camera had been placed on earth for, say, ten million years. Stevens' passage has no such historical reference; the "cloud" is the imagination itself. The rationale for Stevens' adaptation is not far to seek. For Tennyson, as for many of the Victorians, the spiritual crisis of the modern world manifests itself as an issue of historical vision. By breaking from the Christian tradition, the Victorians abandoned a vision of history as a meaningful dramatic structure and were forced to seek secular visions of a historical telos that would secure the spirit from the chaos of random events. Stevens implicitly resituates this spiritual crisis within the epistemological context of high Romanticism, but the central issue for him, as for Tennyson, is whether the world contains a teleological principle that would give shape and meaning to the spectacle of phenomenal change.

The "magnificence" of Stevens' imagery in canto six spreads itself over the spiritual vacancy evoked in canto two. There the shift from anomie to sinister splendor signals itself in the phrase "The season changes." Similarly, the transformations in canto six take place in "the way / A season changes color to no end." The absence of any teleological principle that would give meaning to these changes allows for a sense of idle luxury, but a luxury that cannot sustain the coherence of its elements. It is thus ripe for a dissolution wrought by the irruption of anarchic forces:

> The theatre is filled with flying birds,
> Wild wedges, as of a volcano's smoke, palm-eyed
> And vanishing, a web in a corridor
>
> Or massive portico. A capitol,
> It may be, is emerging or has just
> Collapsed. The denouement has to be postponed . . .

The smooth flow of transformation explodes into a chaos of violently fragmented images—as meaningless as the rise and fall of civilizations. The denouement must be postponed because the climax is premature. In the following stanza, Stevens reorients himself by giving a cryptic directive for the creation of a supreme fiction:

> This is nothing until in a single man contained,
> Nothing until this named thing nameless is
> And is destroyed.

"This" refers to the sort of imaginative activity exemplified in the preceding stanzas. If images are to have any meaning at all, they must cohere within an individual mind, but meaning ultimately derives not from fixed symbols but from *that which cannot be fixed* (*CP,* 353), that is, the first idea.

In the remaining lines of canto six, Stevens allusively identifies its protagonist as the same man who in canto two observes the changes of the north and who in canto three takes refuge in his house. The father's "supernatural preludes" have failed to contain those changes, and in the final stanza, Stevens comes face to face with a foreign absolute:

> He opens the door of his house
> On flames. The scholar of one candle sees
> An Arctic effulgence flaring on the frame
> Of everything he is. And he feels afraid.

As Harold Bloom notes, Stevens derives his persona here from Emerson's "Society and Solitude."[7] Emerson declares that "a scholar is a candle which the love and desire of all men will light" (*RWE,* VII, 11). In "Blue Guitar," Stevens asserted that "A candle is enough to light the world" (*CP,* 172). The confidence of this assertion now palls before the Arctic effulgence. The candle is a light of the mind, and its feeble illumination has been completely overwhelmed by the frigid brilliances of an alien element.

In canto seven the scholar of one candle abdicates the father's throne and takes his place among the worshipers of a supreme imagination. The first four stanzas, describing this imagination, are couched in the interrogative; the fifth stanza affirms that such an imagination does in fact exist:

> Is there an imagination that sits enthroned
> As grim as it is benevolent, the just
> And the unjust, which in the midst of summer stops

---

7. *Ibid.,* 94.

> To imagine winter? When the leaves are dead,
> Does it take its place in the north and enfold itself,
> Goat-leaper, crystalled and luminous, sitting
>
> In highest night? And do these heavens adorn
> And proclaim it, the white creator of black, jetted
> By extinguishings, even of planets as may be,
>
> Even of earth, even of sight, in snow,
> Except as needed by way of majesty,
> In the sky, as crown and diamond cabala?
>
> It leaps through us, through all our heavens leaps.

White is a symbol for pure presence, the primary force that generates its own opposite, black as pure absence. In order to affirm the existence of a mind of minds that can contain the Arctic effulgence, Stevens must render it independent of mortal limitations. Like the shadow of "Chocorua," it is "crystalled and luminous," but as the origin of phenomenal change, it will ultimately consume the human mind that participates in its enkindlings "even of sight, in snow." Stevens has already learned this lesson in "Esthétique du Mal," where pain teaches him that "The ultimate good" is also "The force that destroys us" (*CP,* 324). Because it is an absolute force of creation and destruction, the supreme imagination is indifferent to the merely human concept of justice, but it still needs humanity to reflect its own "majesty." As Stevens says in one of the Adagia, "God is in me or else is not at all (does not exist)" (*OP,* 172). By submitting himself to this transcendental majesty, Stevens passes through the fire and retains of his human self only the bleak crown that symbolizes his dependence on an inhuman god:

> It leaps through us, through all our heavens leaps,
> Extinguishing our planets, one by one,
> Leaving, of where we were and looked, of where
>
> We knew each other and of each other thought,
> A shivering residue, chilled and foregone,
> Except for the crown and mystical cabala.

When the father "leaps from heaven to heaven," he is attempting to assume a power that transcends his human capacity. In the fire of this mystical illumination, there is nothing left of the earthy company with which he has sought to choir it with the naked wind.

In the last two stanzas of the canto, Stevens retreats from this bleak splendor at the edges of oblivion and reestablishes a sense of the human proportions of his enterprise:

> But it dare not leap by chance in its own dark.
> It must change from destiny to slight caprice.
> And thus its jetted tragedy, its stele
>
> And shape and mournful making move to find
> What must unmake it and, at last, what can,
> Say, a flippant communication under the moon.

The referent of "it" is the imagination that sits enthroned. The adjustments this imagination makes are an unmaking of its own absolute power, that is, concessions to the protective illusions of human freedom. Caprice and flippancy are gestures of self-defense against an ultimately inescapable tragedy.

Once Stevens has atoned for the father's hubris, he is able, in canto eight, to draw out the consolatory implications of the tragic vision of canto seven. The "time of innocence" is clearly the "time / That of itself stood still" in the second canto of "Owl":

> There may be always a time of innocence.
> There is never a place. Or if there is no time,
> If it is not a thing of time, nor of place,
>
> Existing in the idea of it, alone,
> In the sense against calamity, it is not
> Less real. For the oldest and coldest philosopher,
>
> There is or may be a time of innocence
> As pure principle. Its nature is its end,
> That it should be, and yet not be, a thing
>
> That pinches the pity of the pitiful man,
> Like a book at evening beautiful but untrue,
> Like a book on rising beautiful and true.
>
> It is like a thing of ether that exists
> Almost as predicate. But it exists,
> It exists, it is visible, it is, it is.

The book that varies in credibility according to the time of the day appears to derive its signification from a passage in Emerson's "Nature." Emerson says that "the difference between the actual and the ideal force of man is happily figured by the schoolmen, in saying, that the knowledge of man is an evening knowledge, *vespertina cognitio,* but that of God is a morning knowledge, *matutina cognitio*" (*RWE*, I, 73). For Stevens, the pure principle is another name for that which cannot be named. Even when it is both beautiful and true, "the supreme poetic idea" (*NA*, 51) remains necessarily inaccessible to any fixed and final formulation. Like the shadow of "Chocorua," the pure principle is "a tragic thing, / Without existence, existing everywhere" (*CP*, 298); and like the perennial moment in "Owl," it is "Less time than place, less place than thought of place" (*CP*, 433).[8] The pure principle is the origin of space and time and is not contained by them. In time it is the ever-becoming present, at once the creation and negation of the moment. In space it is both location and absence. This idea is not easy to grasp, and Stevens begins this canto with hesitant postulations: "There may be. . . . Or if . . . If it is not . . . nor"; then, nonetheless, "it is not / Less real." After this highly qualified assertion, he starts over: "There is or may be." Belief is finally a will to believe that is a fulfillment of desire; it is achieved with the most minimal possible compromise with the modes of human understanding. The difficulty and grace of this vision are that "Its nature is its end." The pure principle does not extend to anything else, has no boundaries or external relations. It is complete within itself. It cannot be said to exist in any rational sense, any sense in which things exist through definition and limitation. Nonetheless, to be conceived at all, it must bear some resemblance to the categories of reason and language. The reticence of Stevens' description, "almost as predicate," is a tacit admission that language cannot unveil its own origin. Language functions through specification, and the pure principle has no limits of form, time, or place. The pure principle can almost be identified by reference to its manifestations or predicates, but not quite. "It is visible," perhaps, but only to a sight that wills its image, as to a mind that wills its conception.

After this effort of affirmation, the metaphysical groping modulates to reverence, and the pure principle realizes itself in a mythic figuration of divine presence:

> So, then, these lights are not a spell of light,
> A saying out of a cloud, but innocence.
> An innocence of the earth and no false sign

---

8. Vendler (*On Extended Wings*, 246) draws attention to the connection between Stevens' auroras and Wordsworth's northern lights, "that manifestation which is 'Here, nowhere, there, and everywhere at once' (*Prelude*, V, 533)."

> Or symbol of malice. That we partake thereof,
> Lie down like children in this holiness,
> As if, awake, we lay in the quiet of sleep,
>
> As if the innocent mother sang in the dark
> Of the room and on an accordion, half-heard,
> Created the time and place in which we breathed . . .

This mythic resolution takes place in the suspended moment of an unfinished proposition. There is no main verb, and the "holiness" of the moment realizes itself in a self-consciously fictive simile. In "A Primitive Like an Orb," Stevens complains that such moments always occur in metaphoric displacements: "Oh as, always too heavy for the sense / To seize, the obscurest as, the distant was" (*CP,* 441). In canto eight of "Auroras," Stevens accepts the necessity of such displacements and thereby realizes "the purpose of the poem." Once he accepts it, the world of external things no longer seems infected by the "poison" of the serpent's self-negating disbelief. Nor do "these lights" appear to be meretricious constructs from within the "cloud" of theatrical contrivances. They are the fulfillment of an inherent good, a teleological principle of sentient relation that organizes phenomenal reality into a meaningful whole. Through his affirmation of this principle, Stevens achieves a tonal poise between apocalyptic terror and archetypal pathos. All time and space converge in a harmonious plenitude of quiet meditation.

Canto eight ends with an ellipsis and canto nine begins with "And," thus subsuming the opening stanzas of the canto within the vision of the innocent mother. The first words "And of each other thought" repeat a phrase from stanza six of canto seven. This repetition resituates normal life from the apocalyptic context of canto seven to the context of mythic resolution. To describe the quality of the life he and his companions have lived, Stevens again adopts the tone of robust jocularity used for the father's festival in canto five:

> And of each other thought—in the idiom
> Of the work, in the idiom of an innocent earth,
> Not of the enigma of the guilty dream.
>
> We were as Danes in Denmark all day long
> And knew each other well, hale-hearted landsmen,
> For whom the outlandish was another day

> Of the week, queerer than Sunday. We thought alike
> And that made brothers of us in a home
> In which we fed on being brothers, fed
> And fattened as on a decorous honeycomb.

With the Danes in Denmark we are back to the resonant eccentricity of normal life.⁹ Stevens avows that the ordinary life is rich in shared meaning, but the phrase "fed / And fattened as on a decorous honeycomb" begins to edge toward a parody of opulent complacency. In the next five lines, Stevens adjusts the tone by reverting to the visionary moment. There is first a catch in thought, as of an idea just coming into consciousness; then, in the following stanza, Stevens synopsizes his visionary experience:

> This drama that we live—We lay sticky with sleep.
> This sense of the activity of fate—
> The rendezvous, when she came alone,
> By her coming became a freedom of the two,
> An isolation which only the two could share.

In "God Is Good," Stevens had described himself as a scholar "seeking celestial / Rendezvous" (*CP*, 285). That rendezvous has been kept, both in "Owl" and in "Auroras." It is, as Stevens says in "Extracts," "a singular romance" (*CP*, 256), an affair altogether segregated from the social life.

The visionary fulfillment Stevens celebrates as "a freedom of the two" is part of "the activity of fate." Another part of this activity, in Stevens' modern mythology, is the approach of death:

> Shall we be found hanging in the trees next spring?
> Of what disaster is this the imminence:
> Bare limbs, bare trees and a wind as sharp as salt?

This bleak foreboding recedes as abruptly as it emerges. In the following stanza, Stevens transcends his dread by elevating himself again to visionary sublimity:

---

9. Baird (*The Dome and the Rock*, 29) points out that the image of the Danes probably derives from Coleridge's description of a trip with Danish sailors. Stevens cites this passage from the *Biographia* in "The Figure of the Youth as Virile Poet": "'*We drank and talked and sung, till we talked and sung altogether; and then we rose and danced on the deck a set of dances*'" (*NA*, 41).

> The stars are putting on their glittering belts.
> They throw around their shoulders cloaks that flash
> Like a great shadow's last embellishment.

The movement of these two stanzas, from sudden terror to visionary peace, closely follows this passage from "The Ancient Sage":

> If utter darkness closed the day, my son—
> But earth's dark forehead flings athwart the heavens
> Her shadow crowned with stars—. (ll. 199–201)

Tennyson's imagery implicitly signals his Romantic lineage, and Stevens would no doubt himself have recalled the source of these images in Shelley and Keats. Shelley represents Intellectual Beauty as "The awful shadow of some unseen Power" that appears only in flickering moments, "Like clouds in starlight widely spread." In "When I Have Fears That I May Cease To Be," Keats provides a prototype for a more active role in the evocation of this unseen power:

> When I behold, upon the night's starr'd face,
>   Huge cloudy symbols of a high romance,
> And think that I shall never live to trace
>   Their shadows, with the magic hand of chance.

Stevens has lived to fulfill this ambition, and he has been able to rely not only on the magic hand of chance but also on the hands of all his Romantic predecessors. Among these predecessors, it is Emerson who provides the most distinct exposition of the principles that inform the Romantic sublime. In "Nature" he declares that nature "always speaks of Spirit. It suggests the absolute. It is a perpetual effect. It is a great shadow pointing always to the sun behind us" (*RWE*, I, 61). Stevens' own "great shadow" implicitly substantiates the bold claim he is to make in "A Collect of Philosophy": "It is very easy to imagine a poetry of ideas in which the particulars of reality would be shadows among the poem's disclosures" (*OP*, 187).

The great shadow of "Auroras" discloses the transcendental spirit, but it offers no release from destruction. In the final stanza of canto nine, Stevens returns to the eminent disaster of his own death. Although his recollection of the transcendental, Romantic sublime cannot effect a complete resolution of his fear, it modulates the harshness of his foreboding:

> It may come tomorrow in the simplest word,
> Almost as part of innocence, almost,
> Almost as the tenderest and the truest part.

Approaching death will be almost as gentle and right as a divine touch or kiss, almost. It will almost be a part of "the innocence of living" (*CP,* 322), but it will retain something of its aspect of evil, for it will happen not to a metaphysical abstraction of freedom and fate but to a human being.

In the subtle tonal ambiguity of "almost," the dramatic enactment of Stevens' visionary quest comes to a close. In the final canto, he attempts to balance the accounts of his enterprise by reducing the human condition to four terms: man, world, happiness, and unhappiness. The asymmetrical character of the formula he selects—"An unhappy people in a happy world"—gives evidence of the unclosable gap between individual need and visionary theodicy. This formula nonetheless answers most closely to the experience that has been enacted. To demonstrate its relative adequacy, Stevens reads through the other alternatives and rejects them:

> An unhappy people in a happy world—
> Read, rabbi, the phases of this difference.
> An unhappy people in an unhappy world—
>
> Here are too many mirrors for misery.
> A happy people in an unhappy world—
> It cannot be. There's nothing there to roll
>
> On the expressive tongue, the finding fang.
> A happy people in a happy world—
> Buffo! A ball, an opera, a bar.
>
> Turn back to where we were when we began:
> An unhappy people in a happy world.
> Now, solemnize the secretive syllables.

The reasons for Stevens' selection among these options are tonal and generic. "An unhappy people in an unhappy world" seems intrinsically repugnant and also lacks any vital tension. This formula would be most suitable for the period of enervation depicted in "The Sun This March." "A happy people in an unhappy world" would be a vapid people, ignorant of evil and drifting inconsequentially through pleasant delusion. "A happy people in a happy world" immediately produces gross hilarity in its appropriate settings. As

Stevens will say in "New Haven," "The strength at the centre is serious" (*CP*, 477). He need not play the clown. "An unhappy people in a happy world" allows for a visionary fulfillment within the transcendental sublime (a happy world) and also invests the poetic hero with a tragic and elegiac dignity.

The formulaic reductiveness of Stevens' summary enforces a tone of semi-comic officiousness that results in the self-conscious affectation of the phrase "solemnize the secretive syllables." This phrase absorbs the need for self-mockery, and in the final stanzas, Stevens shifts into a more lyrically hieratic mode:

> Read to the congregation, for today
> And for tomorrow, this extremity,
> This contrivance of the spectre of the spheres,
>
> Contriving balance to contrive a whole,
> The vital, the never-failing genius,
> Fulfilling his meditations, great and small.
>
> In these unhappy he meditates a whole,
> The full of fortune and the full of fate,
> As if he lived all lives, that he might know,
>
> In hall harridan, not hushful paradise,
> To a haggling of wind and weather, by these lights
> Like a blaze of summer straw, in winter's nick.

Although the repetition of "contrive" emphasizes the inescapably artificial character of his cosmic constructs, Stevens subverts this acknowledgment by representing contrivance as a closed transcendental structure. Contrivance is a "vital" force beyond the individual imagination. The "spectre of the spheres," essential imagination, is at once the object that is contrived and the source of this contrivance. He is one form of the pure principle, and, like this principle, his nature is his end. The final stanza elliptically identifies the imagery of the poem as the chosen locus for the self-realization of this principle. Its purpose is intransitive, "that he might know." The "whole" is a fulfilled teleology that subsists, above or below the fulfillment of ordinary human desires, as a condition of knowledge.

Although he is an inhuman force, the specter of the spheres contains all ordinary human experience. It is "As if he lived all lives, that he might know." By mediating the specter's contrivance, Stevens himself would gain access to all experience throughout time. The specter is equivalent to what both Stevens and Emerson call the "universal mind." In "History," Emerson provides a prototype for Stevens' implicit claim that as visionary protagonist, he speaks for all men: "There is one mind common to all individual men. Every man is an inlet to the same and to all of the same. He that is once admitted to the right of reason is made a freeman of the whole estate. What Plato has thought, he may think; what a saint has felt, he may feel; what at any time has befallen any man, he can understand. Who hath access to this universal mind is a party to all that is or can be done, for this is the only and sovereign agent" (*RWE*, II, 3). In "New Haven," drawing on Emerson's illustration of this idea, Stevens addresses himself as the "ancientest saint ablaze with ancientest truth" (*CP*, 467). In "Things of August," he explicitly defines the universal scope of the visionary protagonist. He recalls the father of "Auroras" and describes him as "The total of human shadows bright as glass" (*CP*, 494).

The supreme fiction is a fiction of "the whole." In "Owl," Stevens articulates the relations among "the forms of thought" that constitute this whole, and in "Auroras" he depicts the problematic relations between the poetic hero and the inhuman imagination within which these forms are subsumed. "A Primitive Like an Orb" completes the climactic phase of Stevens' visionary enterprise. The purpose of this poem is to expound the basic idea of his supreme fiction, the idea that the poet's individual fictions derive from and reflect essential imagination, that is, the world-creating mind of God. The images of "Primitive," like those of "Owl" and "Auroras," are mythic in scope; they represent elemental forces of mind and nature. "Primitive" is not, however, mythic in structure. Nor is it merely a collection of "notes." It is, as Stevens describes it in stanza eleven, "A definition with an illustration," or, more precisely, a definition with several illustrations, all of which are finally subsumed in the image of the giant. This image functions as an intentionally amorphous embodiment of "the spectre of the spheres"; it personifies the contrived balance that constitutes "a happy world."

In tone, "Primitive" is the modal counterpart of "Credences of Summer." It extends the moment of ripeness from midsummer to early autumn and celebrates this moment as "The fulfillment of fulfillments, in opulent, / Last terms; the largest, bulging still with more" (*CP*, 441). The modal opulence of "Primitive" represents another of Stevens' elaborations of the "high romance" sketched by Keats. In the first stanza of "To Autumn," Keats apostrophizes Autumn as a season that conspires to

fill all fruit with ripeness to the core;
To swell the gourd, and plump the hazel shells
With a sweet kernel; to set budding more,
And still more, later flowers for the bees.

In *The Auroras of Autumn,* as the title of the volume suggests, the prevalent seasonal setting is autumn or early winter. "The Beginning," "In a Bad Time," "An Ordinary Evening in New Haven," and the final canto of "Things of August" are early-winter poems. Many of the poems in *The Rock* and the later poems of *Opus Posthumous* are set in deep winter. In "Primitive," Stevens remains within the autumnal phase of mellow fruitfulness. He does not, as in "Credences," follow Keats in a foreboding of autumnal decay. The elegiac sublimity of "Owl" and the tragic heroism of "Auroras" have earned for Stevens the right to expound his achievement in final terms—"For a moment final" (*CP,* 168).

In the title of "A Primitive Like an Orb," Stevens has synthesized the divergent elements within his own visionary development. "A Primitive" signifies the archetypalism that is represented in "Owl's Clover" by the subman, and "an Orb" serves as a geometric figuration for the universal whole that is a construct of the speculative reason. Emerson suggests a similar synthesis in his description of a "primary and aboriginal sentiment" that enables us to come from the circumference to "the centre of the world." In preparing himself to compose "a poem of the whole"—and in the process to integrate his own sensibility—Stevens has frequently received inspiration from Emerson, and "Primitive" implicitly confirms this elective affinity. As we have seen, Emerson may well have contributed to Stevens' conception of an archetypal subconscious memory, and the significance with which Stevens invests the image of the circle probably owes more to Emerson than to anyone else. Santayana also discusses this image, and by comparing his treatment of it with Emerson's, we gain a more definite sense of the way in which—despite Stevens' personal association with Santayana—the ardent American Transcendentalist takes precedence for Stevens over the skeptical Continental aesthete. In discussing the aesthetic "values of geometrical figures," Santayana offers a "definition of space as the possibility of motion" and so assigns a low aesthetic value to the circle. "If a circle is presented, the eye will fall upon its centre, as to the centre of gravity, as it were, of the balanced attractions of all the points; and there will be, in that position, an indifference and sameness of sensation, in whatever direction some accident moves the eye, that accounts very well for the emotional quality of the circle. It is a form which, although beautiful in its purity and simplicity, and wonderful in its continuity, lacks any stimulating quality, and is often ugly in the arts." Santayana argues that because the sense of space depends on the stimulation given to the organs of perception—especially "the tensions in the eye"—the circle has a "dull and stupefying effect."[10] For Emerson, purity, simplicity, and continuity are in themselves stimulating; his mind characteristically operates through emblematic figuration, and the image of the circle sets off infinite associative vibrations. In "Nature" he declares that "the central Unity" of nature "betrays its source in Universal Spirit. . . . It is like a great circle on a sphere, comprising all possible circles; which, however, may be drawn and comprise it in like manner. Every such truth is the absolute Ens seen from one side. But it has innumerable sides" (*RWE*, I, 44). In "Circles" he argues that the circle is "the highest emblem in the cipher of the world," and he cites the same image from Saint Augustine that in "A Collect of Philosophy" Stevens cites from Pascal. "St. Augustine described the nature of God as a circle whose centre was everywhere and its circumference nowhere" (*RWE*, II, 301; see *OP*, 194). Emerson maintains that while knowledge of this emblem originates in the primary organ of perception, the generative center transcends all human knowledge: "The eye is the first circle; the horizon which it forms is the second; and throughout nature this primary figure is repeated without end. . . . Whilst the eternal generation of circles proceeds, the eternal generator abides. That central life is somewhat superior to creation, superior to knowledge and thought, and contains all its circles" (*RWE*, II, 301, 318). In Stevens' rendering of these visionary precepts, "that central life" becomes "the central poem" that "begets the others." Both "that central life" and "the central poem" are conceptually equivalent to what Coleridge calls "the primary IMAGINATION," that is, "the living Power and prime Agent of all human Perception . . . a repetition in the finite mind of the eternal act of creation in the infinite I AM."[11]

In "Credences of Summer," Stevens realizes the fullness of normal poetry

10. Santayana, *The Sense of Beauty*, 88–89.
11. Samuel Taylor Coleridge, *Biographia Literaria*, ed. James Engell and W. Jackson Bate (1983; rpr. Princeton, 1984), 304, vol. VII of *The Collected Works of Samuel Taylor Coleridge*, ed. Kathleen Coburn and Bart Winer.

through a process of exclusion and limitation. Pure poetry, because it is "A difficult apperception" (*CP,* 440), requires an opposite method; in "Primitive," as in Emerson's essay "Circles," definition remains open and gradually expands to encompass everything, including itself. This technique of expanding but ultimately self-reflexive definition determines the structure of "Primitive." In stanzas one, two, four, six, and seven, Stevens directly expounds his thesis:

> The essential poem at the centre of things,
> The arias that spiritual fiddlings make,
> Have gorged the cast-iron of our lives with good.
> We do not prove the existence of the poem.
> It is something seen and known in lesser poems.
> One poem proves another and the whole.
> The essential poem begets the others.
> The central poem is the poem of the whole,
> . . . .
> The roundness that pulls tight the final ring.

Stanza three begins as an elaboration of the ideas in stanza two, then breaks to a nagging doubt about the metaphoric displacements necessary to the realization of the supreme fiction—"the obscurest as, the distant was. . . ." The ellipsis points leave this problem hanging for the moment, but in stanzas five and six, Stevens assimilates "as" to his celebratory description. Stanzas four, five, and six are held together by run-on syntax:

> With these they celebrate the central poem,
> The fulfillment of fulfillments, in opulent,
> Last terms, the largest, bulging still with more,
> V
> Until the used-to earth and sky . . .
> inform
> Each other by sharp informations. . . .
> It is
> As if the central poem became the world,
> VI
> And the world the central poem, each one the mate
> Of the other, as if summer was a spouse,
> Espoused each morning, each long afternoon,

> And the mate of summer: her mirror and her look,
> Her only place and person, a self of her
> That speaks, denouncing separate selves, both one.

It is "as if" there were no "as," as if all displacements were annulled in the speech of the mother who proclaims essential unity. The central poem, here represented by the mother as the one who "speaks," is at first separate from "the world." Then, by way of her mirror, she becomes the world. The mirror suggests opposing entities—reality and the mimetic medium—but as "Her only place and person" it reflects only itself, which is also her self. The principle that makes this paradoxical transumption possible follows immediately: "The essential poem begets the others." By shifting from a static dichotomy—the world and the poem—to an idea of the poem as itself the generative center of the world, Stevens contrives to close the gap between the sign and the signified.

Stanzas seven, eight, and nine form one sentence. Stanzas eight and nine, both beginning with "And," continue to illustrate, through appositives, the thesis with which stanza seven begins: "The central poem is the poem of the whole." The appositives that elaborate on this thesis in stanza seven place natural phenomena on the same ontological footing as all the individual poems of mortal poets and thus complete the integrative process of stanza six:

> The central poem is the poem of the whole,
> The poem of the composition of the whole,
> The composition of blue sea and of green,
> Of blue light and of green, as lesser poems,
> And the miraculous multiplex of lesser poems.

The appositives in the first five lines of stanza eight offer synonyms for the central poem ("A vis, a principle," "an inherent order," a beneficent "nature," "utmost repose"), and in the final line, Stevens presents the "giant, on the horizon, glistening" as the last in this series of synonyms. This metaphor, "an abstraction given head," serves as the binding motif for the remaining four stanzas of the poem.

The loose, appositional progression from the imagery of stanza seven—"The composition of blue sea and of green"—to the image of the giant contains a submerged history of Stevens' visionary enterprise. The starting point discloses itself in Stevens' response to "The Ancient Sage." Stevens' conception of the essential poem is in close kinship to what the sage describes as "such large life" and calls "the Nameless" (l. 57). The sage declares, "Thou canst not prove the Nameless" (l. 57), and Stevens declares, "We do not prove the existence of the poem." Responding to the skeptic's question, "'And yet what sign of aught that lies / Behind the green and blue?'" (ll. 25–26), the sage scoffs at the superficiality of human knowledge, a knowledge that "never yet hath dipt into the abysm, / The Abysm of all Abysms, beneath, within / The blue of sky and sea, the green of earth" (ll. 39–41). Blue and green are elemental colors for Stevens. His emblematic use of these colors to represent an elemental phenomenal presence appears as early as 1914, in "One More Sunset," an unpublished poem from the sequence "Carnet de Voyage": "The changing green and blue / Flow round the changing earth."[12] In Crispin's brave new world, the old mythic structures are dissolved within this elemental phenomenalism. In a faint memorial gesture to the Wordsworth of "The World Is Too Much With Us," the narrator of "Comedian" epitomizes this dissolution through the image of "Triton, dissolved in shifting diaphanes / Of blue and green" (*CP*, 28). Like Crispin, Stevens has sought to cleanse the world of its antiquated myths and to live within an atmosphere of "elemental potencies and pangs" (*CP*, 31). Unlike Crispin, he has also sought to reconstitute these elemental potencies as a new mythic structure. This purpose begins to take firm shape in "Owl's Clover." In "Primitive," the image of the giant evokes the archetypal source that in "Owl's Clover" produces the image of "a sprawling portent." Although it "bears all darkness in its bulk," the portent finally "steps forth, priestly in severity, . . . A wandering orb on a path grown clear" (*OP*, 68, 70). After "Owl's Clover," one of Stevens' primary tasks is to integrate the subconscious source of archetypal images with the speculative reason. Through this integration, he gains access to what, in "Extracts," he calls both the "central heart and mind of minds" (*CP*, 254) and "the pure idea" (*CP*, 256). In "It Must Be Abstract," the pure idea of "Extracts" becomes "the first idea," and Stevens represents this idea as "The pensive giant prone in violet space" (*CP*, 387). In "Chocorua to Its Neighbor," the giant gives place to the shadow who declares, "'My solitaria are the meditations of a central mind.'" After this declaration, the shadow experiences an access of power: "the gigantic bulk of him / Grew strong" (*CP*, 298, 299). In "Primitive," Stevens takes the full measure of this gigantic bulk.

Although it is a single image, the giant of "Primitive" functions as a "late

12. Cited in Buttel, *The Making of "Harmonium,"* 156.

plural" of the first idea, for within this image Stevens combines the essential qualities of the three mythic figures in "Owl." Peace after death, who "stood with our last blood adorned," is "An immaculate personage in nothingness," and the giant, "in bright excellence adorned," is a "giant of nothingness." The mother in "Owl" manifests herself "in the way / Invisible change discovers what is changed," and the giant is "ever changing, living in change." As an image of "utmost repose," the giant is equivalent to the "ever-changing, calmest unity, / The unique composure" of sleep realized. Within this composure a "vanishing-vanished violet . . . wraps round / The giant body the meanings of its folds," and the giant in "Primitive" is "Vested in the serious folds of majesty." (In "Auroras" it is the need for "majesty" that sustains the reciprocal dependence of human sight and the supreme imagination [*CP,* 417].) Like all three of the figures in "Owl," the giant is of a "parental magnitude" and is a "patron of origins." He is, finally, another figuration of the parental space that produces mythic figurations.

Although it is a ubiquitous presence, parental space manifests itself in poetic realizations only at certain privileged moments. In stanzas two and three of "Primitive," Stevens describes these moments, drawing on a long series of his notes toward a supreme fiction. In "Notes" itself, Stevens prefigures the poem of the whole as "The complicate, the amassing harmony" (*CP,* 403). In "Primitive" the particular moment at which this harmony manifests itself occurs as a paradoxical disruption of the mutually exclusive categories of being and nothingness. In "Chocorua," Stevens has embodied this principle of disruption in the shadow that is "Without existence, existing everywhere." Like "The abstract" of "Contrary Theses (II)," it is "suddenly there and gone again":

> We do not prove the existence of the poem.
> It is something seen and known in lesser poems.
> It is the huge, high harmony that sounds
> A little and a little, suddenly,
> By means of a separate sense. It is and it
> Is not and, therefore, is. In the instant of speech,
> The breadth of an accelerando moves,
> Captives the being, widens—and was there.

"The abstract" is a principle of pure relation that devolves into concrete reality. In "Auroras," Stevens calls it a "pure principle," a thing that both is and is not and that is the origin of everything that "is," the world of space and time. In "Notes," Stevens describes mere activity—"the merely going round"—as "a final good, / The way wine comes at a table in a wood" (*CP*, 405). In "Primitive" he uses a similar image of the concrete as a final good, and he situates this good within the activity of the essential poem:

> What milk there is in such captivity,
> What wheaten bread and oaten cake and kind,
> Green guests and table in the woods and songs
> At heart, within an instant's motion, within
> A space grown wide.[13]

As in "Owl" and "Auroras," Stevens must use spatiotemporal metaphors—"an instant's motion," "A space grown wide"—to represent the activity of a principle that transcends space and time. It is the necessity of using such metaphors that generates Stevens' complaint in the remaining lines of the stanza:

> A space grown wide, the inevitable blue
> Of secluded thunder, an illusion, as it was,
> Oh as, always too heavy for the sense
> To seize, the obscurest as, the distant was . . .

The realization of the essential poem remains "an illusion," a fictive construct, but it is a construct that invests illusion with ontological validity, for within this construct the universe is itself the supreme creator of fictions.

By subordinating concrete reality to the essential poem, Stevens effects a definitive theoretical synthesis between pure and normal poetry. At the time of "Notes," Stevens can suggest but is not yet able to articulate fully the hierarchical relations between the two modes. Section three of "Notes" concludes with an encomium, "Fat girl, terrestrial." Although she is found "in difference," he also speaks of her in terms that imply her transumption within a medium that transcends the limitations of normal poetry. He calls her "the irrational distortion": "That's it: the more than rational distortion, / The fiction that results from feeling. Yes, that." The word *feeling* seems to suggest nothing more than a willingness to neglect reason in favor of emotional responsiveness, the lowest form of Romanticism. However, in the final stanza of "Primitive," Stevens repeats the phrase of conclusive conviction—"That's

---

13. In what appears to be a tacit correction of Helen Vendler's judgment on the passage from "Notes," Harold Bloom draws attention to the connection between these two passages (see Vendler, *On Extended Wings*, 201; and Bloom, *The Poems of Our Climate*, 216).

it"—and he represents "the more than rational distortion" as a fictive dialectic on a cosmic scale. He uses the word *change* as a cryptic notation for the process through which the universe fictionalizes itself into existence. Change is the dynamic principle that mediates between being and nothingness, is and is not, presence and absence, thus resolving the giant nonentity of the universe into the world of phenomena:

> That's it. The lover writes, the believer hears,
> The poet mumbles and the painter sees,
> Each one, his fated eccentricity,
> As a part, but part, but tenacious particle,
> Of the skeleton of the ether, the total
> Of letters, prophecies, perceptions, clods
> Of color, the giant of nothingness, each one
> And the giant ever changing, living in change.

This culminating representation of the giant answers to the two basic theoretical requirements of a supreme fiction: it must be abstract and it must change. In order to construct a satisfactory figure, Stevens draws on his own visionary motifs and directly, it seems, on those of Tennyson and Emerson. In "Montrachet" he has said "Amen to thought, our singular skeleton" (*CP*, 260), and in "Auroras" he has affirmed the existence of a "pure principle" that is "like a thing of ether." These two images now combine in a paradoxical image of a philosophical structure that dissolves into pure relation. Stevens' assertion that this abstract giant is "ever changing" echoes a passage from "The Ancient Sage." The skeptic in the poem asserts that all life is but a "'Slight ripple on the boundless deep / That moves, and all is gone.'" The sage replies:

> But that one ripple on the boundless deep
> Feels that the deep is boundless, and itself
> For ever changing form, but evermore
> One with the boundless motion of the deep. (ll. 189–94)

Emerson too declares that whenever one looks at nature, "its outline and texture are changed again" (*RWE*, II, 13) and, like Tennyson, he feels that all phenomenal change is but a ripple on the boundless deep. For Tennyson's ancient sage, a vision of the boundless deep produces a state of mystical quiescence. For Emerson and Stevens, this vision presents itself as a supreme challenge to artistic representation. In "Nature," Emerson declares that "nothing is quite beautiful alone; nothing but is beautiful in the whole. A single object is only so far beautiful as it suggests this universal grace. The poet, the painter, the sculptor, the musician, the architect, seek each to concentrate this radiance of the world on one point, and each in his several work to satisfy the love of beauty which stimulates him to produce" (*RWE,* I, 24). In his own series—the lover, the believer, the poet, and the painter—Stevens commingles this recollection of Emerson with an adaptation of Theseus' declaration in *A Midsummer Night's Dream*: "The lunatic, the lover and the poet / Are of imagination all compact." (Stevens replaces "lunatic" with "believer.") By designating his four examples of imaginative heroism as each a "tenacious particle," Stevens allusively suggests an association between the passage from "Nature" just quoted and two other passages from Emerson. In "Nature," again, Emerson declares that "a leaf, a drop, a crystal, a moment of time, is related to the whole. Each particle is a microcosm, and faithfully renders the likeness of the world" (*RWE,* I, 43). In "The Over-Soul," reformulating this proposition, he declares that "we live in succession, in division, in parts, in particles. Meantime within man is the soul of the whole; the wise silence; the universal beauty, to which every part and particle is equally related; the eternal ONE. And this deep power in which we exist and whose beatitude is all accessible to us, is not only self-sufficing and perfect in every hour, but the act of seeing and the thing seen, the seer and the spectacle, the subject and the object, are one" (*RWE,* II, 269). Stevens' giant of nothingness has no distinct form, but it is no mere vacancy. As the central poem that begets the others, it is what Emerson calls "the eternal generator."

When, in 1954, Stevens says that his work "suggests the possibility of a supreme fiction, recognized as a fiction, in which men could propose to themselves a fulfillment" (*LWS,* 820), it is to the visionary theory exemplified in "Owl," "Auroras," and "Primitive" that he refers. By means of this theory, Stevens solves the spiritual problems he has formulated in poems such as "Anatomy of Monotony" and "Negation." In "Anatomy of Monotony" he represents being and nothingness as two spheres, one contained within the other; the solid world of self and reality is surrounded by an infinite expanse of spiritual vacancy, "And this the spirit sees and is aggrieved" (*CP,* 108). In "Negation" he depicts God as a "Too vague idealist" who strives after a "harmonious whole" but who can achieve only "evanescent symmetries" (*CP,* 97–98). In the cosmology of "Owl," "Auroras," and "Primitive," being and nothingness are dialectical components of a universal spiritual activity. Sentient process is the only reality, and this process culminates in "a poem / Of the whole." The universe drives in to its own center and, through the mediation of "supreme poetry," completes the teleological process of self-recognition.

The Enduring, Visionary Love

"Owl," "Auroras," and "Primitive" establish the definitive terms of Stevens' visionary achievement, and the resolutions within these poems are inherently unstable. The individual's perspective cannot be permanently subsumed within the voluptuous welter of the essential poem, nor can poetic figuration permanently suspend the difference between itself and that which it represents. In "In a Bad Time" (1948), Stevens both confirms the definitive order exemplified by "Auroras" and also suggests the problematic character of his relation to it:

> How mad would he have to be to say, "He beheld
> An order and thereafter he belonged
> To it"? He beheld an order of the northern sky. (*CP*, 426)

Stevens' madness is never without method, and it is the necessity of method—the "secret arrangements of it in the mind" (*CP*, 341)—that leaves him dissatisfied with his visionary achievement. The supreme fiction remains problematic, dependent finally on the will to believe, and so it becomes increasingly vulnerable to Stevens' dread of the "poverty" of old age and his horror before the monstrosity of personal dissolution. In the second stanza of "In a Bad Time," Stevens implicitly concedes that one does belong to one's order, but he suggests a more sinister application of this principle:

> But the beggar gazes on calamity
> And thereafter he belongs to it, to bread
> Hard found, and water tasting of misery.

Stevens never succumbs for long to this threat of a bleakness without splendor. In the final stanza, he exhorts his tragic muse to "Speak loftier lines. / Cry out, 'I am the purple muse.'" In most of the poems he will yet write, Stevens seeks to obey this injunction.

Because visionary perfection is necessarily a contrived and transient balance, it cannot rest in an achieved formulation but must continue to project itself in potential realizations. In a letter of 1948, written after "Primitive," Stevens declares, "I do seek a centre and expect to go on seeking it" (*LWS,* 584). After the three major visionary poems, Stevens' projections figure their possible resolutions in terms and images that derive from the resolutions that have already been achieved. In "Study of Images II" (1949), Stevens depicts the way in which "the centre of images" continues to beget other images, and he remarks that it is

> As if, as if, as if the disparate halves
> Of things were waiting in a betrothal known
> To none, awaiting espousal to the sound
>
> Of right joining, a music of ideas, the burning
> And breeding and bearing birth of harmony,
> The final relation, the marriage of the rest. (*CP,* 464–65)

If by "The final relation" Stevens means the pure principle of sentient relation, the marriage he represents himself as still awaiting has already taken place. It has been "seen and known" in the poems it begets. If by "final" he means placed beyond the compass of change, the marriage would entail a displacement of the supreme fiction that would cancel the conditions on which it depends—dynamic process become fixed entity.

In "Saint John and the Back-Ache" (1948), Stevens depicts dramatically the difficulty of sustaining any final relation and also suggests the way in which the recognition of this difficulty generates apocalyptic prophecy. Saint John, in dialogue with the backache, initially defines the world as "presence." In describing presence, he uses terms similar to those Stevens has used in the second stanza of "Primitive" to describe the expansive moment in which the essential poem manifests itself. "It fills the being before the mind can think. / The effect of the object is beyond the mind's / Extremest pinch" (*CP,* 436–37). Presence is, apparently, "The effect of the object," but not any particular object; Saint John lists several objects, and they all seem to serve as allusions to moments either of anticipation or of dissolution in Stevens' visionary enterprise. "Presence is not the woman, come upon, / Not yet accustomed." Saint John's efforts to explain presence reflect the confusion of a mind under the influence of physical pain. Although the images he lists are not, he says, emblems of presence, they nonetheless help bridge the gap between the mind and external reality. "They help us face the dumbfoundering abyss / Between us and the object." Presence, the effect of the object, has become absence, the abyss. In "Primitive" the giant of nothingness is the locus of both presence and absence, the constituents of change. In "Auroras," Stevens has figured this locus in the image of the serpent that perpetually displaces itself, and he now returns to this image. The "dumbfoundering abyss" is

> The possible nest in the invisible tree,
> Which in a composite season, now unknown,
> Denied, dismissed, may hold a serpent, loud
> In our captious hymns, erect and sinuous,
> Whose venom and whose wisdom will be one.

The prophetic resonance of Saint John's declamation overwhelms the contorted obscurity of his logic, but the backache remains unconvinced.

> It may be, may be. It is possible.
> Presence lies far too deep, for me to know
> Its irrational reaction, as from pain.

Presence and pain are equally irrational distortions. Pain may not be a philosophically unanswerable refutation of a visionary theodicy, but it renders this theodicy practically irrelevant.

There can be no permanent release from evil, but there can be moments in which individual pathos merges with the mythic archetypes and thus elevates itself into an impersonal grandeur of vision. "World Without Peculiarity" (1948) represents one such moment. The poem begins as an unusually direct and poignant expression of personal loss. With the exception of the loss of a child, the kinds of loss Stevens describes are those of the closest human relations. His father "lies now / In the poverty of dirt"; the ghost of his mother "returns and cries on his breast"; and "she that he loved turns cold at his light touch" (*CP,* 453). In the last three stanzas, Stevens effects a reversal, a transformation of grief into fulfillment. He subsumes the image of the real mother—"the thing upon his breast"—within an archetypal image of the earth as itself the ancient mother. The result is that "He, too, is human and difference disappears." When difference disappears, Stevens has access to the "dissociated abundance of being" that is personified in "The Woman in Sunshine" (1948; *CP,* 445). Like the inhuman spirit in "Bouquet of Belle Sçavoir," this woman is the formless origin of definite form, including the form she herself assumes in the poem. Her image, like that of the mother in "Owl," is realized through the simultaneous assertion and negation of images. The mother "stood tall in self not symbol," and the woman in sunshine is composed of neither "the beginning nor end of a form." Her clarity of presence is invisible to the eye. Her dress is "threadless," a self-negating metaphor for sunlight, and she herself is perceived only as the sweet atmosphere of the summer fields. She is not, however, merely a personification of the sensual plenitude of summer. Her presence creates a spiritual atmosphere in which the odor of the summer fields is a manifestation of the archetypal source that invests human experience with the sense of union. She is "invisibly clear, the only love."

The woman in sunshine is a creature of paradox. She is not accessible to reason, but she can be realized in poetic evocation. When summer gives place to autumn and the threat of disintegration, Stevens is sometimes tempted to extend his visionary symbols beyond the limits of that which can be poetically realized. The course of Stevens' yielding to this temptation can be traced in two poems, "The Beginning" (1947) and "A Golden Woman in a Silver Mirror" (1949). In both poems he employs the images of the woman and her mirror, the images by means of which, in stanza six of "Primitive," he closes the gap between the world and the essential poem. "The Beginning" hovers in the empty space between the vivid recollection of summer ripeness and the first chilling intimations of final loss:

> So summer comes in the end to these few stains
> And the rust and rot of the door through which she went.
>
> The house is empty. But here is where she sat
> To comb her dewy hair, a touchless light,
>
> Perplexed by its darker iridescences.
> This was the glass in which she used to look
>
> At the moment's being, without history,
> The self of summer perfectly perceived.
>
> . . . .
>
> The dress is lying, cast-off, on the floor.
>
> Now, the first tutoyers of tragedy
> Speak softly, to begin with, in the eaves. (*CP,* 427–28)

The "self of summer perfectly perceived" is the mother after she has become her own mirror image and has thus become identical with the place she reflects in poetry. After she has gone, her glass remains as a vacant reflection. In "A Golden Woman," Stevens attempts to confront and transcend his fear of death by breaking this glass:

> Suppose this was the root of everything.
> Suppose it turned out to be or that it touched
> An image that was mistress of the world.
>
> For example: Au Château. Un salon. A glass
> The sun steps into, regards and finds itself;
> Or: Gawks of hay . . . Augusta Moon, before
>
> An attic glass, hums of the old Lutheran bells
> At home; or: In the woods, belle Belle alone
> Rattles with fear in unreflecting leaves.
>
> Abba, dark death is the breaking of a glass.
> The dazzled flakes and splinters disappear.
> The seal is relaxed as dirt, perdu. (*CP*, 460)

The rattling of fear in unreflecting leaves echoes the intimate whispers of death from under the eaves, but with a tonal difference. The jumbling of images in the second and third stanzas and the jocularity of the phrase "Gawks of hay" disrupt the tone of visionary meditation with which the poem begins. The French words suggest a manner of elegant insouciance. The declaration "The seal is as relaxed as dirt" recalls the grim poignancy of "the poverty of dirt" in "World Without Peculiarity," but with the word *perdu* poignancy is diverted into snappy drollery. The whispers of tragedy have been transmuted into the cackle of black humor, and in the last two stanzas of the poem black humor transmutes itself into a hieratic recital:

> But the images, disembodied, are not broken.
> They have, or they may have, their glittering crown.
> Sound-soothing pearl and omni-diamond,
>
> Of the most beautiful, the most beautiful maid
> And mother. How long have you lived and looked,
> Ababba, expecting this king's queen to appear?

The breaking of the glass is a breaking of the poet as imager and of the image that is "mistress of the world." By exploiting the word *disembodied* from "The Woman in Sunshine," Stevens has attempted to segregate the individual images of the world from the glass in which these images find themselves. The queen that is mistress of the world has already appeared in many poems; the queen who is still "to appear" is an unrealizable figure situated beyond the impenetrable darkness of the broken glass.

The dissociative legerdemain of "A Golden Woman" transforms the emblems of the supreme fiction into rhetorical icons to be brandished in the face of death. Whatever they gain thereby in hieratic potency must be purchased at the price of their vital pathos, and this loss of vitality generates a necessary reaction in favor of the real and palpable. Commenting on a group of poems that includes "A Golden Woman," Stevens remarks that "after a round of this sort of thing I always feel the need of getting some different sort of satisfaction out of poetry" (*LWS*, 642). The kind of satisfaction he has in mind is that of "normal life, insight into the commonplace, reconciliation with every-day reality" (*LWS*, 643). It is in part an impulse of this sort that motivates the composition of "An Ordinary Evening in New Haven" (1949). While he is writing the poem Stevens explains to one of his correspondents that "here my interest is to try to get as close to the ordinary, the commonplace and the ugly as it is possible for a poet to get. It is not a question of grim reality but of plain reality. The object is of course to purge oneself of anything false. . . . This is not in any sense a turning away from the ideas of Credences of Summer: it is a development of those ideas" (*LWS*, 636–37). These remarks help to explain the initial impetus for "New Haven," but they give little sense of what actually takes place in the poem. In "Credences," Stevens effectively exiles desire for what is not given in the present moment of sensual plenitude. In "New Haven" he attempts to construct a continuum between the "commonplace" and the "miraculous" (*CP*, 470). "Plain reality" serves only as the starting point for a series of dialectical progressions that culminate not in celebratory expositions of a limited telos but in reformulations of the supreme fiction. The moments of resolution in "New Haven" take place exclusively within the realm of pure poetry. They are not moments of "reconciliation with every-day reality"; they are realizations of essential unity. The dominant mythic figure in the poem is not the fat girl but the ancient mother.

In constructing the dialectical progressions of "New Haven," Stevens succumbs to a fundamental confusion of terms. There are two basic dichotomies at work in the poem. One is the opposition between external reality and the individual mind, and the other is the modal polarity between pure and normal poetry. Within a dualistic cosmos, the endless exchanges between reality and the imagination can never resolve themselves into an essential unity. But within a cosmos governed by a transcendent principle of pure sentient relation, the pluralistic world of normal poetry can be contained within the unity of the essential poem. In establishing the conflicts he is to resolve, Stevens repeatedly confuses the terms of one dichotomy with those of the other. He begins with the "plain reality" of a dualistic cosmos, and he concludes with evocations of the essential poem. These evocations depend on the same transcendental assumptions that govern "Description Without Place" and "Primitive." In other words, Stevens poses problems that cannot be solved, or he reaches solutions only by modifying the terms in which the problems have been posed. Stevens' desire to purge himself of anything false is no doubt sincere, but this motive is complicated and in some measure obstructed by yet more urgent motives. Through the confused articulations of "This endlessly elaborating poem" (*CP*, 486), Stevens struggles desperately to escape from the belatedness of his present existence and to reconcile himself to the bleakness of the future.

In his remarks on "New Haven," as in his remarks on "Notes," Stevens disavows any intention of achieving a strict formal unity. He says that "New Haven," "like most long poems, is merely a collection of short ones," and he warns one of his readers that the poem "may seem diffuse and casual" (*LWS*, 640, 719). In fact, "New Haven" is anything but casual, and though it does become diffuse in the later cantos, one may still distinguish a basic structure in the poem. This structure consists of two main movements, one of twelve cantos and one of nineteen. The first twelve cantos are both thematically continuous and dramatically purposeful. As in "Auroras," Stevens enacts a visionary quest that progresses through conflict to resolution. Stevens' affirmation in the last line of canto twelve—"words of the world are the life of the world"—echoes the climactic affirmation of "Description Without Place": "the word is the making of the world" (*CP*, 345); and as in "Description Without Place," this theoretical affirmation is at the same time a mythic affirmation of the "queen that made it seem" (*CP*, 339). The last nineteen cantos are not as coherent in their progression as are the first twelve, but there is a thematic linkage. The fictive hypothesis that concludes the first movement contains the residual dissatisfaction that always attaches to the hypothetical, and this dissatisfaction provides an impetus for the second movement. In canto twenty-eight, by reformulating the conclusions of canto twelve, Stevens effects a partial closure for the whole poem. Full closure is unattainable. Fictive belief remains inherently problematic, and the element of death, introduced in canto sixteen, remains ineluctably alien.

The first version of "New Haven" to be published was the poem of eleven cantos Stevens read at the Connecticut Academy of Arts and Sciences. Stevens' critics have generally and understandably assumed that the short version published by the Academy was the original and that the remaining twenty cantos were added later on. From the evidence given by Louis Martz in Brazeau's oral biography of Stevens, it is now apparent that the poem of eleven cantos is a selection from the longer original. Martz asked Stevens if he would contribute a poem to the Academy's sesquicentennial. Stevens agreed and wrote "New Haven" for the occasion.

He had written many more parts of that poem than the ones he read here. He told me that he had selected sections and put them together specially for the Connecticut Academy to suit the length of time he had to read it. "Now, I read every section as is my custom to my wife as I wrote it. She put her hands over her eyes and said, 'They're not going to understand this.' I was very careful to pick out the sections I thought would go over with an audience. But even so, my wife was terribly concerned about it."[14]

The cantos Stevens selected for the shorter version are I, VI, IX, XI, XII, XVI, XXII, XXVIII, XXX, XXXI, and XXIX. Stevens kept the original order for all except the last canto. The first five cantos constitute an abridgment of the first major movement in the longer poem; and the second movement begins with the introduction of the theme of death in the sixth canto (canto sixteen in the longer version). Through the little fable which concludes the shorter version, Stevens offers a picturesque illustration of his thesis in the fifth canto (canto twelve, longer version): "words of the world are the life of the world" (*CP,* 474). The "wandering mariners" travel from the land of the elm trees to the land of the lemon trees, and in their description of the lemon trees, there was "an alteration / Of words that was a change of nature" (*CP,* 487).

In the first two cantos of the longer poem, Stevens establishes a modal polarity between the poetry of the concrete and the poetry of mythic vision. The initial formulation, in both cantos, is doctrinally defective. Stevens employs the motifs of the supreme fiction, but he situates them within the metaphysical boundaries of a simple dichotomy between external reality and the individual mind. He makes no reference to a transcendental imagination or "mind of minds," and this omission generates a dialectical progression that

---

14. Brazeau, *Wallace Stevens Remembered,* 175. This evidence of intellectual amity between Stevens and his wife may tell another and more appealing side of the story that includes "The hating woman" of "World Without Peculiarity" (*CP,* 454).

will culminate in canto four. Superficially, the movement of the first canto already seems to contain this whole progression. Stevens begins with "The eye's plain version" as "a thing apart" and concludes with a "mythological form" of essential unity, but the visionary conclusion is meretricious. The diction and cadence of the last stanza derive from "Primitive," but the thematic movement of the canto does not actually progress beyond that of "The Bouquet" (1948), for example, or "What We See Is What We Think" (1949). These poems concern themselves only with the opposition between "reality" (unadorned sensory perception) and an imaginative transformation of reality through metaphor. The metaphoric transformations in canto one culminate in "a festival sphere," but they do not resolve that opposition (*CP,* 466).

Cantos one and two are preliminary exercises. In the first line of canto two, Stevens echoes line six of canto one but reverses the hierarchical relation between reality and the imagination: "Of what is this house composed if not of the sun" (canto one); "Suppose these houses are composed of ourselves" (canto two). The activity of the individual mind now becomes the primary, constitutive element of reality, and on the basis of this supposition, Stevens works toward a second realization of visionary fulfillment. The rhetorical vehicle is the word *transparence,* the emblem of spiritual vision introduced in "Owl's Clover": "transparencies of sound, / Sounding in transparent dwellings of the self." By means of this allusion, Stevens creates a facsimile of the

>   sense in which we are poised,
>   Without regard to time or where we are,
>
>   In the perpetual reference, object
>   Of the perpetual meditation, point
>   Of the enduring, visionary love.

The phrase "Without regard to time or where we are" is a subjective reproduction of the transcendental element outside time and space. Stevens sustains the "sense in which we are poised" for the space of one stanza, and in this stanza the sweeping movement of the whole canto comes to poise with breathtaking grace. Because the rhetoric has no adequate doctrinal grounding, however, Stevens quickly loses his balance and stumbles into uncertainty: "Obscure, in colors whether of the sun / Or mind, uncertain in the clearest bells." The supposition that reality is "composed of ourselves" cannot sustain the visionary love, and the object of this love collapses into its source, "the colors of the mind." The "second giant" of canto one—"A recent imagining of reality"—though it takes on the colors "of the sun," also remains part of "ourselves." For the time being, Stevens remains within the metaphysical framework that produces this confusion. He complains that the visionary love is "Obscure"; actually, given this framework, it is not only obscure but factitious.

The first two cantos construct rhetorical approximations of a visionary meditation. In the third canto, Stevens tries to convince himself that such approximations are adequate to his needs, but he concludes the canto with a confession of complete dissatisfaction. In the first stanza, he returns to the point of visionary culmination in the previous canto and, responding to the complaint that follows this culmination, he substitutes the word *desire* for the word *love*:

> The point of vision and desire are the same.
> It is to the hero of midnight that we pray
> On a hill of stones to make beau mont thereof.
>
> If it is misery that infuriates our love,
> If the black of night stands glistening on beau mont,
> Then, ancientest saint ablaze with ancientest truth,
>
> Say next to holiness is the will thereto,
> And next to love is the desire for love,
> The desire for its celestial ease in the heart,
>
> Which nothing can frustrate, that most secure,
> Unlike love in possession of that which was
> To be possessed and is. But this cannot
>
> Possess. It is desire, set deep in the eye,
> Behind all actual seeing, in the actual scene,
> In the street, in a room, on a carpet or a wall,
>
> Always in emptiness that would be filled,
> In denial that cannot contain its blood,
> A porcelain, as yet in the bats thereof.[15]

The "hero of midnight" is a candidate for the leading human role in the supreme fiction, and the "hill of stones" is the plain reality that Stevens has sought, through his rhetorical facsimiles, to transform into the "beau mont"

---

15. Bats are slabs of clay that have not yet been made into porcelain.

of visionary realization. The "black of night" that "stands glistening on beau mont" is the darkness that is not illuminated by epiphany. The ancient saint is still ablaze with the effulgence of visionary experience in "Auroras," and it is on the basis of this lingering glow that Stevens has sought to evoke the visionary love. In "Auroras," by appealing to the pure principle of sentient relation, Stevens creates a spiritual atmosphere in which we "Lie down like children in this holiness" (*CP,* 418). In "New Haven" he has as yet made no such appeal, and holiness remains, for the present, an unattainable object of desire. In "Extracts," Stevens declares that "Stanzas of final peace / Lie in the heart's residuum" (*CP,* 258). He now tries to define the desire for celestial ease as itself an adequate approximation of this final peace. Since "The point of vision" in canto two appears to be a locus of fulfillment, "a sense in which we are poised," desire at first appears to be equivalent to fulfillment. "The point of vision and desire are the same." Acknowledging the "misery" of his unilluminated state, Stevens retreats from this position and argues that desire is "next to" fulfillment, that is, both the prelude to fulfillment and a close second to it in aesthetic and emotional value. The description of "celestial ease" as something "Which nothing can frustrate" recalls the frustration of the previous canto and forces the distinction that desire is "Unlike love in possession." Stevens begins by equating vision and desire, and he concludes in defining desire as mere "emptiness." The reason for this declension reveals itself in an allusive contrast to a passage from "Description Without Place." In this passage Stevens defines sensory perception—the eye's plain version—as

> The lesser seeming original in the blind
> Forward of the eye that, in its backward, sees
> The greater seeming of the major mind. (*CP,* 340)

The "major mind" is the transcendent presence that unifies external reality and the individual mind. Because Stevens has not invoked this transcendent presence, the space "Behind all actual seeing" becomes a mere vacancy, a hollow place in which the rhetorical fullness of the third stanza sets off an aching reverberation.

The progression of the first three cantos synopsizes the spiritual frustrations of Stevens' early poetry. In canto four, Stevens enacts the transition to a fulfillment of religious need that begins in *Ideas of Order* and attains a clear sense of purpose in *Parts of a World*. He first vindicates the conclusion of canto three and then slips around this conclusion to achieve a genuine realization of pure poetry. This realization depends on the intervention of "a diviner opposite":

> The plainness of plain things is savagery,
> As: the last plainness of a man who has fought
> Against illusion and was, in a great grinding
>
> Of growling teeth, and falls at night, snuffed out
> By the obese opiates of sleep. Plain men in plain towns
> Are not precise about the appeasement they need.
>
> They only know a savage assuagement cries
> With a savage voice; and in that cry they hear
> Themselves transposed, muted and comforted
>
> In a savage and subtle and simple harmony,
> A matching and mating of surprised accords,
> A responding to a diviner opposite.

Between the first and third sentences, the heroic plain men who struggle against illusions undergo a metamorphosis and become the protagonists of the supreme fiction. The first sentence evokes the spiritually barren cosmos, described in "Blue Guitar," in which "Day is desire and night is sleep" (*CP*, 167). The third sentence evokes the transcendental realm of the mother's cry and the "huge high harmony" of the essential poem. The urgency of his need does not allow Stevens to give any "precise" account of how this metamorphosis takes place, and the neglect of precision affects the tonal quality of the appeasement he describes. The word *plainness,* at first a synonym for tough-minded or skeptical, metamorphoses into a synonym for unsophisticated or primitive. Similarly, whereas the word *savagery* in the first sentence implies intellectual ruthlessness, the word *savage* in the third sentence implies elemental appetite. Stevens' elemental appetite for visionary fulfillment can be satisfied only through a manifestation of divinity.

The reversal Stevens effects in canto four brings him to a point of balance from which, in cantos five through seven, he will expound the modal polarity that has been governing the poem. Stevens' formulations of this polarity reproduce the confusions in the first four cantos. At the beginning of canto five, Stevens sets out the alternatives that have betrayed him into the emptiness of which he complains in canto three. By the end of canto five, these alternatives have been transformed, enabling him to fill this emptiness with "a savage and subtle and simple harmony." Stevens does not appear to recognize that there is any difference in the dichotomies he formulates, but this difference nonetheless manifests itself in a change of tone. In the first stanza, Stevens adopts a tone of ironic, mocking detachment. In the last stanza, he submits himself, without irony, to the Romantic sublime:

> Inescapable romance, inescapable choice
> Of dreams, disillusion as the last illusion,
> Reality as a thing seen by the mind.
>
> . . . .
>
>   Why, then, inquire
> Who has divided the world, what entrepreneur?
> No man. The self, the chrysalis of all men
>
> Became divided in the leisure of blue day
> And more, in branchings after day. One part
> Held fast tenaciously in common earth
>
> And one from central earth to central sky
> And in moonlit extensions of them in the mind
> Searched out such majesty as it could find.

Within the dichotomy that governs *Harmonium,* metaphysical closure can be achieved only through a self-contradictory privileging of either external reality or the individual mind. The two "dreams" described in the first stanza are the belief that reality, the *Ding an sich,* may be seen as it is, without perceptual distortion, and the belief that our perceptions of reality reflect only our own mental fabric. The dualism that produces this deadlock appears, on the surface, to be nothing but common sense, that is, a conclusion that we draw from our experience of "common earth." In the contrast between "blue day" and "branchings after day," the dualism of mind and reality metamorphoses into the modal polarity of pure and normal poetry. Within this polarity, "common earth," the locus of normal poetry, is comprehended in the region "from central earth to central sky," the locus of pure poetry. The "Inescapable romance" of the first stanza is a delusory fantasy of resolution in an ineluctably divided world. In the romance that is evoked in the last stanza, the parts of the world are unified by the essential poem at the center of things. The words *moonlit extensions* and *majesty* recall the whole history of Stevens' visionary enterprise, from the renunciation of moonlight in "Comedian" to the affirmations of majesty in "Auroras" and "Primitive."

The source of majesty in Stevens' visionary poetry is a transcendent principle of sentient relation—"the pure idea" ("Extracts"), "the first idea" ("Notes"), a "pure principle" ("Auroras"). In "Notes," Stevens represents this principle as informing the whole range of cognitive activity, from simple perception to mythic figuration. The "immaculate beginning" of an "ever-early candor" evolves into the "late plural" of an "immaculate end" (*CP,* 382). In canto six of "New Haven," reconstructing the idea of the immaculate beginning and end, Stevens transforms the modal opposition of the previous canto into a linear progression, and once again he dislocates the initial term of this progression:

> Reality is the beginning not the end,
> Naked Alpha, not the hierophant Omega,
> Of dense investiture, with luminous vassals.
>
> . . . .
>
> Alpha fears men or else Omega's men
> Or else his prolongations of the human.
>
> . . . .
>
>   both alike appoint themselves the choice
> Custodians of the glory of the scene,
> The immaculate interpreters of life.
>
> But that's the difference: in the end and the way
> To the end. Alpha continues to begin.
> Omega is refreshed at every end.

Throughout "New Haven," there is a "difference" between "the end and the way / To the end." The progression in this canto exemplifies the nature of that difference. At the beginning of the canto, "Alpha" and "Omega" are asymmetrical terms. "Reality" is "The eye's plain version" that is "a thing apart," but "Omega" is not the individual imagination. It is the "late plural" that evolves from the "ever-early candor" of the first idea. The Alpha who fears Omega's "prolongations of the human" is a dualist who fears transcendental illusion. In the last two stanzas, Alpha and Omega have become symmetrical. As one of the "immaculate interpreters of life," Alpha now represents the ever-early candor of the first idea. The generalized modal categories in which these distinctions have been subsumed appear finally in canto seven. Stevens speaks of men who display the full truth about themselves, "not merely as to the commonplace / But, also, as to their miraculous," a formulation that echoes Emerson's remark, in "Nature," that "the invariable mark of wisdom is to see the miraculous in the common" (*RWE*, I, 74). In the quasi-technical terminology Emerson borrows from post-Kantian German idealism, the miraculous is equivalent to the "reason" and the commonplace to the "understanding."[16] The problem with Stevens' formulation of a modal continuum between the miraculous and the commonplace in "New Haven" is that Alpha, if it is the singular aspect of the first idea, is not part of the commonplace; and if it is one component of a dualistic cosmos, it can never evolve into the miraculous.

In canto eight, Stevens breaks away from the balanced oppositions of the three previous cantos and begins the ascent toward crisis and resolution that will conclude the first main movement of the poem. This resolution will consist of a synthesis between "the real" and the forms of thought in which Stevens has embodied the transcendental sublime. As he works through the dialectical oppositions that lead to this resolution, the confusions that have attached themselves to the idea of the real continue to operate, and the basic dialectical tension remains between the commonplace and the miraculous. The chief symbol of the miraculous in Stevens' poetry is the ancient mother. Although she has not been called by name, she has appeared incognita as the object of "the enduring, visionary love." Stevens now identifies her more directly:

> We fling ourselves, constantly longing, on this form.
> We descend to the street and inhale a health of air
> To our sepulchral hollows. Love of the real
>
> Is soft in three-four cornered fragrances
> From five-six cornered leaves, and green, the signal
> To the lover, and blue, as of a secret place
>
> In the anonymous color of the universe.
> Our breath is like a desperate element
> That we must calm, the origin of a mother tongue

---

16. On the origin and import of these terms, see Arthur O. Lovejoy, *The Reason, the Understanding, and Time* (Baltimore, 1961).

> With which to speak to her, the capable
> In the midst of foreignness, the syllable
> Of recognition, avowal, impassioned cry.

The words *this form* in the first line refer both to "the real" and to the figure Stevens identifies as "her, the capable." (Frank Doggett rightly associates the feminine figure in this canto with the figures in poems such as "The Candle a Saint" and "Bouquet of Belle Sçavoir.")[17] Like the green queen of "Description Without Place," she is not only a part of the real; she is its sovereign principle. She is herself the breath that at the conclusion of "Montrachet" Stevens invokes as "the single main" (*CP,* 264). In the "sepulchral hollows" of "Owl," the man who breathes "deeply the deep atmosphere / Of sleep" listens to the mother's own "impassioned cry." Stevens now suggests that by speaking his "mother tongue," he speaks through her and for her. It is in this sort of speech, "The cry that contains its converse in itself," that the "savage voice" of canto four makes itself heard.

In canto eight, Stevens defines the kind of speech he will seek to utter in the poem, but the canto closes in a mood "Too fragile, too immediate for any speech," and the fragility of the mother's presence generates a violent reversion to "the real," that is, to the perceptual surface of things prior to poetic transformation. Through this reversion, Stevens proposes to become "clear of uncertainty." Instead, he lapses into "disillusion as the last illusion." Although in a rhetoric more abstract than that of "Nuances of a Theme by Williams" (1918), Stevens regresses to the paradoxical ideal of an unmediated revelation of the thing-in-itself:

>   We seek
> The poem of pure reality, untouched
> By trope or deviation, straight to the word,
> Straight to the transfixing object
>
> At the exactest point at which it is itself,
> Transfixing by being purely what it is,
> A view of New Haven, say, through the certain eye,
>
> The eye made clear of uncertainty, with the sight
> Of simple seeing, without reflection.

---

17. Doggett, *Stevens' Poetry of Thought,* 46.

The problematic character of this ideal reveals itself in the appositional phrases "straight to the word, / Straight to the transfixing object." The word and the object can be brought into an identity only through the agency of the essential poem, and within the essential poem "pure reality" is itself tropic in nature. The object is never exactly "itself"; it is only a point of relation within an infinite complex of relations. The operative force behind these logical problems is an aesthetic ideal of simple immediacy. Stevens is not actually concerned with "the object" for its own sake. He is concerned to establish a standard of perfect realization that can be applied to the figurations of the supreme fiction. "Reality" serves as a fictive locus of simple immediacy, and in the following stanza, Stevens attempts to situate his transcendental constructs within this locus:

>   We seek
> Nothing beyond reality. Within it,
>
> Everything, the spirit's alchemicana
> Included, the spirit that goes roundabout
> And through included, not merely the visible,
>
> The solid, but the movable, the moment,
> The coming on of feasts and the habits of saints,
> The pattern of the heavens and high, night air.

Within the prepositional acrobatics of the fifth stanza, Stevens commingles the dualistic and transcendental paradigms. "Reality" is at once the "solid" external reality of the eye's plain version and also the dynamic process of the essential poem. The "spirit" is both the individual imagination and the transcendent principle that is figured in "The pattern of the heavens and high, night air." When in the last stanza of the poem Stevens declares that reality is not "a solid," he implicitly segregates the transcendental from the dualistic paradigm.

The rough synthesis Stevens effects in canto nine partially dislodges reality from the "solid" world of external objects. Canto ten constitutes a dialectical repudiation of the opposite form of solidity, the reification of the transcendental sublime. Canto ten responds directly to the Yeatsian fantasy in "This Solitude of Cataracts" (1948). In "Cataracts," Stevens expresses a desire to achieve "a permanent realization" and to be "released from destruction, / To be a bronze man breathing under archaic lapis" (*CP,* 425). In canto ten of

"New Haven" he emphatically dissociates himself from this yearning for an artificial immortality. "We are not men of bronze and we are not dead." He accepts the necessity of "constant change," and he thus brings himself to a position from which he can once again, in canto eleven, attempt to synthesize the commonplace and the miraculous. Stevens' excursion into "the metaphysical streets" of New Haven in canto eleven represents a futile effort to evade his dependence on the figurations of his major visionary poems. As he goes walking, "The profoundest forms / Go with the walker," and "These he destroys with shafts of wakening." The "profoundest forms" are "the forms of thought" among which Stevens walks in "The Owl in the Sarcophagus." For the moment he feels himself "Free from their majesty," but he is still "in need of majesty." By identifying the source of this ostensibly new majesty as "The brilliancy at the central of the earth," he inadvertently confirms that he remains bound to the figurations of "Owl" and "Primitive."

Stevens' profession of need in canto eleven recalls the negative definition of love as "desire" in canto three. In canto twelve, desire does not devolve into "emptiness." Stevens synthesizes reality with the "impassioned cry" of "a diviner opposite," and through this synthesis he resolves the dialectical tensions in the first movement of the poem: "The poem is the cry of its occasion, / Part of the res itself and not about it." In these two lines, Stevens formulates with epigrammatic concision a fundamental opposition between two views of language. The view he denies is the positivistic view that language is a system of signs or arbitrary references "about" an objective world of things that exist independently of the names applied to them. The view he affirms is the Romantic, organicist view that poetic language fulfills a need within the "res" itself. The cry that is heard in canto four is uttered simultaneously by the ancient mother and the poet. The mother is the mythic embodiment of parental space, and the poet is the medium through which time and place perfect themselves. In the last three stanzas of canto twelve, Stevens confirms the association between the Romantic view of language and the forms of thought in "Owl." He locates the organic self-generation of language "In the area between is and was," the element in which the ancient mother "held men closely with discovery":

> The mobile and the immobile flickering
> In the area between is and was are leaves,
> Leaves burnished in autumnal burnished trees

> And leaves in whirlings in the gutters, whirlings
> Around and away, resembling the presence of thought,
> Resembling the presences of thoughts, as if,
>
> In the end, in the whole psychology, the self,
> The town, the weather, in a casual litter,
> Together, said words of the world are the life of the world.

The climactic assertion of the last line concludes the first main movement of "New Haven" and at the same time establishes the terms of conflict that will lead to the conclusion of the second movement. In "Primitive," Stevens complains that the essential poem can be realized only through "the obscurest as" (*CP,* 441). His assertion that "words of the world are the life of the world" remains within this realm of fictive hypothesis, the realm of "as if." When, in canto twenty-eight, he again urges that "the theory / Of poetry is the theory of life," he seeks to include the hypothetical aspect of this theory within the theory itself. He suggests that life "As it is" realizes itself "in the intricate evasions of as," but he also concedes that he can offer no definitive verification of this thesis.

The resolutions in the first movement of "New Haven" depend on principles that are essentially religious in character. In cantos thirteen and fourteen, as he begins the second movement of the poem, Stevens adopts two personas—the ephebe and Professor Eucalyptus—and he explicitly defines their purpose as a religious quest. The locus of this quest, for both personas, is the commonplace, and once again the terms in which Stevens poses their problems render the problems insoluble. In canto thirteen the ephebe "seeks out / The perquisites of sanctity," but in this search he chooses to avoid the "perilous" haunts in which these perquisites are actually to be found:

> He is neither priest nor proctor at low eve,
> Under the birds, among the perilous owls,
> In the big X of the returning primitive.

For Stevens, the perquisites of sanctity will continue to be dependent upon the forms of thought in "Owl" and "Primitive." The ephebe, seeking to escape from these forms, defines "a fresh spiritual" in "The difficulty of the visible." The visible, if it is seen "in its idea," leads inescapably to the essential poem; in canto thirty, Stevens will achieve a resolution by redefining this fresh spiritual as "a visibility of thought." In canto fourteen, however, the visible degenerates into that form of Alpha that does not transcend "the object itself":

> The dry eucalyptus seeks out god in the rainy cloud.
> Professor Eucalyptus of New Haven seeks him
> In New Haven with an eye that does not look
> Beyond the object.

The problem posed for Professor Eucalyptus entails a confusion of metaphysical paradigms similar to that in canto one, and the solution he proposes is again to construct a rhetorical facsimile of visionary meditation.

> It is a choice of the commodious adjective
> For what he sees, it comes in the end to that:
> The description that makes it divinity.

By reducing the realization of divinity to a problem of diction, Professor Eucalyptus can only disguise the structural defects in his formulation of the problem. In canto twenty-two, he abandons his project of unification altogether. "Professor Eucalyptus said, 'The search / For reality is as momentous as / The search for god.'" Within one metaphysical paradigm, "reality" is opposed to the "imagination." Within another, the limited telos of sensual fulfillment is opposed to a poetry of religious vision. By connecting the first term of the first dichotomy with the second term of the second dichotomy, Professor Eucalyptus has created a mist through which no visionary illumination can penetrate. He has thus been forced to choose one of his two terms, and the term he chooses, "reality," relegates him to a static dualism. At the end of canto twenty-two, Stevens tries to close the gap between subject and object; he speaks of "the evening star" as simultaneously "an inner light" and a light that "shines / From the sleepy bosom of the real." In a vague, mumbling diction appropriate to this drowsy condition, he declares that this inner light "Searches a possible for its possibleness." There is little likelihood that this sort of possibleness will ever come to much.

After he has defined his purpose as a religious quest, Stevens returns, in canto fifteen, to the problem that remains latent in canto twelve: the hypothetical character of his fictive belief in a transcendental teleology. The terms in which Stevens formulates this problem correspond to the modal limitations he has set for his quest in canto thirteen:

> The instinct for heaven had its counterpart:
> The instinct for earth, for New Haven, for his room,
> The gay tournamonde as of a single world
>
> In which he is and as and is are one.

There are two separate ways in which Stevens can seek to inhabit a world in which "as and is are one." One way is that of the latest freed man, the self-negating effort to construct a reality that is free from metaphoric transposition. The other is to represent the world as a latent consciousness that comes to life only through the figurations of poetry. This is the supreme fiction, and the supreme fiction operates within the realm of pure poetry. In this passage, however, Stevens identifies pure poetry with the transcendental reification of "This Solitude of Cataracts," and he transposes the idea of essential unity to the realm of normal poetry. The "instinct for heaven" signifies the impulse to displace the resolution of all conflict to an ideal sphere totally segregated from ordinary reality—the "empty" and "fatal" sphere Stevens repudiates in canto ten. By defining the alternative to this divided cosmos as "The gay tournamonde as of a single world," Stevens proposes a modal synthesis that can never take place, for normal poetry operates within an atmosphere of "difference" (*CP*, 406).

The conditions Stevens sets for his religious quest suggest a need to escape from the Romantic sublime, and in canto sixteen he introduces a theme that helps to account for this need:

> And yet the wind whimpers oldly of old age
> In the western night. The venerable mask,
>
> In this perfection, occasionally speaks
> And something of death's poverty is heard.
> This should be tragedy's most moving face.
>
> It is a bough in the electric light
> And exhalations in the eaves, so little
> To indicate the total leaflessness.

Death and the Romantic sublime have been intimately associated in Stevens' work since "Sunday Morning": "Death is the mother of beauty, mystical" (*CP*, 69). As Stevens himself approaches closer to death, mystical resolutions of this sort often prove difficult to sustain. In "The Beginning" the "first tutoyers of tragedy / Speak softly, to begin with, in the eaves" (*CP*, 428), but however soft these whisperings, they are terrifying enough to drive Stevens into the occult manipulation of mirrors in "A Golden Woman." In canto sixteen of "New Haven," Stevens attempts to sublimate personal fear within aesthetic affect, but "should" is not *is,* and the aesthetic value of death remains, for the time being, in question. Stevens responds to this question, in canto seventeen, by affirming his own capacity for tragedy:

> The color is almost the color of comedy,
> Not quite. It comes to the point and at the point,
> It fails. The strength at the centre is serious.

The center is at once "The brilliancy at the central of the earth" and the central point of poise in Stevens' own poetic character. Stevens' repudiation of comedy is also a repudiation of the comedian, Crispin, and his critique of paradise. Stevens represents the opposite of comedy, the "serious," through allusions to the emblems of death in "Owl":

> A blank underlies the trials of device,
> The dominant blank, the unapproachable.
> This is the mirror of the high serious:
> Blue verdured into a damask's lofty symbol,
>
> Gold easings and ouncings and fluctuations of thread
> And beetling of belts and lights of general stones,
> Like blessed beams from out a blessed bush
>
> Or the wasted figurations of the wastes
> Of night, time and the imagination,
> Saved and beholden, in a robe of rays.

In "Owl," peace after death stands "Damasked in the originals of green." He is "Adorned with cryptic stones and sliding shines," and his robe bears "the whole spirit sparkling in its cloth." The "beetling of belts" confirms the association between the figure of peace after death in "Owl" and the great shadow in canto nine of "Auroras":

> The stars are putting on their glittering belts.
> They throw around their shoulders cloaks that flash
> Like a great shadow's last embellishment.

In "New Haven," as in "Owl" and "Auroras," Stevens' tragic figurations for "the high serious" are themselves only a "mirror" for "The dominant blank." Death remains inaccessible, and at the end of the canto, Stevens redefines the "serious" as a neutral perception of ordinary reality:

> These fitful sayings are, also, of tragedy:
> The serious reflection is composed
> Neither of comic nor tragic but of commonplace.

This redefinition of the serious seems to suggest that the commonplace is a touchstone of ontological validity, but the sudden repudiation of generic form raises a suspicion that the commonplace actually serves as a refuge from the "foreign absolute" of death (*CP,* 434). This suspicion, if it is justified, helps to explain the modal confusion of canto fifteen. In proposing to resolve the problematic aspects of fictive belief within "The gay tournamonde," Stevens is seeking to escape from the tragic sphere of pure poetry into the happier mode of normal poetry.

After drawing back from peace after death, Stevens wanders through two cantos of meditation on the commonplace, then in canto twenty he attempts to establish a condition of pure potentiality. He represents himself as "A naked being with a naked will / And everything to make." He is not long able to sustain the illusion of complete freedom, and when in canto twenty-one the illusion collapses, he finds himself once again in the "mystical" sphere of the elegiac sublime:

> Romanza out of the black shepherd's isle,
> Like the constant sound of the water of the sea
> In the hearing of the shepherd and his black forms;
>
> Out of the isle, but not of any isle.
> Close to the senses there lies another isle
> And there the senses give and nothing take,
>
> The opposite of Cythère, an isolation
> At the centre, the object of the will, this place,
> The things around—.

As James Baird notes, the black shepherd is Baudelaire. In "Un voyage à Cythère"—a place he calls "cette île triste et noire"—Baudelaire sees an emblem of death as fleshly corruption: a gibbet adorned with a rotting corpse.[18] Cythera is the home of Aphrodite, and Stevens has long known that the fruit of love "comes rotting back to ground" (*CP,* 14). In the island that is "The opposite of Cythère," sexual love is sublimated into visionary passion.

---

18. Baird, *The Dome and the Rock,* 40n; Charles Baudelaire, *Oeuvres Complètes,* ed. Marcel A. Ruff (Paris, 1968), 117.

Stevens' rendezvous with the ancient mother was "An isolation which only the two could share" (*CP,* 419), and his memory of this rendezvous now yields him the courage to declare the primacy of his visionary mode:

> The things around—the alternate romanza
> Out of the surfaces, the windows, the walls,
> The bricks grown brittle in time's poverty,
> The clear. A celestial mode is paramount.

The celestial mode is what, in "A Collect of Philosophy," Stevens calls "the ascent into heaven" (*OP,* 193). This ascent has already passed its apex; prophecy has become retrospection and the future has become a blank. In canto eighteen, Stevens remarks on how difficult it is "To say good-by to the past and to live and to be / In the present state of things." At times he will manage to reconcile himself to "the present state of things," but he will not be able, finally, to say good-bye to the past, for the definitive formulations of his poetic life are now those of the past.

Stevens' celestial mode culminates in the vision of "sleep realized," a vision in which all opposites resolve themselves into "an ever-changing, calmest unity" (*CP,* 433). In the mythic resolution of "Auroras," sleep realized and the ancient mother come together as "An innocence of the earth." In canto twenty-three of "New Haven," Stevens reconstructs this mythic resolution, and he attempts to extend sleep realized into the sleep of death, "the single future of night, the single sleep":

> If, then, New Haven is half sun, what remains
> At evening, after dark, is the other half,
> Lighted by space, big over those that sleep,
> Of the single future of night, the single sleep,
>
> As of a long, inevitable sound,
> A kind of cozening and coaxing sound,
> And the goodness of lying in a maternal sound,
>
> Unfretted by day's separate, several selves,
> Being part of everything come together as one.
> In this identity, disembodiments
>
> Still keep occurring. What is, uncertainly,
> Desire prolongs its adventure to create
> Forms of farewell, furtive among green ferns.

The "cozening and coaxing sound" is that of the canto itself, the soothing, soporific repetition floating in a syntax that is intentionally loose and vague. The word *Of* in "Of the single future of night," though it has no definite antecedent, attaches itself loosely to the preceding word *sleep*. Those who sleep at night sleep "Of" (participate in) the "single sleep" that cancels the alternation of actual day and night. This sleep merges into the "maternal sound" (the mother's accordion) through the phrase "As of." The first object of this phrase is "inevitable sound," and the second object is "the goodness," which is then modified by another "of" that again concludes in "sound." Through the folds of this syntax, the word *single* in "single sleep" comes to be equivalent to the phrase "everything come together as one." The following sentence appeals to other "disembodiments"—such as those of "The Woman in Sunshine" and "A Golden Woman in a Silver Mirror"—as precedents for this kind of transumption within a mythic feminine presence. In the final stanza, the intentional dissociations of the preceding passage are compounded by the syntactical wobbliness of the predication "What is, uncertainly, / Desire prolongs its adventure." "What is, uncertainly" might refer to "Desire," so that we could read: *What may or may not be desire prolongs its adventure*. Or, "What is, uncertainly" might be a detached elliptical assertion, so that we could read: *Whatever is (is real, is present) exists in an uncertain fashion; desire prolongs its adventure*. The evasiveness of this statement is itself a furtive prolongation of the adventure, a prolongation not only in actual time but also into the timeless void of the dominant blank. Stevens' prolongations in this canto may help to allay the anxiety caused by his apprehension of death, but they also reawaken the ontological anxiety of canto three. If desire does not now devolve into emptiness, it is only because the very existence of desire wavers in nebulous ambiguity.

Stevens' evocation of "the goodness of lying in a maternal sound" draws on that strain of Romantic elegy in which Eros, Thanatos, and the maternal principle commingle in voluptuous portrayals of death's seductive appeal. Despite his essential affiliation with the elegiac sublime, Stevens never so completely abandons himself to this seduction as do Keats and Whitman. He could not say, with Keats, that "for many a time / I have been half in love with easeful Death"; nor can he, like Whitman, lose himself "in the loving floating ocean of thee, / Laved in the flood of thy bliss O death" ("Ode to a Nightingale"; "When Lilacs Last in the Dooryard Bloom'd"). In "Prologues to What Is Possible" (1952), when Stevens attempts to envision death as "a point of central arrival" he recoils from it as from something that is "beyond his recognizing" (*CP,* 516).

In canto twenty-four, Stevens seeks to prolong his adventure by recalling an earlier phase of his visionary quest. His point of departure is the annihilation of the Christian God in his own and the preceding generation. As in "Sunday Morning," this God is called Jove. At the beginning of Stevens' poetic career, in the summer of his life, the Christian God, like the ancient Roman father of heaven, had already become an obsolete figure. Because it was no longer a vital form for the imagination, it had to be replaced:

> The consolations of space are nameless things.
> It was after the neurosis of winter. It was
> In the genius of summer that they blew up
>
> The statue of Jove among the boomy clouds.
> It took all day to quieten the sky
> And then to refill its emptiness again.

Although it took all day to quieten and then refill the sky, there was sufficient time "Before the thought of evening had occurred" for the spirit to have reasserted itself in the erotic visionary mode of "The Hand as a Being," a poem in which "Our man beheld the naked, nameless dame" and "She held her hand before him in the air" (*CP,* 271):

> There was a clearing, a readiness for first bells,
> An opening for outpouring, the hand was raised:
> There was a willingness not yet composed,
>
> A knowing that something certain had been proposed,
> Which, without the statue, would be new,
> An escape from repetition.

The new mythic forms that have enabled Stevens to escape from repetition have now themselves become objects of repetitive figuration. In order to escape the fate of Jove, these figurations will become ever more tenuous, dissolving back into the air whence they came.

In "Owl" the mother's "inventions of farewell" give impersonal mythic expression to the principle of change within the essential poem. In canto twenty-three of "New Haven," elegiac detachment begins to degenerate into melancholy reminiscence, and in canto thirty, Stevens renounces elegy in favor of a present reality that, however grim, is more real than is the past:

> The wind has blown the silence of summer away.
> It buzzes beyond the horizon or in the ground:
> In mud under ponds, where the sky used to be reflected.
>
> The barrenness that appears is an exposing.
> It is not part of what is absent, a halt
> For farewells, a sad hanging on for remembrances.
>
> It is a coming on and a coming forth.

In halting for farewells, Stevens has not only been saying good-bye to "the silence of summer" but also lingering within the visionary fulfillments of the elegiac sublime. By embracing poverty, he escapes belatedness and alleviates the ontological guilt that attends his furtive prolongations. In the poetry of his last few years, Stevens will often adopt this stance of severe renunciation. (The "mud under ponds" prefigures the imagery of "The Plain Sense of Things" [1952].) He will not, however, consistently suppress the need to prolong his adventure, and he will frequently reenact the conflict between wistful retrospection and a stern commitment to barren immediacy.

In canto twenty-three, Stevens' visionary mode enters into a phase of decadence. The mingling of life and death, the evocation of essential unity, and the suspension of definite logical relations recall the method of "Owl." In that poem, however, these methods contribute to a poignant intensity of experiential revelation; in canto twenty-three they effect a condition of somnolent dissolution. In canto twenty-seven, Stevens seems to be reacting against this sort of decadence; he restricts his scope to plain reality and to life. He nonetheless retains a subtle connection with his visionary mode: he is, again, the "scholar," and "'He is the consort of the Queen of Fact.'" This queen, despite her unglamorous title, is no kin to the Canon Aspirin's sister:

> "Sunrise is his garment's hem, sunset is hers.
> He is the theorist of life, not death,
> The total excellence of the total book."

If sunrise is his garment's hem and sunset is hers, and if he is the theorist of life, not death, the Queen of Fact appears to be the theorist of death—the ancient mother in her guise as the mother of the dead. If this is so, death itself is the ultimate fact; life is the consort of death, and even in the plain reality of New Haven, life remains bound to an elemental mystery.

The metaphor of life as a "book" brings Stevens back to the conclusion of canto twelve. In canto twenty-eight, elaborating on his thesis that "words of the world are the life of the world," he restates and equivocally reaffirms the doctrine of "Primitive":

> This endlessly elaborating poem
> Displays the theory of poetry,
> As the life of poetry. A more severe,
>
> More harassing master would extemporize
> Subtler, more urgent proof that the theory
> Of poetry is the theory of life,
>
> As it is, in the intricate evasions of as,
> In things seen and unseen, created from nothingness,
> The heavens, the hells, the worlds, the longed-for lands.

Stevens can never be satisfied with the cogency of any theoretical "proof" for the existence of the essential poem. A more harassing master would also be a more dogmatic master, one who was unmindful of the dictum "We do not prove the existence of the poem. / It is something seen and known in lesser poems" (*CP*, 440). The only kind of proof Stevens can offer is the validation of theory through poetic fulfillment.

In the last two cantos, Stevens returns to the immaculate beginning that always evolves into the immaculate end. At the end of canto thirty, he announces that reality has been cleansed of its imaginative incrustations, but he continues to perceive this reality "in its idea" (*CP*, 381). The point of vision is clear, but "It is not an empty clearness, a bottomless sight. / It is a visibility of thought." In "Owl," at the end of the progression initiated by the "visibility of thought," the ever-early candor unfolds itself as "the whiteness that is the ultimate intellect." In the final stanza of "New Haven," reality recedes ever farther from the "solid," and pure poetry, the poetry of "principle," asserts its dominance over the poetry of the concrete:

> It is not in the premise that reality
> Is a solid. It may be a shade that traverses
> A dust, a force that traverses a shade.

Stevens' "premise" has been the necessity of returning to the commonplace; in segregating this premise from the idea that reality is a solid, he appears to be speaking directly to Emerson and defending himself against any possible imputation of materialist illusion. In "The Transcendentalist," Emerson declares, "The materialist, secure in the certainty of sensation, mocks at finespun theories, at star-gazers and dreamers, and believes that his life is solid, that he at least takes nothing for granted, but knows where he stands, and what he does. Yet how easy it is to show him that he also is a phantom walking and working amid phantoms, and that he need only ask a question or two beyond his daily questions to find his solid universe growing dim and impalpable before his sense" (*RWE*, I, 331). Stevens can never resolve the problematic aspects of fictive belief, but neither can he resist the seduction of the abstract. As the solid universe grows dim and impalpable, reality reconstitutes itself as the abstract, and in its fully articulated form, the "force that traverses a shade" is the dynamic principle that animates the giant of nothingness and precipitates the essential poem.

The concluding stanza of "New Haven" offers a modern, minimalist version of the Romantic sublime as it is represented, for example, by the uninhibited rhetoric of "Tintern Abbey":

> And I have felt
> A presence that disturbs me with the joy
> Of elevated thoughts; a sense sublime
> Of something far more deeply interfused,
> Whose dwelling is the light of setting suns,
> And the round ocean and the living air,
> And the blue sky, and in the mind of man:
> A motion and a spirit, that impels
> All thinking things, all objects of all thought,
> And rolls through all things.

The problematic character of Wordsworth's "sense sublime" manifests itself peripherally in the ambiguous signification of the word *interfused*—the "presence" is both identical with and separate from the phenomenal world—and in the sprung parallelism of the prepositional phrase "in the mind of man." In the final stanza of "New Haven," the sense of the problematic has moved from the periphery to the center of the Romantic sublime, a shift that manifests itself in Stevens' substitution of the hypothetical mode—"may be"—for the Emersonian and Wordsworthian indicative.

The driving force in "New Haven" is a need, only partly conscious, to escape from the resolutions of the past. When Stevens returns to the ever-early candor, in canto thirty, he seems to feel that he has reestablished the present in a state of pristine potentiality, but he never actually advances beyond the figurations in the major visionary poems. Because he is determined "to live and to be / In the present state of things," he is unable, at any given point, to rise above the assertions of the moment and attain a comprehensive view of his whole visionary course. In "Things of August," which follows closely upon "New Haven," he takes a more detached, questioning stance, an attitude of probing exploration that is reflected in the freedom and variety of verse structures in the ten cantos of the poem. He frees himself from his fixation on the present state of things and can thereby situate this present state within a definite historical progression.

The problem that motivates the poem appears in the first stanza. Stevens is uncertain whether the sounds of day and night

> Are the instruments on which to play
> Of an old and disused ambit of the soul
> Or of a new aspect, bright in discovery— (*CP,* 489)

In the third canto, Stevens provides a clear formulation of the theoretical context within which this question must be answered. He defines the modal polarity that governs his later poetry—"High poetry and low"—and he decisively aligns himself with the perspective of high poetry. From this perspective, the world appears to be constituted by a transcendent intellective principle, "A nature that is created in what it says, / The peace of the last intelligence." The perspective of "low" or normal poetry is that of the man who "in this intelligence / Mistakes it for a world of objects." This distinction precludes the kind of metaphysical confusion that pervades "New Haven," but it does not enable Stevens to regenerate his visionary drive. The answer to the question posed in canto one is implicitly disclosed in canto five. Stevens' persona, the rabbi, gives a recitation of Stevens' mythic symbols, and the ritual air suggests that Stevens' instruments, though they are not "disused," have lost the capacity for discovering bright new aspects:

> The thinker as reader reads what has been written.
> He wears the words he reads to look upon
> Within his being,
>
> A crown within him of crispest diamonds,
> A reddened garment falling to his feet,
> A hand of light to turn the page.

The diamond crown has a long history in Stevens' visionary poetry. In the "reddened garment," the dress imagery from "The Beginning" and "The Woman in Sunshine" mingles with the depiction of the mother in "Owl"—

"reddened and resolved / From sight." The "hand of light" fuses the image of the hand from "The Hand as a Being" with the light imagery that pervades the visionary poetry and recalls the "luminous pages" on Belshazzar's knee. These symbols have become detached from their contexts; they are mementos of pure poetry, not present realizations of it.

From the beginning of his poetic life, Stevens has struggled to achieve a unified poetic vision. In the climactic moment of "Things of August," in canto eight, he affirms the success of his visionary enterprise, and he identifies the ancient mother as the dominant figure in this enterprise. The evocations of the ancient mother, both in the climax of canto eight and in the denouement of canto ten, are couched in the past tense. In order to achieve resolution in the poem, Stevens must resign himself to the melancholy satisfactions of retrospection:

> When was it that the particles became
> The whole man, that tempers and beliefs became
> Temper and belief and that differences lost
> Difference and were one? It had to be
> In the presence of a solitude of the self,
> An expanse and the abstraction of an expanse,
> A zone of time without the ticking of clocks,
> A color that moved us with forgetfulness.
> When was it that we heard the voice of union?

For Stevens, "solitude" is always a necessary condition of the state within which "The abstract" disengages itself from the contours of the material world. The "zone of time without the ticking of clocks" is a zone in which temporal sequence becomes "an ever-changing, calmest unity." In "Montrachet," at a period when Stevens' visionary fulfillment is yet a remote object of anticipation, the sound of the clock punctuates his fear that this object will never be attained. "Chome! clicks the clock, if there be nothing more" (*CP*, 260). In "The Pure Good of Theory," time is both "The inimical music" and "the enchantered space / In which the enchanted preludes have their place" (*CP*, 330). The complete integration Stevens declares he has achieved could take place only in the realm of transcendental paradox. This is the "element" of "Owl," a zone of time "That of itself stood still, perennial." The "voice" that speaks from within this element is that of the ancient mother:

> Was it as we sat in the park and the archaic form
> Of a woman with a cloud on her shoulder rose
> Against the trees and then against the sky
> And the sense of the archaic touched us at once
> In a movement of the outlines of similarity?

In locating the moment of visionary realization in one specific occasion, Stevens exercises a fictive license: he is actually rendering impressionistically more than one experience. The emphasis on the archaic calls up "The abstract, the archaic queen" of "The Candle a Saint" and thus evokes the whole history of Stevens' liaison with the ancient mother. There is a culminating moment in this liaison, and accordingly Stevens' evocation draws most heavily on "Owl":

> We resembled one another at the sight.
> The forgetful color of the autumn day
> Was full of these archaic forms, giants
> Of sense, evoking one thing in many men,
> Evoking an archaic space, vanishing
> In the space.

The "giants / Of sense" and the "archaic space, vanishing / In the space" recall the "vanishing-vanished violet that wraps round / The giant body the meanings of its folds" (*CP*, 433). The "forms" and "outlines" of Stevens' mythic figures are always approximations. By "Evoking an archaic space," they give momentary substance to the pure idea. The outline they leave behind is not of a fixed system of meanings, but of the integrated poetic persona, "The father":

> In the space, leaving an outline of the size
> Of the impersonal person, the wanderer,
> The father, the ancestor, the bearded peer,
> The total of human shadows bright as glass.

The father is major man. As "the ancestor" who assimilates the irrational source of archetypal images, he is a descendant of the "Great mud-ancestor, oozer and Abraham, / Progenitor wearing the diamond crown of crowns" (*OP*, 64)—who is himself a descendant of the "muddy centre" that was there "before we breathed" (*CP*, 383). In "Asides on the Oboe," Stevens represents the "central man" as "the man of glass, / Who in a million diamonds sums us up," and in canto ten of "Auroras" he associates the father with the specter who "meditates a whole, / The full of fortune and the full of fate, / As if he lived all lives, that he might know."

In the final canto, the affirmations of canto eight modulate into elegy, not only the elegiac sublime of the ancient mother but an elegy for the mother herself. Through his lament for the mother, Stevens finally acknowledges that his visionary ascent has passed its apex and that he is sinking down into darkness:

> The mornings grow silent, the never-tiring wonder.
> The trees are reappearing in poverty.
>
> Without rain, there is the sadness of rain
> And an air of lateness. The moon is a tricorn
>
> Waved in pale adieu. The rex Impolitor
> Will come stamping here, the ruler of less than men,
>
> In less than nature. He is not here yet.
> Here the adult one is still banded with fulgor,
>
> Is still warm with the love with which she came,
> Still touches solemnly with what she was
>
> And willed. She has given too much, but not enough.
> She is exhausted and a little old.

Here the highly wrought abstractions and symbolic convolutions of the major visionary poems have subsided to common experience, the scale of "men" and "nature." Death is a brutal conqueror who will destroy this world, and the ancient mother is a woman who has taught Stevens the secrets of romance. She has given too much for Stevens to be able to resign himself easily to the barrenness that appears, and she has given too little to save him from this barrenness. Although she is the mythic embodiment of "The abstract," she is also the vital principle of Stevens' own imagination, an imagination that is "exhausted and a little old." In the quiet fullness of this recognition, Stevens finds a speech that is free of uncertainty and the strain of willful assertion. Visionary experience has become purely personal experience. Stevens could offer no subtler, more urgent proof that the theory of poetry is the theory of life.

CHAPTER SEVEN

A Final Construction

After the major visionary poems of *The Auroras of Autumn,* Stevens gradually enters a new phase of experience, a passionate confrontation with the poverty of old age. From the evidence of his letters, 1950 marks an epoch in his life, the point at which old age becomes a definitive and inescapable condition. In February of 1950, he reports that he has recently slipped on the ice and had a bad fall (*LWS,* 663). In a letter written in April, he remarks that "only a few months ago I used to say that I felt as if I was still 28 or 30. Recently this has not been true" (*LWS,* 675). Late in 1954, he writes that "the process of growing old accelerates the longer it continues, so that one seems to grow old faster today than one did yesterday" (*LWS,* 856). Old age manifests itself as a decline both of sensual vitality and of visionary power, but in the courage and dignity with which Stevens responds to this calamity, he achieves a final triumph of the imagination. As he hovers on the edges of oblivion he transforms loss and absence into the "Profound poetry of the poor and of the dead" (*CP,* 509).

To the end of his life, Stevens continues to alternate between two distinct modes of poetic perception. At one moment he celebrates the immediate perception of concrete, external reality, and at another moment he seeks to contain this reality within the transcendental element. In poems such as "Final Soliloquy of the Interior Paramour" (1950), "The Rock" (1950), and "To an Old Philosopher in Rome" (1952), he reaffirms the primacy of his celestial mode, but he can no longer look forward to a culminating moment of visionary realization, and in "The World as Meditation" (1952), he redefines the visionary goal as an ever-receding ideal. He cannot, however, always reconcile himself either to reconstructing his previous resolutions or to suspending himself in devotional meditation. Most of his last significant achievements in pure poetry take place in 1950 and 1952. (In 1951, a year in which he made more public appearances than at any other time in his life, Stevens published only one poem, "Madame La Fleurie.")[1] In "The Dove in Spring" (1953), he expresses the frustrated rage of a man who must keep "seeking out his identity / In that which is and is established" (*OP,* 98). In "Farewell Without a Guitar" (1954), he renders this predicament in a mingling of the present and past tense:

> The reflections and repetitions,
> The blows and buffets of fresh senses
> Of the rider that was,
>
> Are a final construction,
> Like glass and sun, of male reality
> And of that other and her desire. (*OP,* 99)

The final construction consists of reflections on and repetitions of established modal forms. The "fresh senses" are senses of what, in "The Green Plant" (1952), Stevens calls "a constant secondariness" (*CP,* 506). The protagonists of both pure and normal poetry have become posthumous figures, "the rider that was." It is no doubt Stevens' frustration with this belated condition that motivates him to write "The Sail of Ulysses" (1954), a long, rhetorical poem in which he attempts, incongruously and unsuccessfully, to adopt the prophetic mantle of the Victorian seer.[2] He envisions a time when the race as a whole will have overcome all limitations and will have achieved "a final order" (*OP,* 101). This millennial prophecy is an anomaly in Stevens' work, and he was himself uncomfortable with the poem. In "Local Objects" (1955), he recovers the visionary mode as a permanent suspension between anticipation and realization.

Stevens' reconstructions of his visionary fulfillments take place against a background of spiritual desolation. In poems such as "The Course of a Particular" (1950), "Lebensweisheitspielerei" (1952), "The Plain Sense of Things" (1952), and "The Region November" (1955), he defines the sort of

---

1. On Stevens' activities in 1951, see Brazeau, *Wallace Stevens Remembered,* xiv, 189.
2. For a discussion of Tennyson's influence on the prophetic mode of this poem, see Joseph Carroll, "The Ancient and the Modern Sage: Tennyson and Stevens," *Victorian Poetry,* XXII (1984), 13–14.

"poverty" he must seek to overcome. The peculiar intensity of these poems of old age derives from their relations, explicit or implicit, to a sublime past. Stevens' stance toward his diminishing range of imaginative possibility is sometimes ironic, sometimes tragic, and sometimes both at once. The way in which these contrary tonalities can come together reveals itself in "Lebensweisheitspielerei," a poem in which he depicts the fading of a heroic world:[3]

> Weaker and weaker, the sunlight falls
> In the afternoon. The proud and the strong
> Have departed.
>
> Those that are left are the unaccomplished,
> The finally human,
> Natives of a dwindled sphere. (*CP,* 504)

The "finally human" are those who are no longer able to participate in a supreme fiction. Although Stevens numbers himself among "the unaccomplished," his pride and his strength do not fail him. The imaginative heroism that has enabled him to achieve his visionary triumphs proves itself against the desolation of the world he has created, and the splendor of the past sublimates itself into an austere pathos:

> Little by little, the poverty
> Of autumnal space becomes
> A look, a few words spoken.
>
> Each person completely touches us
> With what he is and as he is,
> In the stale grandeur of annihilation.

The "poverty / Of autumnal space" is an atmosphere devoid of any transfiguring spiritual presence. Within this spiritual vacancy, the simply human assumes the force of an absolute. In canto twenty-six of "New Haven," Stevens had invoked the fat girl—"the earth, / Seen as inamorata"—and had represented her as being diminished by age, "Shrunk in the poverty of being close" (*CP,* 484). In this dwindled sphere, she "Touches, as one hand touches another hand," and she "whispers humane repose." In "Lebensweisheitspielerei," Stevens subsumes the gentle pathos of this farewell within the

---

3. For a reading that captures this poem's strange and powerful mingling of tonal affects, see Robert Buttel, "'Knowledge [*sic*] on the Edges of Oblivion': Stevens' Late Poems," *Wallace Stevens Journal,* V (1981), 15.

tragic intensity of sure obliteration. At the same time, he subtly merges this pathos with the ironic overtones deriving from the depletion of the transcendental sublime. All these tonal affects resonate in "the stale grandeur of annihilation." The human manifests itself most poignantly on the verge of extinction, and the exaltation of a transcendental fulfillment inverts itself into the negative, ironic sublime of an absorption in nothingness.[4]

The supreme fiction effects an integration of the individual and the whole. In "The Course of a Particular" and "The Region November," Stevens depicts a state of being in which the integrative agency, the pure principle of sentient relation, has ceased to function. The particular to which Stevens refers in "The Course of a Particular" is at once himself and the phenomenon that absorbs his attention: the "cry" of the leaves on a winter day. The course of the poem is a meditation in which Stevens inverts the visionary process through which he comes to a realization of essential unity. As he listens to the sound of the leaves in the wind, he recedes into a state of alienation from the world around him:

> Today the leaves cry, hanging on branches swept by wind,
> Yet the nothingness of winter becomes a little less.
> It is still full of icy shades and shapen snow.
>
> The leaves cry . . . One holds off and merely hears the cry.
> It is a busy cry, concerning someone else.
> And though one says that one is part of everything,
>
> There is a conflict, there is a resistance involved;
> And being part is an exertion that declines:
> One feels the life of that which gives life as it is. (*OP,* 96)

Stevens only gradually clarifies for himself the significance of the cry he hears. The declaration in the ninth line constitutes a climactic recognition. The force that "gives life as it is" is a force of particularity, that is, of "difference." In the first stanza, the cry of the leaves seems to associate itself with "the nothingness of winter" and also, paradoxically, to contribute to the diminution of spiritual negativity. The "icy shades and shapen snow" recall the landscape of "The Snow Man," a recollection that may help to account for the ambiguous mingling of nothingness and the incipient animism in the cry of the leaves. In the second stanza, perhaps because the nothingness of winter

---

4. Weiskel uses the term *negative sublime* in a different sense (see *The Romantic Sublime,* 31, *et passim*).

has become a little less, Stevens suggests that the cry is potentially meaningful, but only to "someone else," and his sense of alienation expands to include the social world. The declaration "being part is an exertion that declines" includes both the world of particular objects and the people who concern themselves with these objects.

Once he has clearly recognized "the life of that which gives life as it is," Stevens drives toward a complete inversion of the pure principle. He drains out the incipient animism in the leaves' cry, which, though it is a meaningless sound, echoes with the ironic pathos of spiritual absence:

> The leaves cry. It is not a cry of divine attention,
> Nor the smoke-drift of puffed-out heroes, nor human cry.
> It is the cry of leaves that do not transcend themselves,
>
> In the absence of fantasia, without meaning more
> Than they are in the final finding of the ear, in the thing
> Itself, until, at last, the cry concerns no one at all.

In Stevens' visionary poetry, man is an object of "divine attention" because he is the special locus of sentience through which the essential poem achieves its "difficult apperception" (*CP,* 440). The divine attention can be realized only through the forms of thought that are also the forms of phenomenal reality. These forms are the "fantasia" of the supreme fiction. The pure principle of sentient relation can articulate itself only in metaphoric displacements, "the intricate evasions of as" (*CP,* 486). The principle of difference manifests itself, here as in "Comedian," in a reduction to the literal, "life as it is." The forms of thought reduce themselves to "the final finding of the ear," and the forms of phenomenal reality reduce themselves to "the thing / Itself." In the absence of fantasia, these two aspects of particularity, the self and the world, are equivalent in their meaninglessness. Stevens repudiates essential unity, but he does not then revert to a celebration of the parts of the world. The failure of transcendental affect leaves him at the nadir of the cycle from Romanticism to indifferentism.

In "The Region November," Stevens again traces the course of a particular. He watches "the treetops, as they sway," and in their swaying, as in the cry of the leaves, he perceives the absence of any sentient relation between man and the world. In order to create a fiction of essential unity, Stevens has had to make "a supreme effort" (*LWS,* 445). In "The Course of a Particular," he attributes his disaffection to the declining power of his own visionary will, but the failure of transcendental affect is also a failure of the divine attention. "God is the centre of the pathetic fallacy" (*LWS,* 444), and in "The Region November," Stevens turns his plaint against God:

> They sway, deeply and loudly, in an effort,
> So much less than feeling, so much less than speech,
>
> Saying and saying, the way things say
> On the level of that which is not yet knowledge:
>
> A revelation not yet intended.
> It is like a critic of God, the world
>
> And human nature, pensively seated
> On the waste throne of his own wilderness. (*OP,* 115)

In the phrase "On the level of that which is not yet knowledge," "not yet" might imply that the swaying of the treetops could still, at some future time, enter the level of sentient relation. However, "not yet" could also imply a permanent suspension on the level of particulars that do not transcend themselves. The phrase "A revelation not yet intended" seems to strengthen the temporal implication, but in the next three lines, the sense of anticipation inverts itself into implicit retrospection. The waste throne in the wilderness has once been a scene of regal splendor:

> A foyer of the spirit in a landscape
> Of the mind, in which we sit
> And wear humanity's bleak crown. (*CP,* 305)

In "Crude Foyer" the critic of paradise stands outside the transcendental region he derides as "false happiness." He denies the very possibility of the Romantic sublime, and he is thus a "comedian." In "The Region November" the critic of God remains within a paradise that has become a wasteland, and he is thus a figure of tragic magnitude.

In "New Haven," Stevens has sought to revitalize his visionary power by turning back to a plain sense of things. In canto thirty, he confronts "The barrenness that appears" after "The last leaf that is going to fall has fallen," and he represents this barrenness as a purification. "The glass of the air becomes an element—. . . It is a visibility of thought." In "The Plain Sense of Things," Stevens restages the imagery of canto thirty—the fallen leaves and the muddy pond—but he does not return to an ever-early candor. He remains within the poverty of autumnal space, and he defines the eye's plain version not as a beginning but as an end of the visionary process:

> After the leaves have fallen, we return
> To a plain sense of things. It is as if
> We had come to an end of the imagination,
> Inanimate in an inert savoir.
>
> It is difficult even to choose the adjective
> For this blank cold, this sadness without cause.
> The great structure has become a minor house.
> No turban walks across the lessened floors.
>
> The greenhouse never so badly needed paint.
> The chimney is fifty years old and slants to one side.
> A fantastic effort has failed, a repetition
> In a repetitiousness of men and flies. (*CP*, 502)

The "inert savoir" is a stagnant consciousness, and the plain sense of things discloses itself as a sense of imaginative inanition. The "great structure" is the "total building" Stevens had envisioned in "The Ultimate Politician" (*CP*, 335). As his imaginative vitality subsides, this visionary structure dissolves into the literal—an actual house in a state of decay. Stevens' "fantastic effort" to create a supreme fiction has failed to fix itself in a permanent realization that would transcend the decay of the natural man. The "romantic intoning" degenerates into a meaningless sound on a level with the buzzing of flies. In the reversal that follows, Stevens does not seek to reconstruct his visionary edifice. Instead, he subverts his figuration of imaginative impotence by elaborating on the figuration itself:

> Yet the absence of the imagination had
> Itself to be imagined. The great pond,
> The plain sense of it, without reflections, leaves,
> Mud, water like dirty glass, expressing silence
>
> Of a sort, silence of a rat come out to see,
> The great pond and its waste of the lilies, all this
> Had to be imagined as an inevitable knowledge,
> Required, as a necessity requires.

In the image of "The great pond," Stevens draws out the metaphor implicit in the phrase "an inert savoir." The plain sense of "things" becomes the plain sense of "it," the inert savoir. The rat that comes out to see serves as a perceptual displacement that reflects the unreflecting surface of the pond, and the inanimate imagination animates itself by reflecting its own stagnation. The resolution Stevens achieves is that of tragic displacement. In "Owl," need and necessity converge in a visionary fulfillment. "These forms are visible to the eye that needs, / Needs out of the whole necessity of sight" (*CP,* 432). In "The Plain Sense of Things," necessity reduces itself to the "inevitable knowledge" of inanition, and the Romantic sublime devolves into tragic fatality.

Stevens' portrayals of the negative sublime establish one generic extreme for his later poetry. The opposite extreme is in "Final Soliloquy of the Interior Paramour," a poem in which Stevens re-creates a sense of a transcendental plenitude. In "Things of August" he has acknowledged that his visionary power has begun to decline; the ancient mother, the medium and symbol of this power, is already receding into memory. In "Final Soliloquy" he calls her back into the present for one of the last times. As the interior paramour, she speaks through the poet, and it is by means of her "miraculous influence" that he once again hears the voice of union. Although they are "there together" in the evening air, she assumes no distinct mythic form. She has become a diffusive presence. Stevens defines his evocation of this presence as "the intensest rendezvous," but the intensity must be carefully nursed into life. He arranges his rendezvous within the sheltered space of a single room, and there the motifs of the supreme fiction must be "Wrapped tightly round us, since we are poor":

> Light the first light of evening, as in a room
> In which we rest and, for small reason, think
> The world imagined is the ultimate good.
>
> This is, therefore, the intensest rendezvous.
> It is in that thought that we collect ourselves,
> Out of all the indifferences, into one thing:
>
> Within a single thing, a single shawl
> Wrapped tightly round us, since we are poor, a warmth,
> A light, a power, the miraculous influence. (*CP,* 524)

The realization of an ultimate good depends on an act of will that barely escapes being canceled by Stevens' recognition of its arbitrariness. It is "for small reason" that we define the world imagined as the ultimate good. The word *therefore* in the fourth line serves to confirm this act of will, and the confirmation enables Stevens to gather his imaginative energy to a single point of concentration. In the final line of the third stanza, this effort of concentration begins to convert itself into the transcendental principle, and in the following stanza the individual will is absorbed within the self-generating order of the essential poem:

> Here, now, we forget each other and ourselves.
> We feel the obscurity of an order, a whole,
> A knowledge, that which arranged the rendezvous.
>
> Within its vital boundary, in the mind.
> We say God and the imagination are one . . .
> How high that highest candle lights the dark.
>
> Out of this same light, out of the central mind,
> We make a dwelling in the evening air,
> In which being there together is enough.

After he has collected himself into one thing, Stevens is able to forget himself within a unitary order that contains its own beginning and end. As in the final strophe of "Owl," he acknowledges that this order subsists only within "the light-bound space of the mind," but this mind, because it reflects the mind of God, contains the whole world. Stevens begins the poem with the lighting of a single light; by the end of the poem this light has become synonymous with "the central mind" that illuminates the evening air. (Alfred Corn notes an echo of "Portia's lines in act V of *The Merchant of Venice*: 'How far that little candle throws his beams! / So shines a good deed in a naughty world.'"[5] Stevens' recollection of this exclamation seems to have associated itself with a recollection of Emerson's declaration, in "Fate," that "the smallest candle fills a mile with its rays, and the papillae of a man run out to every star" [*RWE*, VI, 38].) When Stevens declares "We say God and the imagination are one," he is speaking from the position that is occupied by the shadow in "Chocorua": "'My solitaria / Are the meditations of a central mind'" (*CP*,

---

5. Alfred Corn, "Wallace Stevens and the Poetics of Ineffability," in Peter S. Hawkins and Anne Howland Schotter (eds.), *Ineffability: Naming the Unnamable from Dante to Beckett* (New York, 1984), 184. For a comment on the link between "Final Soliloquy" and "The Candle a Saint," see Baird, *The Dome and the Rock*, 223.

298). As in "Primitive," Stevens speaks in "Last terms," but these terms are no longer bulging with opulence. The final word, *enough,* limits closure to a sufficiency that will not disrupt the fragile serenity of the dwelling he has made.

In order to create a supreme fiction, Stevens has had to effect an integration of the archetypal, ancestral memory and "The abstract." Throughout his major visionary phase, the mother embodies this integration. She is "The abstract, the archaic queen." As his visionary power subsides, this integration begins to give way. In "The Sail of Ulysses," the archaic memory will recede and leave Stevens dependent on lifeless abstractions. "Madame La Fleurie" (1951) represents an opposite form of visionary disintegration. The abstract fades away and the ancient mother degenerates into gruesome caricature. She becomes a mythic embodiment of the earth, and because the earth consumes its own children, she appears as a cannibalistic parent. "Now, he brings all that he saw into the earth, to the waiting parent. / His crisp knowledge is devoured by her, beneath a dew" (*CP,* 507). In the last two lines of the poem, Stevens elaborates on this mythic metaphor with grotesque particularity. "His grief is that his mother should feed on him, himself and what he saw, / In that distant chamber, a bearded queen, wicked in her dead light." Grief resolves itself in horror, and elegiac lyricism is wholly absorbed within the macabre.

"Madame La Fleurie" would be an eccentric conclusion to Stevens' liaison with the ancient mother, and in "The Hermitage at the Centre" (1952), he returns her to the role of the interior paramour. Stevens no longer has the capacity for sustained mythic figuration, but within the miniature scale of this poem he creates a visionary image of exquisite purity. In the first four stanzas, he enacts an abortive effort to bring about a celestial rendezvous. The naked, nameless dame flickers into visible form, but only as a reflection from the past—"Like tales that were told the day before yesterday" (*CP,* 505). Although "She attends the tintinnabula," she has not the strength to sustain her function as the perceptual agent of a festival sphere, and her feebleness betrays itself in the vertiginous imagery and broken syntax of the third stanza: "And the wind sways like a great thing tottering." The imaginative strain becomes too great, and the images dissolve into "unintelligible thought." After failing to revive the erotic visionary mode, Stevens executes a reversal and finds a point of visionary poise by shifting into a more delicate, abstract mode:

> And yet this end and this beginning are one,
> And one last look at the ducks is a look
> At lucent children round her in a ring.

The maternal principle is subsumed within the transcendental circle of light, and the mother once again takes her place as the medium and center of phenomenal presence.

Stevens' "last look at the ducks" is also virtually a last look at the ancient mother. At the end of "The Sail of Ulysses," he will describe her in distinct mythic detail, but only as a figure who is absent from the poem. She "is now seen / In an isolation, separate / From the human in humanity" (*OP*, 104–105). Although he qualifies this isolation by declaring that she is "An inhuman of our features," he cannot bring her vividly to life. In "Farewell Without a Guitar," she appears only as "that other and her desire." Stevens will continue to sustain his visionary mode as a generic norm, but after 1952 there will be no more celestial rendezvous. (Frank Doggett also notes that "Hermitage" is "Stevens' last version of the nameless reclining woman, 'sleek in a natural nakedness.'")[6]

In "Final Soliloquy," Stevens' declining vigor betrays itself both in the carefulness with which he reconstructs his visionary fulfillment and in the cautiousness with which he declares the accomplishment of his purpose. In "Hermitage at the Centre," this decline betrays itself in the slightness of the poem and in the shakiness of Stevens' effort. "The Rock," in contrast, is not only one of the longest but also one of the most vigorous of Stevens' late poems. Nonetheless, this poem too gives evidence that Stevens' visionary power "is exhausted and a little old." In "Final Soliloquy" and the last stanza of "Hermitage," the transcendental presuppositions of pure poetry operate freely—despite Stevens' fatigue—to create images of perfect spiritual quietude. In "The Rock," Stevens' visionary drive once again comes into collision with the obdurate experiential fact of a solid reality outside the "vital boundary" of the mind, and Stevens never fully succeeds in establishing himself at the visionary center. The symbolic significance of the rock itself remains suspended between the perspectives of pure and normal poetry. From the perspective that governs "Credences of Summer," the rock as a symbol of the external world represents "The brilliant mercy of a sure

---

6. Doggett, *Stevens' Poetry of Thought*, 52.

repose," and its "barrenness" is that "Of the fertile thing that can attain no more." From the perspective that governs the final stanza of canto fifteen of "New Haven," the rock signifies a locus of spiritual absence, but Stevens contains and cancels this barrenness within its own spiritual shadow. The "rock of autumn" as "the shadow of bare rock" becomes a "source" for the paradoxical transumptions of pure poetry: "The heaviness we lighten by light will, / By the hand of desire" (*CP*, 476). In the last three stanzas of "*Seventy Years Later*," the first strophe of "The Rock," the rock stands at a point of intersection between the perspectives of pure and normal poetry. The effect of this intersection is to generate powerful but problematic images of the poetic consciousness. As in the first canto of "New Haven," Stevens invokes the rhetoric of the essential poem but fails to disengage this rhetoric from a dualistic conception of the world. In strophe two, "*The Poem as Icon*," he explicitly acknowledges the problematic character of his affirmations, and he undertakes to "find a cure of the ground," that is, to transcend the dichotomy between the mind and the external world. In the course of the strophe, he loses his way, and he concludes by making equivocal terms with the limited telos of "Credences of Summer." In the third strophe, "*Forms of the Rock in a Night-Hymn,*" he returns to the generic range of "Final Soliloquy." Although he reconstructs the significance of the rock and brings himself to repose within the hypothesis of a transcendental mind, he cannot altogether transform this hypothesis into a visionary realization.

"*Seventy Years Later*" is one of Stevens' most dynamic shorter poems. The strophe begins at the end of the imagination and ends in a rapturous figuration of life as a perpetual birth of consciousness. The opening stanzas constitute an ironic fulfillment of the prophecy in "A Postcard from the Volcano" (1936). Stevens had foreseen a time when the children playing among the ruins of his generation would

> say of the mansion that it seems
> As if he that lived there left behind
> A spirit storming in blank walls. (*CP*, 159)

He had represented this view as an error.

> Children picking up our bones
> Will never know that these were once
> As quick as foxes on the hill.

In *"Seventy Years Later,"* Stevens has come to be what he has said the children would perceive, a ghost who stands amazed at the ghastly unreality of the past.

> It is an illusion that we were ever alive,
> Lived in the houses of mothers, arranged ourselves
> By our own motions in a freedom of air. (*CP,* 525)

In order to dispel this sensation of the unreal, Stevens will seek to invest "illusion" with ontological validity. This is the same problem he confronts in "Description Without Place" and "Primitive," and by re-creating the reality of the past, he will involve himself once again in defending the theory of fictive belief.

Stevens' astonishment at the unreality of the past fixes itself on a specific scene, "The meeting at noon at the edge of the field." As he describes it he begins the movement toward a reversal from desolation to visionary affirmation. The idea of "illusion" modulates through a series of synonyms—"invention," "fantastic consciousness," "queer assertion," "theorem"—that gradually alter its connotative force, and the sense of the unreal inverts itself into a sense of creative vitality. The people who meet at noon become "Two figures in a nature of the sun, / In the sun's design of its own happiness." With this last phrase, Stevens takes a crucial theoretical step toward pure poetry. The "invention" of the two people becomes an extension of a transcendental "design." The sun, usually associated with the poetry of normal life, temporarily holds the place of the essential poem. In the next stanza, Stevens shifts from the sun to "the giant of nothingness" that is "ever changing, living in change":

> As if nothingness contained a métier,
> A vital assumption, an impermanence
> In its permanent cold, an illusion so desired
>
> That the green leaves came and covered the high rock,
> That the lilacs came and bloomed, like a blindness cleaned,
> Exclaiming bright sight, as it was satisfied,
>
> In a birth of sight. The blooming and the musk
> Were being alive, an incessant being alive,
> A particular of being, that gross universe.

Stevens' depiction of the birth of sight hovers ambiguously between the dualistic and the transcendental paradigms. The vacancy of the past merges into the universal nothingness from which, in "Primitive," the central poem "begets" the phenomenal world. In the final stanza, the past tense of personal narrative slips into the universal present of "Primitive"—"an incessant being alive"—but "that gross universe" is not yet the essential poem. The rock is an emblem of the external world, and the green leaves, emblems of poetic figuration, only cover the rock; they do not beget or contain it.

In canto eight of "Things of August," Stevens situates the moment of integration within "A zone of time without the ticking of clocks, / A color that moved us with forgetfulness." What he forgets in this zone are the forms of "difference" that inhibit a realization of essential unity. Stevens' moments of visionary fulfillment have never sufficed entirely to annul his desire for "a permanent realization" (*CP,* 425), and in "*The Poem as Icon*" he once again declares his need for a figuration in which all difference can be permanently suspended:

> It is not enough to cover the rock with leaves.
> We must be cured of it by a cure of the ground
> Or a cure of ourselves, that is equal to a cure
> Of the ground, a cure beyond forgetfulness.

Stevens' formulation of the problem already suggests the difficulty he will have in trying to solve it. The problem is to bridge "the dumbfoundering abyss / Between us and the object, external cause" (*CP,* 437). By locating the "cure" in either "the ground" or "ourselves," Stevens presupposes the dualism he seeks to transcend. In stanzas five and eleven, he announces that he has found a cure, but in fact he never escapes from the initial terms in which he poses the problem. In the second and third stanzas, he edges toward a figuration of essential unity by invoking a metaphor from "Description Without Place," but the metaphor never takes form as a transcendental trope. Stevens has represented the supreme fiction as "The spirit of one dwelling in a seed, /Itself that seed's ripe, unpredictable fruit" (*CP,* 341). He now recalls the metaphor of fruit, but fails to activate its theoretical implications:

> And yet the leaves, if they broke into bud,
> If they broke into bloom, if they bore fruit,

> And if we ate the incipient colorings
> Of their fresh culls might be a cure of the ground.
> The fiction of the leaves is the icon
>
> Of the poem, the figuration of blessedness,
> And the icon is the man.

In "Description Without Place," the animating force of the organic metaphor is "The spirit of one." The "fruit" is the supreme fiction, that is, the poem of the whole. Stevens' "fiction of the leaves" originates not in "The spirit of one" but in one spirit, that of "the man." Although he has failed to recover the signification of his metaphor, he draws on its connotative force in order to proclaim a resolution:

>   The pearled chaplet of spring,
> The magnum wreath of summer, time's autumn snood,
> Its copy of the sun, these cover the rock.
> These leaves are the poem, the icon and the man.
> These are a cure of the ground and of ourselves,
>
> In the predicate that there is nothing else.
> They bud and bloom and bear their fruit without change.
> They are more than leaves that cover the barren rock.

The hypothetical "might be a cure" has become the declarative "These are a cure," but up to this point there has been no theoretical advance that would justify the shift of verbal mood. The descriptive seasonal phrases are wonderfully eloquent; nonetheless, the "cure" Stevens announces merely restates the symptoms of the disease. The leaves that cover the rock are only a "copy" of the world, not a generative source. The predication "that there is nothing else" might seem to suggest that "the poem" subsumes all other things, but if so this is a curiously negative rendering of the essential poem. A more likely reading is that in default of any more effective cure, the leaves will have to serve. The assertion that the cycle of fruition continues "without change" answers to the need for a permanent realization, and it also segregates the cycle from the giant that is "ever changing."

   By declaring that the leaves that cover the rock "are more than leaves that cover the barren rock," Stevens implicitly concedes that he has not yet achieved a resolution within the terms he is using. He has not been able to escape from the dualistic conception that constitutes his problem, and in the following stanzas the need for resolution displaces itself into the mode of normal poetry. As he seeks to invest the word *more* with some definite content, the incipient metaphor of essential unity gradually deviates into "the honey of common summer" (*CP,* 316):

> They bud the whitest eye, the pallidest sprout,
> New senses in the engenderings of sense,
> The desire to be at the end of distances,
>
> The body quickened and the mind in root.
> They bloom as a man loves, as he lives in love.
> They bear their fruit so that the year is known,
>
> As if its understanding was brown skin,
> The honey in its pulp, the final found,
> The plenty of the year and of the world.

In "The Ultimate Poem Is Abstract," Stevens contrasts the sense of a central completion with the frustrations that attend "Writhings in wrong obliques and distances" (*CP,* 430). The "desire to be at the end of distances" is a desire to close all gaps within a unifying perspective. After failing to close the gap between the mind and the world, Stevens transposes the ideal of unity into an integration of body and mind. The body that is "quickened" is a body brought vividly to life, and a body so animated provides the "ground" for a "mind in root." This new form of integration, associating itself with the metaphor of fruit, calls up memories of "Le Monocle de Mon Oncle." "This luscious and impeccable fruit of life / Falls, it appears, of its own weight to earth" (*CP,* 14). The "ward of cupido" has long since evolved into "the old man standing on the tower" (*CP,* 16, 374), and the shadings from "Monocle" quickly give place to shadings from "Credences." "The plenty of the year and of the world" evokes the sensual plenitude in which "the distant fails the clairvoyant eye." Within this plenitude, "The utmost must be good and is / And is our fortune and honey hived in the trees." In "Credences," Stevens carefully constructs a limited telos that provides a temporary resting place in the quest for a supreme fiction. "Now the mind lays by its trouble and considers" (*CP,* 372). In the last two stanzas of *The Poem as Icon,* " he attempts to contain this quest within the festival sphere, and the spirit of one loses itself in the multiplicity of figurative forms:

> In this plenty, the poem makes meanings of the rock,
> Of such mixed motion and such imagery
> That its barrenness becomes a thousand things

> And so exists no more. This is the cure
> Of leaves and of the ground and of ourselves.
> His words are both the icon and the man.

The poem "makes meanings of the rock" by articulating its own forms. The barrenness of the rock in itself continues to exist. Within the elaborately circular logic of Stevens' imagery, the basic problem remains unsolved. The "meanings" of the poem are themselves the leaves that "cover the rock," and it is "These leaves" that are supposed to serve as "the cure / Of leaves."

In a letter written in August of 1950, Stevens remarks that he has just reread "The Rock" and that "the last part, which I had liked most, did not please me quite so well as the other parts" (*LWS,* 690). Stevens does not explain either why he initially favored the third strophe or why he later came to like it less, but the nature of the poem suggests a possible explanation. Stevens exercises considerable ingenuity in extricating himself from the perplexities of the preceding strophes, and his success must have given him an initial sense of satisfaction. On looking back at the poem several months later, he may have perceived that for all his cleverness he falls short of a full visionary realization. He is able to delineate the abstract forms of the supreme fiction, but he is not able, as in "Final Soliloquy," to re-create a vivid sense of spiritual presence.

In "*The Poem as Icon,*" Stevens has sought a cure of the ground within the figuration of the leaves. In "*Forms of the Rock in a Night-Hymn,*" he reverses this procedure and takes the rock itself as the focal point for his meditation. In a series of three predications, he dislodges the rock from its position as a simple antithesis to the imagination and situates it as an abstract locus within which he can contrive a whole:

> The rock is the gray particular of man's life.
>
> . . . .
>
> The rock is the stern particular of the air,
> The mirror of the planets, one by one,
> But through man's eye, their silent rhapsodist.
>
> . . . .
>
> The rock is the habitation of the whole,
> Its strength and measure, that which is near, point A
> In a perspective that begins again
> At B: the origin of the mango's rind.

Stevens' quasi-geometric figuration of the whole appears to be an attempt to give poetic illustration to the passage from Whitehead he will quote the following year in "A Collect of Philosophy." "'In a certain sense, everything is everywhere at all times, for every location involves an aspect of itself in every other location. Thus every spatio-temporal standpoint mirrors the world'" (*OP,* 192). Point B, in Stevens' illustration, may be located anywhere. The perspective of the individual extends from "that which is near" to the whole cosmos; "perspective" ceases to signify a particular standpoint, and consciousness becomes a ubiquitous presence. This sentient presence provides a new ground or "origin" for the fruit of which "the understanding was brown skin." These, at least, are the theoretical implications, but they are implications denuded of visionary affect. Stevens says that Whitehead's "words are pretty obviously words from a level where everything is poetic, as if the statement . . . produced in the imagination a universal iridescence." Stevens' own formulation, in contrast, produces the effect of tenuous abstraction. The mango's rind seems artificially attached to this abstraction, and by being overparticularized, the fruit metaphor loses the subtle, allusive suggestiveness it has in strophe two.

As "the habitation of the whole," the rock no longer represents a particular point in space. It has become equivalent to the "nothingness" that is the origin of a self-generating principle of consciousness. Stevens' figuration brings him within sight of a visionary resolution, but he does not effect a complete transition from the perspective of normal poetry to that of pure poetry. In the concluding stanzas, he situates himself on the borderline between these two modes and assumes a posture of devotional meditation:

> It is the rock where tranquil must adduce
> Its tranquil self, the main of things, the mind,
>
> The starting point of the human and the end,
> That in which space itself is contained, the gate
> To the enclosure, day, the things illumined
>
> By day, night and that which night illumines,
> Night and its midnight-minting fragrances,
> Night's hymn of the rock, as in a vivid sleep.

The word *tranquil,* used as a noun, refers both to the state Stevens seeks to achieve and to the visionary construct that makes this state possible: the central point "Where luminous agitations come to rest" (*CP,* 433). The association between "tranquil" and "an ever-changing, calmest unity" has an antecedent in Emerson's "Nature." Commenting on the mental compulsion "to reduce the most diverse to one form," Emerson declares that "when I behold a rich landscape, it is less to my purpose to recite correctly the order and superposition of the strata, than to know why all thought of multitude is lost in a tranquil sense of unity" (*RWE*, I, 67). Stevens himself does not represent the tranquil sense of unity as an accomplished fact. The verb of the main clause—"must adduce"—is prescriptive in form, and the terms of this prescription originate in an ambiguous region where the rock simultaneously signifies the gray particular and the habitation of the whole. The "main of things, the mind" is both the central mind and the individual imagination. The mind "in which space itself is contained" can only be the central mind, but "the gate," an appositive of "mind," is the individual mind. This gate opens into the transcendental enclosure in which space itself is contained. The subtle ambiguity of this modal positioning carries over into the opposition between day and night. The illumination of day is that of normal poetry, and the illumination of night is that of pure poetry. The diction and imagery in the last two stanzas echo those of a passage in Emerson's "American Scholar": "The first in time and the first in importance of the influences upon the mind is that of nature. Every day, the sun; and, after sunset, Night and her stars. . . . There is never a beginning, there is never an end, to the inexplicable continuity of this web of God, but always circular power returning into itself. Therein it resembles his own spirit, whose beginning, whose ending, he never can find,—so entire, so boundless" (*RWE*, I, 84–85). Like Emerson, Stevens presents the two forms of illumination as complementary alternatives, but the poem of the whole subsumes the poetry of normal life, and the strophe concludes in an emphatic evocation of night and sleep.

The resolution Stevens effects at the end of "The Rock" depends upon a willingness to stop short of an actual visionary realization and to accept the repose of devotional meditation. It is within this range, that of potential or hypothetical realization, that Stevens best sustains the visionary mode in the later poems. In the second canto of "New Haven," he had already attempted to conceive of his visionary quest as a "perpetual meditation," but because he had failed to provide an adequate doctrinal grounding for his effort, the "enduring, visionary love" had devolved into "emptiness." In "The World as Meditation" (1952), he returns to the idea of a perpetual meditation, and he now situates this meditation within a transcendental context. As Harold

Bloom notes, Stevens, in his ambiguous, hypothetical depiction of a meeting between Penelope and Ulysses, refigures the visionary consummation between Ozymandias and Nanzia Nunzio in "Notes."[7] After taking off her necklace and "her stone-studded belt," Nanzia Nunzio asks of Ozymandias that he "Clothe me entire in the final filament" (*CP,* 395, 396). In describing the contemplated meeting of Penelope and Ulysses, Stevens declares that "His arms would be her necklace / And her belt, the final fortune of their desire." Stevens' use of a Homeric theme entails a reversal of sexual roles; the object of visionary love becomes a man, and the visionary protagonist becomes a woman:

> Is it Ulysses that approaches from the east,
> The interminable adventurer? The trees are mended.
> That winter is washed away. Someone is moving
>
> On the horizon and lifting himself up above it.
> A form of fire approaches the cretonnes of Penelope,
> Whose mere savage presence awakens the world in which she dwells.
>
> . . . .
>
> The trees had been mended, as an essential exercise
> In an inhuman meditation, larger than her own.
>
> . . . .
>
> But was it Ulysses? Or was it only the warmth of the sun
> On her pillow? The thought kept beating in her like her heart.
> The two kept beating together. It was only day.
>
> It was Ulysses and it was not. Yet they had met,
> Friend and dear friend and a planet's encouragement.
> The barbarous strength within her would never fail. (*CP,* 520–21)

The statement in the first stanza, "The trees are mended," could be taken either as a result of Penelope's expectancy or as a supporting reason for that expectancy. In either case, Penelope's "savage presence" brings the world itself to life and thus brings it within the sphere of pure poetry. "That winter" is like the winter of "The Course of a Particular," a spiritual nothingness that discloses the absence of the divine attention. The "inhuman meditation" that mends the trees restores the world as a harmonious order. Within this order,

---

7. Bloom, *The Poems of Our Climate,* 363–64.

Penelope as the visionary protagonist can sublimate the need for any specific moment of visionary consummation:

> She would talk a little to herself as she combed her hair,
> Repeating his name with its patient syllables,
> Never forgetting him that kept coming constantly so near.

By rendering the moment of vivid anticipation as a constantly repeated condition, Stevens holds the visionary rendezvous in perpetual suspense. In this fashion, he can sustain the visionary mode as a "perpetual reference" for his poetry.

The meeting between Penelope and Ulysses symbolizes the culmination of Stevens' own visionary quest. In "The Poem That Took the Place of a Mountain" (1952), Stevens returns to the time when this culmination still lay ahead of him, and his depiction of the visionary goal helps to clarify the sense in which this culmination both did and did not occur. The poem that took the place of a mountain is "Chocorua to Its Neighbor." By breathing "its oxygen," Stevens evokes the central motif of "Chocorua" and reenters the spirit of his metaphysical metaphor:

> There it was, word for word,
> The poem that took the place of a mountain.
>
> He breathed its oxygen,
> Even when the book lay turned in the dust of his table.
>
> It reminded him how he had needed
> A place to go in his own direction,
>
> How he had recomposed the pines,
> Shifted the rocks and picked his way among clouds,
>
> For the outlook that would be right,
> Where he would be complete in an unexplained completion. (*CP*, 512)

In the fifth stanza, the past-tense narrative shifts into the hypothetical mode of "would" and "could." The exposition of his goal corresponds to what, in "Description Without Place," Stevens had said "might be," a perspective from which the world

>   shrinks to an immediate whole,
> That we do not need to understand, complete
> Without secret arrangements of it in the mind. (*CP*, 341)

This kind of perfect moment has never actually occurred. Stevens has achieved moments of completion, but never without explanations and secret arrangements. Nonetheless, by retrospectively suspending himself in the phase of anticipation, he now contrives a kind of subjunctive existence for the perfect perspective. The elaboration of an ideal possibility becomes a form of fictive realization—yet another secret arrangement.

In his evocation of "Chocorua," Stevens yields himself completely to the romance of retrospective anticipation. In another retrospective poem of 1952, "Looking Across the Fields and Watching the Birds Fly," he evokes the actual fulfillment of his visionary goal, but he presents this achievement from a detached, ambiguously ironic perspective. As he contrasts the consummations of the past with the disaffection of the present, he suspends himself between the positive and negative phases of the cycle from Romanticism to indifferentism. On the one hand he implicitly attributes his present disaffection to a failure of visionary energy, and on the other hand he submits his visionary achievements to the skeptical negations of a critic of paradise.

Stevens' persona in "Looking Across," Mr. Homburg of Concord, provides us with a distinct allusion to the generic and doctrinal lineage of the poem. In "The Over-Soul," Emerson had declared that when we abandon ourselves to "the Supreme Mind," we "come from our remote station on the circumference instantaneously to the centre of the world" (*RWE,* II, 276). In "The Ultimate Poem Is Abstract," Stevens had complained of being "Helplessly at the edge" of the world, and he had declared that "It would be enough / If we were ever, just once, at the middle" (*CP,* 430). At the beginning of "Looking Across," he situates his Emersonian persona "at the edge of things," and as the poem progresses it becomes clear that having once been "at the middle" is not now "enough":

> Among the more irritating minor ideas
> Of Mr. Homburg during his visits home
> To Concord, at the edge of things, was this:
>
> To think away the grass, the trees, the clouds,
> Not to transform them into other things,
> Is only what the sun does every day,
>
> Until we say to ourselves that there may be
> A pensive nature, a mechanical

> And slightly detestable *operandum,* free
> From man's ghost, larger and yet a little like,
> Without his literature and without his gods . . . (*CP,* 517–18)

The kind of spiritual negativity from which Mr. Homburg suffers is similar to that of the anti-master-man, who "brushed away the thunder, then the clouds" (*CP,* 241); but unlike the anti-master-man, Mr. Homburg has no illusions that this negativity will lead to a realization of the ideal. He remembers the lyric vitality of his youth, and he contrasts this vitality with the empty atmosphere in which he now lives:

> No doubt we live beyond ourselves in air,
>
> In an element that does not do for us,
> So well, that which we do for ourselves, too big,
> A thing not planned for imagery or belief,
>
> Not one of the masculine myths we used to make,
> A transparency through which the swallow weaves,
> Without any form or any sense of form,
>
> What we know in what we see.

Starting from this allusion to "Sunday Morning"—"June and evening, tipped / By the consummation of the swallow's wings"—Mr. Homburg progresses to a muted evocation of the mother as motion and discovery, and from this point he moves directly into the majesty of the central mind as parent and patron of origins. The ideal of a perfect lyric integration transposes itself into the ideal of a perfect visionary integration; the transparency of pellucid perception evolves into the transcendental element:

> We hear, what we are, beyond mystic disputation,
> In the tumult of integrations out of the sky,
>
> And what we think, a breathing like the wind,
> A moving part of a motion, a discovery
> Part of a discovery, a change part of a change,
>
> A sharing of color and being part of it.
> The afternoon is visibly a source,
> Too wide, too irised, to be more than calm,
>
> Too much like thinking to be less than thought,
> Obscurest parent, obscurest patriarch,

> A daily majesty of meditation,
> That comes and goes in silences of its own.

The "breathing like the wind" recalls the concluding stanzas of "Montrachet," the shadow's breath in "Chocorua," and the question in canto four of "Auroras": "What company, / In masks, can choir it with the naked wind?" In the climactic moment of "Auroras," the image of breath joins with the image of the ancient mother; it is "As if the innocent mother . . . Created the time and place in which we breathed." In "Owl" the mother

> held men closely with discovery,
> Almost as speed discovers, in the way
> Invisible change discovers what is changed.

All these mythic figurations—"The pure perfections of parental space"—come together in the image of the sky as a sentient presence. The "Obscurest parent" is the essential poem, a force that always reveals itself in "the obscurest as" but that is nonetheless "Vested in the serious folds of majesty."

Stevens' recitation of his own visionary motifs provides a lyric correlative to Emerson's theoretical declamations on the transcendental element. In "Nature," Emerson declares that "man is conscious of a universal soul within or behind his individual life" (*RWE*, I, 27). In describing this universal soul, he subordinates both the natural image of the sky and the archetypal image of the parent to the abstract terms *Reason* and *Spirit*. "And the blue sky in which the private earth is buried, the sky with its eternal calm, and full of everlasting orbs, is the type of Reason. That which intellectually considered we call Reason, considered in relation to nature, we call Spirit. Spirit is the Creator. Spirit hath life in itself. And man in all ages and countries embodies it in his language as the FATHER." Stevens can still participate in the lyric affect of "the sky with its eternal calm" and the archetypal pathos of the father, but he cannot share Emerson's faith in the primacy of capitalized abstractions. Stevens' visionary experience is no less vital than Emerson's, but it is less stable, for Stevens, as a modern man, cannot repose in the authority of formulaic doctrinal propositions.

In the sentence beginning "The afternoon is visibly a source," the evocation of the myths of the past gives place to a present-tense description. The element that is too big for imagery or belief has been transformed into the element of the supreme fiction. Despite this transformation, Mr. Homburg in the following stanzas returns to his point of departure. He is fatigued with the vicissitudes of a majesty "That comes and goes in silences of its own" and that is no more susceptible to control than are the rising and falling of the wind. By reverting to a doctrine of simple realism, he attempts to circumvent the problematic mysticism of the supreme fiction, but the mystical impulse reasserts itself, and the final note is that of an ambiguous Romantic affirmation:

> A new scholar replacing an older one reflects
> A moment on this fantasia. He seeks
> For a human that can be accounted for.
>
> The spirit comes from the body of the world,
> Or so Mr. Homburg thought: the body of a world
> Whose blunt laws make an affectation of mind,
>
> The mannerism of nature caught in a glass
> And there become a spirit's mannerism,
> A glass aswarm with things going as far as they can.

At first sight, the phrase "A new scholar replacing an older one" might seem to signify that Stevens is replacing Emerson, but the "fantasia" on which the new scholar reflects is Stevens' own.[8] As a new scholar, Stevens is replacing—or attempting to replace—his older, Emersonian self, which has created the masculine myths evoked in the preceding stanzas. What he attempts to replace it with is a still older persona, the comedian. Mr. Homburg's initial formulation—"The spirit comes from the body of the world"—recalls Crispin's fatal maxim: "his soil is man's intelligence." The authorial interpolation, "Or so Mr. Homburg thought," suggests Stevens' own ambivalence toward this revived persona, and as Mr. Homburg elaborates on his proposition the perspective of the realist yields once more to that of the Romantic. The "affectation of mind" becomes "The mannerism of nature" and thence "a spirit's mannerism." As in "Primitive," the mother's "glass" serves as a transumptive medium. Once nature has been "caught" in this glass, the generative ground shifts from "body" to "mind," and the "things" of the phenomenal world become things of the spirit.

If Mr. Homburg has been unable to sustain the masculine myths he used to make, neither can he sustain his ironic deprecation of those myths. "To an

---

8. For other efforts to explain the ambiguous relations among Mr. Homburg, Emerson, and Stevens, see Riddel, *The Clairvoyant Eye,* 267; Baird, *The Dome and the Rock,* 70; Bloom, *The Poems of Our Climate,* 358; and La Guardia, *Advance on Chaos,* 160.

Old Philosopher in Rome" (1952) is a eulogistic address that provides Stevens with an occasion to abandon all irony and to represent the masculine myths as a final, total realization. What Stevens does for Santayana in this poem corresponds to what, half a century earlier, Santayana himself had described as the natural inclination of the dying man:

> When a man knows that his life is over, he can look back upon it from a universal standpoint. He has nothing more to live for, but if the energy of his mind remains unimpaired, he will still wish to live, and, being cut off from his personal ambitions, he will impute to himself a kind of vicarious immortality by identifying himself with what is eternal. He speaks of himself as he is, or rather as he was. He sums himself up, and points to his achievement. This I have been, says he, this I have done.
>
> This comprehensive and impartial view, this synthesis and objectification of experience, constitutes the liberation of the soul and the essence of sublimity. That the hero attains it at the end consoles us, as it consoles him, for his hideous misfortunes. Our pity and terror are indeed purged; we go away knowing that, however tangled the net may be in which we feel ourselves caught, there is liberation beyond, and an ultimate peace.[9]

As Santayana suggests, the liberation of the soul serves as a consolation not only for the dying hero but also for those who observe his liberation. By depicting Santayana's final hours as a spiritual triumph, "The human end in the spirit's greatest reach," Stevens allays the frustrations and terrors of his own decline. The human end, death, is subsumed within the end as structural closure. The perspective that governs the poem is established in the first line. By situating Santayana "On the threshold of heaven," Stevens fashions an analogue between the perspective of the dying man and that of the man who walks living among the forms of thought. The temporal progression across the threshold mutates into an atemporal visionary transumption. Heaven serves as an equivalent to "The abstract," and the forms of phenomenal reality become the contours of this abstract:

> On the threshold of heaven, the figures in the street
> Become the figures of heaven, the majestic movement
> Of men growing small in the distances of space,
> Singing with smaller and still smaller sound,

9. Santayana, *The Sense of Beauty*, 238–39.

> Unintelligible absolution and an end—
> The threshold, Rome, and that more merciful Rome
> Beyond, the two alike in the make of the mind.
> It is as if in a human dignity
> Two parallels become one, a perspective, of which
> Men are part both in the inch and in the mile. (*CP,* 508)

In the *Apologia Pro Mente Sua,* a response to his critics, Santayana declares that "for a man of my traditions and tastes, Italy, Rome especially, has an eternal dignity"; and in the same work, he provides Stevens with the image of the two parallels. The basic premise of Santayana's mature philosophy is that "nothing can ever make existence and essence continuous, as nothing can ever make architecture continuous with music: like parallels such orders of being can never flow into one another. But they may be conjoined or superposed; they may be simultaneous dimensions of the same world."[10] Stevens adapts this image to his own distinct vision. He refigures the two parallels as the world and the essential poem, and he associates the essential poem with the traditional idea of heaven. The problematic character of this intersection between the world and the essential poem resolves itself within the "Unintelligible absolution" that recedes into infinity.

The quality of mercy produces a rhetorical dispensation within which Stevens balances "The extreme of the known" and "the extreme / Of the unknown," rendering both extremes, paradoxically, as moments of resolution. Stevens represents "happiness" as an accomplished fact, and yet he projects a happiness—"the celestial possible"—beyond all poetic figuration:

> The bed, the books, the chair, the moving nuns,
> The candle as it evades the sight, these are
> The sources of happiness in the shape of Rome,
> A shape within the ancient circles of shapes,
> And these beneath the shadow of a shape
>
> In a confusion on bed and books, a portent
> On the chair, a moving transparence on the nuns,
> A light on the candle tearing against the wick
> To join a hovering excellence, to escape

---

10. George Santayana, *Apologia Pro Mente Sua,* in Paul Arthur Schilpp (ed.), *The Philosophy of George Santayana* (Evanston, 1940), 603, 525. Peterson cites the latter passage in *The Idealist Tradition,* 86.

From fire and be part only of that of which
Fire is the symbol: the celestial possible.

The image of the candle has a long history in Stevens' work, but the specific use in "An Old Philosopher" suggests that he is recalling a passage from *Scepticism and Animal Faith*. Santayana argues that "the notion of spiritual substances" is "a self-contradictory notion at bottom, because substance is a material and spirit is an entelechy, or perfection of function realized; so that (if I may parody Aristotle), if a candle were a living being, wax would be its substance and light its spirit."[11] Despite his defensive reference to a parody of Aristotle, in order to define the spirit Santayana himself has recourse to the metaphor of light. "By spirit I understand simply the pure light or actuality of thought, common to all intuitions, in which essences are bathed if they are given."[12] For Santayana, essences bathed in the actuality of thought are in fact "given," but existence is not.[13] For Stevens, existence is given, but the celestial possible remains difficult of access. The problematic relationship between the concrete given and the hovering excellence of the essential poem manifests itself in the dual signification of the word *sources*. The first four items in the list of concrete particulars—"The bed, the books, the chair, the moving nuns"—represent places where happiness is actually to be found. The fifth item, "The candle as it evades the sight," signifies a happiness that is yet to be realized. All five items are, at first, subsumed within "the shape of Rome," which is contained within the figurations of the transcendental element: the ancient circles, the shadow, a portent, and a moving transparence. The association among the ancient circles, transparence, and a portent evokes the process through which Stevens has achieved an integration of the transcendental sublime and the visionary subconscious, a process that extends from a letter of 1908 (*LWS*, 136) through "Owl's Clover" and that culminates in "A Primitive Like an Orb." Out of the "confusion" of these figurations, the "light on the candle" emerges as an anomaly that represents the unclosed gaps

---

11. Santayana, *Scepticism and Animal Faith*, 217. Doggett, *Stevens' Poetry of Thought*, 132, cites this passage in reference to "The Candle a Saint."
12. Santayana, *Scepticism and Animal Faith*, 214. A similar objectification of consciousness as a field of light appears in "Of Bright and Blue Birds." Stevens speaks of those privileged moments "in which we pronounce joy like a word of our own" and it is "as if there was a bright *scienza* outside of ourselves" (*CP*, 248).
13. See Santayana, *Scepticism and Animal Faith*, 55, 72–73.

between the real and the transcendental, between anticipation and realization, and between metaphor and the thing-in-itself.

In the light that tears against the wick, the two parallels have separated once again. Stevens now defines these parallels as "two worlds," one the "misery" of a dwindled sphere and the other the "grandeur" of the celestial possible:

> Yet living in two worlds, impenitent
> As to one, and, as to one, most penitent,
> Impatient for the grandeur that you need
>
> In so much misery, and yet finding it
> Only in misery, the afflatus of ruin,
> Profound poetry of the poor and of the dead.

After defining this conflict, Stevens himself yields to the impatience he attributes to Santayana. The transposition of grandeur to the dwindled sphere suggests that he will seek a tonal resolution in the negative sublime. Instead, he chooses to expunge the tragic potential of this conflict and to take refuge in Romantic hyperbole:

> It is poverty's speech that seeks us out the most.
> It is older than the oldest speech of Rome.
> This is the tragic accent of the scene.
>
> And you—it is you that speak it, without speech,
> The loftiest syllables among loftiest things,
> The one invulnerable man among
> Crude captains, the naked majesty, if you like.

As "The one invulnerable man," Santayana ceases to be capable of tragic speech, and the "loftiest syllables" become rhetorically effulgent affirmations. Stevens would presumably consider himself one of the "Crude captains" who are vulnerable to impoverishment. In "The Plain Sense of Things," he declares that "The great structure has become a minor house." In the last two stanzas of "An Old Philosopher," he resituates the great structure at "the end," and he employs the threshold as a locus for a hypothetical totalization:

> It is a kind of total grandeur at the end,
> With every visible thing enlarged and yet
> No more than a bed, a chair and moving nuns,
> The immensest theatre, the pillared porch,
> The book and candle in your ambered room,

> Total grandeur of a total edifice,
> Chosen by an inquisitor of structures
> For himself. He stops upon this threshold,
> As if the design of all his words takes form
> And frame from thinking and is realized.

As in his major visionary poems, Stevens frames his declaration of visionary resolution with a concession to the necessity of metaphoric displacement—"As if the design . . . is realized." Within this concession, the "total grandeur" consists of a reconciliation between antithetical cognitive norms: the simple perception of concrete particulars—"a bed, a chair and moving nuns"—and the passion for structural elaboration. Although Stevens attempts to close all gaps for Santayana, the divergence between existence and essence makes itself felt even in the moment of final affirmation. The architectural metaphor becomes its own referent, and all that is "realized" is an image of structure: "form / And frame."

Within the constant restructuring of the motifs of the supreme fiction, one of the most stable points of reference is the waking sleep. It is in this state—"at sleepy mid-days"—that in "Extracts" the "redeeming thought" comes to life, though "Too vaguely that it be written in character." In "Owl" it is "in the height / Of sleep" that the ultimate intellect becomes accessible, and in "Auroras" it is when "As if, awake, we lay in the quiet of sleep" that Stevens achieves mythic resolution. "The Rock" concludes in "a vivid sleep," and the revelations of the old philosopher in Rome take place when he is "dozing in the depths of wakefulness." In "Prologues to What Is Possible" (1952), it is in the meditative sleep that "things beyond resemblance" can almost be realized (*CP,* 516). At the beginning of "Long and Sluggish Lines" (1952), Stevens expresses his fatigue at the reflections and repetitions of his final phase. "It makes so little difference, at so much more / Than seventy, where one looks, one has been there before" (*CP,* 522). At the end of the poem, he escapes from this sense of belatedness by retreating into sleep as a state of pure potentiality. "You were not born yet when the trees were crystal / Nor are you now, in this wakefulness inside a sleep." At the other pole of his poetic horizon, in the inevitable oscillations from pure to normal poetry, sleep becomes a foil for the "new knowledge of reality" (*CP,* 534) that can be found in immediate sensory perception. In "On the Way to the Bus" (1954), a breath of cold air is "more revealing than / A perception of sleep" (*OP,* 116), and in "Not Ideas About the

Thing But the Thing Itself" (1954), the cry of a bird awakens eager observation precisely because "It was not from the vast ventriloquism / Of sleep's faded papier-mâché" (*CP*, 534). In the later poems, the scope of Stevens' oscillations diminishes, but the oscillation itself never ceases. In one of his latest poems, "Artificial Populations" (1955), Stevens declares that "The center that he sought was a state of mind," and he locates this state of mind in "the wind as it deepens, and late sleep, / And music that lasts long and lives the more" (*OP*, 112, 113).

In the poetry that precedes the major visionary poems, Stevens' dialectical oscillations produce an "amassing harmony" (*CP*, 403). The final poems represent fading echoes of this harmony, and in "Conversation with Three Women of New England" (1954), Stevens seeks to reconcile himself to an oscillation that leads nowhere in particular. He sets out three "modes" of metaphysical vision. The first is the essential poem; the second and third coalesce to form the humanistic naturalism of "Sunday Morning":

> Now, you, for instance, are of this mode: You say
> That in that ever-dark central, wherever it is,
> In the central of earth or sky or air or thought,
> There is a drop that is life's element,
> Sole, single source and minimum patriarch,
> The one thing common to all life, the human
> And inhuman same, the likeness of things unlike.
>
> And you, you say that the capital things of the mind
> Should be as natural as natural objects.
>
> . . . .
>
> And then, finally, it is you that say
> That only in man's definitions of himself,
> Only encompassed in humanity, is he
> Himself. The author of man's canons is man,
> Not some outer patron and imaginer. (*OP*, 108–109)

In canto five of "New Haven," Stevens distinguishes two parts of "The self." One part is that which is "Held fast tenaciously in common earth." The other part is that which in the region

> from central earth to central sky
> And in moonlit extensions of them in the mind
> Searched out such majesty as it could find.

As the archetypal source of both phenomenal and poetic images, the central poem is the integrative agency between the human and the inhuman same. The "humanist," in order to confirm the substantial validity of his experience, denies the existence of any archetypal source possessed of conscious intent. We live in an "island solitude, unsponsored, free" (*CP*, 70). In "Conversation," Stevens commits himself to neither of these metaphysical perspectives. After defining the views of his supposed interlocutors, he assumes the role of neutral mediator:

> In which of these three worlds are the four of us
> The most at home? Or is it enough to have seen
> And felt and known the differences we have seen
> And felt and known in the colors in which we live?

This rhetorical question effects a truce between the premises of Stevens' modal dialectic, but the balance of power is inherently unstable. To see and feel and know is "enough" for Stevens only when one or the other pole of his dialectic manages to free itself from relativistic restriction and assert itself as an absolute.

The tone of "Conversation" is genial tolerance, but the state in which Stevens simply accepts "the differences we have seen" is dangerously close to indifferentism, the state in which "It makes so little difference" what he sees. A sense of visionary purpose is the precondition for a continuing imaginative vitality. It is "the great necessity" (*LWS*, 584), and in "The Sail of Ulysses," Stevens seeks to supply this need by breaking free from his own diminishing oscillations and extending his ambition to the apotheosis of some "'future man / And future place'" (*OP*, 101). "The Sail of Ulysses" was composed as a Phi Beta Kappa address for Columbia University's bicentennial commencement, and its oratorical manner reflects its occasion. Stevens himself recognized that the poem was a failure. "Perhaps I shan't throw it away. But I shall certainly never use it in its present form nor allow anyone to see a copy of it. This is not because I think that knowledge is not a good subject for a poem but because, coupled with birthdays and commencements, it becomes a force of intolerable generalities" (*LWS*, 834–35). While knowledge may not be a bad subject for a poem, the specific sort Stevens wrote about—the final resolution of all the problematic aspects of the supreme fiction—could hardly be presented except in intolerable generalities. Although not only "'Unknown as yet'" but also "'unknowable,'" the future man would provide "'A freedom at last from the mystical, / The beginning of a final order.'" The final order locates itself outside the bounds of poetic figuration altogether. Once all "'misgivings'" have been "'dazzlingly / Resolved,'" "'The ancient symbols will be nothing,'" and "'We shall have gone behind the symbols / To that which they symbolized'" (*OP*, 102). In his major visionary poems, Stevens renders that which cannot be fixed in self-negating mythic images. Once the supreme fiction has been segregated from the ancient symbols, it can be rendered only in "'Plantagenet abstractions'" (*OP*, 103):

> "There is no map of paradise.
> The great Omnium descends on us
> As a free race. We know it, one
> By one, in the right of all. Each man
> Is an approach to the vigilance
> In which the litter of truths becomes
> A whole, the day on which the last star
> Has been counted, the genealogy
> Of gods and men destroyed, the right
> To know established as the right to be."

At the end of section seven, Stevens offers an enigmatic apologia for these abstractions. "'We obey the coaxings of our end.'" In the final section, he confesses that these coaxings are not the inspirations of mythic vision but the frustrations of personal "'poverty.'" He depicts the ancient mother in the form of "'the englistered woman'" and declares that she is not the presiding genius of the poem. The presiding genius is "'the sibyl of the self,'" and Stevens himself calls this figure "'a form that is lame.'" Since she is unable to satisfy his need, he turns again to the ancient mother and, through her, attempts to effect an integration between the human and "'the inhuman more.'" The diction remains abstract, but the appeal to mythic resolution nonetheless serves to moderate the millennialist yearnings of sections four and five. The idea of "'a final order'" gives place to the ambiguous recognition that subsists only "'for a little, lesser time.'"

When the structures of pure poetry lose their affective power, Stevens turns back to the world that must be measured by eye. As he elaborates on this world in poetic figurations, the perceptions of the eye inevitably evolve toward "the main of things, the mind" (*CP*, 528). This movement repeats itself continuously in "New Haven," and in "Local Objects" (1955), Stevens extends the movement so as to encompass the devotional mode that sustains the pure poetry of his final phase. "Local Objects" has the same formal structure as do the cantos of "New Haven"—six tercets—and may be considered as a final contribution to that endlessly elaborating poem. At the beginning of "Local Objects," Stevens once again assumes the stance of a critic of paradise. By the end of the poem, he has already begun reconstructing the landscape of the mind:

> He knew that he was a spirit without a foyer
> And that, in his knowledge, local objects become
> More precious than the most precious objects of home:
>
> The local objects of a world without a foyer,
> Without a remembered past, a present past,
> Or a present future, hoped for in present hope,
>
> Objects not present as a matter of course
> On the dark side of the heavens or the bright,
> In that sphere with so few objects of its own.
>
> Little existed for him but the few things
> For which a fresh name always occurred, as if
> He wanted to make them, keep them from perishing,
>
> The few things, the objects of insight, the integrations
> Of feeling, the things that came of their own accord,
> Because he desired without knowing quite what,
>
> These were the moments of the classic, the beautiful.
> These were that serene he had always been approaching
> As toward an absolute foyer beyond romance. (*OP,* 111–12)

In the first stanza, "local objects" signify those things that are given to the senses, but "the word is the making of the world" (*CP,* 345), and in the fourth stanza, value transposes itself from the objects themselves to the naming of the objects. By the fifth stanza, the meaning of "objects" has changed. The idea of concrete particulars, the objects of perception, has been replaced by the idea of imaginative constructs: "the objects of insight, the integrations / Of feeling." The simple present that is without past or future begins to metamorphose into the "time / That of itself stood still, perennial" (*CP,* 432). Stevens first depicts this visionary present in "Martial Cadenza," where the evening star becomes the emblem of "The present close, the present realized," a present that is

> apart from any past, apart
> From any future, the ever-living and being,
> The ever-breathing and moving, the constant fire. (*CP,* 238)

The evening star is at once a local object and a manifestation of the abstract; it is a spontaneous figuration for those "integrations out of the sky" that constitute "the masculine myths."

The ideal of a spontaneous integration—"the things that come of their own accord"—applies equally to normal and pure poetry, and in the final stanza of "Local Objects" the latest freed man once again assumes the devotional attitude of "The Rock," "The World as Meditation," and "The Poem That Took the Place of a Mountain." As in "The Rock," an adjective of emotional condition becomes a noun: "tranquil" and "that serene." In figuring his relation to that serene as a perpetual approach, Stevens assumes the stance of Penelope, "Never forgetting him that kept coming constantly so near." The "absolute foyer beyond romance" refigures the ideal of a locale "Where he would be complete in an unexplained completion." An "absolute foyer" is an image of Romance, and to place this foyer "beyond romance" is to employ the technique of self-negating images Stevens uses in the major visionary poems. In "Martial Cadenza" he declares that "the present realized" is "Not the symbol but that for which the symbol stands," and in "Owl" the mother of the living and the dead "stood tall in self not symbol." When, in "The Sail of Ulysses," Stevens prophesies a time when "We shall have gone behind the symbols / To that which they symbolized," he displaces visionary paradox into an opposition of present and future. Finally, in "Local Objects," he returns to "his own direction" (*CP,* 512). He defines the absolute foyer not as the millennial resolution but as the object of perpetual reference.

Stevens' poetic ambitions were those of the extreme poet. From attempting to replace God with lyric naturalism, he advances to the apotheosis of poetry and thence of the poet. When in "The Plain Sense of Things" he declares that "A fantastic effort has failed," it is to this unbounded ambition that he refers. Stevens failed to effect a permanent integration with the essential poem. He failed to transform men into gods or earth into paradise. He nonetheless succeeded in creating a mode of poetic experience in which religious awe and Romantic wonder are still possible. Having discarded the outworn myths, he fashioned a fundamental poetry even older than the ancient world, a cosmos in which the forms of thought are elemental potencies, and where divinity is a pure principle. Stevens' visionary mythology lives and has influence only as it manifests itself in the realizations of poetry. It is a fiction, but a fiction that contains the world by designating as the world's essential quality a need to make itself known in the supreme fictions of poetry.

APPENDIX

In the Fold

In Peter Brazeau's oral biography of Stevens, the chaplain who was resident at the Catholic hospital where Stevens died reports that shortly before his death Stevens joined the Catholic church. He explains that the event was not publicized at the time "because his wife was not a Catholic and because it might seem that we got people into the hospital to drag them into the Church at the last minute." While there is no guarantee of the chaplain's veracity, his account seems credible and gains support from the testimony of others. Elias Mengel, a friend of Holly Stevens', went with her to visit her father at the hospital. "Now Holly can't remember this, but I *thought* I saw a copy of the New Testament on his bedside table. I was surprised that he would be reading this." According to Brazeau, "Holly Stevens vigorously denies that her father was converted to Catholicism during his last illness. While at St. Francis Hospital, she recalls, Stevens complained of visits by clergy but he said he was too weak to protest." Stevens may have been embarrassed at his need for official spiritual comfort. With Jim Powers, an old friend who was himself a religious man, Stevens appears to have been less reticent. Powers' wife—the Margaret of "A Fish-Scale Sunrise"—reports that "Holly wrote to me that Julie's [Mrs. Powers' daughter's] St. Christopher medal had been buried with him. Jim . . . said that he also had on his pillow a crucifix that his nurse or somebody had given him. He wanted that out there . . . and he wanted Julie's St. Christopher medal pinned on his pillow right where he could see it."[1]

If one assumes that Stevens had decisively expunged the religious element

---

1. Brazeau, *Wallace Stevens Remembered,* 295, 291, 310, 297.

from his life and work, these disclosures might seem to convict him of a radical inconsequence. If, however, we take account of his own pronouncements on established religion, his deathbed conversion—if such it was—seems natural enough. Although not doctrinally committed, Stevens was always strongly attracted to the church as an institution. From his earliest days in New York, he had a fondness for finding churches and sitting in them to meditate, and in a letter of 1907 he urged his future wife to join a local congregation. While he conceded that churches "do not 'influence' any but the 'stupid,'" he also maintained that "they are beautiful and full of comfort and moral help" (*LWS,* 96). In a fashion that might have been rather confusing to his fiancée, he withdrew the epithet "religious" from his devotion to the church:

It has always been a particular desire of mine to have you join church; and I am very, very glad to know that you are now on the road.—I am not in the least religious. The sun clears my spirit, if I may say that, and an occasional sight of the sea, and thinking of blue valleys, and the odor of the earth, and many things. Such things make a god of a man; but a chapel makes a man of him. Churches are human.—I say my prayers every night—not that I need them now, or that they are anything more than a habit, half-unconscious.

Stevens' equivocal views on the beauty and comfort of churches seem to reflect the influence of Matthew Arnold. As Lucy Beckett points out, one of the main channels through which this influence might have reached Stevens is Santayana. In *Interpretations of Poetry and Religion,* Santayana argues that "religion and poetry are identical in essence, and differ merely in the way in which they are attached to practical affairs. Poetry is called religion when it intervenes in life, and religion, when it merely supervenes upon life, is seen to be nothing but poetry." Like Arnold, Santayana laments that "poetry in order to be religion, in order to be the inspiration of life, must first deny that it is poetry and deceive us about the facts with which we have to deal." Although Christianity has seized "the essence" of human life and thus ought to be "an eternal religion," it "may forfeit that privilege by entangling itself with a particular account of matters of fact, matters irrelevant to its ideal significance."[2]

Stevens' religious sentiments often seem to fluctuate "as the sun shines or

2. Beckett, *Wallace Stevens,* 57, *et passim*; Santayana, *Interpretations of Poetry and Religion,* v, 115–16.

does not" (*CP*, 518), and his terminology is equally unstable. In a journal entry of 1902, Stevens had drawn a contrast between nature and the church similar to that which he later draws in the letter to his fiancée, and he had designated both areas as places of "religious" veneration:

Last night I spent an hour in the dark transept of St. Patrick's Cathedral where I go now and then in my more lonely moods. An old argument with me is that the true religious force in the world is not the church but the world itself: the mysterious callings of Nature and our responses. What incessant murmurs fill that ever-laboring, tireless church! But to-day in my walk I thought that after all there is no conflict of forces but rather a contrast. In the cathedral I felt one presence; on the highway I felt another. Two different deities presented themselves; and, though I have only cloudy visions of either, yet I now feel the distinction between them. The priest in me worshipped one God at one shrine; the poet another God at another shrine. The priest worshipped Mercy and Love; the poet, Beauty and Might. (*LWS*, 58–59)

Both the poet and the priest concern themselves less with dogma than with forms of pathos, and the doctrinal content of Stevens' religion remains very abstract. While on a business trip in 1920, he wrote to his wife, "I should like to go to a pleasant little Episcopalian Church not far from the hotel but my Irish friends will no doubt be here in a short time and might object to my worshipping the principle of things instead of the stuff that makes the mare go round" (*LWS*, 219).

Stevens continued the habit of visiting churches in later years, and he retained a special attachment to St. Patrick's Cathedral. To Anthony Sigmans, who worked under Stevens, this attachment implied no specifically religious orientation:

Mr. Stevens was not a religious man. I was a practicing Catholic. He never discussed religion, except on a rare occasion he would make a comment that he had an enjoyable afternoon yesterday in New York as he sat in St. Patrick's Cathedral and meditated. During his last illness he became a Catholic. There was no publication of it, and the burial rites were brief, without any Catholic ceremony. [Months after Stevens' death Sigmans learned of this from the chaplain at St. Francis Hospital.] I do recall Mr. Stevens saying to me at one time that he belonged to no church, but if he ever joined a church it would be the Catholic Church.[3]

3. Brazeau, *Wallace Stevens Remembered*, 290–91.

(James Baird deserves credit for a sharp intuition on Stevens' aesthetic predilection for Catholicism. "One supposes that, had Stevens been able to accept an orthodoxy of the Christian tradition, he would have embraced Roman Catholicism with its ritual and order, its feasts, its colors of the seasonal year, and its disciplines of meditation.")[4] Anthony Sigmans was not, perhaps, the kind of man to whom Stevens would have divulged his more intimate confidences. Jim Powers seems to have come closer to Stevens, and Margaret Powers reports:

> He and Jim talked an awful lot about religion [over the years]. He knew Jim had a definite faith. Jim had said, "I think Wallace would like to be in a Church but he can't do it." He and Jim sought out these little churches all over Manhattan, mostly Roman. . . . He loved the feeling of the Church, the atmosphere of churches, according to Jim. I'd never been in St. Patrick's, as a matter of fact, and he insisted that we go. We didn't go to a service. We just went in, and he showed me all around the various chapels and the high altar.[5]

Powers' sense of Stevens' reluctant attraction to "a definite faith" finds confirmation in a letter of 1952, where Stevens remarks that "at my age it would be nice to be able to read more and think more and be myself more and to make up my mind about God, say, before it is too late, or at least before he makes up his mind about me" (*LWS,* 763). Stevens has spent a lifetime trying to make up his mind about God. In "Extracts from Addresses to the Academy of Fine Ideas," following Whitman, he had repudiated any orthodox assistance in this effort. "The lean cats of the arches of the churches, / That's the old world. In the new, all men are priests" (*CP,* 254). In a poem of 1952, "St. Armorer's Church from the Outside," he demonstrates that he still has enough independent spiritual vitality to maintain this stance. He contrasts the church, one of "Time's given perfections," to "the need of each generation to be itself, / The need to be actual and as it is" (*CP,* 530):

> St. Armorer's was once an immense success.
> It rose loftily and stood massively; and to lie
> In its church-yard, in the province of St. Armorer's,
> Fixed one for good in geranium-colored day.
>
> What is left has the foreign smell of plaster,
> The closed-in smell of hay.

4. Baird, *The Dome and the Rock,* 305.
5. Brazeau, *Wallace Stevens Remembered,* 297.

St. Armorer's has now fallen into decay, and Stevens affirms his commitment to "this present, / This *vif,* this dizzle-dazzle of being new." One can, nonetheless, detect a note of nostalgic envy for those who have been fixed for good in geranium-colored day.

In his last few weeks, dying of cancer, Stevens seems to have felt the need for mercy and love more strongly than the need for beauty and might. The chaplain's story suggests that Stevens' anxiety to make up his mind about God had reached a critical pitch: "He really wanted to talk. There was something bothering him all the time. He believed strongly in God. When he went to New York, he told me, he used to spend at least a couple of hours at St. Patrick's Cathedral, meditating. He said he got so much peace and enjoyment that he always, when he went to New York, went to St. Patrick's Cathedral. I think he had such a marvelous idea of what God was. The absolute idea of God. 'Everything,' he said, 'has been created. There is only one uncreated.' And that was God." The chaplain says that Stevens felt he "'ought to be in the fold'" but that he hesitated to profess himself a Christian because he was morally repelled by the idea of hell. "'I do think that a merciful God, knowing the weakness of mankind, would not fashion a place like that to punish anyone—not even a dog.'" The chaplain was willing to soft-pedal the issue. "I said, 'As far as we know, we don't know that there's anyone specifically in hell except the devil and his cohorts.'" It may be that this comforting equivocation helped to overcome Stevens' scruples. He continued discussing the issue, "and he was thinking and thinking and thinking. One day he had a bit of a spell. He called for me, and he said, 'I'd better get in the fold now.' And then I baptized him, and the next day I brought him Communion. . . . It was just a few days [later that he died]. He seemed very much at peace, and he would say, 'Now I'm in the fold.'"[6] As Stevens himself stood on the threshold of heaven, he had probably lost the power of fabricating his own myths. "Churches are human," and in submitting himself to an established, traditional mythology, Stevens seems at last to have accepted his position as one of "the unaccomplished, / The finally human" (*CP,* 504).

6. *Ibid.,* 294, 295.

Works Cited

Abrams, M. H. "Structure and Style in the Greater Romantic Lyric." In *From Sensibility to Romanticism: Essays Presented to Frederick A. Pottle,* edited by Frederick W. Hilles and Harold Bloom. London, 1965.
Ackerman, R. D. "Death and Fiction: Stevens' Mother of Beauty." *English Literary History,* L (1983), 401–14.
———. "Desire, Distance, Death: Stevens' Meditative Beginnings." *Texas Studies in Literature and Language,* XXV (1983), 616–31.
Arnold, Matthew. *English Literature and Irish Politics.* Ann Arbor, 1973. Vol. IX of *The Complete Prose Works of Matthew Arnold.* Edited by R. H. Super. 11 vols. 1960–77.
———. *The Poetical Works of Matthew Arnold.* Edited by C. B. Tinker and H. F. Lowry. London, 1950.
Baird, James. *The Dome and the Rock: Structure in the Poetry of Wallace Stevens.* Baltimore, 1968.
Bates, Milton J. "Stevens in Love: The Woman Won, the Woman Lost." *English Literary History,* XLVIII (1981), 231–55.
———. *Wallace Stevens: A Mythology of Self.* Berkeley, 1985.
Baudelaire, Charles. *Oeuvres Complètes.* Edited by Marcel A. Ruff. Paris, 1968.
Beckett, Lucy. *Wallace Stevens.* London, 1974.
Benamou, Michel. *Wallace Stevens and the Symbolist Imagination.* Princeton, 1972.
Bloom, Harold. *Wallace Stevens: The Poems of Our Climate.* Ithaca, 1976.
Bornstein, George. *Transformations of Romanticism in Yeats, Eliot, and Stevens.* Chicago, 1976.
Bové, Paul A. *Destructive Poetics: Heidegger and Modern American Poetry.* New York, 1980.
Brazeau, Peter. *Parts of a World: Wallace Stevens Remembered.* New York, 1983.
———. "Wallace Stevens at the University of Massachusetts: Checklist of an Archive." *Wallace Stevens Journal,* II (1978), 50–54.

Bulfinch, Thomas. *The Age of Fable*. In *Bulfinch's Mythology*. New York, 1934.
Buttel, Robert. "'Knowledge [sic] on the Edges of Oblivion': Stevens' Late Poems." *Wallace Stevens Journal*, V (1981), 11–16.
———. *Wallace Stevens: The Making of "Harmonium."* Princeton, 1967.
Caldwell, Price. "'Sunday Morning': Stevens' Makeshift Romantic Lyric." *Southern Review*, n.s., XV (1979), 933–52.
Carroll, Joseph. "The Ancient and the Modern Sage: Tennyson and Stevens." *Victorian Poetry*, XXII (1984), 1–14.
Coleridge, Samuel Taylor. *Biographia Literaria*. 1983; rpr. Princeton, 1984. Edited by James Engell and W. Jackson Bate. Vol. VII of *The Collected Works of Samuel Taylor Coleridge*. Edited by Kathleen Coburn and Bart Winer. 16 vols. projected.
———. *The Poems of Samuel Taylor Coleridge*. Edited by E. H. Coleridge. London, 1931.
Cook, Eleanor. "Wallace Stevens: 'The Comedian as the Letter C.'" *American Literature*, XLIX (1977), 192–205.
Corn, Alfred. "Wallace Stevens and the Poetics of Ineffability." In *Ineffability: Naming the Unnamable from Dante to Beckett*, edited by Peter S. Hawkins and Anne Howland Schotter. New York, 1984.
Cunningham, J. V. "Tradition and Modernity: Wallace Stevens." *Poetry*, LXXV (December, 1949). Revised and reprinted in *The Collected Essays of J. V. Cunningham*. Chicago, 1976.
Doggett, Frank. *Stevens' Poetry of Thought*. Baltimore, 1966.
———. *Wallace Stevens: The Making of the Poem*. Baltimore, 1980.
Feshbach, Sidney. "Poetic and Human Anxieties in the Early Poetry of Wallace Stevens." *Wallace Stevens Journal*, II (1978), 43–49.
Frye, Northrop. *Anatomy of Criticism: Four Essays*. 1957; rpr. New York, 1965.
Fuchs, Daniel. "Wallace Stevens and Santayana." In *Patterns of Commitment in American Literature*, edited by Marston LaFrance. Toronto, 1967.
Hines, Thomas J. *The Later Poetry of Wallace Stevens: Phenomenological Parallels with Husserl and Heidegger*. Lewisburg, Pa., 1976.
James, William. *A Pluralistic Universe: Hibbert Lectures at Manchester College on the Present Situation in Philosophy*. New York, 1909.
Kant, Immanuel. *Critique of Pure Reason*. Translated by J. M. D. Meiklejohn. New York, 1934.
Keats, John. *Poetical Works*. Edited by H. W. Garrod. 2nd ed. London, 1958.
La Guardia, David M. *Advance on Chaos: The Sanctifying Imagination of Wallace Stevens*. Hanover, N.H., 1983.
Litz, A. Walton. *Introspective Voyager: The Poetic Development of Wallace Stevens*. New York, 1972.
———. "Particles of Order: The Unpublished *Adagia*." In *Wallace Stevens: A Celebration*, edited by Frank Doggett and Robert Buttel. Princeton, 1980.
———. "Wallace Stevens' Defense of Poetry: *La poésie pure*, the New Romantic, and

the Pressure of Reality." In *Romantic and Modern: Revaluations of Literary Tradition,* edited by George Bornstein. Pittsburgh, 1977.
Locke, John. *An Essay Concerning Human Understanding.* Edited by Alexander Campbell Fraser. Vol. I of 2 vols. New York, 1959.
Lovejoy, Arthur O. *The Reason, the Understanding, and Time.* Baltimore, 1961.
Macleod, Glen G. *Wallace Stevens and Company: The "Harmonium" Years, 1913–1923.* Ann Arbor, 1983.
Martz, Louis L. "'From the Journal of Crispin': An Early Version of 'The Comedian as the Letter C.'" In *Wallace Stevens: A Celebration,* edited by Frank Doggett and Robert Buttel. Princeton, 1980.
———. "Wallace Stevens: The World as Meditation." In *Literature and Belief: The English Institute Essays for 1957,* edited by M. H. Abrams. New York, 1958. Reprinted in *Wallace Stevens: A Collection of Critical Essays,* edited by Marie Borroff. Englewood Cliffs, 1963.
Middlebrook, Diane. *Walt Whitman and Wallace Stevens.* Ithaca, 1974.
Miller, J. Hillis. "Wallace Stevens' Poetry of Being." *English Literary History,* XXXI (1964). Reprinted in *The Act of the Mind: Essays on the Poetry of Wallace Stevens,* edited by Roy Harvey Pearce and J. Hillis Miller. Baltimore, 1965.
Morris, Adalaide Kirby. *Wallace Stevens: Imagination and Faith.* Princeton, 1974.
Pack, Robert. "Wallace Stevens' Sufficient Muse." *Southern Review,* n.s., XI (1975), 766–78.
Pearce, Roy Harvey. "The Cry and the Occasion: 'Chocorua to Its Neighbor.'" *Southern Review,* n.s., XV (1979), 777–91.
———. "Toward Decreation: Stevens and the 'Theory of Poetry.'" In *Wallace Stevens: A Celebration,* edited by Frank Doggett and Robert Buttel. Princeton, 1980.
———. "Wallace Stevens: The Last Lesson of the Master." *English Literary History,* XXXI (1964). Reprinted in *The Act of the Mind: Essays on the Poetry of Wallace Stevens,* edited by Roy Harvey Pearce and J. Hillis Miller. Baltimore, 1965.
Perlis, Alan. *Wallace Stevens: A World of Transforming Shapes.* Lewisburg, Pa., 1976.
Peterson, Margaret. *Wallace Stevens and the Idealist Tradition.* Ann Arbor, 1983.
Regueiro, Helen. *The Limits of Imagination: Wordsworth, Yeats, and Stevens.* Ithaca, 1976.
Riddel, Joseph N. *The Clairvoyant Eye: The Poetry and Poetics of Wallace Stevens.* Baton Rouge, 1965.
———. "The Climate of Our Poems." *Wallace Stevens Journal,* VII (1983), 59–75.
Santayana, George. *Apologia Pro Mente Sua.* In *The Philosophy of George Santayana,* edited by Paul Arthur Schilpp. Evanston, 1940.
———. *Interpretations of Poetry and Religion.* New York, 1900.
———. *Scepticism and Animal Faith: Introduction to a System of Philosophy.* New York, 1923.
———. *The Sense of Beauty: Being the Outlines of Aesthetic Theory.* New York, 1896.

Shelley, Percy Bysshe. *Complete Poetical Works of Percy Bysshe Shelley.* Edited by Thomas Hutchinson. New York, 1951.

Simons, Hi. "'The Comedian as the Letter C': Its Sense and Significance." *Southern Review,* n.s., V (1940). Reprinted in *The Achievement of Wallace Stevens,* edited by Ashley Brown and Robert S. Haller. Philadelphia, 1962.

Steiner, Dorothea. "Wallace Stevens: Romantic Traits in Modern Poetic Theory." In *On Poets and Poetry: A Symposium from the Department of English at the University of Salzburg,* edited by James Hogg. Salzburg, Austria, 1974.

Stevens, Holly. *Souvenirs and Prophecies: The Young Wallace Stevens.* New York, 1977.

Tennyson, Alfred. *The Poems of Tennyson.* Edited by Christopher Ricks. London, 1969.

Vendler, Helen Hennessy. *On Extended Wings: Wallace Stevens' Longer Poems.* Cambridge, Mass., 1969.

———. "The Qualified Assertions of Wallace Stevens." In *The Act of the Mind: Essays on the Poetry of Wallace Stevens,* edited by Roy Harvey Pearce and J. Hillis Miller. Baltimore, 1965.

Weiskel, Thomas. *The Romantic Sublime: Studies in the Structure and Psychology of Transcendence.* Baltimore, 1976.

Whitman, Walt. *Leaves of Grass.* Edited by Harold W. Blodgett and Sculley Bradley. New York, 1965.

Winters, Yvor. "Wallace Stevens or the Hedonist's Progress." In *The Anatomy of Nonsense.* Norfolk, Conn., 1943. Reprinted in *In Defense of Reason.* Chicago, 1947.

Woodman, Leonora. *Stanza My Stone: Wallace Stevens and the Hermetic Tradition.* West Lafayette, Ind., 1983.

Wordsworth, William. *The Poetical Works of William Wordsworth.* Edited by Ernest de Selincourt and Helen Darbishire. 5 vols. Oxford, 1940–49.

———. *The Prelude: A Parallel Text.* Edited by J. C. Maxwell. New Haven, 1981.

Index

Index of Stevens' Works

Adagia, 15, 18, 24, 25, 27, 252
Address to the Poetry Society of America, 20
"Adult Epigram," 171
"All the Preludes to Felicity," 246
"American Sublime, The," 72, 83, 206
"Anatomy of Monotony," 50, 55, 63, 132, 144, 146, 269
"Anecdote of Men by the Thousand," 33, 35, 61, 155
"Anecdote of the Jar," 36–37, 113
"Anglais Mort à Florence," 66–67
"Artificial Populations," 333
"Asides on the Oboe," 23, 128, 130–31, 133, 145, 157, 178, 203, 212, 301
Auroras of Autumn, The, 5, 9, 10, 107, 112, 120, 130, 150, 153, 173, 193, 210–11, 214, 261, 303
"Auroras of Autumn, The," 3, 8, 9, 10, 28, 38, 60, 65, 71, 82, 96, 120, 123, 142, 143, 144, 155, 164, 193, 200, 202, 208, 236–60, 261, 266–67, 268, 269–70, 272, 283, 291, 293, 301–302, 326, 332

"Bed of Old John Zeller, The," 16, 158–59, 179
"Beginning, The," 261, 273, 290, 299
"Botanist on Alp (No. 1)," 69–70, 95

"Bouquet, The," 142, 278
"Bouquet of Belle Sçavoir," 148, 149–50, 151, 173, 174, 272, 285
"Brave Man, The," 68
"Candle a Saint, The," 9, 60, 148–49, 151, 163, 173, 183, 188
"Carnet de Voyage," 265
"Chocorua to Its Neighbor," 137, 138, 153, 154, 158, 183, 188, 202–208, 229, 236, 242, 254, 265, 266, 311, 323, 324, 326
Collected Poems, The, 101, 151
"Collect of Philosophy, A," 13, 20, 25, 26, 28, 128, 178, 213, 257, 262, 293, 320
"Comedian as the Letter C, The," 6, 56–62, 63, 66, 75, 94, 115, 116, 124, 131, 132, 153, 155, 179, 265, 283, 307
"Connoisseur of Chaos," 35, 121–24, 126, 132, 135, 154, 159, 187
"Contrary Theses (II)," 145–46, 150, 162, 171, 176, 198
"Conversation with Three Women of New England," 333–34
"Country Words," 118–20, 130, 174, 300
"Course of a Particular, The," 304, 306–307, 322
"Creations of Sound, The," 186
"Credences of Summer," 19, 118, 153, 154,

156, 176, 181–82, 195–97, 198, 201, 260, 261, 262–63, 275, 313–14, 318
"Crude Foyer," 116, 154–58, 159, 173, 244, 246
"Curtains in the House of the Metaphysician, The," 38–40, 200, 248

"Death of a Soldier, The," 84
"Description Without Place," 9, 119–20, 153, 158, 173, 178–79, 182–86, 213, 270, 276, 280, 285, 315, 316, 317, 323–24, 336
"Dezembrum," 111, 112
"Dove in Spring, The," 304
"Duck for Dinner, A," 94–97
"Dutch Graves in Bucks County," 16, 178, 179

"Effects of Analogy," 21–22, 28, 38, 199
"Esthétique du Mal," 60, 133, 154, 156, 158, 178, 179, 187–95, 199, 209, 252, 258, 318
"Evening Without Angels," 71–74, 85, 102, 112, 137, 166, 191, 245
"Examination of the Hero in a Time of War," 93, 130, 132, 133, 200, 206
"Extracts from Addresses to the Academy of Fine Ideas," 3, 109, 128, 131–41, 143, 145, 148, 150, 151, 157, 162, 163, 169, 177, 178, 192, 193, 200, 206, 256, 265, 280, 283, 332, 342

"Fading of the Sun, A," 68–69
"Farewell to Florida," 87–88
"Farewell Without a Guitar," 304, 313
"Figure of the Youth as Virile Poet, The," 3–4, 20–21, 24, 25, 27, 81, 96, 165, 180–81, 199, 254, 256n
"Final Soliloquy of the Interior Paramour," 4, 19, 27, 31, 303, 310–12, 313, 314, 319
"Fish-Scale Sunrise, A," 339
"Flyer's Fall," 178
"Forms of the Rock in a Night-Hymn," 314, 319–21
"From the Packet of Anacharsis," 9, 197–99

"Gallant Chateau," 147
"Ghosts as Cocoons," 146
"Gigantomachia," 168
"Glass of Water, The," 199

"God Is Good. It Is a Beautiful Night," 201, 256
"Golden Woman in a Silver Mirror, A," 273–75, 291, 294
"Good Man, Bad Woman," 147
"Good Man Has No Shape, The," 201
"Greenest Continent, The," 83, 84, 89, 91–93, 95, 102, 114, 157–58
"Green Plant, The," 304

"Hand as a Being, The," 151, 152, 170, 171, 173, 176, 295, 300, 313
Harmonium, 3, 6, 15, 18, 29, 30, 31, 32, 37, 38, 56, 62, 63, 89, 106, 108, 109, 146, 147, 153, 161, 179, 189
"Hermitage at the Centre, The," 312–13
"High-Toned Old Christian Woman, A," 55–56
"Holiday in Reality," 185
"Homunculus et la Belle Etoile," 113, 146
"House Was Quiet and the World Was Calm, The," 201–202
"Human Arrangement," 200
"Hymn from a Watermelon Pavilion," 38, 146

"Idea of Order at Key West, The," 7, 62–63, 64, 74–78, 151, 183, 233
Ideas of Order, 7, 18, 32, 63, 64, 67, 78, 81, 83, 88, 89, 101, 104, 109, 117, 146, 147, 153, 177, 280
"Imagination as Value," 22, 24, 25, 26, 27, 103, 187, 213
"In a Bad Time," 261, 270
"In the Carolinas," 146
"Irrational Element in Poetry, The," 3, 8, 14–20, 25, 99, 170, 175
"It Must Be Abstract," 160, 162–70, 171, 195, 213, 244, 245, 265
"It Must Change," 170, 172
"It Must Give Pleasure," 106, 108, 161, 174–76

"Jasmine's Beautiful Thoughts Underneath the Willow," 37

"Landscape with Boat," 35, 124–28, 132, 161, 239, 325
"Late Hymn from the Myrrh Mountain," 173

"Latest Freed Man, The," 110, 121, 131, 132, 134, 135, 140, 164, 180, 290, 337
"Lebensweisheitspielerei," 10, 304, 305–306, 343
"Less and Less Human, O Savage Spirit," 209–10
"Life on a Battleship," 151
"Like Decorations in a Nigger Cemetery," 62–63, 83–87, 93
"Local Objects," 304, 335–37
"Long and Sluggish Lines," 332
"Looking Across the Fields and Watching the Birds Fly," 51, 324–27, 340–41
"Lunar Paraphrase," 189

"Madame La Fleurie," 146, 304
"Man on the Dump, The," 136
Man with the Blue Guitar, The, 88, 100
"Man with the Blue Guitar, The," 63, 64, 86, 99, 101–105, 109, 114, 136, 143, 153, 166, 177, 180, 188, 205, 209, 251, 261, 281
"Martial Cadenza," 135, 137, 138, 203, 205, 336–37
"Meditation Celestial and Terrestrial," 146, 193
"Men That Are Falling, The," 99–100, 177
"Metaphors of a Magnifico," 36
"Monocle de Mon Oncle, Le," 40–48, 51, 55, 63, 94, 125, 142, 146, 147, 191, 194–95, 292, 318
"Montrachet-Le-Jardin," 37–38, 87, 109, 139, 142–45, 146, 148, 151, 179, 188, 199, 203, 206, 209, 268, 285, 300
"Motive for Metaphor, The," 180
"Mozart, 1935," 88
"Mr. Burnshaw and the Statue," 93–94, 95
"Mrs. Alfred Uruguay," 124, 128, 129–30, 158, 191

"Negation," 32–33, 238, 269
"Noble Rider and the Sound of Words, The," 8, 9, 20, 22, 87, 98, 102, 104, 109, 138–39, 147, 150, 163, 207
"Notes Toward a Supreme Fiction," 4, 5, 9, 20, 21, 95, 96, 106, 117, 124, 128, 142, 146, 153, 154, 156, 158, 160–77, 180, 187, 200, 203, 205, 206–207, 208, 231, 234, 248, 249, 266, 267, 276, 283, 290, 297, 301, 322, 333

"Not Ideas About the Thing But the Thing Itself," 332–33
"Nuances of a Theme by Williams," 34–35, 58, 285

"Of Bright and Blue Birds and the Gala Sun," 117–18, 205, 213, 330*n*
"Of Ideal Time and Choice," 21, 210, 212, 242
"O Florida, Venereal Soil," 146
"Of Modern Poetry," 19, 139, 177, 183
"Old Woman and the Statue, The," 89
"One More Sunset," 265
"On the Road Home," 120–21, 128, 132, 135, 155–56
"On the Way to the Bus," 332
Opus Posthumous, 19, 29, 147, 261
"Ordinary Evening in New Haven, An," 4, 10, 95, 99, 142, 214, 259, 260, 261, 275–99, 305, 307, 308, 314, 321, 333, 335, 336
"Owl in the Sarcophagus, The," 7, 9–10, 19, 26, 27–28, 38, 50, 52, 79–86, 120, 141, 142, 143, 147, 149, 155, 173, 179, 193, 198–99, 200, 202, 206–13, 214–36, 237, 238, 243, 244, 248, 253, 254, 256, 260, 261, 266, 269–70, 272, 285–301, 310, 311, 320, 326, 332, 336, 337
"Owl's Clover," 7, 8, 15–16, 63, 64, 83, 88–89, 100, 104, 109, 120, 130, 133, 142, 147, 151, 153, 170, 177, 179, 203, 261, 265, 278, 301, 330

Parts of a World, 8, 9, 19, 31, 63, 106–109, 112, 120, 131, 133, 141, 151, 152, 153, 154, 177, 214, 232, 244, 280
"Phosphor Reading by His Own Light," 149, 183, 201, 232
"Plain Sense of Things, The," 9, 296, 304, 308–10, 337
"Plus Belles Pages, Les," 142
"Poem as Icon, The," 314, 316–19
"Poems of Our Climate, The," 113, 115–17, 158
"Poem That Took the Place of a Mountain, The," 323–24, 327
"Postcard from the Volcano, A," 314
"Prelude to Objects," 113–14
"Primitive Like an Orb, A," 3, 7, 8, 9, 10, 19,

27, 67, 81, 96, 165, 178, 180, 197, 200, 210, 213, 214, 227n, 255, 260–69, 271, 272, 273, 276, 278, 281, 283, 287, 288, 297, 307, 312, 315, 316, 330
"Prologues to What Is Possible," 332
"Pure Good of Theory, The," 153, 158, 200–201, 300

"Reader, The," 81, 82, 201
"Red Loves Kit," 147
"Region November, The," 304, 306, 307–308
"Relations Between Poetry and Painting, The," 13, 64, 199–200
"Repetitions of a Young Captain," 168, 183
Rock, The, 5, 19, 29, 30, 261
"Rock, The," 4, 86, 96, 142, 303, 313–21, 332, 337

"Sad Strains of a Gay Waltz," 88
"Sailing After Lunch," 64, 67–68, 74, 166
"Sail of Ulysses, The," 95, 152, 304, 312, 313, 334–35, 337
"St. Armorer's Church from the Outside," 86, 342–43
"Saint John and the Back-Ache," 4, 123, 243, 271–72, 316
"Sense of the Sleight-of-Hand Man, The," 111–12, 206
"Seventy Years Later," 314–16
"Six Significant Landscapes," 146
"Sketch of the Ultimate Politician," 31, 159–60, 309
"Snow Man, The," 35, 36, 57–58, 72, 135, 136
"Sombre Figuration," 17, 89, 97–99, 167
"Somnambulisma," 181
"Study of Images II," 271
"Sunday Morning," 6, 23, 40, 47, 48–55, 56, 58, 73, 78, 79, 85, 104, 110, 116, 144, 153, 156, 188, 189, 290, 295, 325, 333, 334
"Sun This March, The," 63, 64–66, 258

"Tea at the Palaz of Hoon," 33, 34, 35, 57, 113, 129
"Things of August," 65, 120, 147, 214, 260, 261, 299–302, 310, 316
"This Solitude of Cataracts," 246, 286, 290, 316
"Thought Revolved, A," 99
"Three Academic Pieces," 21–22, 148
"Thunder by the Musician," 138
"To an Old Philosopher in Rome," 118, 128, 303, 327–32
"To the One of Fictive Music," 116, 147, 172, 173, 185
"To the Roaring Wind," 37
Transport to Summer, 5, 8, 9, 31, 106, 112, 120, 130, 133, 153–54, 171, 173, 177, 187, 210, 214, 232, 244
"Two Illustrations That the World Is What You Make of It," 172
"Two or Three Ideas," 22–23, 24
"Two Versions of the Same Poem," 200, 251

"Ultimate Poem Is Abstract, The," 212–13, 318, 324

"Waving Adieu, Adieu, Adieu," 78–81, 82–83, 132, 140, 188
"Weeping Burgher, The," 179
"Well Dressed Man with a Beard, The," 128, 141, 191
"Woman in Sunshine, The," 272–73, 274, 294, 299
"Woman That Had More Babies Than That, The," 148, 151–52
"Woman Who Blamed Life on a Spaniard, The," 147
"World as Meditation, The," 303, 321–23, 337
"World Without Peculiarity," 52, 146, 147, 272, 274, 277n

General Index

Absence: interplay of presence and, 206, 225, 268, 271–72; black as symbol for, 252; spiritual, 307, 314. *See also* Nothingness

Absolute: poetic, as goal, 1; fiction of, 9, 162, 197, 234, 245; last largeness as, 38, 40; sun as, 87, 145; of action, 100, 131; need for,

118, 334; negative, 124, 161; blank, 129; pure sound as, 139; of sensual experience, 140; instability of, 141; green fish as, 145; physical world as, 150; reductive, 162; death as, 229, 230, 232, 292; Arctic effulgence as, 251; and nature, 257; human as, 305
Abstract, the: as originative element, 145, 146, 149, 171, 176; immanence of, 163; and mythic feminine figure, 171, 183, 302; as pure relation, 266; seduction of, 298; and archetypal memory, 312
Aestheticism, 4, 5, 6, 14, 15, 17, 56, 66, 127
Ananke, 84, 92, 114, 158, 228
Ancestors, 17, 159, 179, 240, 301; great mud-ancestor, 95, 96, 97, 120, 228, 301
Angels, 44, 53, 71, 72, 74, 100, 112, 114, 158, 162
Animism, 35, 104, 112, 190, 306, 307
Apotheosis: Emerson on, 27, 90, 169; of poetry, 86, 337; of the future, 95, 97, 334; and Romantic intoning, 169, 245; excluding speech of, 207; yields to epiphany, 240
Archetypes: and the subconscious, 7, 16; and abstraction, 22, 210; and the feminine figure, 148, 192, 273
Arnold, Matthew, 71, 111–12, 155
Asceticism, 35, 124–26

Baudelaire, Charles, 292
Being: and nothingness, 79, 81, 266, 268; and knowing, 110, 111, 117–18, 205; moving and, 148, 203, 234
Belief: in a fiction, 9, 25–26, 93, 157, 161, 183, 185, 245–46, 276, 289, 292, 298, 315; question of final, 23, 130, 145, 157, 212; to believe beyond, 26, 178; not fixed, 67; need for, 85, 93, 103–104, 254; to be total in, 117, 118, 205, 213; and serpent, 255; beliefs became, 300; element too big for, 325, 326
Blake, William, 207
Bloom, Harold, 4–5, 76, 107, 115
Bible, 26, 44, 48, 53, 54, 119, 248
Bremond, Abbé Henri, 14, 18

Cabala, 82, 96, 97, 252
Cassirer, Ernst, 24

Catholicism, 11, 85, 339–43
Center: search for, 3, 271; of all circles, 9, 198; of poetry, 27; of common life, 62; as a central composition, 70, 74, 83, 95, 198; muddy, 95, 164, 165, 169, 200, 301; generative, 96, 210, 264; of reality, 111; neutral, 125; as central heart, 134, 141, 169, 200, 226, 265; self as, 137; mystical, 144; of the pathetic fallacy, 164, 308; as central sky, 197, 282, 333; in pure and normal poetry, 199–200; of responses, 200, 206; of time, 210, 246; of the world, 213, 261, 324; in sleep realized, 226, 320; strength at, 259, 291; of the universe, 270; as central earth, 282, 287, 291, 333
Chatillon, Sébastien, 247, 248
Christianity: failure of, 6, 48, 134, 250, 295, 340; poetic affects of, 4, 52, 54; God of, 107, 141–42
Church, Henry, 18, 171, 213, 219
Circle: center of, 9, 198; of creation, 27, 211; orb, 89, 98, 261, 265; in the Cabala, 96; in Emerson and Santayana, 261–62
Coleridge, Samuel Taylor: "Dejection: An Ode," 69; "Kubla Khan," 129; *Biographia Literaria,* 256n, 262
Crown: of the moon, 41, 146; and mystical cabala, 82, 97, 252; starless, of Ananke, 92, 95, 158, 228; of crowns, 95, 96, 97, 120, 228, 301; sources for, 96–97; as spirit's diamond coronal, 96, 158, 173, 228, 229; and diamond cabala, 96, 97, 120, 252; of humanity, 155, 158, 244, 246, 308; and weekday coronal, 158, 173, 228–29; and relation, 172–73; wearers of, 228–29; of the father, 240

Death: peace after (as mythic figure), 7, 52, 214, 215, 218, 220, 224, 229–32, 233, 235, 266, 291, 292; syllable between life and, 38, 217, 234; is mother of beauty, 49, 51, 52, 79, 141, 290; in paradise, 52, 158; mythology of modern, 52, 214, 222, 235, 256; fear of, 68, 256, 257–58, 294; mingling of life and, 79, 296; in Whitman, 83, 84, 294; without a heaven, 92, 114; as ultimate evil, 133; dissolves evil, 140–41, 178, 192–93; of soldiers, 177–79; and innocence, 192, 258; transition to, 218–19; remains inaccessible, 230, 276, 291, 294–95; as single sleep, 293–94

Descartes, René, 163, 169

Dialectic: of imagination and reality, 2; of dualism and transcendentalism, 3; of pluralism and monism, 8, 108, 121–24; of pure and normal poetry, 14, 19, 275, 284, 334; of negation and affirmation, 42, 128, 244; in specific works, 48–49, 131, 140, 154, 161–62, 187, 277–78; of conscious and subconscious, 97; of being and knowing, 110, 113; of breadth and order, 135; and supreme fiction, 165–66; of pure idea and particularity, 177; of being and nothingness, 268, 269

Divinity: in self, 23, 49; change in Stevens' idea of, 32; shift in locus of, 52; union of human with, 60; pantheistic, 91, 107, 126–27, 161, 184; and essential imagination, 142; absence of, 307, 308, 322; is a pure principle, 337–38

Doggett, Frank, 2, 11, 16–17, 30

Dualism: struggle against, 1, 22, 35, 37, 161–62, 275, 282, 284, 289, 317; and deconstruction, 2–3; and normal poetry, 3, 19, 275, 282; and transcendentalism, 3, 12, 13, 110, 276, 286, 316; is problematic, 34, 129, 182

Emerson, Ralph Waldo: and the Romantic sublime, 5, 257; influence of, on Stevens, 7; on ancestral memory, 17, 261; on apotheosis, 27, 90, 169; on idealism, 57; on materialism, 57, 156, 297–98; figure of scholar in, 65–66, 251; and transparence, 90–91; on inherent opposites, 122*n*; and central heart, 134, 169, 170; defines transcendentalism, 156; and first idea, 162; and the diva-dame, 171; and the ultimate poem, 213; and the candle, 251, 311; on morning and evening knowledge, 253–54; and the great shadow, 257; on universal mind, 260; and the circle, 261–62; and the giant, 268–69; on miraculous and common, 284; and tranquil unity, 321; and Mr. Homburg, 324–47; on reason and spirit, 326

—works: "Fate," 17, 157, 158, 311; "The Over-Soul," 27, 67, 162, 169, 213, 261, 269, 324; "Nature," 27, 90, 134, 156, 169, 171, 253–54, 262, 268–69, 284, 321, 326; "The Transcendentalist," 57, 156, 297–98; "Compensation," 122*n*; "History," 171, 260, 268; "Experience," 249; "Society and Solitude," 251; "Circles," 262, 263; "The American Scholar," 321

Empiricism, 39, 108. *See also* Materialism; Pluralistic empiricism

Essential imagination: poet as medium of, 86, 150, 183, 260; identified with God, 92, 142, 260; difficulties of, 93, 162; and pure reason, 108; contains mind and sky, 139; as image at its source, 148; final cause of, 158; intersection of human and, 210; as spectre of the spheres, 259

Essential poem: as governing principle, 81, 92, 165; seen in lesser poems, 197, 263, 266; as source of all centers, 199–200; exposition of, 263–70; and normal poetry, 275–76; reality in, 286; absence of proof for, 297; man as medium of, 307; sun holding place of, 315; obscurist parent as, 326; and heaven, 329

Eye: landscape of, 116, 155, 156; world measured by, 132, 156, 335; mind as, 155, 156; blind forward of, 184, 280; that needs, 216, 217, 310; angelic, 245; plain version of, 278, 280, 283, 286

Father, 76, 218, 229, 240, 244–49, 253, 255, 326

Feminine figure: interior paramour, 9, 172, 173, 310, 312; one of fictive music, 43, 147, 185; eternal damsel, 45, 47, 94, 147; celestial paramours, 93–94, 97, 147; development of, 109, 146–52; auroral creature, 143, 145, 146, 148; various guises of, 146–47, 170–74; fat girl, 146, 175–76, 187, 192, 267, 275, 305; naked nameless dame, 152, 170–71, 173, 176, 295, 313; Nanzia Nunzio, 172, 175, 228, 322; maiden Bawda, 175, 247; woman not yet accustomed, 271; that other, 304, 313; Penelope, 322–23, 337

—mother: ancient, 9, 22, 28, 80, 81, 82, 109,

146, 147, 173, 179, 220, 229, 234, 272, 275, 284–85, 287, 293, 296, 300–301, 302, 310, 312, 313; the earthly, and of the dead, 10, 28, 38, 52, 79, 80, 85, 141, 143, 206, 207, 214–25, 232–34, 238, 296, 337; as dominant mythic figure, 9, 22, 28, 173–74, 300–301; innocent, 28, 82, 143, 238, 255, 326; of heaven, 41, 42, 45, 146, 147; and diviner love, 43; of beauty, 49, 51, 79, 141, 290; ocean as, 76; earth as, 109, 146, 147–48, 151, 219–20, 272, 305, 312; summer the drunken, 146, 193; of pathos and pity, 189; and anima, 192; as quick of being, 234; as agent of change, 234, 295; embodies pure principle, 238; as purpose of the poem, 242–43; as father's counterpart, 244, 247; mirror of, 264, 274, 327; and visionary love, 284–85; sound of, 294; and dress imagery, 299–300; elegy for, 302; decline of, 302, 310, 312; last look at, 313; as motion and discovery, 325; as englistered woman, 335
—queen: abstract archaic, 9, 60, 148, 158, 183, 193, 301, 312; regina of the clouds, 41, 45, 146; one of fictive music as, 43; moon as, 60; as single thought, 134, 146; development of, 148, 151; as source of appearances, 173, 276; green, 183, 228, 285; who is still to appear, 274; of Fact, 296; wicked, 312

First idea: archetypal source for, 95; as central principle of the supreme fiction, 162–67; in Emerson, 162, 213; thinker of, 168, 170, 208; giant as, 170, 265; feminine figure as, 173; shadow as late plural of, 207; cannot be fixed, 251; as source of majesty, 283; Omega as late plural of, 283; Alpha as, 284

Giant: development of, 98, 167, 264–66; and the first idea, 167, 170, 264–66; in pure and normal poetry, 168; MacCullough as, 169; as incarnation of the supreme fiction, 177; of nothingness, 178, 180, 210, 266, 268, 269, 272, 298, 315; and the green queen, 183; sleep as, 225, 226, 227; embodies the spectre of the spheres, 260
God: poem equivalent to idea of, 1, 133; wanting to be, 5; Christian, 6, 107, 141–42, 295; as the good, 8, 17; as the ultimate intellect, 10; as mystical motive, 14; as the mystery of life, 18; modern movement away from idea of, 18; as ultimate poetic idea, 18, 20, 21, 26, 32, 213, 254; changes in Stevens' idea of, 18, 32, 269–70; substitutes for, 18, 23, 128, 337; loss of belief in, 23, 93; as world's capital idea, 25; as product of desire, 26; man becoming, 27, 169; identified with the imagination, 27, 31, 311; as an incapable master, 32–33, 238; as an idealist, 32, 269; in Wordsworth, 34; Jove as, 51, 295; and police, 67; as universal being, 90; as origin of individual spirit, 91; identified with essential imagination, 92, 260; and brute necessity, 93; gradual unfolding of, 96; desire for, 100; the thinking of, is smoky dew, 102, 114, 188; absence of, 121, 158; of asceticism, 124; changed to man, 142; immanence of, 163; and pathetic fallacy, 164, 308; equated with the first idea, 165; remains man in humanism, 168; difficulty in forming image of, 174; too human, 188–89; necessity of, 209; as completely closed, 209–10; Whitman and, 229, 245; and the father, 240, 246; in self or not at all, 252; as morning knowledge, 253; as a circle, 262; search for, 289; death of, 295; critic of, 308; web of, 321; of mercy and love, 341; of beauty and might, 341; Stevens' need to decide about, 342, 343; as one uncreated, 343
Gods: death of, 2, 22–23, 51, 114, 191; as a definition of perfection, 23; imagination and, 23, 191; substitute for, 104; without, 325; genealogy of, to be destroyed, 335; men and, 337
Green: night, 148, 149, 183, 202, 232; as motif of pure poetry, 183, 242; originals of, 231, 291; polar, 241; and blue, 227, 264–65; as signal to the lover, 284

Heaven: lyric naturalism substituted for, 6; ascent into, 20, 213, 293; mind that created, 27; mother of, 41, 42, 147; as idea of earth, 45; absence of, 79, 92, 114; they practice for, 83; empty, 86, 91, 97, 101; transparent architecture of, 91–92, 157–58; and nature, 95; collects its bleating lambs, 99; colossal illusion of, 125; instinct for, 290; as equivalent to the abstract, 328; associated with the essential poem, 329

Hell, 175, 244, 297, 343

Human, 208, 305, 343; and divine, 22, 60, 72; rhetoric not contained within, 144; qualitative leap from, 168; annihilation of, 180; height or depth of, 207; repudiation of, 209–10; and inhuman, 209, 210, 313, 333, 334, 335; needed to reflect majesty, 252; as absolute, 305; mother now separate from, 313; beginning and end of, 320; that can be accounted for, 327

Humanism, 23, 114, 168, 333–34

Imagination: generations of, 7, 231, 235; identified with subconscious, 15, 17, 97, 112; life of, 22, 59, 196; that seeks to satisfy the universal mind, 22, 213; identified with the Romantic, 24; and reason, 24, 25, 170; as metaphysics, 24, 25, 27, 187; identified with God, 27, 31, 92, 311; not wholly his own, 38; absence of, 57, 69, 309; moon as symbol of, 59–61; that sits enthroned, 60, 82, 96, 208, 251–52, 253; self-regenerating power of, 62, 64, 190–91; and night, 99; filling the need of, 112; as negative category, 126; affirmation of, 131, 244; high, 138, 139, 245; as absolute, 162; remains unreal, 173; primary, 185, 208, 262; transcendental, 211, 277; failure to become, 240; supreme, 266; end of, 314

Intellect: and subconscious, 15–16, 17; ultimate, 38, 113, 120, 198–99, 225, 228, 234, 241, 297, 332

Intelligence: and soil, 7, 57, 60–61, 94, 155, 327; our different, 18; combining imagination with, 25; and matter, 34, 61; to make new, 61, 115; divine, 102; and nature, 103, 112; of his despair, 187; the truth in, 192

Interior paramour. *See* Feminine figure, interior paramour

James, William, 25–26, 107, 108–109
Jesus, 48, 50, 54, 189
Jung, Carl, 16, 17

Kant, Immanuel, 108, 224*n*
Keats, John: and the elegiac sublime, 5, 51–52, 79–80, 84, 188, 220, 257, 294; moon in, 60; and high romance, 60, 257; transcends personality, 115, 116; mythic feminine figures in, 79–80, 147, 220; on sleep, 228; on autumn, 260–61
—works: "Ode on a Grecian Urn," 51; "The Fall of Hyperion: A Dream," 52, 79–80, 147, 188, 220; "Ode on Melancholy," 52, 79, 80, 220; *Endymion,* 60; "When I Have Fears," 60, 257, 260; "Hyperion: A Fragment," 80, 228; "Sleep and Poetry," 229, 245; "To Autumn," 260–61; "Ode to a Nightingale," 294

Latimer, Ronald Lane, 114
Life: contained by words, 9; as ancient mother, 9, 22, 147; God as mystery of, 18; as problem, 23; of nature, 34; fruit of, 44, 47, 318; and meaninglessness, 54, 61; world of, 72; and chance, 75; mingling of death and, 79, 296; as mediator of ethereal and physical, 95; poet adds to, 104; of life, 111–12; affirmation of, 131; came back, 137; thinking way to, 139, 157; passing from, 143, 217, 218–19, 234; the poem and, 165; description and, 185; innocence of, 192, 258; transcendence of individual, 203, 205; poverty of, 206; mate his life with, 206; such large, 234, 265; denial of, 244; of the world, 276, 297; theory of, 288, 296, 297, 302
Locke, John, 39–40

Major man: as visionary persona, 117, 167–70, 172, 177, 301; two types of, 168, 177
Materialism: Emerson on, 57, 156–57, 297–98; consequences of, 61; cynical, 107. *See also* Intelligence, and soil
Memory: ancestral, 16, 17, 159; transcendental, 52, 141; Mnemosyne, 80; mythic, 81, 179–80, 232; ancient mother's, 81, 217,

218–19, 224, 235; lord of, 89; archetypal, 98, 141, 261, 312
Metaphor: as basis of poetry, 148; the least, minor, vital, 155, 156; validity of, 158; motive for, 180, 200–201; without evasion by, 181, 197; and change, 184; shadow as metaphysical, 202, 204, 242; displacement in, 237, 255, 263, 290, 332; gap between object and, 330–31
Miller, Joaquin, 115
Mind: of minds, 3, 134, 139, 141, 146, 150, 169, 172, 206, 232, 252, 265, 277; the central, 4, 19, 27, 31, 33, 205, 206, 265, 311, 321, 325; of God, 10, 142, 311; the universal, 22, 26, 213, 260; in heaven and on earth, 27; as vital boundary, 31, 311, 313; world as projection of, 33; squamous, 35, 122; as the main of things, 66, 320, 321, 335; acquired transparence, 92, 158; that feeds upon infinity, 60; is an animal, 103; never-resting, 116; landscape of, 116, 155, 208, 308, 336; secret arrangements in, 118, 270, 323; is the unreal, 132; fusion of night and, 137, 203, 204; ultimate poem and, 139; and being satisfied, 139, 141, 157; is the eye, 155, 156; supreme, 162, 213, 324; transcendence of the human, 163–64, 168, 171–72, 205; war between sky and, 177; green, 183; the major, 184, 280; and trouble, 196, 318; is a child, 221, 236; light-bound space of, 236, 311; constitutes reality, 275; integration of body and, 318; contains space, 320, 321
Monistic idealism: William James on, 107; fusion of pluralism and, 110, 145; dialectic of pluralism and, 121–24; and the supreme fiction, 184
Moon: in Wordsworth, 59–60; in Keats, 60, 80; Crispin haunted by, 59, 66, 116; fluctuating between sun and, 60–61, 62; as alien, 102, 140, 188, 192, 209; as symbol of Romantic sublime, 116, 166, 188, 282–83; as mother of pathos and pity, 189; folly of, 191, 193, 194
Mother. *See* Feminine figure—mother
Mythology: and subconscious, 7–8, 17, 96; feminine figure in Stevens', 9, 22, 28, 173–74; of major visionary poems, 9, 213–70; Stevens' analysis of, 22–23; biblical, 44, 118–20; Christian, 48, 51, 85, 190, 343; lyricism and, 51, 82, 133, 325–26; region of, 52; of modern death, 52, 214, 222, 235, 256; of self, 57; in Keats, 79–80, 188, 220; and the elegiac sublime, 81, 220; transcendental, 91, 214; myth before the myth, 95, 164, 165; Ariadne, 96; Demeter and Persephone, 147, 219–20; in Tennyson, 147, 219–20, 231; of parental space, 149, 210, 266; of normal poetry, 175–76; loss of, 190; and mysticism, 202, 234; central emptiness in Stevens', 206; dissolution of, 265; and individual pathos, 272; of essential unity, 278; masculine, 325, 327, 328, 337

New Romanticism: as equivalent to the supreme fiction, 6; touchstones for, 8; definitive form of, 10; world looking forward to, 59, 64; Stevens feeling round for, 62, 64; and ineffectual angels, 74; and celestial paramours, 94; as singular romance, 138; delay in quest for, 199
Night: subman steeped in, 15; consciousness of, 38; as a woman, 60, 146, 148; bare, 74; and imagination, 99; fusion of mind and, 137, 200, 204; undeciphered murmuring of, 143, 144, 151, 206; as elemental parent, 148, 149, 183, 202, 232; old peak of, 152, 192; self-realization of, 201–202; as transcendental element, 216, 217; highest, 252; single future of, 293, 294; identified with pure poetry, 321. *See also* Sleep
Normal poetry: and dualism, 3, 19; alternation of pure and, 10, 187, 332–33; change in Stevens' conception of, 19–20; hierarchical relation of pure and, 19, 131, 177, 180, 197, 199, 297; as final belief, 131; and fat girl, 146; and major man, 168; and motif of center, 199; synthesis of pure and, 267–68; suspension between pure and, 290, 313, 314, 320–21; resolution displaced to, 317–18
Nothingness: and residual animism, 35; as ultimate reality, 55; dialectic of being and, 79, 268; in the Cabala, 96; generative, 96, 180, 315, 316, 320; of death, 178, 210, 230,

235, 266; kinds of, 180; disrupted as category, 266; ironic absorption in, 306

Pantheism, 107, 126–27, 161
Paradise: chant of, 49, 53, 55; of Christianity, 50–51; death in, 52, 158; static, 79; insipid, 85; and the imperfect, 116, 158; critique of, 154–55, 173, 191, 291, 308, 336; of meaning, 158, 191, 195, 210; unknown, 194, 195; as a wasteland, 308; and earth, 337
Parts of a World: Wallace Stevens Remembered, 6, 11, 108, 277, 338, 341, 342, 343
Pascal, Blaise, 199, 262
Pater, Walter, 25, 128
Perfection: and the supreme poetic idea, 21; gods as definition of, 23; of time and place, 27, 186, 208, 287; of parental space, 27, 220, 235, 326; will to, 28; as seed, 135; of central heart, 135, 226; and sound, 138–39; of thought, 201–202, 205, 208; contrived, 270
Place: self-perfection of, 27, 186, 208, 287; created by innocent mother, 28, 82, 238, 255, 326; and soul, 33; not our own, 164; and description, 181, 182; transcendence of, 222, 224, 225, 253; some future, 334
Platonism, 8, 17, 18, 209, 238, 246, 260
Pluralistic empiricism: definition of, 8, 107–108; and essential unity, 8, 199, 275–76; fusion of monism and, 110, 145; dialectic of monism and, 121–24; extreme, 128
Poetry: and philosophy, 11–12, 23–25, 112; cosmic, 13, 14; purpose of, 17–18; fundamental, 22, 213, 337; and belief, 26, 145; and place, 33; and the supreme fiction, 56, 160, 197; Crispin's struggle with, 61–62; universal, 64; is essentially romantic, 68; apotheosis of, 86, 337; inception of, 87; role of modern, 89; and heaven, 101; and pathetic fallacy, 104; metaphor is basis of, 148; archetype of, 148; as medium of essential imagination, 150; theory of, as theory of life, 288, 297, 302
Positivism, 102, 104, 158, 159, 191, 287
Presence: and absence, 35, 225, 268, 271, 272; transparence as, 157; world of sentient, 184, 239; shadow as, 206; divine, 254
Pure idea: as singular romance, 134, 170; remains inaccessible, 143, 150, 163; and the abstract, 145; becomes the first idea, 162–63, 265, 283; and mind of minds, 169, 206; as white center, 198–99
Pure poetry: transcendental character of, 3; motive of, 8; alternation of normal and, 10, 187, 332–33; change in Stevens' conception of, 14, 18, 19–20; and didacticism, 15, 19, 20; as images and music, 15, 23, 24, 47, 68, 128, 153; relative status of normal and, 19, 131, 177, 180, 197, 199, 297; identified with God, 92; development of feminine figure in, 146–52, 174; and major man, 168; green as motif of, 183, 242; and motif of the center, 199–200; abstraction and archetypes merge in, 210; synthesis of normal and, 267–68; and the reified sublime, 290; tragic sphere of, 292; Stevens' last achievements in, 304; suspension between normal and, 313, 314, 320–22; and the devotional mode, 336
Pure principle: as resolution of oppositions, 8; innocence as, 28, 253; as origin of space and time, 254; as name for God, 254, 337–38; as spectre of the spheres, 259; and skeleton of the ether, 268; ceased to function, 306; inversion of, 307
Puvis de Chavannes, Pierre, 198

Queen. *See* Feminine figure—queen

Rabbi, 42, 65, 96, 120, 258
Reality: negative, 2, 126; confusions about, 13; and artifice, 14, 185, 186, 264, 285, 286; forms of thought as, 19, 307; spiritual, 26, 94, 164; as origin of intelligence, 61–62; pressure of, 64, 87, 177; not a solid, 99, 297–98; as emanation of a divine intelligence, 102; center of, 111; of sensual particulars, 121, 141; in objects alone, 132; pure idea as, 145; first ideas as, 163; holiday in, 176, 195; as softest woman, 192–93; is prodigy, 216, 217, 219; as shadows, 257; the abstract devolves into, 266;

sentient process and, 270; plain, 275, 276, 279, 296
—and mind or imagination: marginal to central theme, 1; standard critical dichotomy, 2; contained by transcendent mind, 19, 26, 280; and the last largeness, 40; flow between, 89, 126; as static opposition, 103
Relation: as mediating term, 108, 122; and essential imagination, 108, 139; and the first idea, 162; and diamond crown, 172; and difference, 176, 186, 198; and the abstract, 266
—sentient: animates essential poem, 8; and nature, 34; as pure idea, 162; teleology of, 255; ceased to function, 306–308. See also Pure principle
Religion: Stevens' attitudes toward, 32, 109, 339–43; Stevens' need for, 47–48; vulgar form of, 91; sublimation of, 110; critique of, 188–90; as motivating force, 280, 288
Romanticism: and Stevens' career, 5–7; renewal of, 5–6, 67–68; attenuated forms of, 6, 24, 37; theory of poetry in, 13, 24, 186, 287; and vital mystery, 18; and imagination as metaphysics, 25, 37; religious idiom of, 32; moon as symbol of, 59; as a cycle, 59, 62, 71, 166, 190, 307; feminine figure in, 146, 147–48; lowest form of, 267
Royce, Josiah, 108, 109

Santayana, George: skeptical aestheticism of, 5; and hypothetical belief, 25–26; on sexual passion and beauty, 41; at Harvard, 108–109; and total grandeur, 118, 332; on asceticism, 124; on essence and existence, 127–28, 329, 330, 332; on sentient nature, 164–65; on the circle, 261–62; Stevens' elegy for, 327–32; on poetry and religion, 340
—works: *The Sense of Beauty*, 41, 261–62, 328; *Interpretations of Poetry and Religion*, 41, 124, 340; *Scepticism and Animal Faith*, 117, 127, 164–65, 330; *Apologia Pro Mente Sua*, 329
Schelling, Friedrich Wilhelm Joseph von, 24
Sex, 41, 42, 55, 95, 115, 142
Shadow: the essential, 60, 148, 183, 203; in the mind, 142; prodigious, 184, 202–208; touched him, 188; is a central mind, 205, 206, 265; mode of existence of, 206, 254, 266; a great, 257, 291; in Tennyson, Keats, Shelley, and Emerson, 275
Shakespeare, William, 269, 311
Shelley, Percy Bysshe: and the sublime, 5, 72–73, 74, 91, 231, 257; as ineffectual angel, 71, 74; rhapsodic obscurity of, 75; transcendentalism in, 91; invocation of, 94
—works: "Mont Blanc," 7, 71, 72–73, 75; "The Skylark," 74; "Hymn to Intellectual Beauty," 74, 257; "Hymn of Apollo," 83, 91; "Ozymandias," 172; "A Defense of Poetry," 199; "To Night," 231
Sleep: syllable in distances of, 37, 38; realized, 38, 52, 225, 228, 230, 234, 242, 266, 293; as visionary medium, 38, 39, 225, 228, 332–33; meditating, 59; deep atmosphere of, 120, 285; redeeming thought in, 140; dreamers buried in, 179; as mythic figure, 214–29; height of, 225, 227, 234, 248, 332; awake in quiet of, 238, 255, 332; of death, 293–94
Solipsism, 26, 34, 35, 113, 129
Space: parental, 28, 149, 210, 220, 235, 236, 266, 287, 326; vacant, 72, 83, 206, 280; subordinated to mind, 86, 320, 321; positivistic, 102; non-physical, 194; center of, 200; self-perfection of, 208, 287; transcendence of, 226, 278; of the mind, 236, 311; the father sits in, 244; magnificent, 249; pure principle as origin of, 254, 266–67; Santayana on, 261, 262; archaic, 301
Spirit: in cloth, 7, 291; height and depth of, 20, 150, 207; alienation of, 55, 63, 83, 102, 132, 144, 169; collapse of, 67; empty, 72, 201, 206; search for, 76–77; inhuman, 80, 272; from the sun, 83, 132; and nature, 93, 239, 257, 262; having progeny by, 95; diamond coronal of, 96, 158, 173, 228, 229; foyer of, 116, 155, 157, 163, 308; stratagems of, 118, 182; of one, 184, 316, 318; the shadow's, 208; modern crisis of, 250; alchemicana of, 286; absence of, 322; Emerson on, 326; from body of world,

327; Santayana on, 330; without a foyer, 336
Stevens, Elsie Kachel, 41, 42–43, 44, 48, 147, 272, 277n, 339, 340
Stevens, Margaretha Catherine Zeller, 7, 52–53, 147, 272
Subconscious: and archetypes, 7; subman as, 7–8, 15–16, 97, 100, 167, 179, 192; and imagination, 15, 17, 97, 112; ancestors in, 179–80, 192
Sublime: of celestial grandeur, 5, 78; imagery of, 38, 130, 144, 148–49, 225–26, 249; renewal of, 44; and vacant space, 72, 206; Emerson on, 90; black, 158; transcendental, 259, 284, 286, 306, 330; negative, 206, 306, 331; austere, 241; egotistical, 246; reified, 286–87
—elegiac: and mysticism, 4, 144, 292; in Tennyson, 5, 80–81, 84, 220, 227; in Keats, 5, 51–52, 79–80, 84, 188, 220, 257, 294; in Whitman, 5, 84, 294; and insipid paradise, 51; and death of Stevens' mother, 53; development of, 78–82; lingering in, 296
—Romantic: types of, 5; inversion of, 10, 206; and pure poetry, 19; heaven of, 91–92; in normal poetry, 154, 197; as mode of the supreme fiction, 161; erotic aspects of, 170–73; and Emerson, 257; and death, 290; minimalist, 298; and tragic fatality, 310
Sun: represents realism, 59, 60–61, 62, 73; as a spiritual source, 83, 132; as absolute, 87, 144; solitude of, 91, 92; no shadows in, 101, 180; in its idea, 164, 166; as metaphor of spirit, 257; and the essential poem, 315
Supreme fiction: transcendental character of, 1, 3, 184–85; fulfillment proposed in, 1, 27, 269; definitions of, 1, 13, 26–27, 31, 163, 184, 260, 290; and new Romanticism, 6; elements of, 7, 131; poetry as, 56, 160; is problematic, 118, 207, 270, 327; and good and evil, 133, 193; basic assumption of, 139; and breadth, 152, 210; and the first idea, 162–66; as total building, 175; fruit as metaphor of, 184, 316, 317; as source of poetry, 197; as poem of the whole, 260, 317; decline of, 305

Tennyson, Alfred, Lord: and the elegiac sublime, 5, 80, 81, 84, 219–20, 227; and transcendence of self, 233; and spiritual crisis, 250; and the essential poem, 264–65, 268
—works: "The Ancient Sage," 42, 219, 220, 227, 233, 257, 264–65, 268; *In Memoriam*, 80–81, 227, 249–50; "Demeter and Persephone," 147, 219–20
Thought: the forms of, 19, 52, 80, 208, 217, 221–24, 236, 260, 284, 287, 288, 307, 328, 337; the single, 135, 152; the redeeming, 140, 332; our singular skeleton, 143, 144, 209, 268; is false happiness, 154; end of, 155, 180, 208; stasis of, 163; perfection of, 201, 205, 208; independent of thinker, 205; compromise of, 210, 242; visibility of, 288, 297, 308
Time: self-perfecting of, 27, 186, 208, 287; created by innocent mother, 28, 82, 238, 255, 326; subordinated to mind, 86; flashed again, 137, 203; center of, 200, 210, 246; that stood still, 222, 224, 253, 300, 336; transcendence of, 225, 226, 246, 278; pure principle as origin of, 254, 266–67; as visionary metaphor, 267
Transcendentalism: of the supreme fiction, 1, 184–85; critical responses to, 4–5; in Shelley, 71, 91; in Wordsworth, 71, 226; and pathetic fallacy, 110; and feminine figure, 148–49; Emerson on, 156, 157, 326; as one of two poetic theories, 199; failure of, 307, 308; element of, 325–26, 330
Transparence: lyric and visionary, 51, 325–26; in Emerson, 90–91; source of, 92, 102, 158; is peace, 171; the mother gives, 242, 243; a moving, 329

Victorian period, 54, 95, 250, 304

War, 19, 46, 88, 97–98, 130, 133, 177–79
Whitehead, Alfred North, 320
Whitman, Walt: and the sublime, 5, 84, 246, 297; and natural supernaturalism, 32; ocean in, 76; depiction of, 83–84; and thematic hierarchy, 84, 135; consolatory fantasy in, 85; egotism of, 115, 229, 245,

246; on priests, 134, 342; and central heart, 134–35, 226; and the father, 244–45
—works: "As I Ebb'd with the Ocean of Life," 76; "Out of the Cradle Endlessly Rocking," 76; *Sea-Drift,* 76; *The Sleepers,* 76; "Song of Myself," 84, 85; *Whispers of Heavenly Death,* 85, 229; preface to *Leaves of Grass,* 134; "Song of the Universal," 134, 226; "Chanting the Square Deific," 229, 245; "When Lilacs Last in the Dooryard Bloom'd," 294
Whole: poem of, 3, 211, 261, 263, 264, 266, 270, 317, 321; no language for, 12, 13; obscurity of, 31, 311; creator's struggle toward, 32, 238, 269; Emerson on, 67, 269; world that shrinks to, 118, 184, 213, 323; elixir of, 152; supreme fiction as fiction of, 260, 317; specter meditates, 302; rock as habitation of, 319, 320, 321; and litter of truths, 335
Wordsworth, William: and the sublime, 5, 298; and natural supernaturalism, 32, 48; transcendentalism in, 34; on earthly paradise, 51; moon in, 59–60; animism in, 72, 112; and maternal figure, 147–48; and central heart, 226; and northern lights, 254*n*
—works: *The Prelude,* 33–34, 59–60, 71, 75, 147–48, 254*n*; *The Recluse,* 49, 50, 51; "Westminster Bridge," 102, 104; *The Excursion,* 226; "The World Is Too Much with Us," 265; "Lines Composed a Few Miles Above Tintern Abbey," 298

Yeats, William Butler, 95, 286